The Shadow of the Great Game
The Untold Story of India's Partition

Narendra Singh Sarila was heir to the princely state of Sarila in central India. An ADC to Lord Mountbatten, he later joined the Indian Foreign Service, where he worked from 1948 to 1985. He was a deputy permanent representative in the Indian delegation to the UN. He also served as India's ambassador to Spain, Brazil, Libya, Switzerland and France. He has been a commentator on international affairs and has written for journals such as the *International Herald Tribune* and the *Times of India*.

D1003640

The Shadow of the Great Game

THE UNTOLD STORY OF INDIA'S PARTITION

Narendra Singh Sarila

HarperCollins *Publishers* India
a joint venture with

New Delhi

First published in India in 2005 by
HarperCollins *Publishers* India
a joint venture with
The India Today Group

First published in paperback by HarperCollins *Publishers* India in 2009

ISBN: 978-81-7223-874-2

2 4 6 8 10 9 7 5 3 1

Narendra Singh Sarila asserts the moral
right to be identified as the author of this work.

Cover photograph courtesy of Maj. Gen. U.C. Dubey,
Aditya Arya Archive (www.adityaaryaarchive.com)

HarperCollins *Publishers*
A-53, Sector 57, Noida 201301, India
77-85 Fulham Palace Road, London W6 8JB, United Kingdom
Hazelton Lanes, 55 Avenue Road, Suite 2900, Toronto, Ontario M5R 3L2
and 1995 Markham Road, Scarborough, Ontario M1B 5M8, Canada
25 Ryde Road, Pymble, Sydney, NSW 2073, Australia
31 View Road, Glenfield, Auckland 10, New Zealand
10 East 53rd Street, New York NY 10022, USA

Typeset in 11/13 Sabon
Nikita Overseas Pvt. Ltd.

Printed and bound at
Thomson Press (India) Ltd.

To

My son Samar Singh Sarila
and the younger generation of Indians

Contents

Preface		9
Acknowledgements		13
1	The Great Game	15
2	The Anglo–Muslim League Alliance	34
3	The Pakistan Scheme and Jinnah	65
4	The Churchill–Roosevelt Clash over India	97
5	The Mahatma's Fury	122
6	India, the UK and the USA	145
7	Wavell Plays the Great Game	167
8	Attlee's 'Smoke Screens'	199
9	Nehru in the Saddle	228
10	Mountbatten's Counsellor	269
11	The End Game of Empire	299
12	The Kashmir Imbroglio I: Gilgit and Poonch	330
13	The Kashmir Imbroglio II: At the UN	365
14	Postscript	402
Index		419

Preface

WHILE RESEARCHING IN THE ORIENTAL AND INDIAN COLLECTION OF the British Library, London, in 1997, on another matter, I came across certain documents which revealed that the partition of India in August 1947 may not have been totally unconnected with the British concern that the Great Game between them and the USSR for acquiring influence in the area lying between Turkey and India was likely to recommence with even greater gusto after the Second World War. And to find military bases and partners for the same.

The USSR's powerful victory over Germany in 1945 had increased Joseph Stalin's ambitions to extend his country's influence into territories on its periphery; indeed, he had already started to do so in Eastern Europe. To the Soviet Union's southern border lay the region of the Persian Gulf with its oil fields – *the wells of power* – that were of vital interest to the West. Under the circumstances, Britain could ill afford to lose control over the entire Indian subcontinent that had served as its military base in dominating the Indian Ocean area and the countries around the Persian Gulf for more than half a century and which was also the main source of manpower for the Imperial Army.

Once the British realized that the Indian nationalists who would rule India after its independence would deny them military cooperation under a British Commonwealth defence umbrella, they settled for those willing to do so by using religion for the purpose. Their problem could be solved if Mohammad Ali Jinnah, the leader of the

Muslim League Party, would succeed in his plan to detach the northwest of India abutting Iran, Afghanistan and Sinkiang and establish a separate state there – Pakistan. The proposition was a realizable one as a working relationship had been established between the British authorities in India and Jinnah during the Second World War and he was willing to cooperate with Britain on defence matters if Pakistan was created.

Very little attention has been paid so far to the influence of British strategic concerns on India's partition. Consequently, I thought I would use the recently unsealed documents to make the facts in them available to the public. For this, I researched not only in the Oriental and Indian Collection of the British Library (where David Blake, the curator, was very generous with his time) but also in the Hartley Library in Southampton (where Lord Louis Mountbatten's archives are kept); the Public Records Office in Kew (to which place most British ministers and Foreign Office officials consigned their papers); the archives of the State Department of the USA (covering the period 1942–48 and containing the correspondence of President Franklin Delano Roosevelt with Prime Minister Winston Churchill and with his special envoys in India at that time); the National Archives in Washington; and the Library of the US Congress.

In 1948, as an ADC to the governor-general, Lord Mountbatten, I became familiar with the main locations where the developments had unfolded in New Delhi and Simla and caught glimpses of some of the players. I also gained insights from my father's numerous British friends who had played a role in formulating or implementing British policy towards India. Later on, in the 1960s, while dealing with Pakistan affairs as an Indian diplomat in New Delhi and New York, I came face to face with the attitude of the great powers towards India and Pakistan that had their roots in the events of pre-independence India.

The subject is also fascinating because of the little known facts about the unobtrusive pressure the United States exerted on Britain in favour of India's freedom – and unity – from 1942 onwards. Roosevelt's object was to evolve a post-war order for Asia, free from European colonialism. Churchill trumped this pressure by playing the Muslim, or the Pakistani, card, that the real problem lay in

Hindu–Muslim differences about India's future and not in Britain's unwillingness to accept self-determination for India. American pressure finally contributed in no small measure in persuading Britain to accept the inevitable in India, though the Indians never really recognized this contribution.

The archives are also engrossing because the Indian leaders' conversations with, and written communications to, the viceroys were meticulously recorded by the British and give details of their views and tactics, which do not fully emerge from the Indian records. The Indian nationalists' miscalculations, their upholding ideals divorced from realities and their inexperience in the field of international politics emerge in their own words in the records. It is therefore also a cautionary tale.

The subject is surely also of topical interest. With the end of the Cold War, the retreat of Russia from its Central Asian territories and the deployment of the US forces in strength in the Persian Gulf, the importance of Pakistan as a strategic partner in the Great Game against Russia began to decrease. On the other hand, the Al-Qaida's attacks on the World Trade Center towers in New York and on the Pentagon in Washington on 11 September 2001 brought into sharp focus the menace of Islamic terrorism and the use of Islam for political purposes, i.e., political Islam. The Taliban Government in Afghanistan was set up with the military and diplomatic support of Pakistan. It provided shelter to the Al-Qaida and to Osama bin Laden. The Taliban and bin Laden were influenced by the tenets preached by Indian-born Abdul Al Mawdudi, the leader of the Jamaat-i-Islami, Pakistan, who advocated a government strictly based on the Shariat, a clash of civilizations and jihad against non-believers. Many of the roots of Islamic terrorism sweeeping the world today lie buried in the partition of India.

The successful use of religion by the British to fulfil political and strategic objectives in India was replicated by the Americans in building up the Islamic jihadis in Afghanistan for the same purpose, of keeping the Soviets at bay. There is no gainsaying that nations will ever stop taking advantage of whoever or whatever comes in handy to achieve their immediate vital goals, not the least the US using the Pakistan military to counter the growing influence of the increasing jihadis in Pakistan. Or that the Great Game will not be played out again in Central Asia with different issues at stake and with different sets of partners. However, the Western policies of exploiting political Islam to pressurize India have run their course. The improvement in Indo–US relations since the mid-1990s is the result of these changes in the strategic picture.

Britain was bound to protect its strategic and economic interests from the damaging consequences of its withdrawal from its vast two-century-old Empire in India. How this was done by outmanoeuvring the Indian leaders and partitioning India is the theme of this untold story.

March 2005   Narendra Singh Sarila

Acknowledgements

I AM GRATEFUL TO THE BOARD OF THE BRITISH LIBRARY, LONDON, FOR allowing me to consult material in its custody and particularly the official files of the India Office Records.

I am also grateful to the Hartley Library at the University of Southampton for allowing me to consult material in its custody and to the trustees of the Broadlands Archives for allowing me to quote from documents for which they hold the copyright.

I consulted the United States Foreign Relations documents pertaining to the period covered in this book, for which I am indebted to the concerned agency of the US Government. I thank the staff of the National Archives in Washington D.C. who helped me dig out some documents referred to in this book.

I also consulted the archives of the Nehru Memorial Museum and Library, New Delhi, for which I am indebted to the director. Some of the photographs that appear in this book do so courtesy the NMML and the Public Affairs Section of the US Embassy in India.

Lastly, I am thankful to K.L. Sharma who typed the book from A to Z on the basis of my dictation and handwritten notes and who often acted as a thesaurus. When he showed frustration at my constant revisions, I would remind him of what Han Sui Yen, the well-known writer, once told me: she, on an average, revised her drafts forty times!

Narendra Singh Sarila

1

The Great Game

THE AGREEMENT TO PARTITION INDIA WAS ANNOUNCED IN DELHI ON
3 June 1947. The following week the British Labour Party's Annual
Conference was held in Margate in Britain. There, addressing the
delegates, Ernest Bevin, the British foreign secretary, stated that the
division of India 'would help to consolidate Britain in the Middle
East.'[1]

On the day Bevin spoke, Krishna Menon was staying with Pandit
Jawaharlal Nehru at 7, York Road in Delhi. Settled in London,
Menon then headed the India League in the UK, was a member of
the British Labour Party and the sole interlocutor on behalf of Nehru
with the British socialist leaders. He was the first Indian whom Lord
Louis Mountbatten sought out on being appointed the viceroy of
India in March 1947. Menon's ego had then not inflated to the
extent that was to warp his thinking and judgement after Nehru
made him defence minister. Referring to Bevin's remark, Menon
wrote to Lord Mountbatten at the Viceroy's House on 14 June, in
long hand, as follows (whether or not he did so after consulting
Nehru is not clear from this letter):

Is this frontier [the northwest of India abutting Afghanistan and
Iran] still the hinterland of the Imperial strategy? Does Britain
still think in terms of being able to use this territory and all that
follows from it? There is considerable amount of talking in this

way; and if Kashmir, for one reason or another, chooses to be in Pakistan, that is a further development in this direction. I do not know of British policy in this matter. I do not know whether you would know it either. But if this be the British intent, this is tragic.... As it becomes more evident, the attitude of India would be resentful and Britain's hold on Pakistan would not improve it. I think I have said enough. Perhaps a bit too much.[2]

Menon was raising two important questions. One, whether the British strategy was to use West Pakistan and the princely state of Kashmir as bases to contain the perceived Soviet ambitions towards the warm waters of the Indian Ocean, Afghanistan and the Persian Gulf, as the northwestern region of undivided India had been used for the same purpose for over a century. And two, whether British policy in this regard was so subterranean that even the viceroy of India was kept in the dark about it.

After the czars had incorporated the Muslim sultanates of Khokand, Bokhara and Khiva, including the cities of Tashkand and Samarkand, into their empire in the 1860s and 1870s, that brought Russia's frontier to within a few hundred miles of India (in Kashmir). The northwest frontier of India had become, for the British, the most sensitive of all the frontiers of their vast Empire. And it was here that the pick of the British Indian Army was quartered (and where, incidentally, Winston Churchill had served with the Malakand Field Force in 1898). The British had fought three wars in Afghanistan, incorporated in the 1880s parts of eastern Afghanistan into the North West Frontier Province and Baluchistan (now in Pakistan), built a railway network to the Khyber and Bolan Passes leading to Afghanistan, helped the Dogra Rajput ruler of Jammu under their paramountcy to extend his rule into Kashmir right up to the Sinkiang border, constructed a road from Gilgit in Hunza in northern Kashmir through the 13,000-feet-high Mintaka Pass in the Karakoram mountains to Kashgar in Sinkiang, posted agents there to monitor Russian activities across the border in Uzbekistan and the Pamirs, and bribed and threatened the Shahs of Persia – all in order to keep the areas of India's western approaches from slipping under Russian influence.

★

The British conquest of India, from Bengal (in the east) to the west and north in the nineteenth century, had matched the Russian advance in Central Asia from their heartlands, to the south and east, towards the warm waters of the Indian Ocean. Each of them raised the bogey of the other's expansion to press on further and further, till they stopped on either side of Afghanistan, which, by the beginning of the twentieth century, became the buffer between the two empires. According to one source: 'The Indian revolt or the Great Mutiny of 1857 had heightened British fears of rebellion, conspiracies, whole wars and possible foreign provocations. Amongst likely foreign culprits in the 1860s there was but a single important suspect, the Empire of Russia.'[3] For strategists such as Sir Henry Rawlinson, president of the Royal Geographical and Asiatic Societies, Member of Parliament and holding a lifetime seat in the new five-member India Council: 'If the Czar's officers acquire a foothold in Kabul the disquieting effect will be prodigious. Every native ruler throughout northern India who either has, or fancies he has, a grievance, or is even cramped or incommoded by our orderly Government, will begin intriguing with the Russians; worse, Afghanistan possesses a machinery of agitation singularly adapted for acting on the seething, fermenting, festering, mass of Muslim hostility in India.'[4] (The Muslim was then the British enemy in India, not the Hindu, as later. It was after all the Mughal Empire that the British had smashed while conquering India.)

There was, however, another view, which, along with natural British caution, had kept those subscribing to the forward school in check. 'The less the Afghans see us, less they will dislike us',[5] observed General Frederick Roberts, the conqueror of Kabul. 'India's security lay in the quality of British rule and the contentment of the Raj's subjects and not in foreign adventures',[6] contended Sir John Lawrence, the future governor-general.

In Russia too there was no dearth of believers in a forward policy. 'The position of Russia in Central Asia', declared Foreign Minister Prince Aleksandr Mikaylovich Gorchakov (in St. Petersburg), 'is that of civilized States which are brought into contact with half savage, nomad populations, possessing no fixed organization, or border security and trade relations with whom impel the civilized States to exert a certain authority...they respect only "visible and palpable force".'[7] And Fyodor Dostoyevsky, writing in the *Citizen*, a Petersburg journal, in 1881, exulted: 'Not only did Russia need markets and lands but she would bring science and railroads to a backward people. Asia was to Russia what undiscovered America was to Europe. In Europe we are Asiatics whereas in Asia we too are Europeans. Civilizing mission in Asia will bribe our spirits and drive us thither. It is only necessary that the movement should start. Build only two railroads: begin one in Siberia and then to Central Asia. And at once you will see the consequences...if one fears England then one should sit at home and move nowhere.'[8] Russia had actually gone into Uzbekistan for its cotton, the supplies of which commodity from the southern states of America had been blocked due to the hostilities in the American Civil War.

The intense rivalry between the two most powerful empires in Asia in the nineteenth century was termed by Count K. V. Nesselrode, the foreign minister of Russia, as the *'tournament of shadows'*, because there was no direct Anglo–Russian clash of arms. Rudyard Kipling used the phrase 'the Great Game' in his novel *Kim*, which passed into common usage.

★

The first decade of the twentieth century saw the German eastward thrust, symbolized by the attempt to establish the Berlin–Baghdad railway. This move brought Britain and Russia together in the Entente of 1907 for a while. Even so, the British had to foil Russian attempts to annex northern Persia and to persuade the Persians not to let them build a railway line from Tabriz (now in Iran) to Baluchistan (now in Pakistan) or accept the Russian demand to secede territory 100 miles wide on either side.

After taking over power in Russia in 1917, almost the first thing the communists did in the field of foreign policy was to call a 'Congress of Eastern Peoples' at Baku (situated on the Caspian Sea) in 1920. There they spread the message of fraternity to the non-European people of their neighbouring countries to the south: Turkey, Persia and Afghanistan. Thereafter, the Soviet Union withdrew territorial claims against these countries; in fact, Moscow offered them economic cooperation and signed treaties of friendship and non-aggression with each of them. Only Afghanistan under King Amanullah was influenced by this policy. And a direct air link was established in 1927 between Tashkand and Kabul. Amanullah fell in 1929 after he tried to go too far in emulating Mustafa Kemal Ataturk of Turkey in modernizing Afghanistan's Islamic society. This resulted in a backlash by conservative forces that helped the British.

The First World War (1914–18) resulted in the destruction, at Allied hands, of the most powerful Muslim state, the Ottoman Empire, the seat of the Khalifa, the titular head of the Muslims. This Muslim Empire had acted as a rampart against Russian influence spreading southwards. The British now decided to recruit the Arabs freed from Ottoman rule for the Great Game. The exploits of T.E. Lawrence provide a glimpse into how British agents rallied the desert Arabs. Britain carved out the states of Saudi Arabia, Iraq and Jordan from the remnants of the Ottoman Empire and established more direct control over the territories on the southern side of the Persian Gulf, then known as the Trucial States (now called the Emirates). The British presence in the Trucial States was partly financed by the British Government of India, to which the British political agents posted in these territories also reported. To create the kingdom of Saudi Arabia, the Saudi family was brought from the Nedj desert and installed in power to rule a large part of the Arabian Peninsula and also to guard the holy places. The sons of the Sheikh of Mecca, Faizal and Abdullah, were made the kings of Iraq (the old Mesopotamia), and the newly created state of Jordan, respectively, Kuwait being detached from the former.

The First World War had demonstrated the indispensability of oil in fighting a modern war. Within British reach lay only two areas with big oil fields: Mesopotamia and Persia. After Faisal was installed as king in Iraq, the Iraq Petroleum Company was formed. It contained the predecessors to Exxon and Mobile, Shell, BP and Total (a French company). The great depression that engulfed the world in the 1930s discouraged investment generally. The discovery of oil in Texas, after the war, led to a further postponement in developing Iraq's oil fields. In 1961, the nationalist coup in Iraq resulted in the nationalization of the Iraq Petroleum Company. After Saddam Hussein came to power in in the late 1970s, he diverted the country's funds to build a military machine rather than use them to develop Iraq's oil resources. According to a recent estimate by the Italian oil company, ENI, Iraq's oil reserves may be nearly 300 billion barrels rather than the generally accepted figure of 125 billion barrels.

Persia lay along the soft Muslim underbelly of the Soviet Union. During the course of the Second World War, Britain entered southern Persia and the Soviet Union northern Persia to jointly provide a route by which war material could be supplied by the Allies to the USSR and also to check a possible German thrust beyond the Caucasus. But at the end of the war in 1945 the Soviet Union, while withdrawing from the country, left behind a puppet regime in the Azai area of northern Persia along its border. The territories further north, where the Baku oil field is situated, had already been seized by the czar in the nineteenth century itself. British fears of Soviet ambitions were further fuelled when Joseph Stalin announced in 1946 that his country's requirement of oil had doubled since 1941. 'British interest in southern Persia was centred around oil', Ardershir Zahedi, the son-in-law of the Shah Reza Pahlavi, who became the foreign minister of Iran, once explained to me. 'In the 1920s they had wanted to detach the Iranian province of Khuzestan on the Shat-al-Arab where the British Petroleum Company held concessions and its Abedan refinery is situated and place it under a separate ruler, as they ultimately succeeded to do in Kuwait. Your [Indian] troops led by British officers were used in the region during wars.' Zahedi added: 'It was only after

Mossadeq* nationalized the British Petroleum Company that the British grip on Iran was shaken. After Mossadeq turned pro-communist and was overthrown, a consortium of American and Dutch oil companies together with the British company was formed. This reduced British influence. John Foster Dulles, the US secretary of state (1953–59) was sympathetic to Iran and after that country joined the USA and Britain together with Pakistan, Iraq and Turkey in the CENTO military pact, the nibbling away of Iran's frontiers by the other great powers stopped.'

At the end of the war this is how a venerable British player of the Great Game viewed the prospects:

The strategic movements of the Allies in Iraq and Persia in the Second World War were made possible from the Indian base.... The importance of the Gulf grows greater, not less, as the need for fuel expands, the world contracts and the shadows lengthen from the north. Its stability can be assured only by the close accord between the States which surround this Muslim lake, an accord underwritten by the Great powers whose interests are engaged.[9]

In 1943 an Indian scholar had put the British dilemma in a larger perspective:

The victory of the Allies will see the Soviet Union established as the mightiest power on the Eurasian continent. With her enemy in Europe crushed beyond recovery for a generation and Japan with her continental ambitions foiled for a time, Russia will find it easy to resume her southward march, which was interrupted in the nineties of the last century. The Indian Ocean gives her not merely the outlet to the sea for which she has been working for two centuries, but a commanding position on one of the oceanic areas.... Russia no doubt has no desire to annex the territories of other nations; but integral alliances with other

---

* The prime minister of Iran, Mohammad Mossadeq, in the 1950s.

nations organized on the basis of Soviet republics, is her policy in Asia as well as in Europe.... If India passes into the orbit of the Soviet Union and finds a stable position in that alliance, the latter, already dominant in the Balkans and Central Europe, will become a world organization, such as Lenin could not have dreamed of: irresistible in its power, unequalled in its economic resources and manpower, and having a territorial basis spread over practically the whole of Asia and Europe. The eclipse of the British Empire would be the natural and inevitable outcome.[10]

★

Germany surrendered on 5 May 1945. The same day, Prime Minister Winston Churchill ordered an appraisal of 'the long-term policy required to safeguard the strategic interests of the British Empire in India and the Indian Ocean' by the Post-Hostilities Planning Staff of the War Cabinet. And, on 19 May, this top-secret appraisal report was placed before him. The central point of this report was that Britain *must* retain its military connection with the subcontinent so as to ward off the Soviet Union's threat to the area.

The report cited four reasons for the strategic importance of India to Britain:

Its value as a base from which forces located there could be suitably placed for deployment both within the Indian Ocean area and in the Middle East and the Far East; a transit point for air and sea communications; a large reserve of manpower of good fighting quality; and from the northwest of which British air power could threaten Soviet military installations.[11]

The report also mentions the possibility of detaching Baluchistan from India. (The Baluchistan coast lies to the north of the Gulf of Oman that leads to the Persian Gulf.)

In each and every subsequent appreciation of the British chiefs of staff from then on till India's independence that is available for examination, the emphasis was on the need to *retain* the British military connection with the subcontinent, irrespective of the political and constitutional changes there. Equally, they stressed the special importance of the northwest of India in this context.

It may be noted that the idea of partitioning India in some form, to safeguard British strategic interests, had started to circulate in Whitehall in Churchill's time. Defence and security considerations were therefore uppermost in the minds of British leaders as they considered withdrawal from India. However, sufficient attention has not been paid to this vital factor by historians and political analysts, perhaps because security matters were not debated publicly in Britain.

★

On 18 April 1946, the British chiefs of staff, namely, Field Marshal Viscount Allenbrooke, Air Marshal Arthur William Tedder and Admiral Rhoderick McGrigor, again reported to the British cabinet: 'Recent developments made it appear that Russia is our most probable potential enemy.'[12] And, to meet its threat 'areas on which our war effort will be based and without which it would not be possible for us to fight at all would include India'.[13] Moreover, since Soviet 'policy at present appears to extend her influence to further strategic areas by all means short of major war...we should on no account weaken ourselves by surrendering our influence in the areas of major strategic importance'.[14] Another reason for not totally evacuating from India, they noted, was that 'air fields in northwest India are, except for those in Iraq, the nearest we have to certain important Russian industrial areas in Ural and western Siberia'.[15] They referred to the development of guided missiles that further augmented the menace of the Soviet Air Force operating from the Central Asian plateau. They also mentioned the importance of India as an essential air link to the Far East as, at that point of time, 'few existing types of aircraft [had] sufficient range for long hops'.[16]

The increase in the range and destructive capacity of air power over naval power was demonstrated by the sinking of the British battleships *Repulse* and the *Prince of Wales* by shore-based Japanese aircraft immediately after they left the Singapore naval base for the high seas at the start of the war with Japan. As such the Soviet control of the landmass of Central Asia, where its air power could be based, had acquired much greater significance in strategic calculations.

The commander-in-chief in India, Field Marshal Claude Auchinleck, expressed similar views in a note, which Lord Archibald Wavell, the viceroy, forwarded to the secretary of state on 13 July 1946. Among other things, this note emphasized: 'The principal advantage that Britain and the Commonwealth derive from control of India is strategic.'[17] The C-in-C's note further stated that the greatest asset was India's contribution of two million soldiers. It added that naval bases in India were indispensable for the protection of oil supplies from Persia and the Persian Gulf and its air bases there a necessary link in the Commonwealth air communications to the Far East. The note concluded: 'We [ought to] consider should independent India get influenced by hostile powers such as Russia we could not maintain our power to move freely by sea and air in the northern part of the Indian Ocean areas which is of supreme importance to the British Commonwealth.'[18]

The only difference between these reports and the report of the Post-Hostilities Planning Staff of Churchill's War Cabinet was that the assumption, in the latter, that Britain could continue to be responsible for India for another decade was absent. Soon after, General Lord Hastings Ismay, Churchill's chief of staff during the Second World War (at that time attached to the British Cabinet Secretariat), declared at a meeting of the chiefs of staff: '[It was] tolerably clear that if we evacuate India nothing would remain to prevent Russian infiltration with the consequent possibility of total disruption of the country very soon afterwards.' General Mosley Mayne, who chaired the meeting, 'agreed entirely'.

Lord Wavell, viceroy from 1943 to early 1947, was among the first of the British strategists to grasp the following interrelated factors:

1. India's primary usefulness to Britain was in the field of defence and not any more as a market.
2. Because of its fading power in India, Britain would have to withdraw from India sooner than later after the Second World War.

3. The Congress Party leaders, who would rule India after the British withdrew, were unlikely to cooperate with Britain on military matters and foreign policy, whereas the Muslim League Party, which wanted a partition of India, would be willing to do so.

4. The breach to be caused in Britain's capacity to defend the Middle East and the Indian Ocean area could be plugged if the Muslim League were to succeed in separating India's strategic northwest from the rest of the country, a realizable goal considering the close ties that Lord [Victor Alexander John Hope] Linlithgow, Wavell's predecessor, had built up with the Muslim League leader Mohammad Ali Jinnah during the Second World War.

Lord Wavell had a long discussion with Prime Minister Churchill in March 1945 in London. What was discussed between the two was not recorded except that Wavell noted in his diary that the prime minister had visualized the division of India. That this discussion reinforced his own inclinations in the matter is evident from the course he followed in India immediately thereafter.

Field Marshal Auchinleck had a different view. He held that the unity of the British-built Indian Army, led by British officers, was the surest guarantee against any potential Soviet mischief in the region. Having experienced firsthand the satisfactory cooperation between British and Indian officers, despite some racial problems, as well as the lack of communal animosity among men of various faiths in the Army, he was confident that the British, the Hindus, the Sikhs and the Muslims could pull together in a united India. The chiefs of staff in London supported Auchinleck's view. But this view did not take into account the fact that the Indian National Congress leaders, who would form the government of independent India, were determined to work out their own foreign policy and defence priorities, unhampered by British concerns. In these circumstances, how could the Army of a united India be of any use to Commonwealth defence? As 1946 went by, Wavell's point of view was being increasingly accepted in British military circles. Nehru's oath in the Constituent Assembly to declare India a sovereign independent republic (i.e., to cut off its connection with the Commonwealth) helped in opening their eyes.

★

By early 1947 the British chiefs of staff had become enthusiastic proponents of a Pakistan that would cooperate with Britain in military matters. On 12 May 1947 General Leslie Hollis wrote to Prime Minister Clement Attlee highlighting the views of the chiefs of staff, who wanted 'to deal with...western India* first of all. From the strategic point of view there are overwhelming arguments in favour of a western Pakistan remaining in the Commonwealth [i.e., maintaining defence ties with Britain].'[19] He put forward the following points to buttress his views:

1. We should obtain important strategic facilities [such as] the port of Karachi and air bases in North West India and the support of Muslim manpower.
2. We should be able to ensure the continued independence and integrity [of] Afghanistan.
3. We should increase our prestige and improve our position throughout the Muslim World, and demonstrate, by the assistance Pakistan would receive, the advantages of links with the British Commonwealth.
4. Our link with Pakistan might have a stabilizing effect on India as a whole, since an attack by Hindustan on Pakistan would involve Hindustan in war, not with Pakistan alone, but [also] with the British Commonwealth.
5. The position on the Frontier might well become more settled since relations between the tribes and Pakistan would be easier than they could be with a united India.[20]

---

* Parts of pre-1947 northwest India that were incorporated into West Pakistan.

General Hollis added:

Quite apart from the positive arguments in favour of this course we would draw your attention to the sorry results of refusing an application by Mr Jinnah – which would, in effect, amount to ejecting a numerous and loyal people from the British Commonwealth. We should probably have lost all chance of ever getting strategic facilities anywhere in India (the subcontinent); we should have shattered our reputation in the rest of the Muslim world and could not look for the continued cooperation of Middle Eastern countries. From the military point of view such results would be extremely bad.[21]

To give a flavour of the discussions that resulted in the aforementioned recommendations, are quoted below remarks made by the British Air, Naval and Army chiefs of staff at their meeting. Air Marshal Tedder observed:

We required certain strategic facilities in India, no matter how small these facilities ultimately were. Some were better than none.[22]

Next, Sir John Cunningham, the Naval chief, speaking on whether or not Britain should retain a military link with Pakistan, if India walked out of the British camp, asserted:

It would be insidious to refuse the application of people who had been loyal to the Commonwealth for many years...the result of such a refusal would extend throughout the whole Muslim world.[23]

And Field Marshal Bernard Law Montgomery, the chief of the Imperial General Staff, expressed the following views:

From the broad aspect of Commonwealth strategy it would be a tremendous asset if Pakistan, particularly the northwest, remained within the Commonwealth. The bases, airfields and ports in northwest India would be invaluable to Commonwealth defence. Moreover our presence would make for better civil administration, since British advisers, both civil and military, would ensure the efficiency of the [Pakistan] Provinces and might well attract Hindu States [India and independent princely states] into adopting a similar relationship with the Commonwealth. In addition we should be in a stronger position to support the integrity of Afghanistan...and the sooner this happened the better.[24]

Shortly afterwards, the chiefs of staff prepared another report, which emphasized that British strategic interests in the subcontinent should be focused on Pakistan:

The area of Pakistan [West Pakistan or the northwest of India] is strategically the most important in the continent of India and the majority of our strategic requirements could be met...by an agreement with Pakistan alone. We do not therefore consider that failure to obtain the agreement with India [Hindustan] would cause us to modify any of our requirements...[25]

At this stage, the hope that some large princely states would become independent was still being entertained by the British military:

At first sight it might appear that there would be little object in obtaining air transit rights from Pakistan if we have no similar rights in India [Hindustan]. It may however be possible...to use the territory of independent [princely] Indian States. We will in any case require the right for military aircraft to use bases in Hindustan.[26]

★

Ernest Bevin's remarks, referred to in Krishna Menon's letter to the viceroy (mentioned at the beginning of this chapter), show that the British Labour Party Government, with Clement Attlee as the prime minister, had closed ranks as far as the policy to partition India was concerned. Generally more sympathetic to India and the Congress Party than Churchill's Government, Attlee and his Government, nevertheless, swung around to support the partition of India basically to ensure the defence of Britain's vital interests after the war.

The following unsigned document reflects views that had been gaining ascendancy as India's independence approached. The crux is contained in the following summary:

> The Indus Valley, western Punjab and Baluchistan [the northwest] are vital to any strategic plans for the defence of [the] all-important Muslim belt...the oil supplies of the Middle East. If one looks upon this area as a strategic wall (against Soviet expansionism) the five most important bricks in the wall are: Turkey, Iran, Iraq, Afghanistan and Pakistan.
> Only through the open ocean port of Karachi could the opponents of the Soviet Union take immediate and effective countermeasures. The sea approaches to all other countries will entail navigation in enclosed waters directly menaced by Russian air fleets...not only of the sea lanes of approach, but also the ports of disembarkation.
> If the British Commonwealth and the United States of America are to be in a position to defend their vital interests in the Middle East, then the best and most stable area from which to conduct this defence is from Pakistan territory.
> Pakistan [is] the keystone of the strategic arch of the wide and vulnerable waters of the Indian Ocean.[27]

Who can say that this assessment was not prescient? For, after partition, Pakistan, together with Iran, Iraq, Turkey and Britain first joined the Baghdad Pact and later CENTO (which the USA also joined) to form the brick wall against Soviet ambitions. Later, Pakistan entered into a bilateral military pact with Britain's closest ally, the USA, and provided an air base in Peshawar in the North West Frontier Province to the CIA to enable U2 planes to keep a hawk's eye on military preparations in the Soviet Union. (The existence of this secret base came to light only in 1961 after the US pilot, Gary Powers, who took off from there, was shot down over the Soviet Union.)

In a later and very important 'chukker' of the continuing Great Game, Pakistan, in the 1980s, provided the base from which the US could eject the Soviet forces from Afghanistan, precipitating the break-up of the Soviet Union. If with the establishment of American forces in strength in the Persian Gulf and the prospects of the same happening in the former Muslim territories of the USSR, Western dependence on Pakistan to check Russia has diminished, a half a century's run is all one can reasonably hope for, from the best of strategies.

✶

Krishna Menon, writing in June 1947 to Lord Mountbatten, had wondered whether Britain was following a hidden agenda, whose lid had been slightly raised by Bevin in Margate. Two weeks before Menon wrote to the viceroy, two US diplomats, Ely E. Palmer (envoy extraordinary and minister plenipotentiary to Afghanistan) and R.S. Leach of the State Department, passed through Peshawar, the capital of the North West Frontier Province of British India. They were invited to dine with Sir Olaf Caroe, the British governor of the province. On 26 May 1947 Palmer and Leach reported to the State Department in Washington the substance of their conversation with Sir Olaf. Their report said that the governor asked them to come a little before dinner 'so that they could have a quiet chat'. During this chat, according to the diplomats, 'the Governor first spoke about the "correct" British policy looking towards a united India' but then had 'spoken more frankly' and had emphasized 'the great political importance of the North West Frontier Province and Afghanistan', which he described as 'the uncertain vestibule' in future relations between the Soviet Union and India. He also spoke 'of the danger of Soviet penetration of Gilgit, Chitral and Swat' (all situated on Kashmir's northern border) and then significantly added: 'He would not be unfavorable to the establishment of a separate Pakistan.'[28]

Sir Olaf, before his appointment as governor of the NWFP, had been foreign secretary in Delhi from 1939 to 1946 and hence the principal adviser to two viceroys, Linlithgow and Wavell, on British

India's policy to forestall Soviet expansionism in Afghanistan, Sinkiang and the region of the Persian Gulf. Sir Olaf was really trying to use the Americans' presence in Peshawar to 'educate' the State Department on the usefulness, from a Western point of view, of the creation of Pakistan and Kashmir's adherence to it, as seen by a person with experience in that region. And, in the process, he had let the cat out of the bag.

After his retirement, the British Foreign Office sent Sir Olaf on a lecture tour of America. This tour was, in his own words, an 'attempt to catch and save a way of thought known to many who saw these things from the East, but now in danger of being lost, in the hope that new workers in the vineyards may find in it something worth regard'.[29] In America he lectured on the theme (later collated and published in his book *Wells of Power*) that the Karachi port and the coastline of Baluchistan standing at the mouth of the Persian Gulf were 'vital to its [British] reckoning'. The British base in India – now in Pakistan – had maintained stability in the Middle East since 1801, when Tsar Paul's ambitions first blew the whistle. Russian pressure – 'silent, concentrated, perpetual' – had predated communism, 'the Indian anchor' had been lost, but Pakistan – 'a new India' – had emerged, a Muslim state that could help to establish a defence community of Muslim states and 'show the way for reconciliation between the Western and Islamic models'. Caroe then posed the question: 'Will Islam stand up to communism?' The former foreign secretary of the British Government of India was later to boast that the US secretary of state, John Foster Dulles' phrase 'the northern tier' and his own 'the northern screen' were 'the same idea really'.

It was midway during the Second World War that the British authorities realized that they would have to quit India, their military base for over fifty years, sooner than later. Their thoughts then turned to closing the gap that would result in a Commonwealth defence against a Soviet move to the south, towards the 'the wells of power' and the Indian Ocean. To find a solution, they looked for available opportunities and openings in India in the hallowed British tradition described by Churchill as follows:

We [British] do not think that logic and clear-cut principles are necessarily the sole key to what ought to be done in swiftly changing and indefinable situations.... We assign a larger importance to opportunism and improvisation, seeking rather to live and conquer in accordance with the unfolding events than to aspire to dominate them by fundamental decisions.[30]

So now our attention must turn to the ground realities in India as they obtained at the beginning of the war, which set in motion the events that led to Indian independence and partition.

Notes and References

1. Mountbatten Papers (MB1/E 104, Hartley Library, Southampton).
2. Ibid.
3. Karl Meyer and Shareen Brysac, *Tournament of Shadows* (Counterpoint Press, New York, 1999, p. 152).
4. Henry Rawlinson, *England and Russia* (John Murray, London, 1875, pp. 279–80).
5. Quoted by Sir Penderel Moon, *The British Conquest and Dominion of India*, Vol. 2 (India Research Press, Delhi, 1999, p. 856).
6. View of Sir John Lawrence as paraphrased by Meyer and Brysac, op. cit., p. 155.
7. Gerald Morgan, *Anglo–Russian Rivalry in Central Asia 1810–1895* (Taylor and Francis, London, 1981, p. 120).
8. Fyodor Dostoyevsky, *The Diary of a Writer*, translated by Boris Brasol (Scribner's Sons, New York, 1949, pp. 1051–52).
9. Sir Olaf Caroe, *Wells of Power* (Macmillan, London, 1951, p. 185).
10. K.M. Pannikar, *The Future of South-East Asia* (Asia Publishing House, London, 1943, pp. 69 sqq.) cited in Commonwealth Relations Office (CRO) Document F 15955/8800/85, 1 December 1947, p. 14.
11. Top-secret document, PHP (45) 15 (0) final, 19 May 1945, L/WS/1/983–988 (Oriental and Indian Collection, British Library, London).
12. Top secret, minutes of chiefs of staff (COS) (46) 19(0), 18 April 1946 (OIC, British Library, London).

13. Ibid.
14. Ibid.
15. Ibid.
16. Ibid.
17. Enclosure to Lord Wavell's letter to Lord Frederick Pethick-Lawrence, Simla, 13 July 1946 (OIC, British Library, London).
18. Ibid.
19. Extract from COS (46) 173rd meeting, 29 November 1946, Tp (46), Para 4 (OIC, British Library, London).
20. Ibid.
21. Ibid.
22. Top-secret annexure to minutes of COS (47) 62nd meeting, L/WS/1/1030, pp. 5–12 (OIC, British Library, London).
23. Ibid.
24. Ibid.
25. Top-secret COS memorandum, 7 July 1947, Tp (47) 90, final (OIC, British Library, London).
26. Ibid.
27. Unsigned memorandum dated 19 May 1948, entitled 'The Strategic and Political Importance of Pakistan in the Event of War with the USSR' (Mountbatten Papers, Hartley Library, Southampton).
28. Memorandum in File 845-00/2-2647 (National Archives, Washington, 2 June 1947).
29. Sir Olaf Caroe, article in The Round Table, 1949, and Wells of Power, op. cit.
30. Winston Churchill, Memories of the Second World War, Vol. 6, War Comes to America (Cassel & Co., London, 1950).

2

The Anglo–Muslim League Alliance

IN 1949 I WAS CONVALESCING AFTER AN OPERATION IN THE HOME
outside London of my father's friend Sir Paul Patrick. He had been
a former assistant undersecretary at the India Office before it was
abolished after India gained independence. One day Sir Paul told me
that soon after Adolf Hitler had overrun France in the summer of
1940 and an invasion of the British Isles was imminent, Gandhiji,
during a meeting with Lord Linlithgow, the viceroy, at Simla, stunned
him by saying that the British should have the courage to let Germany
occupy Britain: 'Let them take possession of your beautiful Island,
if Hitler chooses to occupy your homes, vacate them, if he does not
give you free passage out, allow yourself, man, woman and child to
be slaughtered.' Sir Paul then asked me whether Gandhi was turning
senile by that time. Faced with such an impracticable – even unethical –
attitude of the leader of the Indian National Congress Party, no
wonder, Sir Paul said that Lord Linlithgow could not afford to lose
the cooperation and support of Jinnah and the Muslim League to
ensure the successful mobilization of Indian resources for the Second
World War. I must have told Sir Paul some time that we youth in
India believed that the British had gone out of their way to support
the Muslim League or something to that effect. And he was proffering
an explanation for British policy to the son of his friend.

Maulana Abul Kalam Azad, in his book *India Wins Freedom*
refers to this incident and adds to what Sir Paul told me, as follows:

'It was normally his (the Viceroy's) practice to ring the bell for the ADC to come and take Gandhiji to his car. On this occasion he was so surprised that he neither rang the bell nor said good-bye. The result was that Gandhiji walked away from a silent and bewildered Viceroy and had to find his way out to his car all by himself. Gandhiji reported this incident to me with his characteristic humour.'[1]

This incident took place on 29 June 1940. However, misunderstandings between the British and the Congress Party, the main political party fighting for India's freedom, had started to build up right from the beginning of the Second World War. At the time Britain declared war on Germany in September 1939, even though the Central Government in Delhi was in the viceroy's hands, the Congress Party ministries were running the governments in eight out of eleven British provinces* of India and were the foremost partners of Britain in governing the country. They exercised authority over three-fourths of the population of British India and the territories they governed included the British-built port cities of Madras and Bombay, the old Mughal capital of Agra, the ancient cities of Banaras (now called Varanasi) and Patliputra (now called Patna), Lucknow, Ahmedabad and Nagpur and the Pathan stronghold of Peshawar on the Indian side of the Khyber Pass from where the British had played the Great Game to restrain Russian penetration into Central Asia.

The nationalists had taken over power in the aforementioned provinces after their triumph in the provincial elections of 1937 held under the new constitution for an All-India Federation introduced in 1935. This federal scheme provided for self-government at the provincial level and a bicameral legislature at the Centre in which both the eleven British provinces and the 350

---

* India was divided into eleven provinces, ruled directly by the British, and 350 princely states controlled indirectly. By 1939, each British province had an elected legislature (on 14 per cent franchise) and the leader of the majority party ran the government and was called chief minister. The British governors of these provinces had the power to dismiss the ministries and assume control. The chief secretaries in the provinces were mostly British members of the Indian Civil Service (ICS).

princely states* would be represented. The scheme was launched with the consent of Jinnah and the Muslim League. In the Federal Legislature the princes' nominees – none elected, all appointed – were to occupy 110 out of 260 seats in the Upper Chamber and 125 out of 375 seats in the Lower House. Since the elected representatives from British India would belong to various, mutually antagonistic, political parties, the princes' 'battalions', if they remained united, could hold the key to the formation and running of the Central Government. According to Sir Paul's remarks to me, His Majesty's Government's idea was to instal a conservative Indian Government at the Centre that would be able to accommodate essential British interests, besides building up the unity of the country and ensuring its steady progress towards dominion status. It was a recipe for gradualism and for the retention of British influence.

The Federal Legislature and thus the unitary scheme, however, remained stillborn because the Indian princes did not accede to it. Churchill had denounced the scheme in the British Parliament as a 'gigantic quilt of jumbled crochet work...built by pygmies'. He described the notion that India would one day become a dominion as 'criminally mischievous'. He then used intermediaries to travel to India to persuade the princes to stay out of the Federal Legislature, an endeavour that the officers of the Indian Political Service, who dealt with the princes, quietly supported. Had the princes joined the All-India Federation, whatever its shortcomings, a momentum for a unitary India would have been launched and the British would have continued to look towards the princes rather than towards Jinnah. And probably the partition of India would not have taken place.

---

* Less than a dozen princely states were big enough to form viable units, although they lay interspersed with the territories of British provinces. About one hundred of them were of middling size, with annual revenues between US $ 1 million to 5 million at present value. Over two hundred were hardly bigger than Manhattan Island. An overwhelming majority could not possibly stand on their own.

Even so, the introduction of self-government in the British provinces had changed the psychological atmosphere in the country. And this was seen as an important step in Gandhiji's peaceful 'reconquest of India'. The provincial elections had been a setback for Jinnah's Muslim League, which could not get even one-fourth of the seats reserved for Muslims.

The irony of the situation was that within two months of the outbreak of the Second World War, the Congress Party had given up all its gains by resigning from the governments in the provinces. The reasons given by the Congress Party for this grave step were that India had been dragged into the war without any consultation with its elected representatives and that their demand for a declaration about India's freedom after the war and for associating them in some manner or the other with the Central Government in the meantime had been rejected. If the aim of the exercise was to pressurize the British to grant more power to the nationalists forthwith, the result was rather different from that anticipated. Their resignations reduced the British dependence on the Congress Party to mobilize Indian resources for the war and made it less necessary for them to accommodate the party's demands. In other words, the resignations reduced the nationalists' bargaining power with the British authorities. Further, the Congress Party's abdication created a political vacuum in the country that gave an opportunity to the Muslim League, defeated in the elections, to stage a comeback through the back door, by making promises to Britain to cooperate in the war effort. Moreover, it created doubts about the nationalists' commitment to the fight against Hitler and prejudiced opinion against them.

'Had it [the Congress Party] not resigned from its position of vantage in the Provinces the course of Indian history might have been very different.'[2] So says Vapal Panguni Menon, the distinguished civil servant and adviser on constitutional reforms to three viceroys – Linlithgow, Wavell and Mountbatten – in his book *The Transfer of Power in India*. He further says:

> By resigning the Congress Party showed a lamentable political wisdom. There was little chance of its being put out of office: the British Government would surely have hesitated to incur the

odium of dismissing Ministries, which had the overwhelming support of the people. Nor could it have resisted a unanimous demand for a change at the centre, a demand which would have been all the more irresistible after the entry of Japan into the war. In any case it is clear that but for the resignation of the Congress Ministries, Jinnah and the Muslim League would have never attained the position they did.[3]

One of the serious long-term repercussions of the Congress' decision to quit was losing control over the strategic North West Frontier Province. Had this Muslim-majority province remained under Congress Party rule between 1940 and 1946, the plan for the partition of India could not have been put forward. Without the inclusion of the NWFP within its borders, Pakistan would have remained an enclave within India and would have lost its most important asset to the West, that of its strategic value. The inhabitants of this province, mainly Pathans, were under the spell of Khan Abdul Ghaffar Khan, a Congress Party stalwart popularly known as the Frontier Gandhi. The breaking of his spell enabled Jinnah, with British help, to gain a foothold in the province, as we shall soon see.

Jinnah, ensconced in his villa in the tree-clad Malabar Hill in Bombay overlooking the Arabian Sea, was so delighted at the Congress Governments' resignations from the provincial governments that the words 'Himalayan blunder' escaped his lips. And he declared 22 December 1939 as 'Deliverance Day' – deliverance from Congress rule – and immediately went on the offensive to win by diplomacy and bluster what he could never have obtained at that time by popular vote, even of the Muslims of India.

During the First World War, Mahatma Gandhi had supported the Allied war effort. This move had created a soft corner for him in many British hearts, despite Winston Churchill's continuous jibes that he was a charlatan and a humbug. Gandhiji was the first Indian leader the viceroy, Lord Linlithgow, invited for consultations after the start of the Second World War. The meeting took place on

4 September 1939 in Simla, the summer capital of the British Raj, high up in the Himalayas.

> Mr Gandhi explained to me in moving terms the depth of his affection for England and told me that the idea of any enemy defacing Westminster Abbey or Westminster Hall or any monuments of our civilization was one which was intolerable to him and he contemplated the present struggle in his own words with an English heart. I was greatly struck with the depth of his real feeling, his emotion being at times so marked as to make it impossible for him to continue with what he was saying.[4]

So wired the viceroy to Lord Zetland (Laurence John Dumley Dundas), the secretary of state for India in Neville Chamberlain's Government. The viceroy added that Gandhiji had also assured him that he was ready to help with the recruitment of Indians into the Army, as he had done during the First World War.

The British Government received its first shock when Gandhiji failed to get these sentiments translated into the Congress Party's policy; in fact, quite the opposite happened. The Congress leaders met to discuss their attitude to the developing situation at Wardha, Gandhiji's camp in western India, a few days after the above conversation. Jawaharlal Nehru, who had been touring China and had rushed back for the meeting, led with the following argument: 'How can a person bound in chains fight? And if Britain is indeed fighting to uphold freedom should it not logically free India?' He was not a man to knowingly think of, or attempt, blackmail. The provocation for this rhetoric was another. He had visited Europe the previous year and was still seething with anger against the 'class interest-ridden' government of Prime Minister Chamberlain of Britain. Nehru blamed this government for conniving at Francisco Franco's takeover of Spain, for appeasing 'fascist Hitler' at Munich and strangulating the Socialist International, the company of whose members in Europe he had mostly kept. And this was Nehru's way of getting back at Chamberlain, forgetting that once Britain had declared war on Hitler, opposing its war effort on whatever account, in practical terms meant aiding the very fascists he so detested. His anger against His Majesty's Government abated only after the fall of France, when England itself was directly menaced.

★

Subhash Chandra Bose, a rising star from Bengal and Nehru's rival in the Congress Party, also supported the policy of opposing Britain. To him 'Britain's difficulty was India's opportunity'. For some years now, he had been opposing the Mahatma's policy of non-violent non-cooperation as one that was unlikely to yield results and was spoiling to mobilize the masses for a no-holds-barred violent struggle to overthrow British power. A graduate of Cambridge University, like Nehru, Bose was heir to the more revolutionary traditions of Bengal. On his very first meeting with Gandhiji in 1921, he had declared that the Mahatma 'showed a deplorable lack of clarity in his political aims'. Bose's popularity amongst the youth was rising. In 1938, to everyone's surprise, he won the presidentship of the Congress Party, defeating the candidate favoured by Gandhiji. Gandhiji had to work hard to reverse this party decision in the electoral contest the following year. He did so by pushing the equally charismatic, plus a very hard-working and devoted Nehru, to the forefront. In March 1940 Bose formed his own group, the Forward Bloc, and in July 1940 parted company with the Congress Party. Bose, as a result of his subsequent activities perhaps contributed more, in the 1940s, to demoralize the British and break their will to remain in India, than the Congress Party. However, he also contributed to the deepening of the distrust between Britishers and Indians.

Gandhiji was among the few who spoke in favour of unconditional support to Britain in the war at the Congress Party meeting at Wardha. But he failed to press his view in the face of Nehru's emotional appeal and Bose's combative stand. The majority of the Congress leaders, though willing to cooperate with Britain against fascism, wanted a definite declaration from the British that, at the end of the war, India would be freed. They could not rid themselves of memories of the brutal suppression of the freedom movement after the First World War, despite the support the nationalists had given Britain when the hostilities were on. They saw the same pattern emerging again, with the viceroy declaring war on India's behalf without consulting its elected representatives and assuming enabling powers for the duration of the war to interfere in provincial affairs within the competence of the 'popular' governments. The compromise decision taken at Wardha, after several days of deliberations, was that Gandhiji should see the viceroy once again and persuade him to make an unequivocal declaration of British intentions to grant freedom to India as soon as the war ended and, in the meantime, to associate the Congress Party with the Central Government. Gandhiji met the viceroy on 26 September, once again taking the train to the distant Himalayas.

Whereas during his first meeting with the viceroy on 4 September 1939 the atmosphere had been warm, when Gandhiji saw Linlithgow on 26 September, he had turned cold. He brusquely told Gandhiji that there was no prospect of His Majesty's Government agreeing to a declaration of British war aims as demanded by the Congress Party or yielding power at the Centre while Britain was engaged in a life-and-death struggle. 'It was not a question of fighting for democracy,' he explained, 'but of beating Hitler who sought world conquest.' He added that 'the Congress was not the only organization to be considered' because 'there was also the question of the legitimate real claims of other parties and particularly the Princes and the Muslims'. It was a long meeting, during which Gandhiji made the following pitch, as reported by Linlithgow to Zetland: 'If we [the British] could make up our minds to buy Congress we should buy the finest propaganda machine in the East.' It did not move the viceroy. In his report to the secretary of state, he said: 'Their [Congress's] objective is to tie the Muslim community and the Princes tight in constitutional bonds imposed in the first instance with our authority and maintained thereafter in their original rigidity by the majority community.'[5]

✫

Something had obviously happened between 4 and 26 September 1939. And that was Mohammad Ali Jinnah. Jinnah had met the viceroy immediately after Gandhiji on 4 September. While Gandhiji had offered tears and sympathy, Jinnah offered the viceroy the means to win the war and a clear compact. He pledged 'the loyalty of the Muslim community everywhere' (as if he was the sole representative of the Muslims of India) and then, with reference to the Congress ministries in the provinces, told the viceroy: 'Turn them out at once. Nothing else will bring them to their senses. Their object, though you may not believe it...is nothing less than to destroy both you [the British] and us Muslims. They will never stand by you.'[6] And then spelt out his mind:

> Muslim areas should be separated from "Hindu India" and run by Muslims in collaboration with Great Britain.[7]

Jinnah had spoken so candidly to the viceroy because his lieutenant, Khaliq-uz-Zaman, had met Lord Zetland in London a few months earlier. According to Khaliq-uz-Zaman, when he had conveyed to Zetland the desirability of the creation of autonomous Muslim states in the subcontinent that would remain linked with Britain for defence, the British minister showed enough interest to prolong the talk for an hour and a half! The answer Khaliq-uz-Zaman gave to Zetland, when asked about defence, needs to be quoted because it was bound to make the minister feel that the Muslim League would remain dependent upon, and subservient to, Britain: 'If you want to know (about defence) for the period that you are not in any way connected with the administration of the country, then I beg your Lordship not to put that question to me, for God only knows what will happen to us then.'[8]

Gandhiji requested Linlithgow to meet Dr Rajendra Prasad, the Congress president, and Jawaharlal Nehru. The viceroy did so on 3 October 1939. Dr Rajendra Prasad argued: 'If India was to play her part (in the war) she must feel satisfied that she had something to fight for.' He also asserted that 'the Muslim League did not represent the mind of Islam'; i.e., Jinnah did not represent all the Muslims. Nehru pressed for a declaration of war aims so as 'to persuade the people that something big had happened and to produce a sufficient psychological disturbance to produce real enthusiasm for the war'. But then he dwelt at some length on how changes brought about by the war would modify the concept of the Empire itself. This touched a raw nerve in the viceroy, who retorted: 'If the war was to transform the British Empire, it might make a difference to the fortunes of the Congress as well if they were now to decide to commit themselves to active opposition to Government.... They would be well advised in their own interest to avoid a break.'[9]

✶

From then on, the records in the British archives show that with each meeting Linlithgow held with Gandhiji and Jinnah, he gravitated more and more towards the latter. Jinnah's stand that he would ask his co-religionists to oppose the type of declaration demanded by the Congress Party, on the plea that it would harm Muslim interests, was very convenient for his purpose. It would help stall the Congress Party pressure for the same as well as of those members of the Labour Party in England who desired to accommodate the nationalists.

When Gandhiji met Linlithgow next on 5 October 1939, he unfolded a plan to help Britain and bypass the obstacles created by some of his Congress Party colleagues (that is not generally known to the public). According to Linlithgow's report to Zetland, Gandhiji began by saying that Nehru maintained that if we obtained freedom, India would have to go in for a first-class army, a large air force, battleships and everything 'tiptop', 'to which he [Gandhi] had told them that if that is where Congress is leading India, I can go no further with them.' According to Linlithgow, Gandhi then said:

I [Linlithgow] must not feel surprised if in a few days it came out that he [Gandhi] had broken away from his friends. He had desired, since he and I had come so close together, himself to tell me these things in advance. Meanwhile he hoped that I would go quietly ahead on the line I had already taken. If by any chance a greater part of the Congress were to follow him (on the path of non-violence) then of course his own path and perhaps mine [Linlithgow's] also would be greatly eased...I thanked him and asked no more.[10]

Judging from the exchange of views between Linlithgow and Jinnah later on the same day, it becomes evident that Gandhiji's démarche had made no impression on the viceroy. For Gandhiji this was a way to help Britain, however tortuous the approach (and indeed he did everything to keep the Congress Party from obstructing the war effort, until 1942, when the Cripps* offer, with the embryo of Pakistan hidden in it, made him emote like a jilted lover). For Linlithgow, if Gandhiji were a true friend, he would have dug in his heels and forced the Congress Party to cooperate with the British war effort.

'Jinnah', the viceroy reported, began by 'expressing great gratitude for what I had done to assist [him] in keeping his Party together'.[11] Jinnah was referring to the pressure Linlithgow had applied on Sikandar Hayat Khan, the chief minister of the Punjab, to fall in line with Jinnah. Linlithgow's disciplining Sikandar Hayat Khan was no small help. Besides being a staunch friend of the British, he was the premier of a province from which 50 per cent of the British Indian Army was recruited and a major figure in Indian politics. Though a member of the Muslim League, Sikandar Hayat Khan believed that his government, as well as the unity of his prosperous province, was being threatened by Jinnah's policy of pitting the Muslims against the Hindus and the Sikhs, all of whom supported his coalition government in the Punjab. And lived amicably in it. Linlithgow's perspective was different. After acknowledging Jinnah's thanks, he told him:

> It was clearly unsatisfactory that while one of the two great parties was well organized and well equipped to pursue its objectives and express its aims, that the other equally of great importance should be masked and prevented from securing its full expression by failure to secure an adequate mouthpiece. It was in the public interest that the Muslim point of view should be fully and competently expressed.[12]

---

* As part of the Stafford Cripps' mission to India in early 1942.

The viceroy then sought Jinnah's opinion on the Congress Party's demands for a declaration of British objectives in India after the war and on the expansion of the council to accommodate political parties. It was now Jinnah's turn to scratch Linlithgow's back. Neither was necessary, Jinnah replied and added that he would refuse 'to reach agreement either with the Congress or the government unless the plan of creating a united India was abandoned, and effective protection was given to the Muslim minorities in the Provinces'.[13] Linlithgow, by citing this 'Muslim objection', could now deflect the Congress Party's demands as well as those of the Labour Party critics at home.

Reinforced with this pledge of Jinnah, Linlithgow, on 17 October 1939, proceeded to issue a statement on British policy in India that brought about the Anglo–Congress Party rupture. This statement promised that, after the war, consultations would be held with representatives of various communities, parties and interests in British India and also with the Indian princes, to secure their cooperation in the framing of such modifications in the stalled federal scheme as may be agreed upon. And, in the meantime, to set up 'a consultative group' of the representatives of the political parties and princes.[14] All this was very far from the Congress Party's demands and was condemned by it as a reiteration of the same old imperialist policy of prevarication. And on 23 October, in a huff, the Congress ministries in the provinces decided to quit. Linlithgow, under London's pressure, tried to placate the nationalists by suggesting an expansion of the Viceroy's Executive Council to include political leaders, but the Congress Party went ahead with its resignations. This walking out by the Congress Party from the provincial governments was interpreted by many in England as its refusal to support Britain in its life-and-death struggle against the Axis powers. It turned out to be a watershed in Indo–British relations.

*

There had been considerable support in England for the Congress Party's demand for a British declaration on its post-war policy on India, with the Labour Party leader, Clement Attlee, wanting the viceroy to respond to it 'with imaginative insight'.[15] According to a private telegram from Zetland to Linlithgow, Stafford Cripps in a letter to Nehru had urged him to stand firm and not to recede by an inch from the position he had taken (on the declaration), which Zetland termed 'all very naughty and extremely mischievous'.[16]

On the other hand, the mood of the British establishment in India that surrounded the viceroy was different. When Desmond Young, the editor of the *Pioneer* newspaper, had got Nehru to agree to terms for the Congress Party's cooperation in the war which he wanted to show to Linlithgow, Sir John Gilbert Laithwaite, the viceroy's private secretary, turned down his request for an interview with the viceroy, with the words: 'Surely you don't believe a word these fellows say. You are only wasting the Viceroy's time.'[17] And Laithwaite also headed off other Britishers such as Malcom Darling, a senior British civil servant, who tried to intervene to prevent a rupture. For the British establishment in India, which was appalled that the Congress Party had been given power by London to govern over large parts of India, this was an easy way to get them off their backs.

After the administration of the Congress-run provinces was taken over by the government, Linlithgow began to lean even more towards the Muslim League. He calculated that in view of the Congress Party's earlier commitment against Nazism and fascism, it would be hesitant to start a campaign of civil disobedience. Further that international opinion would condemn any action by this party that might thwart the war effort. The government was also confident that it had ample resources to crush any civil disobedience movement that the nationalists might launch.

When Gandhiji saw Linlithgow next on 4 November 1939 he regretted the turn things had taken, promised to continue to work towards a settlement and made several suggestions.[18] However, all of them floundered as Linlithgow's insisted that the Muslims and the princes would have to be first brought on board. When the viceroy saw Jinnah the same day the atmosphere was completely different. Referring to Jinnah's public rejection of a declaration of British objectives in India after the war, Linlithgow thanked him for the 'very valuable help he had given by standing firm against the Congress claims' and added that he was 'duly grateful'.[19] In his telegram on his discussions with Zetland, he reported: 'If Jinnah and the Congress had confronted me with a joint demand on this [the British declaration], the strain upon me and upon HMG would indeed have been very great.'[20]

Jinnah, after accepting Linlithgow's thanks, made certain remarks that were bound to sound like music to any Britisher at that time and would be lapped up in London. 'He [Jinnah] was extremely doubtful as to the capacity of India and Indians to look after themselves', reported Linlithgow. And added: 'If the British by any chance be beaten in the war and driven out of India, India would break into a hundred pieces in three months and lie open, in addition, to external invasion.' After offering this bouquet, Jinnah came to the point he had come to make. Referring to the recent debate in the House of Lords, he said:

> Prominent personages, who were quite likely to be in the [British] Cabinet after the war, had frankly urged that in India [the] majority must rule and the minority take their medicine.... When the opposition at home came into power they would force democratic government on India and anaesthetize the Muslims.[21]

Therefore, what he wanted was an undertaking from HMG that the Muslim community would not be compelled in any future dispensation to accept something it did not want. Linlithgow kept silent on this subject, but promised to forward this view to London for consideration.

Jinnah saw the viceroy again on 12 January 1940 and advised on the form the British undertaking should take: 'If you say that you would make no new pronouncement or new constitutional departure unless the Muslims approved, he [Jinnah] would be attacked as the arch supporter of Imperialism and for playing our [British] game. Therefore the formulation should be that any pronouncement of a future advance would have to receive the approval of the two communities.'[22] And then delivered the following broadside against the Congress Party that he knew would be more conducive to clinch his argument than any other on the basis of merit: 'Show Congress that they can get nothing further out of you and once they know that, they will be more likely to come to a settlement and even if they don't, what do you lose?'[23] It is well to record here that whatever the sentiments of Jinnah on his ability to manipulate the viceroy, the latter was quite sure that he was using the former.

'He [Jinnah] represents a minority and a minority that can only hold its own with our assistance'[24]

was how Linlithgow later put it to the secretary of state.

The next day Linlithgow was in Bombay and sent for Jinnah to seek his help in installing a Muslim League Ministry in the North West Frontier Province – the crucial province – from which the Congress Party Government had walked out in October 1939. Jinnah agreed to go to Lahore and make the effort. The collaboration between the British and Jinnah was now growing day by day. Linlithgow then told him that he was under pressure from England not to 'indefinitely postpone normality'; in other words, he should try to bring back a measure of popular participation in government. The Muslim League chief's reply, as reported by the viceroy, was as follows: 'The Hindus were not capable of running a government as we will find for ourselves before we had finished.'[25] And when Linlithgow drew his attention to an article by John Gunther, the American journalist, on Nehru, that had just appeared in the *Life* magazine in the United States, and asked him to do something to contradict such pro-Congress propaganda, Jinnah replied that he had no funds to do so, thereby leaving whatever had to be done in this context to his new British partner.[26]

At his next meeting with Gandhiji on 5 February 1940 Linlithgow unfolded his country's plan to bring about 'normality' that the British Cabinet was pressing for. According to his report he told Gandhiji that despite his earlier announcement to suspend negotiations for the All-India Federation, HMG was now willing to resume them even during the war, and that such a federation could most appropriately be used as a means to achieve the goal of self-government within the Empire – by which he signalled Britain's continued support for a unitary constitution, a significant point. Linlithgow's report continues: 'Gandhi responded to this by repeating the Congress stand that "there was no sufficient ground to render further discussions profitable".' Linlithgow claimed that he, nevertheless, persisted: 'The whole business was something that had to grow' – that some movement on the part of the Congress Party would start a process of mutual accommodation. But Gandhiji remained silent and another opportunity for holding a dialogue and for stemming the Jinnah tide was lost. Reported Linlithgow to Zetland: 'The most probable explanation of the Congress attitude is that if they can but hold out for a little longer we may suffer such strong pressure from public opinion at home that we shall offer them a better bargain.'[27]

The viceroy saw Jinnah later the same day. Jinnah complained that the viceroy never appeared to break with Gandhiji, which created 'dreadful suspense'. He threatened: 'If the Congress Governments returned to provincial office there will be civil war in India.' Then taking up Linlithgow's request of the previous month to instal a Muslim League Ministry in the North West Frontier Province, he observed that he required the support of the governor, Sir George Cunningham, to be able to do so. And added: 'There could be no better advertisement of the real position in India whether before the country or throughout the world than that a non-Congress Ministry should be set up in the North West Frontier [Province].'[28] Naturally, because a Congress Party Ministry in a 95 per cent Muslim-majority province was embarrassing to him – and to his plans for partition. And the viceroy agreed to ask the governor of NWFP to help Jinnah. It was to block further British initiatives of the type Linlithgow had made to Gandhiji and to keep the ball under his own feet that Jinnah now decided to come out openly with his 'two-nation theory' and place it on the negotiating table.

★

The Congress Party, stranded in the wilderness, also now decided to issue a threat. The Congress Party Working Committee meeting at Patna at the end of February 1940 described the war as an 'imperialist war' and resolved that 'the withdrawal of Congress Ministries [from the provinces] must naturally be followed by civil disobedience to which the Congress will unhesitatingly resort as soon as the Congress organization is considered fit enough for the purpose.' This resolution was confirmed at the Ramgarh session of the Congress Party in March that year. Widely criticized in India as 'completely ignoring the realities of the internal and international situation', it provided Jinnah with the perfect backdrop for his move on Pakistan, which he made a few days later.

Eleven days before he gave the call for the partition of India, Jinnah took the viceroy into confidence regarding his plans on 13 March 1940. According to Linlithgow's report to Zetland, Jinnah told him:

> Given the development of the war [its possible extension into Asia] there was much to be said for our [British and Muslims] getting together…[but] if we wished for their [Muslims'] definite and effective help we must not sell the pass behind their backs…. He and his friends were clear that Muslims were not a minority but a nation, that democracy (i.e., majority rule) for India was impossible, and they were anxious not to let us get ourselves in a position in which our hold over India was deliberately and progressively withdrawn so that in the end the control of the country would be handed over to Hindu Raj. He [Jinnah] was quite prepared to contemplate the possibility that we might have to stay here much longer than was anticipated for the job of keeping the ring…. He wanted Muslim areas to be run by Muslims in collaboration with Great Britain, and that Muslims would be able to safeguard "because of their military power even those of their community who were domiciled in the Hindu areas".[29]

Jinnah's audacious remark that Muslims in their own state would be able to safeguard even their co-religionists left behind in India and his call for a continued British presence in the subcontinent after partition amounted to invoking a full-fledged Anglo–Muslim League alliance against a 'Congress–Hindu India' of the future.

Linlithgow replied to Jinnah as follows:

His Majesty's Government's presence would be needed in India longer than even some imagined [and this could be] in a manner as little out of tune with Indian aspirations as possible [and] in such a tripartite arrangement [Muslims, Hindus and the princes]...Britain would have the predominant responsibility for defence.[30]

Jinnah preferred instead a separate Muslim state dependent on British support to safeguard British interests. And that is what happened in the end.

Jinnah, on 24 March 1940, proclaimed at Lahore that 'the Muslims are a separate nation according to any definition of a nation and they must have their own homelands, their territory and their states'. He suggested grouping the geographically contiguous areas in which the Muslims were numerically in a majority as in the northwest and eastern zones, to constitute autonomous and sovereign states with such territorial adjustments as may be necessary. No Muslim leader had so far proposed that a sovereign and separate Muslim state (or states) be founded in India in provinces where Muslims were in a numerical majority. The reasons for this were not hard to seek. But before we delve into these, let us continue to follow the British–Jinnah dialogue on the one hand and the ups and downs of the Congress Party policies on the other, which were contributing to the forging of the Anglo–Muslim League alliance.

The British reaction to Jinnah's announcement becomes evident from the exchanges between the viceroy and the secretary of state on it. On 4 April 1940 Linlithgow wired Zetland:

I am not too keen to start talking about a period after which British rule will have ceased in India. I suspect that day is very remote.... It would [however] be politically unfortunate to criticize it [Jinnah's plan].... The wise tactics would be to keep our hands free until a critical moment is reached in future constitutional discussions.[31]

And in a subsequent telegram advised: 'Any constitutional progress for India must be preceded by internal agreement...to strike a balance.' In other words, use Jinnah's plan to forestall the Congress Party and its supporters in England. Zetland agreed:

> I do not feel much uneasiness about provoking Congress which has largely shot its bolt.... I feel the greatest possible uneasiness...over any measure that might provoke [the] Muslim League, in view of the uncertainties as regards the Middle East.... I would deprecate any step which might be interpreted as weighing scale in favour of Hindus by giving an insufficient weight to Muslim Leaguers.[32]

Meanwhile, there had been some adverse comments in the United States on Jinnah's proposal to partition India. On this, Linlithgow advised Zetland 'to make some play with the extent to which we have...continued insistence on Indian unity which you and I have repeatedly stressed'. He, however, warned that 'any condemnation of Jinnah's scheme will at once irritate Muslim feelings and will be seized on by Congress'.[33]

The secretary of state made a statement in the House of Lords on 18 April 1940. This was in response to Jinnah's repeated pleas for a guarantee to the minorities. Zetland was equally responding to Linlithgow's advice to ignore the Pakistan scheme but yet keep Jinnah in play:

> I cannot believe that any government or Parliament in this country would admit to impose by force upon, for example, 80 million Muslim subjects of His Majesty in India a form of constitution under which they would live peacefully and contentedly.[34]

On 19 April, Linlithgow underlined this particular portion of the secretary of state's speech and sent it to Jinnah.

The viceroy was, by that stage, so taken up with the idea of building up Jinnah as the spokesman of the Muslims in India that when Sikandar Hayat Khan, the premier of the Punjab, once again brought to the attention of the British governor of the province, Henry Craik, the danger that the Pakistan scheme would pose to the peace and unity of his province, Linlithgow asked the governor to just ignore him. By encouraging separatist forces in the Punjab in order to build up the strength of the Muslim League in India against the Congress Party, Linlithgow was playing a dangerous game of brinkmanship. And he cannot be entirely absolved of the blame for the communal carnage that subsequently engulfed the province in 1947, well after he had retired to his castle in Scotland.

In May 1940 as the German panzers smashed through the low countries and raced towards Paris, Winston Churchill replaced Neville Chamberlain as the prime minister of Great Britain and Leopold Amery, who had been two years senior to Churchill at the Harrow School and who had hurled the Cromwellian words 'in the name of God, Go!' at Chamberlain, on the floor of the House of Commons, succeeded Lord Zetland as secretary of state for India. Churchill proved a great war leader and probably saved the world from Hitler. But his assumption of office was ominous for India, which, as was well known, was his blind spot. Amery, his friend, has been quoted as wondering

> whether on the subject of India he is really quite sane – there is no relation between his manner, physical and intellectual on this theme and the equability and dominant good sense he displayed on issues directly affecting the conduct of the war.[35]

Churchill and his Tory friends had earlier sabotaged the scheme for an All-India Federation, which had been launched by his own Conservative Party Government in 1935, fearful that it may ultimately lead to dominion status for India. To Churchill 'India was a geographical expression, a land that was no more a single country than the equator'; he had no qualms regarding how many pieces it was broken up into. After hearing him speak at a cabinet meeting, Lord Wavell, the future viceroy, noted in his diary: 'Churchill hates

India and everything to do with it.'[36] Churchill himself is on record as saying: 'I hate Indians – they are a beastly people with a beastly religion'.[37] And, of course, Gandhiji was always Churchill's bugbear, whom he termed 'an enemy' and 'a thoroughly evil force'. Many Englishmen of those times, 'temperamentally, by upbringing, and by instinct', were believers 'in a racially based imperialism', as the historian Patrick French points out. However, Churchill's feelings about India were far more intemperate.

On taking over as prime minister, Churchill was too busy rallying England to face up to the German invasion to interfere in Amery's handling of India. But even so, he insisted that telegrams exchanged between him and Linlithgow be shown to him, a practice not followed by his predecessor. Churchill's objective was, no doubt, to block any constitutional advance his secretary of state, who prided himself on being an egghead, might think up. And indeed the fidgety nature of Amery can be discerned in an early telegram he sent to Linlithgow asking him whether there was any chance of enlisting Jawarharlal Nehru as 'the recruiter in chief', i.e., of winning him over. After all, Nehru like himself and his chief, was an old Harrow boy. (And be it noted in tribute to the old school tie that when Nehru was sentenced to three years of rigorous imprisonment by a British magistrate later the same year, Amery and Churchill enquired from Linlithgow whether the sentence did not appear too harsh – a concern quite out of character for Churchill for Indian leaders.)

★

By June 1940 the Congress Party's capacity to negotiate on the basis of realistic and easily understandable policies had further deteriorated. As noted at the beginning of this chapter, on 29 June 1940, Gandhiji had told Linlithgow (much to his amazement) that Britain should resist Hitler's invasion exclusively through non-violent action, even if it meant self-annihilation. The next day Gandhiji wrote a letter to the viceroy, which said:

> You are losing: if you persist it will only result in greater bloodshed. Hitler is not a bad man. If you call it off to-day he will follow

suit. If you want to send me to Germany or anywhere else I am at your disposal.[38]

Linlithgow's reply brings one down to terra firma:

We are engaged in a struggle. As long as we do not achieve our aim we are not going to budge. Everything is going to be all right.[39]

Gandhiji had become extra loud in preaching non-violence during the summer of 1940. This was partly to head off the challenge posed by Subhash Chandra Bose. What, however, remains inexplicable is why he started counselling Britain to adopt non-violent non-cooperation as the best method of fighting Hitler. Such advice, given to a people at a time when they were bracing themselves to offer 'blood, toil, tears and sweat', with their leader promising 'we shall go on to the end...whatever the cost may be...we shall never surrender', played right into the hands of Churchill's friends who saw the Mahatma as the arch saboteur of the British Empire.

Nehru saw the danger of Gandhiji's going too far with his 'non-violence'. After the fall of France, he was able to impress upon his colleagues the risks to India and the world if Hitler were to overwhelm Britain. He devised a formula that might open the way for a dialogue with Britain and lead to cooperation in the war effort. A new resolution was passed by the Congress Party in July 1940. While this resolution pressed for a British declaration granting complete independence after the war, it laid aside 'the creed of non-violence in the sphere of national defence', which had been the party's most important declared reason for its inability to have anything to do with the war. Gandhiji resigned from the leadership of the party so as not to compromise his own absolute opposition to violence by association with it (apparently forgetting that at the beginning of the war, it was he who had offered unconditional support to the war effort).

Linlithgow was 'against running after the Congress' and preferred a policy 'of lying back'.[40] In his dispatches during this period, he shows greater interest in hunting and fishing than in responding to any initiatives from the Congress Party's side. For example, he reported his satisfaction at landing a thirty-six-and-a-half pound Mahaseer in the UP forests and his anxiety to bag a Ghond stag.[41] The reasons for the viceroy's relaxed mood were not far to seek. Around 200,000 recruits were offering themselves for military service each month, out of which only about 50,000 could be absorbed by the defence forces. Moreover, Indian industrialists, including the Congress Party financiers, such as Ghanshyam Das Birla, were fully engaged in producing goods for the Army, if not out of loyalty to the King Emperor than out of devotion to their own pockets. What more help could the Congress Party in Linlithgow's estimation give to Britain at this time, except to get in his way if its leaders were asked to join his government?

Jinnah met the viceroy on 27 June 1940. He had apparently received intelligence with regard to Amery's plans to come out with a declaration on HMG's policy on India in the wake of the formation of the new government. He pressed Linlithgow 'for a declaration on agreement between the principal communities as precedent to the implementation of any constitutional scheme'. Referring to Zetland's April statement in the House of Lords, he demanded a firmer guarantee to ensure that 'the likes of Cripps and Wedgewood Benn* in England at some future date would not sell the Muslims to the Hindus'.[42] Jinnah's views were accepted by the War Cabinet, though Churchill warned against 'any far-reaching declaration'. The upshot was the British declaration made by Linlithgow on 8 August 1940 and, at Jinnah's request, repeated by Amery in the House of Commons on 14 August. It offered dominion status after the war; an expansion of the Viceroy's Executive Council to accommodate representatives of political parties; a War Consultative Committee which would include some princes; and a guarantee to the minorities as follows:

It goes without saying that they [the HMG] could not contemplate transfer of their present responsibilities for the peace and welfare of India to any system of Government whose

---

* Both socialists.

authority is directly denied by large and powerful elements in India's national life. Nor could they be parties to the coercion of such elements into submission to such a Government.[43]

The British forever afterwards interpreted the aforementioned statement as His Majesty's Government's firm commitment not only to the Muslims of India but also to Jinnah as the sole spokesman of the Muslims of India, thus virtually according him veto powers over future Indian constitutional developments. The declaration therefore turned out to be an important milestone in the British efforts to build up Jinnah and forge the Anglo–Muslim League alliance. In all subsequent negotiations for Indian independence, Jinnah flung this declaration at the British negotiators who questioned his demand for Pakistan or suggested a settlement of communal differences in an elected Constituent Assembly instead of directly with him. And after the Labour Party replaced the Conservative Party in power in England in 1945, British civil servants in London and New Delhi were ever ready to point to this British declaration in order to curb any propensity on the part of their new masters to bypass Jinnah.

Jinnah and his party in 1940 did not, in fact, represent all the Muslims of India and even within the Muslim League there was serious opposition to his separatist policies. Sikandar Hayat Khan and Fazal-ul-Haq, the Muslim League premiers of the Punjab and Bengal – the major provinces claimed by Jinnah for Pakistan – were totally opposed to the concept of a Muslim nation. Sikandar Hayat Khan called it 'Jinnahstan'. It was therefore not unreasonable for the Congress Party to insist that unless a settlement was reached with the elected representatives of the Muslim community as a whole, preferably in an elected Constituent Assembly functioning outside British influence, there could be no finality to it, since Jinnah could not be considered the sole representative of the Muslims.

The British declaration of 8 August 1940 came as a rude shock to the Congress leaders. The veto power given to Jinnah on India's constitutional developments would increase his intransigence. Their reaction was to revoke their own offer made after the fall of France to lay aside their creed of non-violence for national defence, which they had hoped would clear the way for cooperation with the Allies during the war. However, Gandhiji was worried that in their frustration some Congressmen might go too far and start an agitation against the government, which he had promised the viceroy he would discourage. So he worked out a strategy that would enable the Congress Party to show to the public that it was giving no quarter to the British authorities and yet take no action that would really hinder the war effort, which stand Subhash Chandra Bose compared to 'running with the hare and hunting with the hound'.

To prepare the ground for his new approach, Gandhiji wrote to the viceroy on 29 August 1940 that his desire not to embarrass the British Government during the war 'could not be carried to the extent of the Congress Party committing hara-kiri'. And when he saw Linlithgow on 27 September 1940, he reiterated his view and insisted that he had the right of freedom of speech to dissuade the people from recruitment on the ground that his party was committed to only non-violent action. 'A person had a right not to join the army but not the privilege to propagate the same', Linlithgow argued back, reporting to London that 'to preach non-violence in this way was unlikely to remain an academic question but impinge on the war effort'.[44] Making an issue of his freedom to preach non-violence, Gandhiji, on 17 October 1940, launched what was termed 'Individual Peaceful Disobedience'.

Under this movement, important Congress leaders, one after the other, would speak in public to protest against recruitment into the Army, and get arrested. There would be no mass stir; merely protest by selected individuals. The Congress Party opened its innings by sending in Vinobha Bhave, Gandhiji's staunchest disciple of non-violence, who got promptly 'stumped'; in other words, he was put behind bars. Nehru followed as number two. After he too landed in jail, Sardar Vallabhbhai Patel was sent in. And so on and so forth till all the top stars of the Congress Party got themselves picked up and packed into British prisons. Gandhiji then retired to his ashram and devoted himself to social work and the spinning wheel, leaving the viceroy to handle the complexities of defence preparedness without any embarrassment from the Congress Party's side.

Louis Fisher characterized this agitation as one launched 'to save face'. The director of British Intelligence had a different view of the Gandhian policy in 1940. In one of his reports, he quotes Nehru as saying: 'No one expects Gandhiji's movement to bring success, but its moral value is what counts.' The director then added: 'After the war is over any ban [on the Congress] will be lifted, Congress leaders will be released and at the next elections Congress will sweep the polls. Today they want to embarrass the Government morally. Gandhiji's plan serves this purpose.'[45]

Some Indians at least were less than convinced about the moral ascendancy of the Congress Party's policy. Chamanlal Sitalvad, a well-known barrister, wrote in the *Statesman* on 7 October 1940 as follows: 'Gandhiji says that the Congress [Party] is as much opposed to victory for Nazism as any Britisher can be, nevertheless he demands liberty to carry on anti-war propaganda that must weaken the war effort and thus assist the enemy. Gandhiji proclaims the Congress [Party] would rather die in the act of proclaiming its faith in the creed of non-violence than departing from it. Had Mr Gandhi momentarily forgotten this creed when on the outbreak of the war he expressed himself to the effect that India would give unconditional support to Britain in the prosecution of the war? The Congress [Party] says in the Poona Resolution that they will give all help to Britain in the war if there was a declaration of the independence for India and responsible government was set up at the Centre. If these conditions can be fulfilled then the Congress [Party] was prepared to give the go-by to their creed of non-violence and participate in the war.'

The number of Congressmen arrested during Gandhiji's 'Individual Civil Disobedience' reached a peak of 15,000 by the summer of 1941. 'The movement caused no excitement and attracted little attention and owing to the muzzling of the press was hardly known to be in progress. So the movement dragged on for a year with dwindling numbers participating. The effect on India's war effort was nil.'[46] Nor did Gandhiji's movement deter Indians from taking advantage of the opportunities for employment: ultimately, the strength of the British Indian armed forces rose from about 190,000 at the beginning of the war to almost two million towards the end. And when it was decided to release the demoralized

Congressmen at the end of 1941 – Nehru and Azad were released on 3 December – Churchill called it: 'Surrender at the moment of success.'

Whatever the conceived benefits of the 'Individual Peaceful Disobedience' to the nationalists, it led to considerable gains for Jinnah and the Muslim League. According to one Muslim leader: 'While the Congress civil disobedience was lingering along [sic], the Muslim League through speeches, pamphlets and personal contacts had started making rapid progress in the cities and towns.' And believing that in the final reckoning violence, not non-violence, would pay, the League started to build up a force called the Muslim National Guards whose volunteers took to escorting Jinnah to public functions with drawn swords[47] – the sword of Islam. Linlithgow repeatedly turned down Jinnah's pleas to accept the principle of Pakistan, insisting that this must be left 'as an open question for post-war discussion', but did everything possible to bolster Jinnah and 'to shepherd all the Muslims into the [Muslim League] fold', as he put it, in a report to London.[48] This was no easy task considering the personal and policy differences among Muslim leaders. According to Linlithgow, Sikandar Hayat Khan told him that Jinnah was frightened that Hitler would win the war and he would find himself in trouble. He gave other instances of Jinnah's chickenheartedness. Linlithgow faced opposition to Jinnah from the Bengal Muslim League premier, Fazal-ul-Haq, as well. But the viceroy's faith in Jinnah as the best instrument to fight the Congress Party never wavered.

Lord Linlithgow, the son of a former British governor of Australia, was sent out to India in 1936 to inaugurate the 1935 Constitution that he had taken the lead to finalize as chairman of the Joint Parliamentary Committee. It was ironical that circumstances instead led him to bury the same. Nehru described Lord Linlithgow as 'slow of mind, solid as a rock and with almost a rock's lack of awareness'.[49] Leo Amery compared the six-and-a-half-foot-tall and pernickety Scottish peer with a huge double chin to a ponderous elephant who possessed 'an elephant's cunning'. According to him, Hopie (as Linlithgow was called by his friends) did 'a great piece of work in all essentials; he had broken the Congress attempt to force it into a disastrous surrender'.[50] With the help of the Congress Party-hating civil servants who surrounded him – and with no little help from the Congress Party itself – he had indeed built up the Anglo–Muslim League alliance and headed off any possibility of an Anglo–Congress Party *rapprochement*. Disbelieving that the British would have to leave India in the foreseeable future, he displayed no real enthusiasm for Pakistan, but by making concessions to Jinnah, to keep him in play against the Congress Party, he created the conditions on the ground that made partition possible a few years later. 'It is possible, though by no means certain,' contends a British historian, 'that if from the outset the British had made it clear that they would never countenance the partition of India, the demand for Pakistan would have been dropped.'[51]

Under the British system, everything that was discussed with Indian leaders was communicated day to day to London almost verbatim. If the viceroy saw Jinnah and Gandhiji the same day, his dispatch might run into twenty-five to thirty pages. Hence, Jinnah's repeated pleas for the prolongation of the British presence in India and his sallies against the 'Hindu Congress' – the enemy – were reaching the highest echelons of the British Government and creating a niche for Jinnah in British hearts, more so because they knew he was dependent upon them. Jinnah's reach on the ground did not extend to all the Muslims in India, leave alone that enjoyed countrywide by the Congress Party. But his consistency and directness, as opposed to the contradictions and confusability of the Congress Party policies, particularly as they appear in cold print in Linlithgow's telegrams and letters, created an aura of his strength and integrity. These meticulously maintained records were always available to British ministers and viceroys who dealt with India then and in subsequent years and played a part in firming up Britain's position in favour of the Muslim League and against the Congress Party.

It would be appropriate to end this chapter by quoting how V.P. Menon viewed the situation:

The Congress opposition to the war effort and the [Muslim] League's de facto support for it had convinced the British that Hindus generally were their enemies and the Muslims their friends. And this consideration must have added force to the silent but effective official support for the policy of partition.[52]

Soon Japan would strike Pearl Harbor and, in one fell swoop, conquer the British Empire in Asia, east of India. This would change the ball game for the British as well as for the Indians, not the least because it brought the USA into the arena. However, before we come to that, let us cast a glance at Jinnah's scheme for a separate state or states for the Muslims of India, as proposed by him on 24 March 1940, and at Jinnah's own enigmatic personality.

Notes and References

1. Maulana Abul Kalam Azad, *India Wins Freedom* (Orient Longman, Delhi, first published 1958, p. 35; revised edition 1988).

2. V.P. Menon, *Transfer of Power in India* (Longman Green, London, 1957, p. 52).

3. Ibid.

4. MSS/EUR F 115/8, Vol. V, p. 96 [Oriental and Indian Collection (OIC), British Library, London].

5. Ibid., pp. 149–50.

6. Ibid., pp. 100–02.

7. Ibid.

8. Khaliq-uz-Zaman, *Pathway to Pakistan* (Longman Green, London, 1961, p. 206).

9. MSS/EUR 125/8, Vol. IV, pp. 161(a) to (k) (OIC, British Library, London).

10. Ibid., pp. 169 (a) to (e).

11. Ibid., pp. 169 (e) to 170.

12. Ibid.

13. Ibid.

14. V.P. Menon, op. cit., p. 66.

15. Sir Penderel Moon, *The British Conquest and Dominion of India*, Vol. 2 (India Research Press, Delhi, 1999, p. 1088).

16. MSS/EUR/125/8, Vol. IV, viceroy to secretary of state, 26 October 1939 (OIC, British Library, London).

17. Desmond Young, *Try Anything Twice* (Hamish Hamilton, London, 1963, pp. 245–46) and Sir Penderel Moon, *Divide and Quit* (University of California Press, Berkeley, 1961, p. 25).

18. MSS/EUR/125/8, Vol. IV, p. 199 (i), note of viceroy's interview with Gandhiji, 4 November 1939 (OIC, British Library, London).

19. Ibid., note of viceroy's interview with Jinnah.

20. Ibid., pp. 199 (j), (k) and (l).

21. MSS/EUR F 125/9, Vol. V, pp. 41–45 (OIC, British Library, London).

22. Ibid.

23. Ibid.

24. MSS/EUR F 125/12, TOP (transfer of power), Vol. III, p. 769 (OIC, British Library, London).

25. MSS/EUR F 125/9, Vol. V, pp. 45–49, note on viceroy's talk with Jinnah in Bombay, 13 January 1940 (OIC, British Library, London).

26. Ibid.

27. Ibid., p. 91, viceroy's telegram (Para 6) to secretary of state, 6 February 1940, on his talk with Gandhiji and Jinnah on 5 February 1940.

28. Ibid.

29. MSS/EUR F 125/8, Vol. V, pp. 191–95, note of viceroy's interview with Jinnah, 13 March 1940 (OIC, British Library, London).

30. Ibid.

31. Ibid., telegram from viceroy to secretary of state, 4 April 1940.

32. Ibid., p. 140, telegram (Para 3) from secretary of state to viceroy.

33. MSS/EUR F 125/9, Vol. V, pp. 91–92, viceroy to secretary of state, 6 April 1940.

34. See V.P. Menon, op. cit., p. 85, for text of Amery's statement in the House of Lords, 18 April 1940.

35. W.J. Barnds, *Pakistan and the Great Powers* (Pall Mall, London, 1972, p. 993).

36. Lord Archibald Wavell, *The Viceroy's Journal* (Oxford University Press, London, 1977).

37. Koenraad Elst, *The Saffron Swastika: The Notion of 'Hindu Fascism'*, Vol. 1 (Voice of India, New Delhi, 2001, p. 532).

38. Robert Payne, *Life and Death of Gandhi* (Rupa, Delhi, 1979, pp. 486–89).

39. Ibid.

40. MSS/EUR/9/5, p. 127, viceroy to secretary of state (OIC, British Library, London).

41. Ibid., p. 124.
42. File L/P&J/8/507, Jinnah's interview with Linlithgow, 27 June 1940, at Simla.
43. V.P. Menon, op. cit., p. 93.
44. MSS EUR F 125/19, Vol. V, viceroy's telegram, 27 September 1940.
45. Director, Intelligence Bureau, commentary, 21 May 1940 (OIC, British Library, London).
46. Sir Penderel Moon, *The British Conquest and Dominion of India*, Vol. 2, p. 1097.
47. Patrick French, *Liberty or Death: India's Journey to Independence and Division* (HarperCollins, London, 1995, pp. 132–33).
48. MSS/EUR F/125/9, Vol. V, p. 291.
49. Jawaharlal Nehru, *Discovery of India* (Oxford University Press, Delhi, 1990, p. 437).
50. Amery to Anthony Eden, TOP, Vol. III, S.No. 695, L/PO/8/9a–9, May 1943, pp. 109–15.
51. Sir Penderel Moon, *The British Conquest and Dominion* of India, Vol. 2, pp. 109–23.
52. V.P. Menon, op. cit., p. 438.

3

The Pakistan Scheme and Jinnah

IN THE SUMMER OF 1940, LEOPOLD AMERY, THE SECRETARY OF STATE for India, wrote a secret private letter to Lord Linlithgow, the viceroy, in which he noted:

> If our [British] tradition is freedom-loving and our domestic development centuries ahead of the continent, that is largely because we are an island. If the Prussian tradition is one of militarism and aggression, it is largely because Prussia had never had any natural frontiers. Now India has a very natural frontier at present. On the other hand, within herself she has no natural or geographic or racial or communal frontiers – the northwestern piece of Pakistan would include a formidable Sikh minority. The northeastern part has a Muslim majority so narrow that its setting up as a State or part of a wider Muslim State seems absurd. Then there is the large Muslim minority in the United Provinces, the position of Muslim princes with Hindu subjects and vice versa. In fact, an all-out Pakistan scheme seems to me to be the prelude to continuous internal warfare in India.[1]

Britain, in 1940, hoped to stay on in India for many decades more. Therefore, its leaders had no interest in the creation of a sovereign state of any denomination in the subcontinent, Muslim, Hindu or any other. Also, at the beginning of the war the Muslims of India had not yet been linked up in the British mind with its post-war defence strategy. That came later. The reason why the viceroy was befriending Jinnah in 1940 was with the limited aim of encouraging him to oppose the Congress Party's demands that Britain make an unambiguous commitment to grant independence to India at the end of the war and, in the meantime, to include members of political parties in the Viceroy's Executive Council.

First of all, the Muslims, by and large, were also not enamoured of Jinnah's scheme. Any scheme for a separate Muslim state in India, to be created on the basis of British provinces in which Muslims were in a majority (i.e., in the North West Frontier Province, the Punjab, Sind, Baluchistan and Bengal) would exclude from it about 25 to 30 million Muslims who lived in provinces in which they were in a minority (i.e., in the United Provinces, Bihar, the Central Provinces, Bombay, Madras, Orissa and the capital city of Delhi). Further, it was in the Muslim-minority provinces of British India that fear of Hindu domination under a democratic constitution, i.e., rule by the majority, had started to surface and the cry of 'Islam in danger' could be whipped up. In the Muslim-majority provinces, earmarked for a separate Muslim state by Jinnah, Muslims dominated political life and were running the governments there. They neither feared Hindu domination under a democratic constitution nor were they interested in a *separate* Muslim state. This is proved by the fact that Jinnah's Muslim League Party was unable to win absolute majorities in elections in the Muslim-majority provinces right up to independence in August 1947. So, Jinnah's scheme would foist Pakistan on those not interested in it and leave out those who might welcome it.

Secondly, the sentiment of those Muslim leaders who wished to escape Hindu domination was not for the withdrawal, and confinement, of Islamic power to the two corners of the subcontinent. This would mean abandoning the heartlands of India such as Delhi, Agra and Lucknow, from where Muslim rulers had held sway over many parts of the country for more than 600 years, until defeated by the British. These were the places where the most famous and magnificent symbols of past Muslim power and glory, both secular and religious, such as the great forts of Delhi and Agra, the Taj Mahal, the Jama Masjid, amongst others, were situated. It would mean to them not only an ignominious retreat but also the betrayal of centuries of Muslim conquest and rule in India. 'A Pakistan without Delhi is a body without [a] heart' was the sentiment that Patrick French, the historian, encountered even more than half a century after partition.

Thirdly, Jinnah's scheme appeared unnecessarily defeatist to many Muslims. The non-Muslims were divided into various faiths, such as Christianity, Zoroastrianism, Sikhism, Jainism, Buddhism and animism and the Hindus, though in a great majority, were divided into castes and subcastes and a proportion of them were impregnated with pacifist and passive philosophies. On the other hand, the 85 to 90 million Muslims, i.e., more than a fourth of the total population of the country, belonged to one faith.*

In such a situation, the Muslims could not only hope to avoid being dominated but also establish a measure of political ascendancy in a united free India. Moreover, major Muslim princes, including the Nizam of Hyderabad, with a state as large as France, could be expected to cooperate with them to maintain the balance between the Muslims and the non-Muslims.

Fourthly, the Muslim fundamentalist groups were particularly opposed to Pakistan, however anomalous that may sound. The leading Sunni thinker and preacher of this time was Abdul Al Mawdudi of Hyderabad. In 1941, it was he who formed the Jamaat-i-Islami, an organization whose influence during the last fifty years has spread far and wide over the Muslim world. Besides opposing Pakistan for some of the reasons given earlier, Mawdudi was against the type of sovereign authority on the Western model that Jinnah proposed to instal in Pakistan. He also considered Jinnah unfit to guide the Muslims of India because of the latter's lack of religious knowledge and his Western ways of thinking. He was for adopting chapter and verse the system of political organization as decreed by the Prophet. Mawdudi's

---

* Most Indian Muslims are Sunnis with a history of conflict with Shia Muslims. But in a struggle against non-believers, the Sunnis and Shias were likely to make common cause with each other. It needs to be pointed out that the Agha Khan and Jinnah, two leading politicians of India, were Shias, belonging to the Khoja sect.

views were pan-Islamic and not India-centric. He foresaw a clash between the Muslims and the non-Muslims of the world – 'a clash of civilizations'. Mawdudi's ideas have inspired ideologues and jihadis such as Omar Abdullah, the leader of the Taliban, and Osama bin Laden himself.*

Several Muslim groups indeed held a meeting in Delhi after Jinnah gave his call for the partition of India to denounce his proposal. There was a long tradition of opposition by the Ulema – Muslim religious scholars – and their followers to British Christian rule. These religious scholars were influenced, among other Islamic religious movements, by the tenets of the Wahhabi creed (founded by Mohammad ibn Abd al Wahhal of Najd in Saudi Arabia). The Jamaat-ul-Ulema (the Congress of the Learned), founded in the 1920s, was a byproduct of such thinking. In the same decade, the Jamaat leader Maulana Shoam Noamani of Azamgarh established the Deoband and the Nadwain Tul Ulema seminaries in the United Provinces. The impeccable anti-British credentials of the Ulema and their followers can be judged from the fact that they had exhorted their followers to support the Mutiny of 1857 and, after the British forces reconquered Delhi, about 27,000 of their members were executed in the capital and its vicinity alone. Many Ulemas felt a certain affinity for the Indian nationalists of the Congress Party because they were also fighting British domination.

---

* Despite his earlier reservations about Jinnah's scheme, Mawdudi shifted his headquarters to Pakistan after it came into existence (Jamaat-i-Hind became a separate organization), and after Pakistan agreed to call itself an Islamic state in 1956 (though in name only), the Jamaat found a justification to start obtaining financial help from the government. It also became an important conduit for funds from Saudi Arabia and the Gulf countries to the subcontinent for funding *madrasas* (Islamic schools) and preaching fundamentalist views. In the 1980s the Jamaat became the instrument of the ISI (Inter-services Intelligence, Pakistan's secret service) to further Pakistan's policy in Afghanistan, Tajikistan and India, where it worked through the terrorist group Hizb-ul-Mujahideen in Kashmir and in other parts of India. It was in the *madrasas* and camps set up by the Jamaat-i-Islami in Pakistan's northwest frontier region that fundamentalist ideological and military training was imparted to Afghani, Pakistani and youths of other countries who served the Taliban and later Al-Qaida and Osama bin Laden.

Another Muslim group, the Ahrars, was influenced by the teachings of the Persia-born Maulana Afghani. Under his inspiration they worked to create a bridge between the Pathans of the North West Frontier Province and the Pathans of Afghanistan on the one hand and the Indian National Congress Party on the other. The objective was to jointly oppose the dethroning of the Ottoman Sultan, the Khalifa or the spiritual leader of the Muslims, by the British after the First World War. The movement they launched came to be known as the Khilafat Movement. Even after Mustafa Kemal Ataturk became the president of Turkey in 1923, and formally abolished the caliphate in 1924, the Pathans of the NWFP and Ahrars retained their links with the Congress Party.

Fifthly, quite a few Muslims feared the possibility of relocation as a result of partition for economic reasons. The All-India Momin Conference, an association of weavers, opposed the scheme because it might result in their being uprooted and losing their long-developed and assured markets. The same was true of many other Muslims engaged in cottage industries. The Shias were, by and large, more educated and held more government posts than the Sunnis. They did not feel that they would improve their prospects if Pakistan were created. In an overwhelmingly Sunni Pakistan they would face more pressure exerted by that sect than in the large polyglot and multireligious India. Consequently, the Shia Political Conference also participated in the Muslims' protest against Jinnah's scheme.

The only person who suggested the partition of India before Jinnah did so in 1940 was one thirty-six-year old individual named Rahmat Ali (1897–1951). In 1933 he published a pamphlet from Cambridge in England titled 'Now or Never'. In this pamphlet, he proposed the creation of a separate sovereign state in the northwestern region of India. He also coined the word 'Pakistan'* for it. But the idea was so unpopular among Muslims that he was totally ignored.

---

* 'Pak' means pure; thus Pakistan referred to a country that did not contain people of an impure or a different faith.

However, the word 'Pakistan' stuck and was adopted for Jinnah's scheme a decade later. No member of the Muslim League delegation, then in London for the Round Table Conference, met Rahmat Ali. When he sought an interview with Jinnah, the latter refused to see him.

Stanley Wolpert, the well-known American historian, in his book *Jinnah of Pakistan* speculates whether Rahmat Ali's ideas might not have been inspired by the die-hard British Conservatives. Churchill and his friends were dead set against an All-India Federation that was being considered by the British Government in the wake of the Round Table Conferences of the early 1930s. They feared that whatever the safeguards incorporated in such a federation, it might encourage the Indian parties and religious groups to work together and start India's slide towards political unity and self-rule. They would rather have three mutually antagonistic entities emerging in India: 'A Muslimstan, a Hindustan and a Princestan', as described by Linlithgow to Jinnah on 13 March 1940 and later by Churchill to Lord Wavell. Such a trifurcation would 'institutionalize' differences among the Muslims, the Hindus and the princes and would enable Britain, by playing one against the other, to rule for decades to come.

A few years later Rahmat Ali amended his scheme to include, besides northwest India and Afghanistan, 'the heterogeneous Muslim belt all the way from Central Asia to the Bosphorus, the original Pakistan'. This suggests that Rahmat Ali was a loose cannon. It cannot be said for certain that his 1933 ideas were inspired by Churchill's friends.

How then did Jinnah tackle the critics of his scheme, especially the Muslim Leaguers and Muslim fundamentalists? How did he square the circle? First, although Muslims may not have been enamoured of partition, there was to be found, among their elite, the sort of amorphous feelings as conveyed by the Agha Khan to Lord Zetland in 1940:

> After all there was a certain obligation on His Majesty's Government not to put the Muslim community or other minorities and the princes under a worse position than they had occupied when the British had come to India.[2]

Therefore, there existed a foundation for Jinnah to build upon. Jinnah had taken care, when announcing his scheme in Lahore, to ensure that its parameters were kept obscure and fluid. He left open the possibility of the creation of a large and powerful state, which the Muslims could be proud of. The Muslim League plan revealed in 1942 included the North West Frontier Province, Baluchistan, the Punjab and the neighbouring Delhi province – even though it did not have a Muslim majority – and Sind, in the west and Bengal, including Calcutta, and Assam – even though it also did not have a Muslim majority – in the east. The plan also included Hyderabad and all the other Muslim-ruled princely states. (Later, a corridor to connect the two wings of the proposed Muslim state was added to the plan.) Such a large Pakistan would be more than equal to Hindustan, even if all the princely states ruled by Hindu princes joined the latter. Such a possibility was remote, as made out by the League, because the chancellor of the Chamber of Princes, Nawab Muhammad Hamidullah of Bhopal, was working for the creation of a third sovereign state – a Princestan – consisting of the territories of all the Indian princes.

After the idea of a separate Princestan collapsed, Jinnah encouraged the Nawab of Bhopal to try and persuade those non-Muslim Indian princes whose states lay between West Pakistan and Bhopal in Central India to join Pakistan; but more on this topic later. All such activity and propaganda succeeded in creating in the Indian Muslim mind an ambiguity about the future boundaries of Pakistan until the very end of British rule. This saved Jinnah embarrassment and revolt by his followers in the Muslim-minority provinces, who would have been left high and dry.

Jinnah's ardent supporters spread the message that without creating a powerful independent Muslim state in the subcontinent with its own armed forces, free to seek the support of foreign powers, the Muslims' position in a post-British united India would gradually deteriorate and their identity would be threatened. Therefore, Jinnah's adherents emphasized that the retreat of Muslim power to the two wings of the subcontinent should be seen as a strategic move, with the avowed goal to consolidate and advance as opportunities presented themsleves after British withdrawal. Jinnah had given a hint of this type of militant thinking to Lord Linlithgow as early as 13 March 1940, when he told them: 'The Muslim areas would be poorer, but because of the Muslims' military power and British collaboration, they will be able to safeguard even those of their community domiciled in the Hindu areas.'[3]

*

On 31 March 1940, Sir Francis Mudie, the chief secretary in the United Provinces, reported what two prominent members of the Muslim League, Khaliq-uz-Zaman (the same person we met earlier talking to Lord Zetland) and M.B. Kidwai told him:

> During the late regime [the Congress Party Government in UP till October 1939] they [the Muslims] were powerless vis-à-vis the Congress [Hindus] because of the implied sanction of the British army. If each of these dominions [Pakistan and India] had an army of its own, that position would change. The UP Muslims would then look after themselves against a UP Congress Government relying on their own resources.[4]

The superior fighting prowess of the believers in Islam is entrenched in Muslim lore. A future minister of Pakistan, Ghanzafar Ali, in a speech in Lahore on 7 February 1947 (available in the British Archives), further developed the point that Jinnah had made to Linlithgow as follows:

> Mohammad Mir Qasim and Mahmud of Ghazni invaded India with armies composed of only a few thousand and yet were able to overpower lakhs of Hindus; God willing, a few lakhs of Muslims will yet overpower crores of Hindus.[5]

Sir Firoz Khan Noon, a future Muslim League prime minister of Pakistan, has been recorded as declaring that if the Muslims were driven to fight, 'the havoc they will cause will put to shame what Chenghez Khan and [his grandson] Halaku did'.[6]

Sayed Ain-ud-Din had served as a district magistrate of Lucknow, the capital of the United Provinces, in the pre-independence era. In 1945 or 1946 he told my father that his acquaintances in the Muslim League were assuring him that, with England's help, Pakistan would become strong and since there would be Hindus in Pakistan and Muslims in India, this factor would restrain the Hindus from acting against the Muslims left behind in India. This was the League's 'hostage theory' to calm the Muslims who, under Jinnah's scheme, would be left in India. Nevertheless, Ain-ud-Din migrated to Pakistan after it was founded. (He later became the administrator of the Karachi airport.)

The Congress Party did not pass any resolution to counter Jinnah's scheme even though it was the most direct attack on the party's fundamental policy to work for a united India and especially when the scheme contained inherent contradictions that could be exposed. For instance: How could the scheme be justified on the basis of the two-nation theory when nearly 25 to 30 million Muslims would be left out of the Islamic state? Did the Muslim-majority provinces earmarked for Pakistan want it at all? Would the creation of Pakistan settle the communal problem in either dominion, or exacerbate it? What would be the economic consequences of partition? Would a division of India strengthen or weaken the defence of the subcontinent, which had natural boundaries based on mountains and seas? Would not partition enable foreign countries, other than Britain, to fish in troubled waters?

Could the Congress Party's silence be attributed to the reasons given by Jawaharlal Nehru, namely, that 'to consider it [the Pakistan scheme] seriously would merely encourage diverse, separatist and disruptive forces', and therefore it was best to dismiss it as a 'mad scheme that would not last a day', as he put it? If so, this attitude was a measure of the nationalists' escapism and arrogance. Gandhiji termed Jinnah's two-nation theory 'an untruth', but waited till 1944 to explain to the public what he meant by this term. Then in an open letter to Jinnah he contended that it was not true that the Hindus and the Muslims of India were two separate nations because an overwhelming majority of the Indian Muslims (over 90 per cent actually) were descendants from converts and there was no precedent in the history of the world that a change of religion changed the nationality of a person.

★

The facts given above and in Chapter 2 might suggest that Mohammad Ali Jinnah was a dyed-in-the-wool Islamic fundamentalist whose life's aim was to divide Muslims from Hindus by carving out an Islamic state in the subcontinent. Moreover, it may appear that he had no scruples in permitting the use of violence to achieve this end. The irony is that for the first sixty years of his life Jinnah (until the mid-1930s) fought for Hindu–Muslim political unity and for the emergence of a united, independent India and worked to achieve these objectives through peaceful constitutional means.

On his return to India as a full-fledged barrister (Lincoln's Inn) in 1896, Jinnah chose Bombay as his place of residence, although he was born in Kathiawad in Gujarat, the same state as Gandhiji, and his parents had settled in Karachi. From the very beginning, besides pursuing his career at the Bombay Bar, he took a lot of interest in politics. At that time, there were two conflicting political currents influencing educated Indian Muslims. One represented the continuing old jihad against Christians, which in the Indian context meant against the British, who ruled over more Muslims than any other power, including the Ottoman Turks. The other represented the Muslims' efforts to seek reconciliation with Britain after their decisive defeat at the hands of the British in the nineteenth century and to forge an alliance with them against the majority Hindu population.

★

The Europeans (i.e., the Portuguese) had reached India in the late fifteenth century, spurred by the papal bull to get 'rearwards of the land of the Moors' (the Muslims) who then controlled large chunks of the territories between Europe and Asia. (Trade, of course, went hand in hand.) The French were not far behind. The British, however, defeated the Portuguese and later the French. Throughout the eighteenth century, the British fought against Muslim rulers who then held sway over much of the country. Akbar's policy of reconciling the Hindus in the sixteenth century, which was reversed by Aurangzeb in the seventeenth, got reversed once more thereafter. As the grip of the Mughal Empire in the subcontinent weakened from the end of the seventeenth century onwards, the local Muslim satraps who emerged, became more dependent upon the support of the majority community in their domains. This state of affairs triggered off a process of Hindu–Muslim reconciliation in the political field. Muslims and Hindus fought side by side against the British in the eighteenth century. In fact, the commander-in-chief of Bengal's Nawab Siraj-ud-Daula's army, which faced Robert Clive at the decisive Battle of Plassey in 1757, was a Hindu general.

The year of the Mutiny, 1857, marked a watershed. Until then the Muslim was Britain's enemy number one in India. Thereafter, the British identified a new enemy, namely, the growing Indian middle class, who were imbibing Western ideas of democracy, and a majority of whom happened to be educated Hindus. This change in British perceptions encouraged many Muslims to clutch the proffered British hand of friendship and bury the old hatchet. Syed Ahmad Khan (1817–98) was the most prominent Muslim to represent this view. He exhorted the Muslims to ally themselves with their old enemy and distance themselves from the majority community. (He was knighted by Empress Victoria.) It is worth noting that a British Member of Parliament, John Bright, had, as early as 1858, suggested the break-up of the Indian Empire and placing some parts *under Muslim control*. The notion of 'divide and rule' had come rather naturally to the Imperial power. With British help Sir Syed Ahmad Khan, in 1877, founded the Anglo-Oriental College at Aligarh, about 100 km southeast of Delhi. The declared aim of this institution was 'to produce an educated upper class of Muslims who might lead their people out of despair and ignorance towards humanism and intelligent government'. The course content and the teaching patterns at the Aligarh College under its first principal, Theodore Beck, were Muslim centric. They had a profound influence on the Muslim elite who flocked to this college from all over India.

After Sir Syed, the Agha Khan donned the mantle as spokesman of Anglo–Muslim cooperation. He was the leader of a Shia sect of traders (incidentally, the same sect into which Jinnah was born) who were spread over many parts of the British Empire and were dependent on British protection. By frequently visiting England – he lived on the French Riviera – and deploying his considerable diplomatic talents, and not the least because of his love of the favourite British sport of horse racing, Agha had achieved an entrée into the highest British political and social circles. In his book *India in Transition*, he has described the position of the Muslims of India under British rule at the end of the nineteenth century as follows:

> The average Indian Muslim looked upon himself as a member of a universal religious brotherhood, sojourning in a land in which a neutral government with a neutral outlook kept law and order and justice.... While his allegiance was to Queen Victoria his political self-respect was satisfied by the existence of the Sultans of Constantinople and Fez and of the Shah and Khadive [a title equivalent to lord] of Tehran and Cairo [respectively]. The fact that the British Government was a mainstay support in the diplomatic arena of the independent Mohammadan States was naturally a source of continued gratification to him.[7]

It was the Agha Khan, who, in 1883, first put forward the idea of separate electorates for Muslims, i.e., that a certain number of seats in every election should be reserved for Muslim candidates and the Muslim electorate should vote exclusively for these Muslim candidates, as against 'the principle of election pure and simple'. Under such a system Muslim candidates would not be required to seek support from people belonging to other religions or to pay heed to the interests of their non-Muslim compatriots. The normal elective process is one of the best ways to bring about harmony among antagonistic groups as it knits together people by making them politically interdependent. The setting up of separate electorates, on the other hand, is a sure way to tear people politically apart.

★

The Muslim League Party was launched by the Agha Khan and some landlords of Bengal in 1906. On 1 October of that year, the League petitioned the viceroy for the introduction of separate electorates for Muslims. The deputation received a hearty welcome from Lord Gilbert Elliot Minto and the viceregal staff. Lady Minto noted the development as follows: 'Nothing less than the pulling back of 62 million of people from joining the ranks of the seditious opposition.'[8]

The young Jinnah was not impressed by either of these two currents: neither the continuing jihad against Christian Britain nor the one of befriending the British at the expense of India's majority community.

I got a glimpse of the young Jinnah from M.C. Chagla, who was for nearly two decades, i.e., up to the end of the 1920s, Jinnah's junior in his legal firm in Bombay and a collaborator in the Muslim League. Chagla later became the chief justice of the Bombay High Court and on retirement an ambassador and a foreign minister. Chagla said that Jinnah rose in his profession and acquired wealth by the sheer dint of his hard work, discipline and a burning passion to shine and prove himself in any task he undertook, although outwardly he remained taciturn, detached and aloof. He was oversensitive to anyone slighting him. His integrity was beyond reproach. He moved mostly in the company of rich Parsis* who were more Europeanized than other Indians. He spoke neither Urdu nor Hindi and addressed public meetings in English, even if the crowd did not understand a word of what he was saying. Jinnah was not a practising Muslim. He never read the Quran or performed the Haj; he did not follow the Quranic precepts of prayer. He did not abstain from drinking alcohol or eating pork, taboo for Muslims.

---

* A majority of Parsis nowadays live in Bombay. They follow the Zoroastrian faith and their ancestors had to flee Persia in the ninth and tenth centuries A.D. to India to escape conversion by the Islamic hordes from Arabia. Over the years, many Parsis have achieved both fame and glory in modern India. For instance: Dadabhai Naoroji (an eminent freedom fighter and reformer); Jamshedji Tata (an illutrious industrialist); Homi Bhabha (a renowned physicist); and Field Marshal Sam Manekshaw, who led the Indian Army that defeated Pakistan in the 1971 Bangladesh war. Prime Minister Rajiv Gandhi's father, Feroze Gandhi, was a Parsi.

He saw himself as a modern, secular man. Chagla's references to Jinnah's ego and his ambition to be always number one give a clue to his later metamorphosis.

Jinnah reacted strongly against the League's demand for separate electorates for Muslims describing it 'as a poisonous dose to divide the nation against itself'.[9] However, after such electorates were introduced, he did not hesitate to contest elections to the Imperial Legislative Council from the reserved Muslim seat for Bombay. In 1910, he became the first non-official Muslim to sit on that body. Jinnah's participation in public affairs as a representative of the Bombay Muslims brought him in touch with Muslim politics for the first time. The experience that he gained here fired his imagination in the direction of dominating Muslim politics and he joined the Muslim League in 1913. His aim at that time was to ride two horses – those of the Congress Party and the League at the same time – in order to establish a cooperative relationship between the two. 'Cooperation to [sic] the cause of our motherland...should be our guiding principle', he told his supporters.[10]

Jinnah was the leading light behind the forging of the Lucknow Pact between the Muslim League and the Congress Party in 1916. Under this pact, the Congress accepted reservation of seats for a certain percentage of 'Muslim members' in each of the Provincial Legislative Councils in return for the League's general support. This understanding avoided a Hindu–Muslim rift in the wake of the introduction of separate electorates. He advised the Muslims not to be 'scared away' by 'your enemies' from cooperation with the Hindus, 'which is essential for the establishment of self-government'.[11]

Jinnah's difficulties with regard to the Congress Party began soon after Gandhiji returned from South Africa in 1915 and assumed the leadership of that party. Jinnah was then thirty-nine and Gandhiji forty-five. Until then the Congress Party had at the forefront leaders who, like Jinnah, believed in fighting the British through constitutional means. Jinnah profoundly disagreed with Gandhiji's policy of mass movements to arouse the masses to fight British rule, though, of course, through non-violent action. Jinnah believed that it was dangerous to play with the emotions of ignorant and illiterate masses.

In his view, the advantage of bringing the weight of numbers into play against British power was not a sufficient ground to abandon gradualism and constitutional methods and risk 'political anarchy and communal chaos' as a consequence. To Gandhiji, on the other hand, the social, economic and moral uplift of the masses – a non-violent cultural revolution – was very important to achieve not only political goals but also freedom. Jinnah was astonished by Gandhiji's rapid success at mobilizing people of all classes, castes and creeds, including Muslims, throughout the length and breadth of the country. But Jinnah stuck to his own formula.

Jinnah soon found himself being squeezed out by Gandhiji not only from the Congress Party's platform but also from that of the Muslim League, as the Mahatma successfully exploited Muslim sentiment against the dethroning of the Ottoman Sultan, the Khalifa, by Britain, after the First World War. Gandhiji's objective was to build bridges between the Muslims and the Congress Party by extending support to the former on this issue. Jinnah looked askance at a policy that gave a fillip to pan-Islamic sentiments and which, in the long run, might come in the way of genuine Hindu–Muslim cooperation. Jinnah had walked out of the Muslim League meeting that endorsed the Khilafat movement, saying it was against the constitution of the League to oppose the government's foreign policy.

Jinnah's first clash with Gandhiji took place with regard to the policy of recruitment of Indians for the British Indian Army during the First World War. Gandhiji was helping with such recruitment on the pattern of his support to the South African Government in the Boer War, despite his oppostion to the same government's apartheid policy. 'Seek yee first the Recruiting Office and everything will be added unto you', he wrote to Jinnah.[12] On the other hand, Jinnah's position was made clear in his following statement: 'I say that if you [British] wish us to help you to facilitate to stimulate the recruiting, you must make the educated people feel that they are the citizens of the Empire and the King's equal subjects.... We want action and immediate deeds.'[13] It is worth recording that during the Second World War, Gandhiji used Jinnah's above argument to oppose recruitment, while Jinnah used Gandhiji's aforementioned stand for urging cooperation with the British war effort. Was it the two men, or the situation, that had changed?

In 1920 Jinnah wrote to Gandhiji that his 'extreme programme must lead to disaster…. Your methods have already caused split and division in almost every institution that you approached hitherto, and in the public life of the country not only amongst Hindus and Muslims but between Hindus and Hindus and Muslims and Muslims and even between fathers and sons'.[14] This outburst came after the disagreement between Gandhiji and Jinnah had come out in the open at the December 1920 Nagpur Congress Party session. Gandhiji had spoken from the platform in favour of dissolving 'the British connection'. Jinnah immediately objected that it would be impractical and dangerous to do so without a greater amount of preparation for independence. When he said 'I appeal to you to cry halt before it is too late', he was 'howled down with cries of shame and "political imposter"'. When he argued back, referring to Gandhiji as 'Mr Gandhi', the audience yelled: 'No; Mahatma Gandhi!'. Gandhiji, refused to intervene, and the boos, hisses and catcalls of the audience 'drove Jinnah from the platform'.[15] All these events took place in the presence of Ruttie, his young wife, who then hero-worshipped him and whom he had brought to Nagpur to acquaint her with the Indian political scene.*

Ruttie was the beautiful daughter of a Parsi magnate of Bombay, Sir Dinshaw Petit. When Jinnah married her in 1916, she was half his age. He had wooed her for two years despite the opposition of her father, who happened to be his friend. She was irrepressibly vivacious, always looking out for new ways to amuse herself. Her husband's rising stature in national politics was a fascinating game for her. Jinnah's deep humiliation at the crowded 1920 Congress session was not what she was expecting; nor indeed he. It left a deep scar on the psyche of both. Once, when the newly married couple was asked to dine at Government House in Bombay at a time when Lord Willingdon (Freeman Freeman-Thomas) and Lady Willingdon

---

* Earlier that year Gandhiji had irritated Jinnah by writing a letter to Ruttie asking her to coax him to learn Hindustani or Gujarati.

occupied it, Ruttie had appeared in a rather low-cut French dress that somewhat exposed her bosom. As the guests settled down at the table Lady Willingdon asked one of the bearers to fetch a shawl, saying that 'Mrs Jinnah might be feeling a bit cold'. On hearing these words, Jinnah bristled from across the table: 'When Mrs Jinnah feels cold she will say so', he retorted and got up from the dining table and both left the Government House.[16] At Nagpur too both got up and left the *pandal*, the meeting's enclosure.

It must be said in defence of the howling Nagpur crowds that they did not take him seriously. Here was a handsome man, wearing a beautiful girl on his arm, a monocle dangling on the lapel of his London-tailored double-breasted suit, complete with matching two-toned shoes, addressing them in English. This image did not fit in with their idea of a committed leader whom they expected to wear *swadeshi* (home-spun) cloth, appear to practise self-abnegation and speak in Urdu or Hindi.

Despite such provocations, Jinnah did not leave the Congress Party. He continued to attend its policy sessions, where he argued against the advisability of launching the mass satyagraha movement of 1921 that Gandhiji was planning in the wake of the general mood of anger and resentment at the extension of the Emergency Powers Act (the Rowlatt Act) beyond the war. This move had signalled Britain's coercive intentions even after the unbridled massacre of innocent people by Reginald Dyer at Jallianwala Bagh in Amritsar in April 1919. Jinnah also protested against the British policy, but in a different manner. He resigned his seat on the Imperial Legislative Council, in the deliberations of which he had come to acquire considerable weight. He had already resigned from the Muslim League Party as a protest against its refusal to follow him in opposing the Khilafat agitation.

*

The 1921 satyagraha, which had mobilized the populace beyond anybody's expectations, was abruptly abandoned by Gandhiji from his prison (where he had been confined for sedition) after it resulted in violence in a place called Chauri Chaura (in UP), where twelve (some accounts put the number at twenty-two) police constables were burnt to death by a mob. One can well imagine Jinnah's comment on the episode: 'Inevitable, dear Chagla, inevitable.' Gandhiji did not launch a mass movement for a decade thereafter, leaving constitutionalists such as Motilal Nehru, the father of Jawaharlal, to try their luck, while he himself concentrated on social problems such as village cleanliness and abolition of the caste system. Meanwhile, Gandhiji's popularity continued to steadily rise all over India.

Throughout the 1920s Jinnah's alienation from the Congress Party continued apace. At the same time, his hold on the Muslim League in particular and on the Muslims in general also weakened.

In 1924, as soon as Jinnah was elected to represent the Muslims of Bombay in the Legislative Assembly (inaugurated under the new constitution promulgated in 1919), he tried to forge a common front with the twenty-three independents in the assembly and the twenty-five members of the Swaraj Party led by Motilal Nehru and C.R. Das, who had entered the assembly despite Gandhiji's policy of non-cooperation with the same. Jointly, these two groups could outvote the British official representatives and force the pace towards early self-government. However, C.R. Das's death and Motilal Nehru's reluctance to collaborate too closely with Jinnah, because of the Mahatma's reservations about him, negated Jinnah's efforts.

In 1927 His Majesty's Government sent out a commission headed by Sir John Simon (Clement Attlee, a future prime minister, was one of its members). This commission was boycotted by the Congress Party, as it did not include any Indian. Jinnah decided that the Muslim League, which he had rejoined by then, would also boycott the Simon Commission for the same reason. This gesture was applauded by Gandhiji.

The Earl of Birkenhead (Frederick Edwin Smith), the secretary of state, wrote to the viceroy on 19 July 1928: 'I should widely advertise all the interviews with Muslims.' He added that Simon's brief was 'to terrify the immense Hindu population by the apprehension that the Commission...may present a report altogether destructive of the Hindu position, thereby securing a solid Muslim support and leaving Jinnah high and dry.'[17]

In February 1928 an All-India-All-Party Conference was held in Delhi to suggest reforms – essentially, a single Indian formula – to take the wind out of Simon's sails. Jinnah represented the Muslim League at this widely attended conference, which was presided over by Dr Mukhtar Ahmed Ansari, the president of the Congress Party. The conference agreed to demand 'full responsible government' and thus bypass those in favour of dominion status (like Jinnah) and those for outright independence (like Jawaharlal Nehru).

On the issue of Muslim rights and representation, Jinnah had persuaded the Muslim League and some other Muslim leaders in 1927 to agree to give up separate electorates in return for the Congress Party's acceptance of the following concessions: (1) one-third (33 per cent) Muslim seats in the Central Legislature instead of the existing 27 per cent; (2) the separation of Sind from the Bombay Presidency; and (3) the recognition of North West Frontier Province and Baluchistan as separate entities with their own provincial legislatures (they were then being administered centrally). The acceptance of concessions (2) and (3) would enable Muslims to dominate governments in five British provinces (the aforementioned three plus Bengal and the Punjab). This formula was a major contribution by Jinnah to reduce communal differences. If Muslim candidates would have to get the support of non-Muslims to get elected as in a normal democracy, they would be forced to tone down, if not give up, emphasizing merely issues of Muslim interest. Such a development would bring national and economic developmental issues to the forefront. To begin with, the Congress Party welcomed this formula. However, at the All-Party Conference, the Congress Party leaders changed their stand and did not accept the concessions. Even a small increase (from 27 per cent to 33 per cent) in Muslim representation at the Centre was unwelcome to them.

Thereafter, the Congress Party appointed a commission under Motilal Nehru to draft the salient features of a joint draft constitution, which eventually came to be known as the Nehru Report. This report proposed the abolition of separate electorates, without agreeing to the concessions suggested by Jinnah. Jinnah felt betrayed and refused to meet Motilal Nehru in an attempt to work out a compromise on the differences. For his part, Motilal Nehru saw no reason to yield to Jinnah because many members of the Muslim League had notified him that they were willing to accept the Nehru Report as it stood. In 1928 Motilal Nehru was angling for his son, Jawaharlal, to be elected as president of the Congress Party. This could also have been a reason why he wished to play safe with the Congress leaders, including Gandhiji. In fairness to Motilal Nehru, it must be stated that, because his hands were tied on the issue of the increase in Muslim representation at the Centre, he was willing to let separate electorates continue. But Chagla, representing Jinnah, a strong nationalist, prevailed upon him to demand joint electorates – a stand Jinnah repudiated. Thus began his break with Chagla.

The next meeting of the All-Party Conference was scheduled to be held in Calcutta on 28 December 1928. Chagla has written that 'Jinnah was in favour of outright rejection [of the Nehru Report]', but finally decided to attend the meeting, however, withdrawing his proposal to abolish separate electorates. Jinnah presented his case at the Calcutta meeting, which the Mahatma did not attend, as follows: 'Here I am not speaking as a Musalman but as an Indian.... Would you be content with a few Musalmans agreeing with the Report? Would you be content if I were to say I am with you? Do you want or do you not want the Muslim India to go along with you?' He meant that he could *not* carry other Muslim leaders on the issue of separate electorates without the acceptance of the increase in Muslim representation.[18] Sir Tej Bahadur Sapru, representing the moderates, called Jinnah 'a spoilt child, a naughty child', adding 'I am prepared to say give him what he wants and be finished with it'. R. Jaikar, the deputy leader of the Nationalist Party in the assembly and a spokesman of the Hindu Mahasabha at the Calcutta conference, opposed any concessions whatsoever: 'One important fact to remember...is that well-known Muslims like the esteemed patriots Maulana Abul Kalam Azad, Dr Ansari, Sir Ali Imam, Raja Sahib of Mahmoodabad and Mr [Saif-ud-din] Kitchlu have given their full consent to the compromise embodied in the Nehru Report.... Mr Jinnah therefore represents, if I may say so without offence, a small minority of Muslims.'[19]

Such remarks deeply hurt Jinnah; they were difficult for him to swallow. Nevertheless, he continued: 'I am not asking for these modifications because I am a naughty child...I am asking you for this adjustment because I think it is the best and fair to the Musalmans.... We are all sons of this land. We have to live together. We have to work together and whatever our differences may be, let us at any rate not create more bad blood'. Wolpert observes: 'A born thespian that he was, Jinnah spoke his lines to a packed, if not always friendly, house, before each curtain fell on a major act of his political life. Nagpur had ended act one. Calcutta finished act two.'[20]

After his humiliation at Calcutta, Jinnah took the next train to Delhi where the All-India Muslim Conference, presided over by the Agha Khan, was due to begin on 1 January 1929. The Agha Khan welcomed Jinnah as the return of the proverbial prodigal son. But Jinnah could not see any signs of welcome in the eyes of the Agha Khan's friends who had started to consider him an agent of the Congress Party. That the Agha Khan's Muslim Conference was so well attended was proof enough of Jinnah's and his League's declining clout amongst Muslims. Jinnah did not commit himself to the manifesto produced by this conference, which recommended a loose federal system for India, separate electorates and further Muslim 'weightage' in provincial governments and in the Central Government as well as in the civil services. Jinnah was not comfortable amongst those who had continued to follow the tenets of Sir Syed Ahmad Khan. But events appeared to be pushing him to do so.

When he was facing this major crisis in his political life, Jinnah suffered another ignominy, another deep blow to his ego: his beautiful young wife, Ruttie, left him in 1928 and moved to live separately in the Taj Mahal Hotel at Bombay. It was not so much her death a year later, but this desertion, that adversely affected him. Although staggered, it made him all the more determined to gird his loins and to succeed in his public life. But how?

*

Lord Irwin (Edward Frederick Lindley Wood) was the first viceroy to consult Jinnah on the course that Britain should adopt in India. Then, in 1929, a silver lining in the clouds appeared.

Ramsay Macdonald, the Labour Party leader with whom Jinnah had a fairly good rapport, became the prime minister of Great Britain. Jinnah immediately wrote to him, spelling out his ideas for India's future. His main thrust was that Britain should pledge that India would be granted full responsible government (dominion status). Such an assurance, he emphasized, would deflate the Congress Party, which was demanding independence. This demand, he warned, was gaining ground. He also suggested that the British prime minister convene a round table conference, in which Indian and British leaders would participate to discuss India's future constitutional advance. A recommendation for calling a round table conference was, at the same time, made by the viceroy to His Majesty's Government. Ramsay MacDonald replied to Jinnah through a private letter, agreeing that dominion status for India should be the goal. The British prime minister's letter brought some cheer to Jinnah in that his voice still found an echo in some quarters. Eventually, Jinnah attended the first Round Table Conference (in London in 1930), in which both British and Indian leaders took part.

It was after the third Round Table Conference of 1933 that Jinnah decided to settle down in London to practise before the highest judicial authority in the British Empire, the Privy Council, and distance himself from Indian politics. This decision reflected the measure of his disappointment with the Round Table Conferences. Since the Congress Party had boycotted the first conference in 1930, it had been like enacting *Hamlet* without the Prince of Denmark. However, there had been, more or less, a joint demand by the Indian delegation, including by the princes, for the formation of an All-India Federation. In his opening statement, Jinnah said: 'We are here to witness the birth of a new Dominion of India'. These words brought frowns on the brows of the English delegates and failed to evoke applause from the other Muslim delegates. Lord Irwin's hope that Jinnah would weld the Muslims together was not fulfilled. Lord Malcolm Hailey, ex-governor of the Punjab as well as the United Provinces, who was the Government of India's senior consultative official at this conference wrote in his report to the viceroy, Lord Irwin, from London on Jinnah's performance:

The Agha Khan does not give them [the Muslims] a lead, but professes himself willing to follow the majority. Jinnah is of course a good deal mistrusted; he did not at the opening of the Conference say what his party had agreed. And they [the other Muslims] are a little sore in consequence. He declined to give the Conference Secretariat a copy of his speech in advance as all the others had done. But then Jinnah of course was always the perfect little bounder and as slippery as the eels which his forefathers purveyed in Bombay market.[21]

At the second Round Table Conference in 1931, Jinnah again failed to make a mark. He was overshadowed by Gandhiji (who attended this time) on the one hand and by the Agha Khan on the other, so much so that for the third Round Table Conference his name was dropped from the list of Muslim delegates. Meanwhile, Ramsay Macdonald was replaced by Stanley Baldwin, the Conservative leader, as prime minister.

Jinnah's lonely existence in London – admittedly as a successful and wealthy barrister with a house on Hampstead Heath surrounded by eight acres of garden, a chauffeur-driven Bentley, occasional evenings at the theatre and dinners with friends at the Carlton Grill (a fashionable restaurant) – does not appear to have satisfied him. Long walks on the Heath gave him pause to rethink his life. At the Round Table Conference he had seen, firsthand, the influence the Agha Khan had come to wield through his ability to wheel and deal. The Agha Khan, by cooperating with the British, was able to further the interests of his Khoja sect as well as of himself. The members of this sect were successful in setting up business establishments and shops throughout the Empire and he was recognized as the leading Indian Muslim. It was to him that Jinnah turned when he sought sponsorship for a Conservative seat in the House of Commons. (He had been earlier rejected for a Labour seat.) The Agha Khan tried but did not succeed. The exercise, however, put Jinnah in touch with some important Conservative figures.

Sir Martin Gilbert, the British historian and biographer of Winston Churchill, recently revealed that he had come across

Jinnah's letters of 1946 to Churchill. Since Churchill was then out of office and did not wish to be seen in touch with Indian politicians, he had asked Jinnah to address his letters to a lady employed at Chartwell Manor, Churchill's home in Kent. Letters to her would receive no attention. She was one Elizabeth Giliat. Precisely when this connection started, I do not know. However, Jinnah's sudden breaking away from the Federal Scheme, which Churchill opposed, in 1937, his confidence and boldness in coming out with the Pakistan scheme that Churchill favoured in 1940 and his coddling by Viceroys Linlithgow and Wavell, both Churchill's admirers between 1940 and 1946, are undisputed facts. Jinnah admitted during the Simla Conference in 1945 that he was receiving advice from London (see Chapter 7).*

A man, so interested in power and so dynamic, was bound to get bored with his legal practice, dabbling in stocks on the London Exchange and acquiring real estate. His trips to India to argue cases between 1933 and 1936 helped him to keep in touch with his staunch supporters, who continued to plead with him to return home and lead the Muslims. In 1933 Liaqat Ali Khan, an Oxford-educated zamindar from the United Provinces, and his vivacious wife, called on him at his house in Hampstead Heath. Liaqat Ali Khan had been with him at the fateful Calcutta confrontation of 1928. Her, he had never seen. He responded to the begum's flattery that he had the unique ability to 'save the situation'. When Jinnah, unsure of his capacity to move the masses like Gandhiji could, demurred, Liaqat Ali promised to arrange the means to win them over. However, how this objective was to be achieved was probably not fully revealed to him, for Jinnah, in 1933, might have baulked at whipping up fanaticism and intercommunal disharmony to inflame and unite the Muslims behind him. It was only in 1936 that the process started by Liaqat Ali Khan bore fruit. The elections scheduled for 1937, under the freshly promulgated Act of 1935, offered a challenge. He sold his London house and the Bentley, though he retained his stocks

---

* See the transcript of the remarks made by Sir Martin Gilbert, OBE, FRSL, on 28 January 2005, available at the India International Centre, New Delhi.

in the London Stock Exchange and his rented properties in Mayfair, and returned to Bombay.* According to Mohammad Yunus (the nephew of Khan Abdul Ghaffar Khan), his brother Abdul Aziz, at the behest of the home secretary in the Government of India, gave up his seat in the assembly to make way for Jinnah.

On his return to India, Jinnah immediately started to reorganize the Muslim League Party. Until then there were hardly any League cells in the districts; nor was there any coordination with other important Muslim leaders. Consequently, Jinnah constituted the League's central and provincial parliamentary boards, recruited volunteers from the Aligarh Muslim University to spread the League's message and travelled around the country to unite the Muslim leaders behind him. By accepting the supremacy of Fazal-ul-Haq, the leader of the Peasants' and Tenants' Party in Bengal, of Sir Sikandar Hayat Khan, the Unionist Party's leader in the Punjab, and of Ghulam Hussain in Sind, Jinnah established a framework of cooperation with them. In the United Provinces, he persuaded Khaliq-uz-Zaman to merge his Muslim Unity Board with the League for fighting the elections. To build up funds for the party, he befriended and recruited wealthy Muslims. Hence he made M.A. Isfahani, the industrialist from Calcutta, his principal adviser for Bengal and the Nawab of Mahmoodabad, the richest Muslim landlord of United Provinces, the treasurer of the Muslim League. In Bombay, his native city, he had always been supported by members of his sect, most of whom were prosperous traders. That his popularity in cosmopolitan Bombay was high becomes clear from the fact that he was repeatedly elected to the Central Assembly by that city *in absentia*.

Despite all these measures, the Muslim League suffered a rout under Jinnah's leadership in the provincial elections of 1937. This serious setback was a terrible blow to his self-esteem – he had been

---

* His standard legal fee by 1936 was Rs 1500 per day (equivalent to at least Rs 90,000 in today's terms) the highest in India. He earned Rs 24,000 per annum from his rented flats in Mayfair (equivalent now to Rs 14 lakh) and Rs 40,000 per annum from dividends in the Stock Exchange (equivalent now to Rs 24 lakh). He was one of the elite group of Indian tax-payers whose income required 'super tax' as well as 'supplementary tax' payments, and like many very wealthy Indians, he was at times several years late in remitting his taxes.[22]

beaten once again. The League was able to win only 108 out of the 485 seats reserved for Muslims in the British provinces, thereby establishing that it did not represent even a quarter of the Muslims of India. The followers of the Jamaat-ul-Ulema and the Ahrars did not support the Muslim League and in the newly carved North West Frontier Province, a 95 per cent Muslim province, the Pathans humiliated him by voting for the Congress Party. Ultimately, the Congress Party formed governments in eight out of the eleven British provinces.

✯

In defeat defiance, yes; but how to vanquish the rising Congress monolith and how to humiliate the arrogant Nehru, whose vigorous campaigning had done him in? How, indeed, to defy the game of numbers? At this point of time, the vision of a renowned poet came to his rescue. Mohammad Iqbal, now close to the end of his life, had started writing to him to work for a separate Muslim state in order to recapture the old Muslim glory in Hindustan. Jinnah was not much interested in recapturing past glory, but now began to wonder whether the partition of India may not be the only way to achieve power and glory for himself: if he could not dominate the whole Hindustan, he could at least settle for ruling a part of it. Accordingly, his rhetoric against the Congress Party sharpened: 'We [the Muslims] do not want to be reduced to the position of the Negroes in America', he contended and went on to further dramatize the dangers facing the Muslims.[23]

It is axiomatic that the massive Congress Party victory contributed to the Muslim League's recovery in 1938–39. The insecurity that the Congress victory created amongst Muslim leaders, including those opposed to the League and Jinnah, resulted in their moving towards each other. For example, Sir Sikandar Hayat Khan, premier of the Punjab, whose Unionist Party ruled the province through a coalition with Sikh and Hindu parties and who differed with the League's communal approach, asked his partymen to simultaneously become members of the Muslim League. Sir Sikandar's move was a major gain for Jinnah. Similarly, Fazal-ul-Haq of Bengal and other provincial Muslim leaders began to show interest in establishing closer contact with the League.

The Muslims' concern about the growing power of the Congress Party was given a sharper focus with the party's decision not to form coalition governments with the Muslim League in the United Provinces and Bombay. Khaliq-uz-Zaman, a former Congressman and also third in the Muslim League hierarchy after Jinnah and Liaqat Ali Khan, hoped that his party would obtain two berths in the Congress Party Government in the United Provinces – one which he would keep for himself – and forge a Congress–League coalition in the province. B.G. Kher, a Congress leader from Bombay, also wanted a coalition with the League and to induct some Muslim League leaders into his cabinet. Jawaharlal Nehru, the Congress president, however, saw no reason to accommodate League leaders unless they joined the Congress Party. This attitude served to increase the feeling amongst Muslim leaders that if the Congress Party ever came to rule India, they could not expect any consideration whatsoever. It turned Khaliq-uz-Zaman into a bitter enemy of the Congress Party. He soon did everything in his power to pit the Muslims against the Hindus in the United Provinces and to embarrass the Congress Party Government there. However, the view of several historians that this Congress decision, i.e., not to form coalitions with the League, was the single most important factor that resulted in the partition of the country overlooks the importance of developments that took place during the Second World War.

The Congress victory at the hustings also alerted the British. They now began to fear that the elections to the All-India Federal Legislature may result in the Congress Party coming to dominate the Centre too. In the Lower House of the bicameral Federal Legislature, one-third of the seats were reserved for Muslims* and an equal number for the nominees of the rulers of princely states. Since, in the provincial elections, the Muslim League had won less than one-fourth of the seats reserved for Muslims, there was no gainsaying that the formula worked out to block the Congress Party at the

---

* Muslims were elected through separate electorates; the elections were held on a 14 per cent franchise.

Centre by packing this body with dependable Muslims and princes' nominees would not go haywire. If even half the Muslim legislators cooperated with the Congress Party, there was a possibility that this party could achieve a majority in the Lower House. The shift in the British view on the formation of the federation was not lost on Jinnah. Lord Brabourne (John Ulick Knatchbull), the acting viceroy, reported to the secretary of state, Lord Zetland, on 18 August 1938:

> Jinnah ended up with the startling suggestion that "we should keep the Centre as it was now; that we should make friends with the Muslims by protecting them in the Congress Provinces and that if we did that, the Muslims would protect us at the Centre".[24]

This development marked the beginning of the policy of 'mutual support' between Jinnah and the British, which had far-reaching consequences for India.

There was another factor that was soon to come into play. His doctors told Jinnah that the patch on his lung, first noticed in 1928, had spread and that he was terminally ill. (The cancer came later.) He kept this fact to himself, although he took the precaution of writing and depositing his last will and testament with his Bombay lawyer on 19 May 1939. Whatever had to be done, had now to be done fast.[25]

The opportunity came a few months later, when at the commencement of the war, the Congress ministries walked out of provincial governments and the British looked desperately for support for the war effort towards the Muslim League and, by logical extension, to Jinnah. And he boldly grasped it (as recounted in Chapter 2).

★

After Pakistan was formed and his ambition fulfilled, Jinnah could afford to dispense with the theories that he had developed in the previous decade to achieve his goal. In reality, he had remained the same old Jinnah who believed in secularism in politics, who was opposed to communalism and had no faith in religion. Speaking in the Pakistan Constituent Assembly in Karachi on 11 August 1947, he discussed the pros and cons of a united India and said: 'Maybe that view [for a united India] is correct. Maybe it is not. That remains to be seen.' This statement gives a truer picture of his ambiguous feelings about the creation of Pakistan than all the dogmatic bombast he had been indulging in about the two-nation theory in his search to fulfil personal ambition. Further, he told the Constituent Assembly, much to the amazement of Muslim Leaguers and others: 'You may belong to any religion or caste or creed – that has nothing to do with the business of the State.... In course of time Hindus would cease to be Hindus and Muslims would cease to be Muslims, not in the religious sense because that is the personal faith of each individual, but in the political sense as citizens of the State.'[26]

To the end of his life, Jinnah showed no respect for Quranic principles and tenets. In his will, he bequeathed certain monies on the basis of interest that would accrue and willed the whole of his property, instead of one-third, the maximum permitted under the Shariat. He was indifferent to the importance of the holy month of Ramzan to the Muslims. For example, to welcome Lord and Lady Mountbatten during their visit to Karachi to inaugurate the creation of Pakistan on 14 August 1947, he ordered an official luncheon. Since he did not practise the Islamic faith, he forgot that the luncheon had fallen in the month of Ramzan, during which the Muslims fast from dawn to sunset. The luncheon had to be changed to a dinner party at the last minute.[27]

Towards the end of the 1930s he acquired two elegant houses. The first was a large mansion with Italian marble floors in Malabar Hill, Bombay, which, after partition, became the UK Deputy High Commissioner's residence. The second was an architectural gem surrounded by gardens that he purchased in the heart of Edwin Lutyen's leafy New Delhi, that is today the Royal Dutch Embassy. These houses were not acquired for his progeny; he had no son and, by this time, he had distanced himself from his only daughter, willing her merely a paltry sum. For whom then were these opulent acquisitions, but to satisfy his vanity? The same trait is reflected by his purchasing an ivory-coloured Packard car in which he moved about in Delhi at a relaxed, royal speed. And, of course, in his decision to become the first governor-general of Pakistan, 'His Excellency', in the very town of Karachi, in which in the 1880s, he lived as a simple student called 'Jinnahbhai'.

As Lord Mountbatten, resplendent in his naval uniform, decorations, Garter and all, marched to the dais to inaugurate Pakistan, he noted that there was only one special chair there. The viceroy's first thought was that it would be inappropriate for Jinnah, who was to become the governor-general of Pakistan, not to have an equally important chair as himself. He was taken aback when Jinnah promptly sat down on the special chair and motioned Mountbatten to take the one by its side.* Maybe he wished to pay back Mountbatten for the humiliations he had suffered at British hands in his early days, or for forcing him to accept a truncated Pakistan, despite all the help he gave them against the Congress Party during the war. But most likely it was megalomania in his old age.

If Colonel Elahi Baksh, the doctor who attended on Jinnah during the last phase of his illness in August–September 1948 at Ziarat near Quetta, is to be believed, he heard his patient say: 'I have made it [Pakistan] but I am convinced that I have committed the greatest blunder of my life.' And, around the same period, Liaqat Ali Khan, the prime minister of Pakistan, upon emerging one day from the sick man's room after receiving a tongue-lashing, was heard to murmur: 'The old man has now discovered his mistake.' Was this Jinnah's final metamorphosis?[28]

---

* The above is based on what Lord Mountbatten told me in Broadlands (in Hampshire), a few years before his death. The Report on the Last Viceroyalty, dated 16 August 1947 to London, reads: 'The following day I addressed the Pakistan Constituent Assembly...Jinnah had wanted to take the principal seat himself as President of the Constituent Assembly, but I refused to give up my rights as Viceroy and he eventually gave way.'

Notes and References

1. MSS/EUR F 9/5, S. No. 32, p. 190 (Oriental and Indian Collection, British Library, London).
2. MSS/EUR F 129/V, Zetland's letter to the viceroy, May 1940, Para 27 (OIC, British Library, London).
3. MSS/EUR F 125/8, Vol. V, pp. 191–95 (OIC, British Library, London).
4. India Office Records (IOR), L/P&J/8 506, note by Francis Mudie, chief secretary, UP, on his talk with Khaliq-uz-Zaman and M.B. Kidwai, 31 March 1940.
5. Transfer of power (TOP) IX, S. No. 396, p. 170, Sardar Patel to Lord Wavell, 14 February 1947, enclosing a cutting from *Free Press Journal*, dated 8 February 1947 giving excerpts from Ghanzafar Ali's speech in Lahore.
6. S.K. Majumdar, *Jinnah and Gandhi* (Minerva Associates, Calcutta, 2000, pp. 205–06), quoted by Rafiq Zakaria in *The Man Who Divided India* (Popular Prakashan, Bombay, 2001).
7. See Hector Bolitho, *Jinnah* (John Murray, London, 1954, p. 41).
8. Mary (Countess of Minto), *India, Minto and Morley* (Macmillan, London, 1934, pp. 47–48).
9. Hector Bolitho, op. cit., p. 42.
10. Rafiq Zakaria, op. cit., p. 12, and Agha Khan, *Memoirs* (Simon & Schuster, New York, 1954, pp. 122–23).
11. Ibid., p.19.
12. Syed S. Pirzada (ed.), *Quaid-i-Azam Jinnah's Correspondence*, 3rd revised edition (National West Publishing Company, Karachi, year not available, p. 159).
13. Ibid., p. 82. Jinnah to Gandhiji, 4 July 1918.
14. Ibid., pp. 181–88.
15. Ibid., pp. 264–65.
16. Stanley Wolpert, *Jinnah of Pakistan*, ninth edition (Oxford University Press, London, 2002, pp. 71–72). (This is based on a *Times of India* report dated 13 January 1921.) *Dr Naeem Qureshi Papers* (Pakistan Historical Society, Vol. IV. 1, p. 229) and Jamil-ud-Din, *Glimpses of Quaid-i-Azam* (Education Press, Karachi, 1960, p. 2).
17. John Campbell, *F.E. Smith: Earl of Birkenhead* (Pimlico, London, 1983, p. 515). Birkenhead to the viceroy, Lord Irwin, 19 January 1928. MSS EUR D 703.

18. Stanley Wolpert, op. cit., pp. 100–02 (based on an account by Syed S. Pirzada, op. cit., pp. 426–29 and 432–35).

19. Ibid.

20. Ibid.

21. MSS/EUR/22, 34, Lord Hailey to Lord Irwin, 14 November 1930 (India Office Records, London).

22. Stanley Wolpert, op. cit., pp. 159–60 (based on papers in the National Archives of Pakistan, F/77) quoted by Z.H. Zaidi, 'M.A. Jinnah – The Man' (National Archives of Pakistan, Quaid-i-Azam Papers, IV. 1, Vol. III, p. 45).

23. Stanley Wolpert, op. cit., pp. 166–67.

24. Ibid., pp. 161–62 (based on *Memoirs* of the Second Marquis of Zetland, John Murray, London, 1956). The fact that Jinnah met the acting viceroy at Simla on 16 August 1938 is confirmed by document F/1095 in the National Archives of Pakistan.

25. Stanley Wolpert, op. cit., pp. 170–71.

26. Hector Bolitho, op. cit., p. 210, and speeches of Quaid-i-Azam (Ministry of Information and Broadcasting, Karachi, 1950, pp. 133–36).

27. Report on 'The Last Viceroyalty', 16 August 1947, No. 17, p. 249 (OIC, British Library, London).

28. Member of Parliament Dr M. Hashim Kidwai's letter printed in *The Times of India*, 27 July 1988, on the basis of reports published in *Frontier Post*, Peshawar, and *Muslim India*, New Delhi.

4

The Churchill–Roosevelt Clash
over India

THE NEWS OF THE JAPANESE ATTACK ON PEARL HARBOR WAS RECEIVED
in London on the evening of 7 December 1941. Winston Churchill
records in his memoirs his feelings of relief and elation that Japan
had, by this act, drawn the United States into the war: 'So we had
won after all...Britain would live. The Commonwealth and Empire
would live. We should not be wiped out. Our history would not
end.... Being saturated and satisfied with emotion and sensation I
went to bed and slept the sleep of the saved and thankful.'[1]

On waking up the next morning, his first act was to plan to go
to Washington to review with President Franklin Delano Roosevelt
'the whole war plan in the light of reality and new facts as well as
the problems of production and distribution'. It was during this visit,
recounts Churchill, that Roosevelt 'first raised the Indian problem
with me on the usual American lines', meaning on anti-'Empire'
lines. He continues: 'I reacted so strongly at such length that he
never raised it verbally again.'[2]

On the way to the United States on board the brand new
battleship, the *Duke of York*, while dodging German U-boats in the
Atlantic, he had premonitions of the coming 'Indian danger'. On
7 January 1942, he cautioned Clement Attlee, the deputy prime
minister and in charge in London in his absence, as follows:

I hope my colleagues will realize the danger of raising constitutional issues, still more of making constitutional changes, in India at a moment when [the] enemy is upon the frontier. The idea that we should "get more out of India" by putting the Congress in charge at this juncture seems ill-founded. Yet that is what it would come to if any electoral or Parliamentary foundation is chosen. Bringing hostile political elements into the defence machine will paralyse action.... The Indian troops are fighting splendidly, but it must be remembered that their allegiance is to the King Emperor, and that the rule of the Congress and Hindu priesthood machine would never be tolerated by a fighting race.[3]

Immediately after getting back to London, worried that Roosevelt would return to the Indian situation, Churchill asked the War Cabinet to develop a policy to forestall American pressure for self-government in India. As he writes: 'The concern of the Americans with the strategy of a world war was bringing them into touch with political issues on which they had strong opinions and little experience.... In countries where there is only one race broad and lofty views are taken on the colour question. Similarly, states which have no overseas colonies or possessions are capable of rising to moods of great elevation and detachment about the affairs of those who have.'[4] Roosevelt's interest in India was based on enlisting popular support there against the advancing Japanese, ensuring India's freedom and the subsequent building up, after the war, of a post-colonial order in Asia.

The central point of the top-secret recommendation that was submitted to Churchill and the War Cabinet by the secretary of state for India, Leopold Amery, on 28 January 1942, was as follows:

The talk of Hindu and Muslim communities as majority and minority is a dangerous misuse of terms because it tends to imply that the right of the numerically smaller community to have its individuality respected is less than that of the larger. It is, after all, in defence of that right that we are at war today. Yet this fundamental issue has been throughout ignored by the Congress

Party – which, in spite of the efforts to keep a Muslim element in its façade is essentially a Hindu Party.... We have in the 1940 declaration [that gave to the minorities a veto on India's constitutional development] the only long-term policy which can achieve a settlement. We cannot go back on the pledges which it embodies: Our business is to stand by it and expound it confidently and with conviction and not apologetically. On that ground we can weather the immediate storm which is sweeping down upon India.... There is no immediate further interim constitutional advance that we can make.[5]

From India, the viceroy, Lord Linlithgow, advised that a time of military reverses was not the best time to offer concessions. He went on to add:

India and Burma have no natural association with the Empire, from which they are alien by race, history and religion, and for which neither of them has any natural affection, and both are in the Empire because they are conquered countries which have been brought there by force, kept there by our control, and which hitherto it has suited them to remain under our protection.[6]

The views of Amery and Linlithgow were after Churchill's own heart. However, he had to contend with the opposition of his deputy in the War Cabinet, namely, Attlee:

India has been profoundly affected by the changed relationship between Europeans and Asiatics which began with the defeat of Russia by Japan at the beginning of the century. The hitherto axiomatic acceptance of the innate superiority of the European over the Asiatic sustained a severe blow.... The reverses which we and the Americans are sustaining from the Japanese at the present time will continue this process.... The fact that we are – necessarily – driven to a belated recognition of China as an equal and of Chinese as fellow fighters for civilization against barbarism makes the Indian ask why he, too, cannot be master in his own house. Similarly, the success against the Axis of a semi-oriental people, the Russians, lends weight to the hypothesis that the East is now asserting itself against the long dominance of the West. A Pan-Asiatic movement led by Japan has been recognized as a danger; a Pan-Asiatic bloc of our Allies [meaning with China and India] is a possibility that should not be ignored. Incidentally, American sentiment has always leaned strongly to the idea of Indian freedom.

The Secretary of State thinks we may weather the immediate storms. Such a hand-to-mouth policy is not statesmanship. All [of] India was not the fruits of conquest; large parts of it came under our rule to escape from tyranny and anarchy.... We are condemned by Indians not by the measure of Indian ethical conceptions but by our own which we have taught them to accept. My conclusion therefore is that a representative with power to negotiate within wide limits should be sent to India now, either as a special envoy or in replacement of the present Viceroy, and that a Cabinet Committee should be appointed to draw up terms of reference and powers.[7]

This line of thinking placed Churchill in a cleft. According to Amery, pressure on Churchill from Roosevelt and on Attlee and company from their own party, plus the admission of Sir Stafford Cripps to the War Cabinet, suddenly opened 'the sluice gates'. However, with typical aplomb and cunning Churchill used Amery's and Attlee's concepts to forge a bold policy that would (1) help to deflect American pressure for immediate self-government in India, (2) give a new turn to Britain's policy in the subcontinent, (3) put the Congress Party in a dilemma and (4) appease Churchill's coalition partners of the Labour Party. Cripps, a leading socialist member of the War Cabinet and the leader of the House of Commons, who knew Gandhiji and Nehru – in 1939 he had been a guest at the latter's home in Allahabad – would be sent out to India to make an offer to the Indian people on HMG's behalf. Attlee was also to be roped in for the cause by being made the head of the newly constituted India Committee of the War Cabinet. Of course, neither Churchill nor Amery nurtured any hope – or wish – that the Cripps Mission would succeed. Moreover, Churchill did not have any great admiration for Cripps: 'The trouble is his chest is a cage in which two squirrels are at war, his conscience and his career.'[8] Churchill was not at all disappointed, as we shall see later, when Cripps failed. The offer that was initially worked out in London and would be later made by Sir Stafford in India may be summarized as follows:

Immediately after the war India could have full independence inside or outside the Commonwealth on the basis of a constitution framed by the Indians themselves. And in the interim period leaders of Indian political parties would be asked to enter the Viceroy's Executive Council and enjoy considerable autonomy except for the conduct of the war that would remain in British hands. [These concessions would catch the American eye.] However, there would be a caveat to all this. The Indians must accept the right of any British Indian Province, or Princely State, to stay out of the proposed Indian Union at independence if it so chose, and that the proposal was to be "accepted as a whole or rejected as a whole", which meant that the Indian Parties' agreement to assume office in the Government of India would commit them to accept the principle of the partition of India, when British withdrew after the war.[9]

The philosophy and the strategy behind the Cripps offer were devised by the India Committee, in London, during early 1942. On 21 February, Amery wrote to the viceroy on how to get round the criticism that 'we are deliberately holding up all progress by giving a blackmailing veto to the minorities'. The way out, he suggested, lay in the 'provincial option' that was 'normally accepted in the Dominions...namely, that if there are sufficient provinces who want to get together and form a dominion, the dissenting provinces should be free to stand out and either come in after a period of option, or be set up at the end of it, as a Dominion of their own'.[10] This line was approved by Churchill on 26 February[11] and adopted by the War Cabinet, with Attlee in the chair, on 27 February.[12]

'This approach represented a radical departure from the policy adopted by Britain in India so far', observed V.P. Menon in his authoritative work *The Transfer of Power in India*. He also noted:

'It had never before been contemplated that the accession of the British Provinces to an Indian Federation or Union would be optional.'[13] By adopting this line, Britain was accepting the rights of the provinces to 'walk out' of the country. Indeed, this option opened the constitutional path for the creation of Pakistan. From this theory, the British never afterwards resiled. In the Cripps offer of 1942, in the Cabinet Mission plan of 1946 and in Attlee's announcement on British withdrawal on 20 February 1947, the right of the British provinces to walk out was a consistent feature.

London adopted this approach in February 1942, independent of any advice from the viceroy, which would have been based on the contingencies prevalent in India. It is important to note this fact, because of the general belief that the British devised the theory of the 'provincial option' to meet Muslim pressure.

★

On 10 March 1942, a fortnight before Sir Stafford Cripps landed in Delhi, Amery informed Linlithgow on the significance of the new plan. This let the cat out of the bag:

As for the Congress their adverse reaction may be all the greater when they discover that the nest [the offer] contains Pakistan Cookoo's [sic] egg.[14]

In his secret report on his mission, while recording his conversation with Jinnah in Delhi on 25 March 1942, Cripps noted:

I think he [Jinnah] was rather surprised in the distance that it [the British offer] went to meet the Pakistan case.[15]

It is another matter that the public face of British policy remained quite different. Concluding the debate on the Cripps mission in the House of Commons, Amery announced with fervour: 'Our ideal remains a united India.'

In the concluding chapter of his book, The Transfer of Power in India, V.P. Menon writes:

When in 1942 HMG's offer was announced, the opinion was widely expressed that the British were bent upon the division of the country; that they wanted to create a Middle-Eastern sphere of influence and in pursuance of that policy wished to bring about the creation of a separate Pakistan. This would [be in] accord with their policy of protecting the Straits [of Hormuz] on the Persian Gulf and the Suez Canal from Russian influence and with their new but overwhelming interest in oil of Iran, Iraq and Arabia.[16]

Whether strategic considerations had entered Churchill's calculations at this time or they evolved a little later cannot be said for certain. Evidence suggests that by 1945 defence had certainly become the prime factor for Britain's India policy.

However, before Churchill could send Cripps off to India to make his offer, President Roosevelt intervened. General Chiang Kai-shek of China had wired to Roosevelt from Chunking on 25 February 1942 that after his recent visit to India (with Madam Chiang) he had come to the conclusion that 'if the British Government does not fundamentally change its policy toward India, it would be like presenting India to the enemy. If the Japanese should know of the real situation and attack India, they would be virtually unopposed'. Chiang then referred to British mismanagement in the Malay states and pointed out that Britain '...should voluntarily give the Indians real power and...not allow different parties in India to cause confusion'.[17] On the same day, Roosevelt wired the US ambassador in Britain, John G. Winant, that he was 'concerned about the situation in India especially as the British defence [against the advancing Japanese] will not have sufficiently enthusiastic support from the people of India themselves'.[18] He then instructed the ambassador as follows:

In the greatest confidence could you or Averil Harriman [the president's special representative in London] or both let me have a slant on what the Prime Minister thinks about new relationships between Britain and India? I hesitate to send him a direct message because, in a strict sense, it is not our business. It is, however, of great interest to us from the point of view of the conduct of the war.[19]

★

Things had been coming to a boil in Washington. Earlier the same month, President Roosevelt had decided to send an Economic and War Supplies Mission to India headed by Colonel Louis Johnson (formerly assistant secretary in the War Department), in the capacity of his personal representative, to endeavour to boost war production there. The Americans feared that it may not be easy to convince the British Government that India should be made self-sufficient in war production because of fears of losing the Indian markets after the war. The State Department had advised that: 'We once more take up with the British the necessity of making a statement of policy with respect to India. It would seem that the logical thing to do was to have Churchill announce in London that the British plans contemplated the introduction of India as a full member of the United Nations and that by pre-arrangement, the United States – perhaps through the President – promptly and vigorously welcome the step.' As a preamble to this recommendation, the State Department noted: 'The Secretary of State Cordell Hull has taken up with the British Government twice in 1941 the possibility of a prompt recognition of India's aspirations to freer existence and membership of the British family of nations and the President had indicated his sympathy with this general line.' And that 'under existing conditions any such programme [as contemplated in the Louis Johnson Mission] is not likely to get very far unless the political situation is handled with extreme vigor.'[20]

Washington had also, at the same time, received a message from the US ambassador in London that there was wide division among the members of the British Cabinet on the Indian question. But perhaps the strongest pressure on Roosevelt to take some action by exerting pressure on Britain with regard to India had come from the rumblings in the Senate's Foreign Relations Committee. This committee had, unanimously, with such important senators as Thomas Connally, Arthur H. Vandenberg, Nathan Green and Dewey la Follet pitching in, expressed the view that the 'Allies should fully utilize the manpower of China and of India as sources of military strength' and that 'Indians would not have the desire to fight just in order to prolong England's mastery over them'.[21] The overwhelming sentiment within the committee was that the US had done so much for England through lend-lease that it could now justifiably participate in British Empire counsels and demand autonomy status for India.

Roosevelt, on 12 March 1942, explained to Sir Girja Shanker Bajpai, the Indian agent general, his policy vis-à-vis India. He pointed out that India needed the inspiration of 'new thought'. He added that Indian self-government should evolve through a process of trial and error; a date for independence needed to the fixed and the UK and the USA should support China and India in post-war Asia.[22]

Roosevelt's message to Churchill was delivered by Averil Harriman, the dapper millionaire of great charm and discretion who had given up business and polo to serve his country. Harriman carried out numerous difficult tasks for several American presidents in the last century. For such a man to voice the opinion that the assignment now handed to him was the most trying of all the assignments that Roosevelt had ever given him shows he was well aware of Churchill's rigid views on India. Harriman was later to marry Pamela Churchill, the wife of the prime minister's son, Randolph, and Lord Beaverbrook (Maxwell Aitken) had remarked: 'To have FDR's Personal Representative, the man charged with keeping Britain safe, sleeping with the Prime Minister's daughter-in-law was a wonderful stroke of luck.'[23]

When Harriman broached the subject on 26 February 1942, Prime Minister Churchill immediately replied that the political initiative that the British were planning to take in India would be discussed by the cabinet that very day. And then fired the opening salvo of his campaign by volunteering the following information that Harriman passed on to Roosevelt in a telegram the same day:

Approximately 75 per cent of the Indian troops are Muslims.... The Muslim population exceeds 100 million. The fighting people of India are from the northern provinces largely antagonistic to the Congress movement. The big population of the low-lying centre and south have not the vigor to fight anybody. The Prime Minister will not therefore take any political step which would alienate the Muslims.... There is ample manpower in India willing to fight. The problem is training and equipping.[24]

Now, the fact was that only 35 per cent of the Indian troops were Muslims (as Lord Wavell, commander-in-chief in India had cabled to London the same week). But then, as Churchill was to tell Roosevelt in another context later: 'In war the truth must sometimes have an escort of lies.'[25] The prime minister followed up his discussions with Harriman with a telegram to Roosevelt (on 4 March):

We are earnestly considering whether a declaration of Dominion status after the war carrying with it if desired the right to secede should be made at this critical juncture. We must not on any account break with the Muslims who represent a hundred million people and the main army elements on which we must rely for the immediate fighting.... We have also to consider our duty towards 30 to 40 million untouchables and our treaties with the princely states of India, perhaps 80 million. Naturally we do not want to throw India into chaos on the eve of invasion...[26]

To this telegram, he appended a memorandum written by the military secretary at the India Office, which read as follows:

Indian soldiers are voluntary mercenaries. They take pride in their profession in which a leading element is personal loyalty to the British Officers and general loyalty to the British Raj. Any indication of a fundamental change in the conditions or the authority under which they have accepted service, whether as affecting their material prospects or their creed as soldiers of the British Crown, cannot fail to have at once an unsettling effect.[27]

In order 'to let the Americans see the Muslim side of the picture', he enclosed a note by Jinnah, which stated: 'The virtual transfer of power immediately to a Hindu All-India Government [meaning to a majority Congress Party Government] would practically decide at once far-reaching constitutional issues in breach of the pledges given to the Muslims and other minorities in the British Government's declaration of 8 August 1940 which promised no constitutional change, interim or final, without Muslim agreement and would torpedo the Muslim claim for Pakistan which is their article of faith.'

Churchill followed up this note with another telegram to Roosevelt on 7 March: 'We are still persevering to find some conciliatory and inspiring process, but I have to be careful that we do not disturb British politics at a moment when things are increasingly aquiver.'[28] And, in addition, he summarized the Punjab governor's views to the viceroy: 'Responsible section of Moslems hold [the] unshakeable view that until [a] constitution acceptable to Moslem India is devised, Britain must continue to hold the ropes. They will certainly be worried at [a] constitution [that] would place power in hands of Hindus, whom they already suspect of pro-Japanese tendencies. They will therefore be diverted from working for defence of India as a whole and seek to align themselves elsewhere.'[29]

President Roosevelt was, however, not convinced. On 10 March 1942, he wired back to Churchill: 'Of course all of you good people know far more about [the problem] than I do.' He then launched into a lengthy discourse about the process of trial and error through which the thirteen American colonies had passed during the US Revolution from 1775 to 1783 before agreeing to federate. He suggested that representative groups in India be recognized as a temporary 'dominion government' until a year after the end of the war, when the same body 'could also be charged to consider a more permanent government after that'. Roosevelt added that such a move would be strictly in line with the changes that had taken place in the world over the past half a century and also with the democratic processes followed by all those who were fighting Nazism. He ended his message as follows: 'It is, strictly speaking, none of my business, except in so far as it is a part and parcel of the successful fight that you and I are waging.'[30]

The US State Department had, in the meantime, advised Cordell Hull, the secretary of state, that Gandhiji's pacifist influence was on the wane and the Congress Party could therefore be persuaded to join in the war effort: 'Many party members considered the satyagraha [the individual non-violence] movement unrealistic and ineffective, and opposition to it was growing.... Apparently, he [Gandhiji] realized that he could not prevent the adoption of the resolution but felt that his non-violent principles would not permit him to participate in a policy of co-operation with the war effort. He therefore renounced his active leadership in the party but was able to nominate Nehru as his "legal heir".'[31]

★

Sir Stafford Cripps landed in Delhi on 22 March 1942 and made his offer eight days later. I distinctly remember hearing Sir Stafford's broadcast in the evening news of All-India Radio in my school that day (30 March). And I was struck by one word in his broadcast, i.e., the *'peoples'* (of India). I had never before thought of, or heard, the people of India being described in the plural. And it was on the implication of this very thesis that India contained more than one nation, that Cripps' offer got stuck.

George R. Merrell, the officer in charge of the American Commissariat in Delhi, could recognize the nub of the problem and telegraphed the secretary of state on 2 April 1942:

> The Congress will oppose the scheme on the ground that it unnecessarily presupposes vivisection of the country whereas the declaration should only promise Dominion Status and a Constituent Assembly after the war leaving details to be worked out by the Indian leaders themsleves.[32]

The same day India's agent general in Washington, Sir Girja Shanker Bajpai, sent out a subtle warning to the viceroy that he had been summoned by the US president and that 'Mr Roosevelt seemed to think that the plan regarding immediate federation does not go far enough'.[33]

H.V. Hodson, the reforms commissioner and the main adviser to the viceroy on constitutional affairs, has recorded in his memoirs that, before Cripps left for India, Linlithgow, on his advice, had 'objected strongly' to the idea of 'the provincial option' clause. According to Hodson, this clause, 'while being no substitute for safeguards for Muslims in Hindu-majority Provinces would be taken as acceptance of Pakistan as regards the Muslim-majority Provinces and would have a particularly disruptive effect in the Punjab, above all amongst the Sikh minority there'. The viceroy was also against disturbing the status quo in the Punjab, from where 50 per cent of the Army was recruited. Hodson has recounted that there was a 'fierce Ministerial dispute on the issue which had threatened to split the War Cabinet', but that Churchill and the protagonists of Pakistan had prevailed and 'the package deal (consisting of the provincial option) was no longer negotiable'.[34]

On 6 April 1942, while Cripps was still in India, the first Japanese bombs fell on Indian soil at Visakhapatnam and Kakinada (then in the Madras Province and now in Andhra Pradesh), situated on the east coast of India. Only eight anti-aircraft guns were believed to be available in the whole of India at that time. Moreover, no planes were available to counter the raids. The Japanese were in complete control of the Bay of Bengal and had sunk a good deal of British shipping there. In Burma the British forces were in full retreat, through dense forests and mountains, into northeast India. After the ineffectual resistance put up by the British to the Japanese both in the Malay states and Burma, there was not much confidence in their ability to defend India.

Colonel Louis Johnson had by now landed in New Delhi and flung himself into the negotiations with typical American vigour, apparently making an immediate impact on Jawaharlal Nehru. The colonel posed the question: Could there not be a compromise on the interim arrangements so favourable to the Congress that it would make them forget their long-term concern about the 'provincial option' and induce them to enter the war on the Allies' side? And Cripps, in a desperate bid to bring the Congress Party on board, agreed to dangle before them the possibility of an immediate cabinet type of government with a restricted viceregal veto, even though the granting of this concession went beyond his brief.

A compromise was reached with Nehru on the control over defence; this would remain in the hands of the 'British Commander-in-Chief for the duration of the war'. But Linlithgow protested directly to Churchill against Nehru's efforts, which were supported by Cripps and Johnson, to abridge his (Linlithgow's) veto powers to overrule the Interim Government, which would mean the virtual transfer of power into Indian hands and Britain's loss of control over Indian affairs. Churchill firmly put his foot down against any such moves (or 'Crippery' as the British civil servants in India had started to call Sir Stafford's efforts). 'In your natural desire to reach a settlement with Congress you may be drawn into positions far different from any the Cabinet approved before you set forth,'[35] wired Churchill to Cripps on 10 April. Actually, since the viceregal veto powers over the Viceroy's Executive Council were derived from an Act of the British Parliament, they could not be modified without a reference to it. There could, of course, be a gentleman's agreement not to use these powers, but this depended on the viceroy's concurrence, which was absolutely and predictably not forthcoming.

At Cripps' request, the Congress Party had agreed not to make public their objections to the 'provincial option' or to the long-term proposals in the offer, as long as the discussions on the immediate issue of the formation of the national government were underway. But after Cripps threw in the towel on 11 April 1942, the Congress leaders publicized their objections against both Britain's long-term and short-term proposals. Immediately thereafter, Cripps abruptly left India, somewhat in a huff.

The Congress Party resolution (11 April) opposed the Cripps offer because of its 'acceptance beforehand of the novel principles of non-accession for a Province...[which would be] a severe blow to the conception of Indian unity'. However, there appears the following sentence in the same resolution: 'Nevertheless the [Congress Working] Committee cannot think in terms of compelling the people in any territorial unit to remain in an Indian union against their declared and established will.'[36]

Sir George Cunningham, the governor of the NWFP, had warned the viceroy that, according to Meher Chand Khanna (later the Indian minister for relief and rehabilitation), 'the fundamental objection felt by the Congress to Sir S. Cripps' proposals was the Pakistan element in them. Congress could not, however, bring this element too much to the forefront without stultifying a good deal that they have preached in the past about rights of self-determination. So they manoeuvred for a breakdown on other issues'.[37] But since the party considered India one and indivisible, and the principle of self-determination as not applicable to parts of states, why had it raised a doubt about its own commitment to India's unity? The same 'bone of ambiguity', the result of loose thinking, would get stuck in the Congress Party's throat on other occasions as well. Such contradictions amongst Congress Party's leaders stood out in stark contrast to Jinnah's clear-cut formulations, which adhered to a uniform line of reasoning, and projected an impression of strength of his position, even when it was inherently weak.

According to Hodson: 'The Cripps offer was a compromise which had been accepted to avert a Cabinet crisis but not all Ministers hoped with equal vigour that it would succeed. To some it had been primarily a public relations exercise to appease American opinion, a section of the British opinion, and moderate Indian opinion rather than an all-out attempt to bring Congress and other parties into [the] Indian Government. When Mr Churchill learnt of the breakdown of the Delhi negotiations he put [on] an act of sham tears before his guests at Chequers [Churchill's country house], not troubling to conceal his own pleasure. But this is very different from the allegation that he sabotaged the mission.'[38]

Leo Amery summarized his reaction vis-à-vis Cripps' failure to Linlithgow as follows: 'So far as the effect outside India is concerned it seems likely to be all to the good. For the first time America will have learnt something about the complexities of Indian affairs and of the intransigence of the Congress politicians and their underlying refusal to face responsibility'. He added: 'What a relief now that it is over.'[39] A deluge of comments on Cripps' failed mission followed, but the one attributed to the gamekeeper of Linlithgow's estate in Scotland takes the cake: 'The cheek of the man [Cripps] to think that he could do in a fortnight what His Lordship has not been able to do in six years.'[40]

★

Churchill informed Roosevelt of Cripps' failure on 11 April itself: 'I feel absolutely satisfied we have done our utmost', read his message. The British PM also endorsed a telegram he had sent to Cripps, in which he had stated: 'The effect throughout Britain and in the United States has been wholly beneficial. The fact that the break comes on the broadest issues and not entangled formulas about defence is a great advantage...the foundations have been laid for the future progress of the people of India.'[41]

Roosevelt replied to Churchill the same day:

> I am sorry to say that I can't agree with the point of view that public opinion in the United States believes that the negotiations have failed on broad general terms. The general impression here is quite contrary.
>
> The feeling almost universally held is that the deadlock has been caused by the unwillingness of the British Government to concede to the Indians the right of self-government, notwithstanding the willingness of the Indians to entrust technical, military and naval defence control to the competent British authorities. American public opinion can't understand why, if the British Government is willing to permit the component parts of India to secede from the British Empire after the war, it is not willing to permit them to enjoy what is tantamount to self-government during the war. I feel I must raise this issue before you very frankly.... If the present negotiations are allowed to collapse as presented to the American people and India should subsequently be successfully invaded by Japan with attendant serious military or naval defeat for our side the prejudicial reaction on American public opinion can hardly be overestimated. Consequently would it not be possible for you to have Cripps postpone his departure on the ground that you personally have sent him instructions to make a final effort to find a common ground of understanding?[42]

Churchill then dug in his heels. His reply, dispatched the next day, ran as follows: 'You know the weight I attach to everything you say to me but I did not think I could take responsibility for the defence of India if everything is again to be thrown into the melting pot at this critical juncture.'[43] Besides, he pointed out that Cripps had already left India. This exchange occurred just before General George Marshall was due to reach London to thrash out with Churchill the details of the Anglo–American plans for the invasion of Europe: whether there should be a landing across the Channel as the Americans preferred, or an invasion first of North Africa as Churchill was insisting upon. With such crucial issues at stake, Roosevelt did not think it advisable at that time to press Churchill further on India.

Colonel Louis Johnson's presence in New Delhi during the Cripps mission had given the US president a trustworthy source of information on the events that created doubts in his and Cordell Hull's mind whether or not Churchill had really wanted the mission to succeed. On 4 April Johnson had wired the following message to Hull: 'Unless the President feels that he can intercede with Churchill it seems the Cripps mission is doomed to failure', adding that 'Cripps so believes too'.[44] And as the negotiations collapsed on 11 April, Johnson informed Hull: 'Cripps with embarrassment told me that he could not change [the] draft [of the British offer] without Churchill's approval'. He added that 'Churchill had cabled him that he will give no approval unless Wavell [the commander-in-chief in India] and Viceroy endorsed the change'. Johnson then concluded: 'London wanted a Congress refusal.'[45]

Johnson passed on his impressions to Washington (i.e., to the secretary of state) on other matters as well. For example, he found the 'industrial and political situation here much more difficult than I was advised before arrival'. Also, he felt that 'Indian industrialists can raise war production two and a half times and China was willing to place orders in India but Civil Servants and ten or twelve British industrialists who dominate Indian policy in London are against it'. He also reported that the 'Muslim League [was being] used by Britain as a counterforce to [the] Congress' and that 'Wavell hates and distrusts Nehru'.[46] (How Churchill had Johnson eventually evicted from his post in India is related later.)

Johnson's impressions were largely corroborated by the report sent to the US administration by two other sources, namely, Edgar Snow and Louis Fisher.

Snow, best known as a China hand (author of *Red Star over China*, Grove Press edition, New York, 1989), had been visiting India regularly since 1931. President Roosevelt met Snow in February 1942 and encouraged him to go to India once again, but this time as a war correspondent and 'write when you hear anything interesting' and also 'to ask Nehru to write me a letter and tell me exactly what he wants me to do for India'.[47]

Fisher, a renowned writer, was helped by Sumner Wells, the assistant secretary of state, in getting a flight to India in order 'to appraise the political situation there following the failure of the Cripps offer'. He spent a week with Gandhiji in Sevagram in June 1942. His book, *The Great Challenge* (Associated Faculty Press, Utah, 1971), records his journey and his experiences.

The British were, meanwhile, making every effort to convince Roosevelt that the blame for the failure of the British initiative fell squarely on Indian shoulders. They also tried to drive home the point that it was *not* Britain's reluctance to hand over power that was delaying self-government in India but the *lack of agreement* among the diverse political elements in India.

While Halifax stonewalled enquiries by Cordell Hull as to whether the US could be of any assistance in India, a campaign was mounted through others, i.e., non-Britishers, to explain 'the complications of the Indian situation' to the president. For instance, Graham Spry, a Canadian national who had accompanied Cripps to India, was brought to Washington to give an eyewitness account of what exactly had transpired in Delhi. According to a note written by Spry on 15 May 1942, the US president, at the outset, posed two questions: (1) Had any restrictions been placed on Cripps' instructions during the later stages? (2) Had Colonel Johnson been helpful 'because some of your people over there thought he was interfering'?

The British had anticipated the first query, and Spry immediately produced a message from Sir Stafford, which he read out to Roosevelt: 'Please convey to the President my personal assurance that throughout the Indian negotiations I was loyally supported by the War Cabinet, the Viceroy and the Commander-in-Chief.' This statement, was of course not quite accurate (as the earlier discussion has shown), and Winston Churchill himself, in the House of Commons on 12 September 1946 admitted that: 'His Majesty's Government had not been willing to support Sir Stafford Cripps to the extent to which he himself was prepared to go.'

To the second question, Spry smoothly replied that Sir Stafford was 'most grateful' for the colonel's help who, he emphasized, had throughout acted strictly in his personal capacity as an intermediary. Spry's responses appeared to take a load off the president's mind and made him more receptive to the other information on India furnished to him by the Canadian.

Spry recorded the other remarks made to him by the president as follows: 'Nehru seemed to wish the negotiations to succeed... Gandhiji's "resurgence" had caused some surprise...I think our people began to see it is not easy.' The last observation signified that the British had got their message through. A perusal of the US State Department papers shows that Spry used his time in Washington to explain to American officials that the defence of India did not depend upon obtaining the support of the Congress Party, as was its claim, and that about 50,000 Indian volunteers were joining the Army each month, despite Gandhiji and Nehru standing aside, which was the ground reality.[48]

The Indian agent general in Washington, Sir Girja Shanker Bajpai, a member of the elite Indian Civil Service and till lately a member of the Viceroy's Executive Council, had been attached to the British Embassy simultaneously with the appointment of an American commissioner in Delhi in 1941. On 24 April 1942, when questioned by Wallace Murray, the adviser on political relations in the State Department, as to why the Cripps Mission had failed, he replied that the major cause was the difference in the views of Jawaharlal Nehru and C. Rajagopalachari (another eminent Congress leader from South India) on the one hand and Gandhiji on the other. 'I am sorry to say', he added, 'that some members of the party [Congress] reasoned that if the British lose and the Japanese succeed in occupying India the Indians would be in a better position to negotiate a satisfactory settlement with the Japanese than they would have been if they had fallen in with the British proposals.'[49] For his role in the United States during the war, Nehru termed Bajpai 'a goose of British Imperialism'. Nevertheless, Nehru appointed Bajpai as the first secretary-general of the Indian Ministry of External Affairs after independence. And it was Bajpai who was instrumental in setting up the Foreign Service of free India.

According to an assessment prepared by the British Embassy in Washington,

the Cripps Mission had made a solid contribution against American doubts that Britain is incompetent to administer Indian affairs. The most enduring improvements in opinion [here] due to the mission were, first, that the Indian problem and Indian politics were not open to simple interpretations or solutions, and second that the British government professed at least the right intentions for the future when hostilities had ended. The good intentions may be suspect, and it is widely held that the British "reactionaries" did not believe in, and will not, allow the proposals to be implemented. But the American people are not so unreasonable as to want that constitutional experiments detrimental to the war should be embarked upon [for the present].... Successful military operations based on India will almost certainly strengthen the British position.[50]

After the collapse of the Cripps Mission, despite repeated pleadings of Chiang Kai-shek and Cordell Hull and the threatened agitation in India, President Roosevelt did not take any further initiative on India. It is clear from the State Department records that Roosevelt faced a dilemma. On the one hand, he was thinking as to what could be the American position in Asia after the war. This required him to pay special attention to a liberated China and a freed India and to use the principle embodied in the Atlantic Charter as a lever to prevail upon European countries to grant freedom to their Asian colonies and to exercise care not to identify the USA with British policy in Asia. On the other hand, Britain had become America's closest and most useful strategic partner in the war against Germany and Japan, not the least because of its far-flung political influence, military bases and the resourcefulness of its people. Roosevelt felt that this wartime partnership could prove even more useful after the war to maintain peace in the world, on American terms. Churchill's dominant personality was part of this dilemma. He did not agree with Churchill's ambitions to maintain the British Empire by hook or by crook and to keep India under its control after the war. However, he saw Churchill as America's staunchest friend in all the world and a British leader willing to bind Britain to America forever. Under the circumstances, he had to walk a tightrope. And we will discover in a later chapter how he and his advisers accomplished the task when a few months later Churchill and Gandhiji clashed during the Quit India movement.

It would be worthwhile to consider here whether or not the Congress Party leaders had made a mistake in turning down the Cripps offer. Admittedly, by accepting the offer they would be agreeing to the principle of the possible division of the country at the time of British withdrawal. If the Muslim League-controlled provinces and some of the larger princely states (such as Hyderabad, Kashmir, Mysore and Travancore) decided to exercise 'the provincial option' and opted out of the Indian Union at that time, such a step could have Balkanized the country.

Such speculation was, however, hypothetical; the immediate, practical gains to the nationalists from the Cripps offer were tangible. The offer provided an opportunity for the Congress Party to get back to power in the governments of British provinces from where they had resigned in 1939. This would help them regain the political initiative in the country. Even more importantly, it provided an opportunity for them to enter the Viceroy's Executive Council at the Centre. Such a step, whatever the constraints to their free functioning in the council, would signal their joining the Allied cause.

The upshot of it would be a powerful swell of public opinion in their favour in the USA and Britain. Such a development would make it virtually impossible for the British Tories to resist granting India independence at the end of the war. Also, the question of the partition of the country would be sidelined.

If the Congress Party had agreed to enter the Interim Government, reserving its position on the long-term 'provincial option', Churchill could not very well take the stand with the US president, or indeed with his own country's Labour Party, that he would not take the help of the largest political organization in India to stop the advancing Japanese because that body would not agree in advance to some commitment in the future, i.e., after the war, which, in any case, as Edmund Burke put it 'never leaves where it found a nation'. Indeed, when the time came to consider future constitutional developments in India, Churchill would not be there, for he fell from power in 1945.

Nor did the Congress Party pay sufficient attention to the fact that the Muslim majorities in the two relatively large and crucial provinces, the Punjab and Bengal, might not opt out of the Indian Union. In fact, the Muslim chief ministers of these provinces, Sir Sikandar Hayat Khan and Fazal-ul-Haq, were opposed at that time to the idea of Pakistan. In the Punjab the scheme threatened the coalition government consisting of all the communities, which formed the base of Sir Sikandar's power. In Bengal the Muslim majority (51 per cent as against 49 per cent Hindus and others) was too slender to ensure a certain vote for Pakistan. The larger princely states could attempt to break away, but such a possibility would be lessened if the nationalists were part of the Interim Government and thus able to exercise influence within such a government, rather than if they remained in the wilderness.

*

For his part, Nehru, with Colonel Johnson's help, did try to work out a compromise on the contested issues, as related earlier. Abandoning his earlier reservations to support England in the war, he had now swung around to become a protagonist of the Allied cause and wished his countrymen to throw their weight behind the British in their struggle against Hitler and the Japanese. However, as he informed Cripps and Johnson, he could not count on his party colleagues to back him. The unvarnished truth is that the Mahatma stood in the way. So, with Churchill and Linlithgow opposed to the Cripps offer on the one hand and Gandhiji on the other, whatever its pros and cons, it hardly had any chance of succeeding. Why the Mahatma adopted such a dismissive attitude to the offer and the riposte he worked out to combat Churchill and company are dealt with in the next chapter.

To sum up: After losing Singapore to Japan, Churchill came under pressure from Roosevelt to seek Gandhiji's and Nehru's help to defend India. Churchill deflected this pressure by making an offer that appeared to concede self-government to the Indians, but, by insisting on the 'provincial option', turned the course in Pakistan's direction. If the forging of the Linlithgow–Jinnah alliance in 1940 was the first step that opened the way for the creation of Pakistan, Churchill's putting forward the idea of the 'provincial option' in 1942, was the second step towards this goal.

On the other hand, if the Congress Party leaders had used the Cripps proposal to get into the seats of power in the provinces and the Centre, there was a reasonable chance that they could have turned the tables on Churchill. If the first grave error the Congress Party committed at the end game of Empire was to resign from provincial ministries in 1939, which left the field open for Jinnah, its second was to spurn the Cripps offer.

Notes and References

1. Winston Churchill, *Memories of the Second World War*, Vol. 6, *War Comes to America* (Cassel & Co., London, 1950, pp. 209–10).
2. Ibid., p. 188.
3. Ibid., pp. 286–87.

4. Ibid., p. 188.

5. Transfer of power (TOP), Vol. I, S. No. 43, p. 82.

6. War Cabinet Paper, 42/43, pp. 104–05, viceroy to secretary of state, quoted in TOP, Vol. I, S. No. 60, Para 10.

7. TOP, Vol. I, S. No. 60.

8. Churchill on Cripps, cited in Charles McMoran Wilson (aka Lord Moran), *Winston Churchill – The Struggle for Survival* (Constable, London, 1966, p. 74).

9. For text of Cripps' offer, see V.P. Menon, *Transfer of Power in India* (Longman Green, London, 1957, p. 124).

10. TOP, Vol. I, S. No. 163, 21 February 1942.

11. Ibid., S. No. 185.

12. Ibid., S. No. 191.

13. V.P. Menon, op. cit., pp. 437–38.

14. TOP, Vol. I, S. No. 296.

15. War Cabinet Papers, WP (42) 283, L/P&J/8/510, 6 July 1942. Memorandum by Cripps, para on negotiation with Muslim League, pp. 407–16.

16. V.P. Menon, op. cit., p. 138.

17. US FR 1942, Vol. 1, pp. 604–05.

18. Ibid., p. 604.

19. Ibid.

20. Ibid., pp. 602–04. Memorandum by the assistant secretary of state (Adolf A. Berle), dated 17 February 1942.

21. Ibid., p. 607, assistant secretary of state, Breckinridge Long's note.

22. TOP, Vol. I, S. No. 318.

23. Christopher Ogden, *Life of the Party: The Biography of Pamela Digby Churchill Hayward Harriman* (Little Brown and Co., London, 1994, pp. 122–23).

24. US FR, 1942, Vol. 1, Harriman to Roosevelt, p. 608.

25. Winston Churchill, *Memories of the Second World War*, Vol. 10, *Assault from the Air* (Cassel & Co., London, 1950, p. 54).

26. TOP, Vol. I, S. No. 207, Churchill to Roosevelt, telegram dated 4 March 1942.

27. Ibid., enclosure to above.

28. Ibid., S. No. 271, Churchill to Roosevelt, telegram dated 7 March 1942.

29. Ibid., enclosure to above.
30. US FR, 1942, Vol. 1, pp. 615–16, Roosevelt to Churchill, telegram dated 10 March 1942.
31. Ibid., pp. 601–02, US State Department memo, dated 5 February 1942.
32. Ibid., p. 624. Merrell's telegram to secretary of state, dated 2 April 1942.
33. TOP, Vol. I, S. No. 508, Bajpai's telegram to viceroy, dated 2 April 1942.
34. H. V. Hodson, *The Great Divide: Britain-India-Pakistan* (Oxford University Press edition, Delhi, 2000, p. 94).
35. TOP, Vol. I, S. No. 582, Churchill to Cripps, telegram dated 10 April 1942.
36. Ibid., S. No. 605, Resolution of Congress Working Committee issued 11 April 1942.
37. Ibid., S. No. 673 and MSS/EUR/F 125/77, governor of NWFP's letter to viceroy, dated 23 April 1942.
38. Hodson, op. cit., p. 103.
39. TOP, Vol. I, S. No. 610, MSS EUR 125–11, 11 April 1942.
40. Patrick French, *Liberty or Death: India's Journey to Independence and Division* (HarperCollins, London, 1995, p. 148).
41. US FR 1942, Vol. I, p. 632, Churchill to Roosevelt, telegram dated 11 April 1942.
42. Ibid., p. 633, Roosevelt to Churchill, telegram via Harry Hopkins (personal aide to Roosevelt), dated 11 April 1942.
43. Ibid., p. 634, Churchill to Roosevelt, telegram dated 12 April 1942.
44. Ibid., p. 629, Johnson's telegram to secretary of state, dated 4 April 1942.
45. Ibid., p. 631, Johnson's telegram, dated 11 April 1942.
46. Ibid., pp. 630–32, Johnson's telegrams to secretary of state from 13 April to 4 May 1942.
47. Edgar Snow, *Journey to the Beginning* (Random House, New York, 1958, p. 54).
48. TOP, Vol. II, S. No. 61, notes by Spry on interview with Roosevelt, 15 May 1942.
49. US FR 1942, Vol. I, memo of conversation of adviser on political relations in the US State Department (Wallace Murray) with Bajpai, 24 April 1942.
50. British Embassy in Washington, 'Appreciation on US Attitude towards India', Paras 33–41 [Oriental and Indian Collection (OIC), British Library, London].

5

The Mahatma's Fury

BY INTRODUCING THE IDEA OF THE 'PROVINCIAL OPTION', CHURCHILL
had marked out the constitutional path by which the Muslims and
the princely states could achieve self-determination and separation
from an Indian Union, if and when Britain withdrew from the
subcontinent. As he himself put it, this path 'laid the foundation for
the future progress of the peoples of India'.

After failing to persuade the Congress Party leaders to
unconditionally support Britain in the war, Gandhiji had given his
word to the viceroy on 5 October 1939 that he would try to ensure
that they did not obstruct the British war effort in India in any
tangible way. And he believed that by persuading the party to adopt
a generally passive role, even at the risk of weakening it, he had lived
up to his promise all through 1940 and 1941. Admittedly, the Congress
Party Governments had resigned from the provincial ministries in
British provinces and the party had continued to pass resolutions
demanding instant independence and to raise slogans against violence
and war, which had landed quite a few of the leaders in prison.
However, India, by and large, had remained calm during this period,
while Britain built up its war strength in the country.* On the other

---

* About two-and-a-half million men from the subcontinent (33 per cent of
  whom were Muslims) fought in the Allied armed forces.

hand, Gandhiji had now begun to feel that his supposed partner, the British viceroy, had betrayed him and used this period of relative peace to build up the separatist Jinnah against other Muslim leaders who favoured a united India and had indeed forged an alliance with the Muslim League Party. If the British declaration of 8 August 1940, giving veto powers to the minorities on future constitutional developments, had dealt a heavy blow, the Cripps proposal, by sowing the seeds of partition, was the proverbial last straw. Gandhiji, therefore, felt that he had to rethink his approach.

It was another matter that Linlithgow saw it all somewhat differently. The Congress Party's resignations from provincial ministries seemed to him a definite instance of its non-cooperation with the war effort, even if its other provocations were to be ignored. And since he felt quite confident of smashing any agitation that the Congress Party might launch, its supposed restraint in the domain was nothing to be grateful for. Then, if Gandhiji had indeed been serious about unconditional support to Britain in the war, how could he, a few months later, oppose the same war on the ground that it violated his principle of non-violence? Furthermore, as he had reported to Lord Zetland, Jinnah was dependent on him, and therefore, a better bet.

Before considering Gandhiji's new approach, let us cast a glance at the activities of the ex-president of the Congress Party, Subhash Chandra Bose. Bose today is seen as one leader of the Indian freedom movement who dared to fight the British with the sword and was not implicated in the creation of Pakistan. One fine January morning in 1941, Bose, who had been confined by the British authorities to his home in Calcutta, disappeared, to their great consternation. After he broke with the Congress Party and raised the slogan 'Britain's difficulty is India's opportunity', and formed his own group, the Forward Bloc, disavowing Gandhian non-violence and pacifism, he had first been imprisoned and then kept under close police surveillance. While in prison, his popularity had steadily risen, especially amongst the urban youth of all communities. For example, the Muslim students of Calcutta University threatened to launch an agitation for his release. Linlithgow, while reporting this event to Amery on 20 July 1940, warned that both the chief minister of

Bengal, Fazal-ul-Haq, and his opponent, Nizam-ud-din, the two top Muslim leaders of Bengal, were vying for Bose's support, no doubt to Jinnah's discomfiture and the viceroy's own.[1]

After a while Bose surfaced in Berlin. This sent a thrill through the country, not because of any sympathy for Nazi Germany but because Bose was seen to have delivered a slap on the British face. By 1942, Bose's flight had turned into the stuff of which legends are made, and the reasons were not far to seek. 'Without actually being on the ground here it is difficult if not impossible to appreciate how distrust and hatred of the British have developed even during past three months', wrote the chargé d'affaires of the American Mission in New Delhi to the secretary of state in Washington on 21 July 1942.[2]

Bose had escaped from Calcutta to Peshawar by train, disguised as a Muslim gentleman. And then he crossed into Afghanistan through unused mountain tracks. Once in Kabul, dressed like an Afghan, he headed for the Italian Embassy, likely to be less rigorously watched by British Intelligence than the German Embassy. The Italian ambassador, Alberto Quaroni (according to the account of the ambassador's son) treated him somewhat like a hot potato and passed him on to his German counterpart, who then made all the arrangements for Bose's onward journey. From Kabul he was sent to Berlin through the USSR, which was then still at peace with Germany, as Stalin waited for Hitler to pounce upon Britain, and Churchill marked time for Hitler to attack the Soviet Union.

Ambassador Quaroni had been wisely cautious, for when Bose, after reaching Europe, travelled to Rome to see Benito Mussolini, Count Galaezzo Ciano, the Italian foreign minister, noted in his diary: 'The value of the upstart is not clear.'[3] In Hitler's race-conscious Germany, Bose was used, not honoured. His demand for a 'free Indian government' was rejected; instead, he was allowed to start a 'Free India Centre', from where he could beam anti-British propaganda to India over the German radio. The salutation 'Jai Hind' – victory to India – that he originated and broadcast from Berlin, and which remains a common greeting amongst Indians to this day, was perhaps his most tangible contribution to India's cause from Germany. Even so, Gandhiji was worried about Bose's activities.[4]

According to a British Intelligence report, Gandhiji told Congress workers at a private gathering in Bombay: 'I have an idea that the Forward Bloc is a tremendous organization in India, Subhash has risked much for us but if he means to set up a government in India then he will have to be resisted.'[5]

Hitler had no faith in the Indians' capacity to rule themselves. The Fuehrer evidently did not want Bose to stay on in Germany longer than necessary. In 1943 Bose was transported by submarine round the Cape of Good Hope and entrusted to the care of Germany's new ally, Japan, for whatever use that country could make of him. In Southeast Asia, Bose blossomed, and, as we shall see in a later chapter, played an important role in demoralizing the British military establishment in India. Indeed, it is a toss-up whether Gandhiji's or Bose's influence during the period 1945–46 – even after Bose's death – played a more important role in destabilizing British rule in India.

The fresh approach that Gandhiji was evolving and which ultimately crystallized into the Quit India resolution of 8 August 1942 can best be discerned from the draft for a resolution that he sent for adoption to the closed-door session of the Congress Working Committee meeting at Allahabad a fortnight after Sir Stafford Cripps had returned to England. He sent the draft through the secure hands of the faithful Mira-ben (whose original name was Madeleine Slade) but this document, as well as the minutes of the discussion that took place on its contents, fell into the hands of the British Intelligence, courtesy two communist members of the Congress Party. (They are available in the unsealed British archives.) The Indian Communist Party had switched its loyalty from the nationalists to the British after Hitler attacked the Soviet Union in August 1941.

Gandhiji's points in the draft resolution may be summarized as follows:

(1) The British be asked to clear out forthwith;
(2) if the British could not be persuaded to go, they would have to be thrown out;

(3) once the British were removed India would avoid being invaded because Japan's quarrel was with Britain and not with India;

(4) if Japan invaded India, it would meet with non-violent resistance; and

(5) the stationing of foreign soldiers, including American, on Indian soil was a grave menace to Indian freedom.

Nehru, according to the minutes of the meeting of the Congress Working Committee, opposed these views:

> If we said to Japan that her fight was with British Imperialism and not us she would say: "We are glad the British Army is withdrawn; we recognize your independence, but we want certain facilities now, we shall defend you against aggression, we want aerodromes, freedom to pass our troops through your country, this is necessary in self-defence".... If Bapu's* [Gandhiji's] approach is accepted we become passive partners of the Axis powers.

J.B. Kriplani, a senior Congress leader, objected: 'Why should it mean passage of armies through India? Just as we call upon the British and the Americans to withdraw their armies so also we ask others to keep out of our frontiers.' To this objection, Nehru retorted: 'You can't stop Japan by non-violent non-cooperation. The Japanese armies will make India a battleground and go to Iraq, Persia and throttle China and make the Russian situation more difficult.... The British will refuse our demand [to quit] for military reasons apart from others. They cannot allow India to be used by Japan against them.... They will treat India as an enemy country and reduce it to dust and ashes, they will do here what they did in Rangoon.'

Dr Rajendra Prasad (who later became the president of independent India) was adamant but ambiguous in his stand: 'We cannot produce the proper atmosphere [in the country] unless we adopt Bapu's draft.' A report by Denys Pilditch, director of the

---

* Bapu is an affectionate term for 'father' in India.

British Intelligence Service, revealed Dr Rajendra Prasad's real thoughts. In a smaller enclave he had expressed the following view: 'It would be easier to oust the Japanese from India after ridding themselves of the British, whose imperialism was too deep-rooted.' Another freedom fighter, Achyut Patwardhan, also supported Gandhiji but for reasons not entirely Gandhian: 'I would reconsider the position if the Allies could defeat the Axis.' Acharya Narendra Deo, a senior leader, then chipped in with bravado: 'We have to make it clear that [the] Japanese threat has not unnerved us.... We can tell the British to go leaving us to our fate.' Vishvanath Das declared: 'The protest against the introduction of American soldiers in the country is also proper.'

C. Rajagopalachari opposed Gandhiji's views: 'Do not run into the arms of Japan, which is what the resolution comes to.' Vallabhbhai Patel, who emerged as the most successful and practical statesman in the last two years before independence, was, in 1942, completely subservient to Gandhiji: 'I place myself in the hands of Gandhiji. I feel he is instinctively right in the lead he gives in all critical situations.' Others, including the president of the Congress Party, Maulana Abul Kalam Azad, differed in varying degrees with Gandhiji's view, but none had the guts to speak forcefully against it and, in their interventions, often slipped into irrelevancies or began contradicting themselves. For example, Azad said: 'Gandhiji's prescription is the only alternative, though I doubt its effectiveness.' He suggested no alternative. It was at this meeting that Nehru stated: 'It is Gandhiji's feeling that Japan and Germany will win. This feeling unconsciously governs his thinking.' This statement was picked up by London from the British Intelligence report and quoted to Roosevelt to denounce Gandhiji as 'a fifth columnist' or a 'quisling'.

The minutes of the meeting show that the hotly contested draft containing Gandhiji's advice was adopted by a majority vote by the Congress Working Committee in the forenoon session. However, the same afternoon, the CWC was reconvened by the president, Maulana Azad, and the draft changed, with the same gentlemen abruptly reversing their stand without discussion. This reversal came about after Nehru threatened that as he was committed to oppose the Axis powers he would have to openly disassociate himself from the resolution if it was not amended. As a result, the following two sentences were expunged from this resolution: 'Japan's quarrel is not with India' and 'the Committee desires to assure the Japanese Government and people that India bears no enmity with [sic] Japan'. The following text was added in support of Britain's effort to defend India against a Japanese invasion, but in a compromise formulation rather escapist and shifty:

> In places wherein the British and the invading forces are fighting our non-cooperation will be fruitless and unnecessary. Not to put any obstacles in the way of the British forces will often be the only way to demonstrate our non-cooperation with the invader.[6]

The above record allows us a peep into how those leading the fight for India's independence were going about their business.

The Home Department of Linlithgow's Government forwarded the entire CWC proceedings (in the form of a report) to the secretary of state in London, cautioning that Gandhiji 'was in a desperate mood'. The report also warned: 'We hear a good deal of fifth column activities in Burma...and it looks as if we must be prepared for similar behaviour by the Hindu population in this country.' Nehru's statement that Gandhiji believed that Japan and Germany would win came in particularly handy for British propaganda in the USA. The following points were then suggested for widespread dissemination, with the claim that each of them could be proved on the basis of the evidence available:

(1) The long-term object of the Congress is to establish a permanent Congress–Hindu bourgeois domination in India.

(2) The cause of the Congress hostility to us [British] is because of our effort to ensure fair play for all.

(3) The Congress Party's hostility to the Allied cause is to obtain their long-term objective through Japan's victory, if it cannot be obtained from Britain.

(4) The Cripps proposals were rejected because they did not give control [to the Congress Party] over defence or power to make independent terms with Japan.

The report also advises: 'Attack Gandhi's policy, but not Gandhi himself; emphasize prejudice to American war effort and American troops that would result from Gandhi's plan and dispel suggestions in American quarters that the agitation would compel HMG to make political concessions.'[7]

The British Intelligence Department did not accord much credibility to Nehru's pro-Allied efforts in the committee: 'The final draft as published may fairly be regarded as [Nehru] merely disguising what Gandhi wishes to proclaim openly.' Pilditch put forth another explanation for Nehru's pro-Allied stance: 'Nehru suffered from a confusion of impulses in which now the anti-British, now the anti-Japanese prevailed; he was at that time presumably under the influence of the anti-Japanese impulse.'[8]

At the beginning of the war in 1939, Nehru had opposed joining Britain (in the war) for reasons explained in an earlier chapter. By 1942, however, his views had stabilized on the premise that opposition to British rule in India did not mean opposition to the Allies' struggle against the Axis' aggressors. The German attack on the Soviet Union had helped. Even more did China's plight after the Japanese assault. In 1939 he had visited China and there met the generalissimo, Chiang Kai-shek, and the beautiful and articulate Madame Chiang, with whom he began a correspondence. In February 1942, Madame Chiang visited India with her husband and pleaded her country's cause with Nehru, pronouncing him as 'a man of world vision'. And, after the failure of the Cripps Mission, she took up India's cause with President Roosevelt wiring him directly, on 23 April 1942, that 'British newspapers conveying that Cripps did not fail but prepared ground for better Indo–British relations in the future, according to Nehru, was untrue'.[9] In 1940, Nehru had spoken in favour of a confederation made up of China, Iran, Afghanistan and India. He never lost faith in Asian solidarity, based on a Sino–Indian rapport, till China attacked India in October 1962.

Nehru's pro-Allied attitude at that point of time was also influenced by Colonel Louis Johnson, who became a conduit between him and the American administration. For example, on Johnson's advice, Nehru, on 13 April 1942, wired the US president to explain the reasons for the Congress's rejection of the Cripps offer:

> We desired an opportunity to be given to us to organize a real national and popular resistance to the aggressor and invader...the least we considered essential was the formation of a truly national government.... Still we shall do our utmost not to submit to Japanese or any other aggressor's invasion.[10]

He received a prompt reply that expressed the president's 'deep gratification at the message and confidence that all of the people of India will make every possible effective effort to resist Japanese aggression'. It should be remembered that Roosevelt had burnt his fingers in attempting to persuade Churchill to grant self-government to India, and, consequently, on the substance of the message, he kept silent.[11]

*

London did not totally accept Linlithgow's view that there was absolutely nothing to be done with Nehru. On his return to London after his failed mission, Cripps told Churchill that before his departure from Delhi, Nehru had assured him that: 'We are not going to surrender to the invader. In spite of what has happened we are not going to embarrass the British war effort in India. The problem for us is how to organize our own.'[12] Mid-1942 was the worst time for the British in the war. Could they hope for Nehru's support and, in any case, by contacting him, find out how far Gandhiji intended to go with his 'rebellion'?

Sir Edward Villiers had been a member of the Bengal Legislative Council, president of the European Association of India and vice-chairman of the British Union of India in the 1920s and 1930s and had spent twenty-four years in India. In 1942 he was working for the Ministry of Information in London. He travelled to Wardha (now in Maharashtra), where Gandhiji's ashram was situated and where Jawaharlal Nehru was then staying. On 5 July he held a fairly long discussion with Nehru, broken by a gap, during which the latter went to meet Gandhiji. In a detailed report on his talk with Nehru, Villiers began as follows: 'The interview took five hours owing to Nehru's habit of taking half an hour to answer every point made or question asked.... His [Nehru's] political attitude, where it is not merely a reflex of Gandhi's, is very largely conditioned by his vision of the Great Imperial India of the past. He told me that he thought there were only four countries which held any great future: America, Russia, China and India. He was certain that England at all events was finished.'[13]

When Villiers raised the Cripps Mission proposals, Nehru replied that, under the suggested formula, there was no certainty that Britain would withdraw from India after the war in view of their 'repeated broken promises as regards to India's future self-government' and accused England 'of deliberately driving a wedge between Hindus and the Muslims'. This statement gave Villiers the opportunity to drive home his central point:

If the Congress [Party] was prepared without reservations or conditions so far as India and her problems were concerned, to enter the war whole-heartedly on the side of the Allies...she should so place herself in the eyes of the British and American people that even if our [British] Government wanted to go back on its expressed intentions [to grant self-government to India at the end of the war] it would be absolutely impossible for it to do so. Moreover, he [Nehru] himself would be proclaimed and in fact would be a great leader.[14]

Villiers records that Nehru appeared to waver: 'He is not altogether happy about the effect which the Congress Party attitude was having on the American and Russian opinion, but eventually his intervening visit to Gandhi had knocked off the wavering out of him.'[15]

When Villiers finally asked whether he could see Gandhiji, Nehru replied that the old man was feeling too tired. Nevertheless, Villiers reported on the possibility of the Congressmen revolting as follows: 'They were unlikely to start an agitation because they were hoping for some further move to be made by England which will enable them to encroach a little further.' He recommended 'a stony silence' as the best policy in the circumstances. Villiers concluded his memorandum as follows: 'I got the feeling more and more as the conversation proceeded that he [Nehru] was thinking resentfully of India's great past and dreaming more and more of a future India which should take her place in the world as one of the four great coming powers. He referred to this four or five times. If this supposition is correct I imagine he is likely to become more and more intransigent.'[16]

Villiers' memorandum is filed along with Sir Stafford Cripps' private papers. Whether it was sent to him by his Tory cabinet colleagues to stop his own wavering, or whether he was part of the exercise, one cannot say. However, Villiers' assessment provided yet another piece of evidence to the supporters of the Muslim League in England, for instance, Churchill, that the hope that a united self-governing India led by the Congress Party would cooperate with Britain on foreign policy and defence policy was nothing but a mirage. Indeed, an independent India under Nehru and company might turn out to be a hostile force.

Gandhiji's views, as we have already seen, had become strident after the failure of the Cripps Mission. From 10 May 1942 onwards, writing in his newspaper, *Harijan*, he started to sound the alarm against the partition of India ('I consider the vivisection of India to be a sin')[17] and to propound the view that 'the British presence in India was an invitation to Japan and their withdrawal will remove the bait'. On 26 May he exclaimed: 'Hitherto [the British] rulers have said we would gladly retire after we know to whom we should hand over; my answer is leave India to God. If that is too much then leave her to anarchy.'[18] The upshot of his writings and speeches and the fact that he had complete control over the Congress Party apparatus led to a rapid drift towards a confrontation with Britain. The party's dependence on Gandhiji rested on the masses' blind faith in him that had nothing to do with their understanding of, or support for, his day-to-day strategies.[19]

On 14 July 1942, the Congress Party Working Committee passed a resolution, the pith of which was that the British should withdraw and a provisional government formed, consisting of representatives of all sections of the people of India who would then discuss future relations between Britain and India 'as allies in a common task of meeting aggression'. But in the event of the British rejecting this resolution, 'the Congress would be reluctantly compelled to utilize all its accumulated non-violent strength in [a] widespread struggle under the leadership of Gandhiji.'[20] The resolution gave Britain time till 7 August to take a decision on this matter, when the All-India Congress Committee would meet to discuss the CWC resolution.

★

While all these momentous and historic events were taking place, Mohammad Ali Jinnah sat peacefully in his Bombay home, content to issue a statement on the Congress resolution of 14 July: 'It was the culminating point in the policy and programme of Mr Gandhi and his Hindu Congress of blackmailing the British.' Jinnah then demanded 'an immediate declaration from the British Government guaranteeing to the Muslims the right of self-determination and a pledge that they will abide by the verdict of a plebiscite of Muslims and give effect to the Pakistan scheme'.[21] He was preparing the ground to coordinate his policies with Britain on the probable launching of mass agitation by the Congress soon.

George R. Merrell, in charge of the American Mission in Delhi, in his report to Washington on 14 July, analysed the Congress resolution as follows: 'While it asks for complete transfer of power, it is replete with conciliatory passages and gestures [and proposes the convening of] a Constituent Assembly acceptable to all sections of the people [including the Muslim League].' However, he added: 'The Congress demand [for the immediate transfer of power] as contained in the resolution is unrealistic in the middle of the war.' The American diplomat's report continued: 'In a statement to the press Gandhi said "there is no room left for negotiations". I interpret this as pure bombast and I am convinced Congress would accept compromise.... Nehru is passing through Delhi on Thursday and the first secretary in the American Mission is dining with him that evening after which a further report will be submitted.'[22] On Jinnah's statement, Merrell, in his report of 17 July, stated: 'Gandhi is correct that Jinnah has not disclosed the implications of Pakistan nor made attempt to negotiate with Congress' and 'Jinnah knows that many of his followers are uncertain about Pakistan'.[23]

HMG's assessment was, however, somewhat different. Its reaction to the above resolution was rigid and uncompromising. Leopold Amery, in the House of Commons, and Sir Stafford Cripps, in a broadcast to the American people, made it clear that the government would not flinch from taking every possible step to meet the Congress Party's challenge, which decision was also officially conveyed by Clement Attlee to President Roosevelt, as stated in an earlier chapter.

It was on 8 August 1942, in Bombay, that the Congress Party in a full meeting of its Working Committee passed the famous Quit India resolution calling for a mass non-violent agitation and also for mass non-cooperation on the widest possible scale to force Britain to quit India immediately. Mahatma Gandhi's address was impassioned and uncharacteristically bellicose. He declared:

> Freedom immediately, this very night, before dawn if it can be had.... Congress must win freedom or be wiped out in the attempt. Here is a mantra, a short one that I give you – "Do or Die". We shall not live to see the perpetuation of our slavery.[24]

The British were fully prepared to meet the situation on the two fronts that they had to cover: the internal – Indian – and the external – American. On the Indian front, the British were so very ready and confident that Amery pushed the green light button by telegraphing Linlithgow the following ditty:

> Twice armed is he that has his quarrel just.
> But thrice armed is he who gets his blow in first.[25]

With the prompt arrest of the Mahatma and the other members of the Working Committee (except Rajagopalachari), the plans of Gandhiji's non-violent struggle against the government were never carried out. Instead, the movement fell into the hands of the revolutionaries, the opponents of Gandhiji's non-violent methods. The outburst of violence and sabotage, which took the revolutionaries a few weeks to organize, was directed principally against communications and transport. This outburst resulted in the destruction of 250 railway stations and almost an equal number of post offices and police stations. Also, large sections of railway lines and telephone and telegraph wires were ripped away. The railway tracks and the telegraph and telephone systems through Bihar were damaged to such an extent that the communications and war supplies to the eastern front were totally cut off for a little while. It took fifty-seven battalions and severe repressive measures, such as the machine-gunning of mobs from aircraft to restore order. Some 60,000 persons were held and about a thousand killed. Even though the uprising was mostly confined to the Gangetic valley, with its epicentre in Bihar, Linlithgow judged it to be the most serious revolt against British rule since the Great Mutiny of 1857. The British moved fast and managed to break the backbone of the revolt by November 1942.

The Quit India crisis unfolded at a critical moment for Britain in the war. Earlier in the year, they had been beaten in East Asia with nearly a hundred thousand of their troops captured by Japan, whose forces, having achieved total mastery over the Bay of Bengal, were now poised to attack India from Burma. Then in June, in North Africa, Tobruk fell and 33,000 British troops were captured, thereby exposing Egypt to General Erwin Rommel's Afrika Corps. In Europe the German panzers were tearing deep into Soviet land, swiftly approaching the gates of the oilfields of the Caucasus. Would the Japanese, after crossing India, join up with the Germans somewhere in the Middle East? Churchill and the American generals were at loggerheads on whether to launch an offensive across the Channel into France in order to relieve the Soviet Union or to first land forces in North Africa to counter General Rommel, thereby providing relief to the British in the Middle East. 'During this month of July (1942)', wrote Churchill in his memoirs, 'I was politically at my weakest and without a glean of military success.' Indeed, on the day the Quit India movement was launched in India, the British prime minister was in

Cairo, shuffling the commanders. He replaced General Claude Auchinleck with General Harold Alexander as commander-in-chief in the Middle East and Neil Ritchie with Bernard Montgomery as commander of the 8th Army then stationed in the African desert. Consequently, it was not unnatural for the British Government and the British public to react to Gandhiji's and the Indian Congress Party's move with not only exasperation but also anger. They considered this move as a stab in the back at the moment of their direst peril. In fact, the British civil servants in India and Churchill's friends in England attributed the worst possible motives to Gandhiji's intentions. Even those individuals other than the India baiters in England were aghast at Gandhiji's move. The *Daily Herald* of London, the official mouthpiece of the British Labour Party, had come out with an editorial after the Congress had taken the decision to launch the movement that succinctly summarized the feelings of the anti-Tory lobby in England:

> If you persist in demands which are at this moment impossible to grant, you will cripple your cause and humble the influence of us who are your proud and faithful advocates. You will do worse, you will convey to the world the impression that India's leaders are incapable of distinguishing between the ideal of the United Nations and the petty standards of nationalism, that you rate political strategy higher than the prospect of liberty, equality and fraternity with the progressive peoples of the world.[26]

Admittedly, the slogan 'Quit India' was catchy and mobilized public opinion on a large scale against British rule. Even children in the streets yelled '*Quit India*' at passing Englishmen. Such spontaneous reactions contributed to the general mood that freedom was round the corner. However, by and large, the movement proved counterproductive. The relative speed with which the Quit India movement was suppressed tilted world opinion towards the British view that the Congress Party's hold on the Indian masses perhaps was not as formidable as had been believed. Such a development boosted British support for Jinnah and the Muslim League and enhanced faith in Linlithgow for having had the sagacity to forge the

Anglo–Muslim League alliance in advance. And later, with the failure of Japan to invade India and close the supply channel to China, the prevailing situation made Roosevelt all the more disinclined to press Britain to grant independence to India at that point of time. If the Quit India movement was not very effective, it did not remain non-violent for long, thus losing the Gandhian 'high ground'; it contradicted the whole Gandhian approach since 1915, which had been to woo the British public to put the Raj authorities on the defensive. Indeed, with Japan knocking at India's door, the War Cabinet in Britain and the viceroy in Delhi would face no opposition from public opinion in England and have no scruples in ruthlessly suppressing any agitation in India. It was a foolish and inopportune challenge to the British, for all the organized and armed forces were on the other side, as Nehru was to write later. But, at that time, he deferred to Gandhiji, against his better judgement, as he did on many other occasions.

Gandhiji and his colleagues did not think through the results of their action. They knew that their chances of driving out the British by launching such an agitation were minimal. Would not their action push Britain further into Jinnah's arms; that it may actually help bring about the very situation – partition – they wished to avoid the most? The Mahatma's policy was in total contrast to Jinnah's tactics, who, from a far weaker position, used the bait of cooperation with Britain on the one hand and the threat of the use of force, i.e., direct communal action, on the other, to successfully achieve his ends.

Robert Payne, Gandhi's biographer, has attributed the Mahatma's excursion into bellicosity (and unreality) in 1942 to nerves brought on by the shock of a world conflagration and his own impotence to do anything about it. Here was the greatest challenge ever offered to the efficacy of non-violent non-cooperation, and he had been consigned to redundancy. Payne has referred to two letters that Gandhiji wrote to Hitler to prove his contention. In the first letter, dated 23 July 1939, Gandhiji pleaded: 'Will you listen to the appeal of one who had deliberately shunned the method of war not without success?' And in the second, much longer letter, dated 24 December 1941, after roundly condemning Hitler's policies, he wrote: 'We have no doubt about your bravery or devotion to your fatherland, nor we believe that you are the monster described by opponents. In the non-violent technique there is no such thing as defeat. It is do or die without killing or hurting.... I had intended to address a joint appeal both to you and Signor Mussolini.'[27]

Of course, he was equidistant with his advice to *all* the belligerents, for, had he not, in June 1940, as noted in an earlier chapter, advised the viceroy that Britain should oppose Hitler with non-violent non-cooperation even at the risk of self-annihilation, which had left Linlithgow stunned and speechless? It was while he was in such a frame of mind that he expressed the view that he 'expected the Jews to pray for Hitler, who was not beyond redemption', on which Payne has made the following comment: 'In the quiet of the ashram the greater quiet of the gas chambers was inconceivable; he did not have and could not have any imaginative conception of their plight, nor had he much conception of dictatorships.'[28]

Was Gandhiji so anaesthetized by the longing to test his theory of satyagraha during the great war that he indulged in flights of fancy as Payne has concluded? Or was he so worried about losing his hold on the Congress Party to militants such as Subhash Chandra Bose that he had taken this desperate plunge? Or was it simply panic induced by the Cripps proposals that Britain was out to partition India and frustrate his life's work?

Anyway, Gandhiji's militant mood did not last for long. By the end of the year, he was corresponding, from his place of confinement, with the viceroy, each holding the other responsible for the events that had taken place. Gandhiji accused Linlithgow of imprisoning him without giving him a hearing and the viceroy blamed the Mahatma for the violence that his actions had unleashed and which he (Gandhiji) even then was unwilling to condemn. Alongside these somewhat grim exchanges, we find Gandhiji congratulating the viceroy on the marriage of his daughter and requesting that his condolences be conveyed to Lord Halifax in Washington on the loss of his son in the war.

It was, however, the fast that he undertook for twenty-one days, from 9 February 1943 onwards, to 'crucify the flesh' as he put it, and the nationwide wave of anguish and anxiety for his well-being on the possibility of his death that was generated, which finally helped him regain his equilibrium. People all over India waited with baited breath for the daily bulletins issued on his health, thereby affirming not only the mystical hold he still exercised on the masses but also his indispensability to the Indian freedom movement, despite his failing judgement. Indeed, Linlithgow was more worried about the consequences of the anti-British emotion that could have swept the country if Gandhiji died in British custody than he had been at the prospect of the turmoil that could have erupted from the Quit India movement in August 1942.

Linlithgow, by early 1943, had started to call himself 'Churchill of the East'. And according to a report dated 18 February sent by the US president's special representative to India, Ambassador William Phillips (who had replaced Colonel Johnson and had reached India in January 1943), Linlithgow told him in the middle of Gandhiji's fast, when he appeared to be dying: 'Should he die there will be a certain amount of trouble to cope with but at the end of six months this would pass and the atmosphere will become clear and progress made easier...Gandhi had always sabotaged all efforts made by the British Government.'[29] Phillips, while writing to Roosevelt on 23 February, said of Linlithgow: 'Perhaps he is [a] chip off the old block that the Americans knew something about in 1772 [during their war of independence].'[30] Churchill remained inflexible as ever. While Gandhiji's life hung in the balance, he wired to Linlithgow: 'Have heard that Gandhi usually has glucose in his water when doing his various fasting antics. Would it be possible to verify this?'[31] And was heard to remark: 'I do not think Gandhi has the slightest intention of dying and I imagine he has been eating better meals than I have for the last week.'[32]

★

Mahatma Gandhi was the most influential Indian leader of the twentieth century. As soon as he returned from South Africa, he reached out to the masses finding a formula satyagraha or non-violent non-cooperation not only to bring them into the battle against the Raj but also to revive the self-confidence of a downtrodden race. By laying emphasis on tolerance and pluralism, he sought to knit together the multitudes on basically indigenous values, which were also fundamental to democracy. At the same time, he tried to weed out the most obnoxious features of Hindu society such as a general lack of social responsibility, of which untouchability and unconcern for people beyond one's kith and kin were offshoots. And his spinning wheel (*charkha*) was a symbol of self-reliance and self-determination. The more he adopted the simple life and dress of the villager, the more he appeared different – superior, a Mahatma to them. And a formidable mystique developed around his personality.

Mahatma Gandhi's message that the powerless were not necessarily without power spread around the globe, igniting three of the century's great revolutions – against imperialism, racism and economic exploitation – and inspired leaders in diverse countries. One of them, South Africa's Nelson Mandela, has stated: 'At a time when Freud was liberating sex, Gandhi was reining it in, when Marx was pitting workers against capitalists, Gandhi was reconciling them; when the dominant European thought had dropped God and soul out of the social reckoning he was centralizing society in God and soul; and when the ideologies of the colonized had virtually disappeared, he revived them and empowered them with a potency that liberated and redeemed.'

At the core of the great man's confusion at this stage of his life was whether or not or how far to continue to adhere to the policy of non-violence in a situation that was changing from a purely colonial struggle to something different, more akin to one faced by independent states in their dealings with other states. The true power of satyagraha lay in provoking deep moral stirrings in the oppressor by the willingness of the oppressed to withstand all atrocities, even to the extent of calmly facing self-annihilation. It is a tenet for action by individuals who thereby risk only their own or their nearest and dearest ones' lives; it cannot serve as a gospel for leaders of sovereign states to fight aggression by another country.

No leader of a country can afford 'to turn the other cheek' to an invading army and risk defeat for his country and the annihilation of perhaps millions. Non-violence could be used to fight racialism (as in South Africa) or colonialism (as in India) practised by people who are capable of doubting the morality of their own policies and actions. It cannot be a policy to fight pressures exerted by people with totally different ethical values or by fundamentalists or jihadis. Nor can it be a policy for free nations to defend their integrity from aggression or diplomatic blackmail.

In an article in *Harijan* (24 May 1942), Gandhiji wrote that the 'Indian army will be disbanded with the withdrawal of the British Power'. We also have on record that he expressed different views on this matter at different times. 'My belief is', observed Vincent Sheean, his biographer, 'that Gandhiji himself in the course of his long pilgrimage learnt a great deal about the obstinacy of facts; and that his burning enthusiasm for the Tolstoy doctrine was somewhat modified. He said to me two days before he died: "Mind you no ordinary government can get along without the use of force." '[33] On 29 October 1947, Gandhiji told Mountbatten and Lieutenant General L.P. Sen (who was directing military operations in Kashmir) that Indian troops would have 'to do or die in Kashmir'.[34]

It was unfortunate for the country that he could not sort out this confusion in his mind or draw a clear line between tolerance and appeasement as India became independent.

Gandhiji's attempts, in the later part of his life, to mediate between the viceroy and the Congress Party carried an air of unreality and were misunderstood by the British side. And, after partition (in August 1947), his endeavours to woo Pakistan through appeasement became controversial in his own country, justifying Sir V. S. Naipaul's remark: 'It was India's luck Gandhi was never responsible for the running of the country.' His most controversial act was his fast in January 1948, at the height of the war with Pakistan to force independent India's Government not to delay, as it had decided to do, the payment of a sum of Rs 55 crore (equivalent to about US $500 million, in today's terms), which India owed to Pakistan as part of latter's assets, agreed to at the time of partition. The Indian leaders' reason was that this money was likely to be straightaway used to buy arms by Pakistan to shoot down Indian soldiers.

★

Sir Richard Attenborough's universally acclaimed 1982 film did not adequately portray the later Gandhi. His dedication, discipline, courage and humour never deserted him, but he was beginning to retreat into areas of action requiring renunciation and moral fortitude rather than analysis and strategic foresight. After 1946 he flung himself into the riot-torn areas at the risk of his life in order to stop the killings and to alleviate human suffering, irrespective of political considerations. Perhaps such humane endeavours of individuals were the noblest of all, but it was the earlier Gandhi of the 1920s and 1930s sharp, clear-sighted, practical and original who had, by his ability to find solutions to seemingly intractable problems, mesmerized the Indian masses.

Probably the last great service Gandhiji rendered to the country was as far back as in 1932. Then, from his place of confinement in Poona, he successfully combated the British proposal to accord separate electorates to the depressed classes, i.e., the lowest castes. According to this proposal, the depressed classes were to be given reserved seats in future elected bodies for which the candidates and voters could belong only to the depressed classes. Separate electorates for Muslims, introduced in 1909, had gradually contributed to Muslim separatism in India. The new British proposal now threatened to politically split the caste-ridden Hindu society. Gandhiji fought back by announcing that if the proposal were carried through, he would fast unto death. At the same time, he tried to negotiate with Dr B.R. Ambedkar, the leader of the lowest castes, whether or not he would be satisfied if the Congress Party gave the depressed classes seats from amongst its own quota; in fact, more in number than the British had envisaged for them. This negotiation turned out to be successful and the so-called 'Poona Pact' that emerged left the British with no option but to retreat.

The lowest castes today constitute about 20 per cent (about 200 million) of the total Indian population, whereas, half a century ago, they constituted only about 6 per cent (about 24 million) of the total population. No politician who wishes to get elected these days can possibly ignore them. The election process in India, more than any other factor, is helping to purge the caste system. However, if separate electorates for the lowest castes, like those earlier for the Muslims, had been institutionalized, the elective process, instead of knitting together the upper and the lower castes by making them politically interdependent, would have torn them further apart with each election.

'His preaching against the evils of caste, and the advantage of village sanitation, gives a truer impression of the deepest in Gandhi than political campaigns or negotiations with those in power which generated the bulk of the written historical record of his life', points out another one of his biographers, Judith Brown.[35]

Notes and References

1. MSS EUR 125/9, Vol. V, viceroy to secretary of state, dated 21 July 1942.
2. US FR 1942, Vol. I, p. 693, Merrell to secretary of state, dated 21 July 1942.
3. TOP II, S. No. 90, from Intelligence Bureau's report of 26 May 1942, p. 131.
4. Ibid., p. 35.
5. Ibid.
6. TOP II, S. No. 113 (also MSS EUR F 125/105) dated 31 May 1942, enclosure to No. 113 gives the entire proceedings of the Congress Working Committee meeting held at Allahabad at the end of April 1942.
7. TOP II, S. No. 132 (L/P&J/8/596 F 207–87), p. 189, 7 June 1942. Note by Home Department, Government of India, to secretary of state.
8. Ibid., pp. 187–88.
9. US FR 1942, Vol. I, p. 639. Madame Chiang Kai-shek to President Roosevelt, dated 23 April 1942.
10. Ibid., p. 635. Nehru's message to Roosevelt (via Colonel Johnson), dated 13 April 1942.
11. Ibid., p 637.
12. Winston Churchill, *Memories of the Second World War*, Vol. 7, *The Onslaught on Japan* (Cassel & Co., London, 1950, p. 199).

13. Most secret memorandum by Sir Edward Villiers, 5 July 1942, on talks with Jawaharlal Nehru at Wardha, CAS 127–43, Public Records Office, London.
14. Ibid.
15. Ibid.
16. Ibid.
17. *Harijan*, 24 May 1942.
18. Ibid., 26 May 1942.
19. TOP II, S. No. 66–67 (OIC, British Library, London).
20. Ibid., S. No. 265, resolution of the Congress Working Committee, dated 14 July 1942, p. 387.
21. V. P. Menon, *Transfer of Power in India* (Longman Green, London, 1957, p. 153).
22. US FR 1942, Vol. I, p. 679, Merrell's telegram to secretary of state, dated 14 July 1942.
23. Ibid., dated 17 July 1942, p. 683.
24. Patrick French, *Liberty or Death: India's Journey to Independence and Division* (HarperCollins, London, 1995, p. 154).
25. Penderel Moon, *The British Conquest and Dominion of India*, Vol. 2 (India Research Press, Delhi, 1999, p. 1114).
26. Editorial in *Daily Herald*, London, cited in V.P. Menon, op. cit., p. 142.
27. Robert Payne, *Life and Death of Gandhi* (Rupa, Delhi, 1979, pp. 485–88).
28. Ibid., p. 486.
29. US FR 1943, Vol. IV, pp. 195–96. William Phillips, personal representative of President Roosevelt in India to the secretary of state, 18 February 1943.
30. Ibid., p. 203.
31. Winston Churchill, *Road to Victory: 1941–45* (The Churchill Centre, London, 1986, p. 343).
32. TOP, Vol. IV, p. 738, Churchill to Field Marshal Jan Christian Smuts.
33. Vincent Sheean, *Mahatma Gandhi* (Publication Division, Government of India, New Delhi, year not available).
34. MB/E/193/2, University of Southampton, UK, and Lieutenant General L.P. Sen, *Slender Was the Thread* (Orient Longman, New Delhi, 1969, p. 56).
35. Judith Brown, cited in Patrick French, op. cit., p. 104.

6

India, the UK and the USA

As THE CRIPPS MISSION FLOUNDERED, CORDELL HULL, THE US secretary of state, summoned Lord Halifax (the British ambassador) and asked anxiously what was likely to happen next. 'Nothing', calmly answered the ambassador.[1] Of course, something did happen, which had long-term consequences for India. But Gandhiji's fury at the Cripps offer, let loose on 8 August 1942, neither debilitated the Allies' supplies of war material to China via India nor did it diminish British India's preparedness against Japan, which was, after all, what the American secretary of state was primarily concerned about.

It was on 21 May 1942 that Cordell Hull got wind of Gandhiji's plan. That day he received a message from George Merrell, in charge of the American Commissariat in Delhi, 'that Gandhi is planning to launch massive civil disobedience in near future'. Merrell also reported that 'when [Gandhiji was] warned that such a programme could...make India an easy prey for the Japanese, [he] is reliably reported to have been unmoved'.[2] On 25 May the secretary of state received another report from Merrell that, when J.L. Berry, the US Mission's secretary, met Nehru, he found him 'unable or unwilling to state his position [which] leads me to suspect he is veering to his master's [Gandhiji's] point of view'.[3] Meanwhile, the US State Department had received from its New Delhi office copies of Gandhiji's articles in *Harijan*, which, from 10 May 1942 onwards, had taken a decidedly strident tone, as noted in the last chapter.

On 3 June 1942, Cordell Hull again sent for Halifax and enquired about the 'disquieting reports' that were emanating from Delhi, to which the ambassador replied impassively that he would find out and let him know.[4] Faced with a taciturn Halifax, Hull, on 15 June, tackled Sir Girja Shanker Bajpai, the Indian agent general. Bajpai explained to his interlocutor that Gandhiji's influence was not all that great and the US should concentrate on supplying India with tanks and airplanes, which 'would take care of the situation against a possible Japanese attack', which he added, he 'did not anticipate within the next few months'.[5]

★

Most Congress Party leaders did not pay much attention to foreign affairs; nor indeed did Gandhiji. However, Nehru, who did, was concerned about the American and Chinese reactions to Gandhiji's moves. Indeed, he wished they would persuade Britain to restart talks with the Congress Party so that the possibilities of averting the crisis could be explored. On 4 June 1942, he sent a message to Colonel Louis Johnson (who had by then returned to Washington), which read as follows:

> Though Gandhiji does not wish to embarrass the war situation and will not start a movement unless forced to do so, the recognition of India's independence is now essential to successfully fight the war and utilize India's great resources for it.[6]

This message, however, failed to breach the Halifax–Bajpai front in Washington. On 18 June Cordell Hull had Johnson send the following reply to Nehru: 'You should know that Mr Gandhi's statements are being misunderstood in the United States and are being construed as opposing our war aims.'[7]

Nehru then somehow persuaded Gandhiji to accept that if India was granted freedom, Britain and America could retain their forces in the country to fight the Japanese. Nehru believed that such a clarification was necessary if China and America were to be persuaded to prevail upon Churchill to grant self-government to India in the middle of the war. Gandhiji's telegram to Chiang Kai-shek, drafted by Nehru, was a long one. Its main points are contained in the following excerpts:

A Japanese domination of either India or China would be equally injurious to the other country and to world peace.... Free India will agree that Allied powers under treaty with us keep their armed forces in India and use the country as a base for operations against the threatened Japanese attack...I am straining every nerve to avoid a conflict with British authorities but if in the vindication of the freedom which has become an immediate desideratum, this has become inevitable I should not hesitate to run any risk however great.[8]

Nehru then persuaded Gandhiji to write to Roosevelt as well, and make the same proposition, which he did on 1 July 1942:

Under foreign rule we can make no effective contribution of any kind to this war except as harlots. The policy of the Indian National Congress admittedly the largest political organization of the longest standing in India is largely guided by me.... The Allied declaration that the Allies are fighting to make the world safe for freedom of the individual and for democracy sounds hollow as long as India [and] for that matter Africa are exploited by Great Britain and America has the Negro problem in her own home.... Allied troops will remain in India during the war under treaty with the free India Government that may be formed by the people of India without any outside interference direct or indirect...I write this to enlist your active sympathy.[9]

Chiang's reply, dated 8 July 1942, was received through the Chinese consul general in Delhi. Chiang requested the Mahatma to hold his hand on any agitation because of the recent heavy reverses that the British had suffered in North Africa.[10] This message along with the Congress Party leaders' lingering hopes that Britain may yet reopen talks with them resulted in the Quit India movement being postponed till August.

On 25 July 1942 Chiang Kai-shek then sent a three-page-long telegram to the US president and also asked his foreign minister, T.V. Soong, who was then in Washington, to deliver a verbal message. The telegram, amongst other things, said:

> The Indian people have been expecting the US to come out and take a stand on the side of justice and equity.... The Indian people are by nature of a passive disposition but are apt to go to extremes.... By showing sympathy, they can be influenced...a laisser-faire policy would cause them to despair...[and] danger [would be] of the situation getting out of control.[11]

Foreign Minister Soong made three points orally to Sumner Wells, the US undersecretary of state. These Chiang thought too sensitive to be put down on paper. The first point was that the 'Indian Congress actually represents the desire of the Indian people'. Secondly, 'that the question of India is regarded by all Asia as a test case'. Thirdly, that 'the US and China acting together can influence the situation'.[12]

Wells supported the Chinese démarche, recommending to his president, on 29 July 1942, a joint Sino–US intervention to bring about 'some satisfactory arrangement [in India] which would hold during the war period'. Roosevelt, however, decided to transmit Chiang's entire message to Churchill and requested him 'to let me have as soon as possible your thoughts and any suggestions you may wish to offer with regard to nature of the reply I should make to him'.[13] To Gandhiji, Roosevelt replied on 1 August as follows:*

> US has always supported policies of fair dealing and of fair play. War has come as a result of the Axis Powers' dreams of world conquest...I shall hope that our (mutual) interest in democracy and righteousness will enable your countrymen and mine to make common cause against a common enemy.[14]

---

* This message could not be delivered to Gandhiji because he had been arrested before it reached India. When he was released in 1944, the American Commissariat advised that the message had lost all relevance and may merely rub the British the wrong way. Roosevelt insisted that it be delivered all the same.

Roosevelt's message to Churchill arrived in London when the prime minister was away in the Middle East. Attlee thought that the matter was too urgent to be left pending even for a few days. Immediately, Leopold Amery, the secretary of state for India, sent for John G. Winant, the US ambassador, who reported to Hull on 29 July 1942 as follows:

First he [Amery] explained the service that Britain had rendered to India. His emphasis is always on the divisions in India, both religious and political, underlining the minority problem.... The Indian Congress would not be the sole party with which England would ultimately deal.... If Congress revolts after 7 August [the] British would arrest Gandhi and other political leaders. If similar effort was made within England same measures would be taken. Amery then asserted confidently: "Agitation will not affect the Indian war effort or recruitment."[15]

On 7 August Attlee sent off a lengthy telegram to the president enclosing the minutes of the Congress Working Committee of 29 April 1942 (which have been referred to in the previous chapter) to prove that the Congress was defeatist and particularly Gandhiji was so, and no reliance could be placed on them at this juncture. Attlee then warned that 'if Congress agitated, the consequences could be grave and thus rigorous steps would be necessary to suppress the movement at the very outset'.[16] Roosevelt's notation to Hull on this telegram read as follows: 'Frankly I think it is best not to reply to it. What is your view? – FDR'.[17]

On receiving Attlee's telegram, Roosevelt did not wait for Churchill's reply before answering Chiang, on 8 August 1942:

I agree with you [but] the British feel that their position is fair and in any case the suggestions coming from us would undermine the authority of the only existing government in India and create the very crisis we wish to avoid.... We could further consider the matter should the course of events in India in the next week or two reach a more serious stage.[18]

He added the following in a further message to Chiang on 12 August: 'Under the Atlantic Charter, the US supports "independence for those who aspire for independence".'[19]

Churchill replied to Roosevelt on 13 August. As may be expected, he was furious:

> All Chiang's talk of Congress leaders wishing us to quit in order that they may help the Allies is eyewash.... You could remind Chiang that Gandhi was prepared to negotiate with Japan on the free passage for Japanese troops through India to join with Hitler. Personally I have no doubt that in addition, there would have been an understanding that the Congress would have the use of sufficient Japanese troops to keep down composite majority of 90 million Muslims, 40 million untouchables and 90 million in the Indian states. The style of his message prompts me to say *"Cherchez la femme"*. It may well be that ensuing weeks will show how very little real influence Hindu Congress has over the masses in India.[20]

Churchill had taken liberty with facts, but, in the last paragraph, he had thrown down the gauntlet: that the coming struggle would prove the Congress Party's lack of support amongst Indians. '*Cherchez la femme*' – look for the woman – was what Louis XIV used to say whenever there was a whiff of scandal in his court. '*La femme*' in Churchill's message was obviously a reference to Madame Chiang Kai-shek and to her influence on the generalissimo as well as her enthusiasm for Nehru.

Churchill, in the meantime, had succeeded in breaking up the Nehru–Johnson nexus by arranging, through Harry Hopkins, the president's friend and most influential adviser, for Johnson's recall from India. On 31 May 1942, Churchill had wired to Hopkins:

> There are rumours that the President will invite Pt. Nehru to the United States. I hope there is no truth in this, and that anyway the President will consult me beforehand. We do not at all relish the prospect of Johnson's return to India. The Viceroy is much perturbed at the prospect. We are fighting to defend this

vast mass of helpless Indians from imminent invasion. I know you will remember my many difficulties.[21]

And by August 1942 Johnson's fate was sealed, and Roosevelt began looking for a replacement.

★

The ire of English officialdom in India against the Americans had been rising after Colonel Johnson's arrival in Delhi. Their general attitude is well conveyed in a telegram from Sir Maurice Hallet, the governor of United Provinces, to the viceroy: 'America will compel us to hand over [power] to Congress...it is extremely dangerous that the idea should get around that Roosevelt disapproves of HMG policy in regard to India and is even willing to interfere in that policy.'[22] Linlithgow forwarded this telegram to London with the following comment: 'A difficult people and we are bound to have a great deal more difficulty I think once the war is over...I of course and you are only too well aware of the difficulties presented to us by American sentimentalism and ignorance of the Indian problem.'[23]

The American assessment, based on the reports of the US Mission in Delhi at that time, was that the British would find it difficult to suppress the agitation in India but would not negotiate with the Congress Party because of their 'belief based on British and American Intelligence reports that there is no chance of a Japanese invasion' and also 'because they could rely on the intransigence of Jinnah'. Cordell Hull, after the Quit India movement had been launched, had proposed to Roosevelt that Britain would be well advised to 'repeat with full emphasis its proposal of Independence of India at the end of the war'.[24] However, as indicated in his letter to Chiang, Roosevelt's policy had turned to waiting and watching and applying pressure on Britain, but only with great caution.

Around this time the President Roosevelt's assistant, Lauchlin Currie, passed through India on his way back from China. He noticed the danger of American forces and American attitudes in India getting identified with British policy in the minds of the Indians and wired his chief:

This tendency endangers your moral leadership in Asia and therefore America's ability to exert its influence for acceptable and just settlement in post-war Asia. It is to Britain's own long-term interest that Asiatic belief in American disinterestedness be preserved. The thing to be avoided at all costs is the shedding of Indian blood by American troops.[25]

Roosevelt, who, ever alert to the US' image and future role in Asia, immediately issued a directive to the American forces in India that 'their sole purpose is to prosecute the war of the United Nations against the Axis powers' and to 'take scrupulous care to avoid any appearance of participation in India's internal political problems'. The president sent a copy of this directive to Chiang Kai-shek to further reassure him about American policy.

☆

The previous year, on 12 August 1941, Roosevelt and Churchill had signed the Atlantic Charter. This charter laid down certain common principles that the US and the UK wanted to follow for a better future for the world and included the declaration that *'they* [the US and the UK] *respect the right of all peoples to choose the form of government under which they will live* [italics added]'.

On 7 August 1942 the British Embassy in Washington reported to London that, on the first anniversary of the signing of the Atlantic Charter, the United States was planning to propose that telegrams be exchanged between the president and the prime minister and that the president's telegram would state that the charter applied to Asia and Africa as well as to Europe. When this message reached Churchill on 9 August 1942, he was in Cairo. But he immediately wired Roosevelt:

Charter's proposed application to Asia and Africa requires much thought. Grave embarrassment will be caused to the defence of India at the present time by such a statement.... Here in the Middle East the Arabs might claim by majority they would expel the Jews from Palestine. I am strongly wedded to the Zionist policy of which I was one of the authors. This is only one of the unforeseen cases which will arise from new and further declarations.[26]

By raising the Jewish issue, Churchill obviously hoped to temper American enthusiasm to apply the Atlantic Charter to India and the rest of the British Empire. The charter's first anniversary passed off without any controversy, but, on 24 August 1942, Cordell Hull summoned Halifax and told him bluntly that the 'Atlantic Charter should be applied universally including to the British Empire and there will be difficulties if it was applied in separate compartments, so to speak'. 'A very impressive view', answered Halifax, and the matter rested there.[27]

Raising the question of freedom under the Atlantic Charter had been one way of applying indirect pressure on Britain. Another was to draw British attention to the growing public opinion in the US in support of India in the wake of the Quit India movement. On 17 September 1942, Cordell Hull drew the British ambassador's attention to the 'prospect in this country [of] a general movement of agitation against Great Britain and in favour of independence of India, which might create complications in one way or another later on'. Hull specifically referred to the necessity for more moderate and sympathetic speeches (by British statesmen) that would clarify 'that the British Government desired to resume its course going forward with its programme for Indian independence just as quickly as this movement of violence terminated'. In his memorandum of this conversation, Hull noted: 'He [the ambassador] must have known that I was referring to two recent speeches one by the Prime Minister and the other by the Secretary of State for India.'[28] In these speeches Churchill and Amery had lambasted Gandhiji and the other Indian leaders and asserted that 'what we have, we keep'.

The release in the US of selected sections of the draft resolution sent by the Mahatma to the Congress Working Committee at Allahabad on 29 April 1942, which had fallen into British hands, had proved to be a shot in the arm for the British campaign in the US to paint Gandhiji as pro-Japanese and project him as a threat to the Allied war effort. The British built their propaganda around the theme that 'it was not a question whether Great Britain is prepared to give India her freedom but whether India is in a position to exercise it, in view of the serious differences between the Hindus represented by the Congress Party and the Muslims represented by the Muslim League'.

The New York Times and other major newspapers were willing to recognize Britain's difficulties at a time when it was fighting for survival. On the other hand, Edgar Snow and Louis Fisher were vociferously raising the question about the ideals that the US was fighting for. They wanted India to serve as a test case for how Washington would want Asia to emerge after the war. Their writings in the *Nation* and the *Saturday Evening Post*, their lectures at various fora and, especially, their close contacts with the US administration influenced American policy, though the general public, by and large, remained unacquainted with their views. Snow developed upon the points he had made in his book *Battle for Asia* (Random House, New York, 1941) to highlight that Britain was blocking India's industrialization so as to preserve its hold over the Indian market after the war. (The same theme was echoed in a memorandum sent by the assistant secretary of state for the Near East to the secretary of state, Cordell Hull.) In his article entitled 'Why Cripps Failed', which appeared in September 1942, Fisher observed that the will to transfer power was simply not there. Nevertheless, in the same article, he also warned the Indian nationalists that if the continued civil disobedience threatened the Allied war effort, such a state of affairs could reduce American public support for their freedom movement.

In September 1942, Halifax wired London that the general feeling (even in friendly quarters) was 'that if HMG were to appear indifferent to the making of further constructive efforts to find a solution, US opinion would conclude that we were not trying to rally India for active prosecution of the war.'[29] Halifax had earlier warned London of the 'slipping back' of the gains made with the US public opinion after the Cripps Mission failed. Around the same time, the *London Times* contended, in an editorial, that the increase in critical American opinion on the Indian question 'has been so great that it threatens seriously to affect Anglo–American relations'. The same anxiety was reflected in another report of this period sent by the

British Embassy in the US to London: 'India has become the first test which the American, friendly or unfriendly, at once applies to British Imperial policy. In the main it is critical, and it is frequently shot through with emotion.'[30]

★

The American Government, at this stage, decided to twist the British lion's tail by yet another stratagem. By September 1942 the Quit India movement had turned violent, rupturing communications and transport to the eastern parts of India, which served as the base for supplies to China and to the Japanese front on the Indo–Burmese border. The British repression to break the movement was then at its peak. At that very moment, without giving any notice to the British, the Americans stopped the deliveries of supplies being made under the Anglo–US lend-lease agreement to India.[31] According to Auriol Weigold, an Australian educationist, who, in 2000, made a survey of Anglo–American relations in the post-Cripps period, the reports of the American Mission in Delhi and the writings of Snow and Fisher contributed to this serious development, although the concerns of the American chiefs of staff that these supplies may be looted or lost in the turmoil that had engulfed India were also taken into account. Halifax, knowing fully well that the agitation would shortly be smashed, took no action on the American move.[32]

After the Quit India movement was crushed by November 1942 and the fear of a Japanese invasion of India receded, India went off the blip in the US press. And public interest in Indian developments faded once again. By the end of 1942, Churchill had, for all practical purposes, won the 'press war' on India in the United States. However, he remained deeply concerned that a new crisis might develop in India that could once again raise the temperature in the US and persuade the government there to renew pressure on him that would strain Anglo–US relations, particularly because he had no desire to withdraw from India then or later. One consequence of this was that, in early 1943, the British Government commissioned a high-powered survey (to be conducted by Sir Frederick Puckle, an official of the British Ministry of Information) to pinpoint the reasons for this special American interest in Indian affairs, so that this aspect could be dealt with appropriately. According to Puckle:

> India has been an abiding factor in Anglo–American relations…and it may well be that the influence of the Indian question may be more dangerous to the preservation of good relations between Britain and the USA at the peace table than it has ever been before…. For, if we are honest, we must admit that there is no reasonable hope that the end of the hostilities will bring us any nearer to the day when we can say that our obligations and promises to India have been discharged. There is a long and difficult road yet to be travelled and on our journey along it we shall become more and more exposed to charges of dishonesty and insincerity from our ill-wishers everywhere. In these days American cooperation, sympathy and understanding will be invaluable, and without them India may be a most adverse [sic] factor in our mutual relations and a serious obstacle to Anglo–American collaboration for the satisfactory settlement of the world's affairs. This is the real importance of India in the USA, its influence on Anglo–American relations both now and in the future.[33]

Puckle analysed the reasons for the Anglo–American misunderstanding as follows:

> In the whirl of crosscurrents, floating rubbish and sunken snags which make up the stream of American opinion on the subject of India, two things steadily catch the attention, the interest and the ignorance. The interest is because of the old psychology of the frontiers which still influences America and makes them utterly disinclined to believe that there is no quick and simple way out of a deadlock in India or anywhere else…. It is also there because of the presence of American troops in India and their view that China's deliverance will come from their base in India…America has suffered two major disasters in this war, Pearl Harbor and Pearl Buck, the second because of the sentimentalism she has spread in the public about China and India.[34]

He then goes on to enumerate the important 'pressure groups' in America, which played a role:

For the anti-imperialists the British are par excellence the great imperialists, therefore the British are oppressing India; for the American neo-imperialists like Mr Henry Luce of *Time, Life* and *Fortune*, who see the coming years as the "American Century", India is just another of the muddles into which a decadent Britain has got herself, to be cleared up now by the world power, the USA; for big business and not the least the anti-New Dealers, Roosevelt is the enemy, and he is of course in Mr Churchill's pocket and since Churchill is the prime enemy of Indian freedom India becomes the stick with which to beat the President.[35]

Puckle continues:

Finally there is jealousy: Our alleged failure in India is not unpleasing to many Americans, who are not fundamentally anti-British. The Americans are fundamentally concerned...not for India but for themselves, perhaps for the world; India is seen to be our responsibility but their business as well. This sort of a tentative view makes American policy dependent upon American public opinion and critical American public opinion creates complications. In India in particular American criticism of Britain heartens the Congress Party, frightens the Muslims and discourages our supporters.... It can hardly be questioned that both HMG in London and the Government of India in Delhi are at times embarrassed by the tone of American comment by its effect both on their supporters and on their opponents. On the other hand, the censorship decreed by the Government of India creates suspicion in America that the state of things in India is much worse than is allowed to be known. The failure of Mr Gandhi's fast has rubbed some of the gloss off a romantic figure and driven India off from the front pages of the newspapers. But any new incident would revive the adverse interest because India embodies the idea of the British Empire: few people worry at all about Trinidad, Kenya or the Gold Coast.... Whenever there is any matter on which America and Britain are at odds; the lion hunter, when he goes out after his quarry, may vary the charge in his right barrel to suit the circumstances, but in the left there will always be India.[36]

Now, one way for this British conundrum to be solved would be to make the American public disenchanted with India, more precisely with the Congress Party – to Churchill always the Hindu party – or, for the Indian nationalists to become distrustful of American intentions or both. In April 1942 Churchill had tasted success in warding off American pressure by sowing doubt in American minds about the Congress Party's commitment to the Allied cause and by emphasizing the necessity to depend on 'loyal and robust' Muslim support. 'By now', according to R. Moore, the historian, 'Churchill had come to see the Congress–Muslim League conflict as a pillar of the Raj'.[37] So, there would certainly be other topics with which to sow Indo–American discord, but from then on, whenever an Englishman went out after this particular prey, whatever the arguments he loaded in his right barrel, in the left there would always be Pakistan.

★

By January 1943, William Phillips, the successor to Colonel Johnson, had arrived in Delhi as the US president's special representative in India. The instructions issued to him by the president best illustrate American policy on the role that they saw for themselves in the wake of the altercation with Churchill vis-à-vis the Quit India movement. These may be summarized as follows:

> To become partisan of either Great Britain or India would seriously handicap us in dealing with the other side. Objectionable pressure on Great Britain would probably result in no progress but only in disturbance to the unity of command and of operations both during and following the war. On the other hand, while conscious of the complexities of the Indian situation, we have to keep in mind our policy of freedom for all dependent peoples

as illustrated in our cooperating with the Philippines for the purpose of their freedom and as incorporated in the Atlantic Charter. And talking bluntly to British officials as long as they understand that this was being done in a thoroughly friendly way can be helpful. The British have raised the question why our professed interest in protecting the integrity of the French Empire is at variance with our attitude towards the British Empire. Our view is that the positions of the two Empires are dissimilar and hence the question does not arise.[38]

Phillips' tenure in India lasted for four months. At the end of April 1943, he was recalled on the pretext of consultations and sent on another assignment by the president, though officially he retained his post in India. Phillips was recalled because, in the midst of the growing Indo–British embroilment (renewed by Gandhiji's fast in February 1943), the presence of Roosevelt's representative in Delhi, whom Linlithgow would not permit to even call on Gandhiji or intercede in any way, was creating misunderstanding regarding the president's policy and position with respect to India in particular and Asia in general. The British by then had crushed the Quit India movement and with the increase in American naval and air pressure on Japan in the Pacific, the possibility of that country successfully invading India had become remote. Churchill and Linlithgow were now fully confident of retaining India well after the end of the war and were in no mood to encourage anyone, even if he be the American president's representative, to say or do anything that might instigate the Indian leaders or give ideas to the Americans to pressure Britain to start a dialogue with them. Phillips warned Washington that the US had to safeguard 'our own position in India as [a] military base against Japan as well as our future relations with all coloured races. If the Viceroy can obstruct the representative of President to see Gandhi, Indians will lose confidence in his capacity to accomplish anything'.[39] Roosevelt, upon reading this message, instructed Cordell Hull in February 1943 to bluntly tell Halifax to convey to London that 'Gandhi should not be allowed to die in prison', but Phillips was instructed not to make public in India this concern expressed by the president for the Mahatma.[40]

Rendered immobile, Phillips, in his reports to Washington, was, nevertheless, able to convey the flavour of the prevailing situation in India at that time: 'They [the Englishmen in India] seem unaware of the changing attitudes in England and cannot really envisage a free India fit to govern itself [and] point to illiteracy, Indians' disinterest in self-government and interest only in food and protection, Hindu–Muslim differences and the possibility of civil war as soon as the British leave, as factors that had to be taken into account in considering self-government for India.' These views, reported Phillips, 'have the effect of convincing Indian leaders that the British promises to withdraw are worthless'.[41] On 15 February 1943, he reported that when the American correspondents in Delhi complained to Sir Reginald Maxwell (the home member in the Viceroy's Executive Council) about press censorship that did not even permit them to send abroad reports on Gandhiji's fast that appeared freely in the local press, the reply they received was that 'the Congress is the enemy' and that 'they would not be permitted to send out dispatches which place Gandhi or Congress in a favourable light'.[42] There were voices in the State Department seeking a more active American role. Wallace Murray, the adviser on political affairs, noted: 'We will be in a very vulnerable position in the future if we adopted [an] overcautious attitude in the situations of this kind merely because we fear that the British might not like it.'[43] However, the undersecretary, Sumner Wells, ruled out any modification to the policy being followed.

★

On 7 April 1943, Phillips held a meeting with Jinnah that lasted almost four hours, after which he wired the following message to Washington: 'Jinnah twice reiterated his willingness to help in every way towards victory...he would not stand against any plan which could further the war effort, and that his reservations to British plans were "defensive" only, by which "I interpret as meaning that the right to Pakistan must be maintained".'[44] Phillips left without his being able to meet any Congress leader, except C. Rajagopalachari, who was free. One can only speculate as to whether any of them would have been as forthright as Jinnah in telling the American what his countrymen most wanted to hear at that point of time.

In his reports dated 19 April 1943 and 14 May 1943 to Roosevelt, before leaving, Phillips recorded his impressions of his sojourn in India, which can be summarized as follows:

(1) The British are "sitting pretty", completely successful in suppressing dissent;
(2) with the Congress Party men in jail, the Congress Party's influence [is] decreasing and [that] of the Muslim League increasing;
(3) if one looks for excuses not to change the status quo in a vast country like India, some can always be found;
(4) Indians are coming to believe that America stands solidly with Britain;
(5) Indian leaders are wondering whether the Atlantic Charter is only for the benefit of the white races;
(6) a feeling of frustration, discouragement and helplessness [is] endemic amongst Indians;
(7) despite everything "America is still looked upon as the one and only hope"; and
(8) that "in view of our military position in India we should have a voice in these Indian affairs".[45]

On Phillips' departure from India, the Muslim League's official organ gave him a kick in the pants: 'PHILLIPS FAILS TO IMPRESS US OFFICIALS' ran the caption of the news item in the *Dawn*.[46] On 25 September 1943, Merrell informed Hull that there was a pro-Japan feeling in Bengal because it was hoped the Japanese would bring Burmese rice to relieve the acute famine* and also that there was distrust of America because of close Anglo–US collaboration.[47] On 8 October Merrell further reported as follows: 'There was growing disappointment with the US, famine adding to the bitterness,

---

* According to estimates, almost three million people died in Bengal due to starvation.

and anti-British feeling is at a new high.'[48] On 18 October, in yet another report, he stated that, in an off-the-cuff interview, the viceroy, Linlithgow, had told an Indian journalist whom he knew well that 'the British must continue to rule for another fifty years; [it] would take that long for Indians to learn to govern themselves'.[49]

The same month, the British news agency *Reuters* carried a news item that suggested that the US was indifferent to the Bengal famine. When this item came to Hull's notice, he was furious, and wired to Merrell that in view of the close connection between the British authorities and Reuters, the US saw this story as 'an attempt by the British to shift the blame for the famine as far as public opinion is concerned to the alleged indifference of the US Government'. Hull asked Merrell to clarify in India that, under the US–British agreement, all 'shipping between the United States and India is under British control and it therefore rests with the British Government to determine to what extent available supplies may be utilized for the transportation in India which might be sent from this country'.[50]

Colonel Louis Johnson, Roosevelt's first representative in India, had succeeded in establishing contacts with Nehru, which had created a channel between the Americans and the Congress Party for the first time. However, the colonel's overzealous and open support for the nationalists during the Cripps negotiations had given an opportunity to Churchill to seek his recall from India. Roosevelt's directive to Phillips, his successor, to help the cause of Indian freedom only through friendly pressure acceptable to British officials, gave Linlithgow the means to restrict Phillips' contacts in India, which created misunderstandings in India about American policy. It was unknown in India, for example, that Phillips had made several efforts to meet the Congress Party leaders but was prevented from doing so by the viceroy. The fact that he was forbidden by the US State Department even to mention this aspect to the Indians was the extent to which the British had succeeded in intimidating the Americans.

Most Indians, even the educated ones, had a most perfunctory knowledge of America and Americans at that time. American history taught in the universities ended with the battle of Yorktown and the American independence from Britain. People were more knowledgeable about Canada and Australia – which were part of the British Empire – than about the USA or indeed about neighbouring countries or territories, such as China, Central Asia, Afghanistan or Persia. Whatever curiosity about America that existed came from acquaintance with American cars and Hollywood films. Fords and Chevrolets, with their higher clearances, were better suited for the rough Indian roads than English cars and ruled the roads. Hollywood was the main source of information about the new world, even though these films never reached the villages, where 80 per cent of the people lived. When newsreels on events connected with the war began to be shown in picture houses, people were aghast to know that America, not Britain, was, in fact, the senior partner in the war!

The Indian villagers, when they got an occasional glimpse of the Americans, lumped them together with the British as 'Whites' or 'red-faced monkeys'. The Indians educated in England were to be found in the higher civil services, in the legal profession, in the universities and some even in politics. They had imbibed in Oxford and Cambridge or in the leftist London School of Economics the prejudices of their fellow English students of the pre-First World War days about the Americans: that they were ignorant, uncouth and callous, which views they had found rather fashionable to wear on their lapels during the Raj. To those Indian communists who had joined the teaching and journalistic professions, the US was a capitalist country which was out to snatch India from the British clutches into its own. After Hitler attacked the Soviet Union, the Indian communists had started to support the British, who not only lifted the ban on their party, as recounted earlier, but also chose to close their eyes and shut their ears to their anti-American propaganda. The important group of socialists in the Congress Party were no great friends of capitalist America either. On the other hand, Gandhiji hardly displayed any interest in the United States, which lead was followed by most Congressmen. Nehru was an exception. He sought President Roosevelt's help to achieve advances in Indian constitutional reform. But he later came to distrust the Americans.

Indian princes, except for one maharaja – Holkar of Indore – who had an American wife, were not interested in America, which, admittedly, back in the 1940s, did not have the same allure as it has today. Moreover, the US was too far away from India for excursions. Their interests outside India remained focused on England and the Continent: in England for political reasons to nurture their treaty rights on which their positions rested and in the Continent for pleasure: Paris of the Belle Epoque and the newly founded resorts on the Riveria.

So, there was enough disinterest in, and ignorance of, America, with some bias against it thrown in too, that could well sway India in an anti-American direction, despite there being no conflict of interest between the two countries; actually quite the opposite. There was another disturbing factor. Neither Indian leaders nor informed Indian public opinion had sufficiently focused on the hard realities of survival in our predatory world, when India would be entirely on its own, with the British security umbrella cast away. And ignorance, overidealism and swaggering abounded. Meanwhile, the vision of the Father of the Nation that a sovereign state could survive without armed forces added hugely to the complications. It was not easy for foreigners, especially for the matter-of-fact, not-too-well-informed and demanding Americans, in such circumstances, to work out mutuality of interests with Indians easily, and the possibilities of misunderstandings remained enormous.

Propaganda by itself cannot swing public opinion or alignments; self-interest always does. Churchill had trumped Roosevelt's intervention for self-government in India by playing 'the Pakistan card', i.e., by highlighting the value of the Muslim connection to the West. Soon after Indian independence and partition, the Iron Curtain descended over Eastern Europe and the Cold War began. At the same time, a new Muslim state, abutting Iran and Afghanistan and thus consisting of areas of the greatest strategic importance to the West to resist the perceived Soviet threat to the oilfields of the Middle East, and willing to cooperate with US strategy, had come into being. This turn of events changed the American vision about the subcontinent. Even so the 'good boy' India in American eyes did not become the 'bad boy'; nor did India entirely disappear as an adversarial factor in

Anglo–US relations, till Pakistan, largely through the good offices of the British, became a firm US ally in the Cold War.

Notes and References

1. US FR 1942, Vol. I, p. 623. Cordell Hull's talk with Halifax, 1 August 1942.
2. Ibid., p. 663. Merrell to Hull, 21 May 1942.
3. Ibid., p. 664. Merrell to Hull, 25 May 1942.
4. Ibid., p. 667. Hull's conversation with Halifax, 3 June 1942.
5. Ibid., p. 670. Hull's talk with Bajpai, 15 June 1942.
6. Ibid., pp. 667–68. Nehru's message to Roosevelt (via Johnson), 4 June 1942.
7. Ibid., p. 674. Hull/Johnson's message to Nehru, 18 June 1942.
8. Ibid., pp. 674–76. Gandhiji's message to Chiang Kai-shek, 21 June 1942.
9. Ibid., p. 677. Gandhiji's message to Roosevelt, 1 July 1942. Copy in Franklin D. Roosevelt Library, New York.
10. Chiang Kai-shek's reply to Gandhiji, 8 July 1942, through S.H. Shen, Chinese consul general in Delhi.
11. US FR 1942, Vol. II, p. 695. Chiang Kai-shek to Roosevelt, 25 July 1942.
12. Ibid., p. 698. Chiang Kai-shek's oral message to Roosevelt via Foreign Minister Soong, 25 July 1942.
13. Ibid., pp. 699–700. Wells' note to Roosevelt, 29 July 1942 and Roosevelt's telegram to Churchill, the same day.
14. Ibid., p. 713. Roosevelt's reply to Gandhiji, 1 August 1942.
15. Ibid., p. 700. Winant to Hull, 29 July 1942.
16. Ibid., p. 703. Attlee's message to Roosevelt, 7 August 1942.
17. Ibid., see note on p. 705.
18. Ibid., p. 705. Roosevelt's reply to Chiang Kai-shek, 8 August 1942.
19. Ibid., p. 715. Roosevelt's message to Chiang Kai-shek, 12 August 1942.
20. TOP, Vol. II, S. No. 532. Churchill to Roosevelt, 13 August 1942.
21. Ibid., S. No. 112. Churchill to Harry Hopkins, 31 May 1942.
22. Ibid., S. No. 695. Hallet's telegram to viceroy.
23. Ibid.
24. US FR 1942, Vol. I, p. 721. Hull's memo to Roosevelt, 15 August 1942.
25. Ibid., pp. 712–14. Currie to Roosevelt, 11 August 1942.

26. TOP, Vol. II, p. 477. Churchill to Roosevelt, 9 August 1942.
27. US FR 1942, Vol. I, pp. 726–27. Hull's conversation with Halifax, 24 August 1942.
28. Ibid., p. 733. Hull's conversation with Halifax, 17 September 1942.
29. Ibid., pp. 740–71. As related by Bajpai's to Adolf A. Berle, US State Department, 13 October 1942.
30. British Embassy's appreciation on 'American Attitude towards India', Paras 33 to 42, pp. 21–24 (OIC, British Library, London).
31. US FR 1942, Vol. I, p. 735, Bajpai's conversation with Berle, US State Department, 2 October 1942.
32. South Asia, University of Canberra, Vol. XXIII, No. 2, 2000, pp. 63–68.
33. Survey of American opinion on India, dated 8 May 1943, by Sir Frederick Puckle (OIC, British Library, London).
34. Ibid.
35. Ibid.
36. Ibid.
37. R. Moore, South Asia, University of Canberra, Vol. XXIII, No. 2, 2000, pp. 66 and 76.
38. US FR 1942, Vol. I, p. 746. Roosevelt's instructions to William Phillips contained in telegram to Ambassador Winant, 20 November 1942.
39. US FR 1943, Vol. IV, pp. 196–97. Phillips to Roosevelt, 19 February 1943.
40. Ibid., p. 199. Hull's conversation with Halifax, 20 February 1943.
41. Ibid., pp. 180–83. Phillips to Roosevelt, 22 January 1943.
42. Ibid., p. 193. Sir Reginald Maxwell's talk with American correspondents, 15 February 1943.
43. Ibid., p. 212. Wallace Murray, US State Department's memo to Sumner Wells, 6 April 1943.
44. Ibid., pp. 213–14. Phillips to Roosevelt, 7 April 1943.
45. Ibid., pp. 217–22. Phillips' reports to Roosevelt, 19 April 1943 and 14 May 1943.
46. Ibid., pp. 223–24, Merrell to Hull, 27 May 1943.
47. Ibid., p. 301. Merrell to Hull, 25 September 1943.
48. Ibid., p. 230. Merrell to Hull, 8 October 1943.
49. Ibid., p. 231. Merrell to Hull, 18 October 1943.
50. Ibid., pp. 304, 306 and 307. Hull to Merrell, 9 and 13 October 1943.

7

Wavell Plays the Great Game

IN THE BRITISH ADMINISTRATIVE SYSTEM, THE MAN ON THE SPOT traditionally enjoyed considerable authority. This was more so for a person appointed the viceroy of India and who occupied the most important post in the British Empire, outside the British Isles at that time. We have seen in an earlier chapter how the viceroy, Lord Linlithgow, in 1942 blocked certain proposals made by a British minister, and one as eminent as Sir Stafford Cripps, by appealing directly to the prime minister. Due weight was attached to the viceroy's views also because he had at his beck and call a team of tried officials with vast experience of India. This team was made up of secretaries of the various departments of the government, the governors of British provinces and the residents in the princely states – largely drawn from the prestigious Indian Civil Service – and his efficient Directorate of Intelligence. Moreover, the commander-in-chief in India, who controlled the British Indian Army, sat as a member in the Viceroy's Executive Council. The prestige and authority that the British Parliament and Government sought to bestow on the viceroy were evident from the magnificent building in which he was housed – the largest dwelling for a couple in the entire world at that time – and from the other trappings of pomp and pageantry to fit the status of one standing in for the King Emperor.

It is necessary to provide such a background because a viceroy with definite views had the means to influence high-level policy back home and, indeed, create realities on the ground in India that could not then be ignored. A viceroy running away with the bit between his teeth absolved the ministers of direct responsibility for actions that might involve them in controversy in Parliament and the press and sometimes from taking hard decisions. If Linlithgow took the initiative in 1940–41 to build up Jinnah as the sole spokesman of the Muslims of India and forge an alliance with his Muslim League Party, his successor, Lord Archibald Wavell, in February 1946, produced the blueprint detailing the areas of British India that should go to Pakistan. This blueprint was implemented at the time of the British withdrawal from India in 1947, even though it was kept secret to avoid any impression of a British initiative or hand in the division of India.

Secret archives cannot be depended upon to reveal the entire picture. Many decisions that are taken by governments are never committed to paper or, if so committed, are not revealed, even after the prohibitionary period for keeping them under wraps has lapsed. For instance, Lord Mountbatten's reports to London, sent after 15 August 1947, while he was the governor-general of India, have not been unsealed even after almost sixty years, thereby depriving us from information surrounding British policy on Kashmir.

While going through the actual files – with the first drafts and the corrections made in them, all retained – I came across top-secret dispatches that were supplemented by private or demi-official letters that contained the real views of the writer; these do not figure in the transfer of power documents series that have been published. Ministers and officials were careful not to commit to paper, even in top-secret documents, views that dealt with sensitive matters at variance with the government's public posture or those that could be judged as 'unprincipled'. Moreover, the influence exerted on decisions by powerful individuals unconnected directly with the issue – say, a Lord Beaverbrook, the press baron and Churchill's ally – may never be recorded. Therefore, the true course of policy can, at times, only be fathomed by taking into account the action taken by the concerned officials and from circumstantial evidence. The partition of India was a particularly sensitive issue. The Britishers of the post-war generation – particularly the Labour

Party leaders – sought to live down their country's reputation for 'divide and rule' and HMG had also to reckon with American public opinion that was against the division of India, because they felt this might help the communists.

∗

Field Marshal Wavell was not a member of the aristocracy, from whose ranks most of the viceroys were drawn. He belonged to a class of society – the upper middle class – which, according to a British historian 'was the mainstay of the British Raj and largely responsible for its character'.[1] Wavell was the first soldier to hold the office of the viceroy after the British Crown took over the governance of India from the East India Company in 1858. Before his appointment to the viceroyalty in September 1943, he was commander-in-chief in India and had supervised the defence of the British Empire in South-east Asia against Japan. Earlier, he had been the commander of the British forces in the crucial front of the Middle East, where his victories over the Italians in Abyssinia and Cyrenica, in North Africa, at the start of the war had made him quite a popular hero in Britain. On coming to power Churchill had removed him from the Middle East command and sent him to the relatively calm waters – before the Japanese attack – of India and Asia. And after the British defeat at Japanese hands in South-east Asia, kicked him upstairs, in an honourable way, to the viceroyalty. Churchill considered Wavell overcautious and defeatist, 'eminently suited to run a provincial golf club',[2] he once said. Churchill expected him to take no political initiatives in India during the course of the war. Wavell, on the other hand, remained in awe of his chief, 'the bigger man than either Roosevelt or Stalin', he noted in his diary,[3] but he used to complain that 'Churchill was always expecting rabbits to come out of empty hats'.[4] The irony is that one whom Churchill considered so mediocre has come to be acknowledged by several historians as the most important viceroy of India since Lord Curzon. His forte was his lack of illusions; and his achievement, the division of India.

Before Wavell left London to take up his post in India, Field Marshal Jan Christian Smuts, the prime minister of South Africa and

Churchill's trusted counsellor, sought him out. And, according to Wavell, confided in him what was in Churchill's mind about India that he did not wish to express to him directly when he had offered him the viceroyalty at a tête-à-tête dinner in the basement of 10, Downing Street. As Smuts put it: 'The PM is not thinking beyond the end of the war – about India or anything else – and is alarmed lest by raising the Indian issue I should split the Conservative Party in Parliament and cause him trouble.'[5] Therefore, for the first year in office Wavell did not make any political move, even though he had come to firmly believe that to let things slide in India was not in Britain's best interests.

Wavell profoundly disagreed with his predecessor's view, expressed to him just before Linlithgow left Delhi, that Britain 'would have to continue responsibility for India for at least thirty years' and that 'the country was in pretty good trim...[with] Gandhi and the Congress leaders out of the way in prison and the Muslims immensely strengthened during the last three or four years'.[6] Wavell's assessment was that the British position was deteriorating fast and that a plan was needed for an organized and orderly retreat that would, nevertheless, protect Britain's most important asset in India, which he saw as the military base that it provided to control the Middle East and the vast Indian Ocean region and from where fighting manpower was recruited. One would do well to bear in mind what an Indian scholar has stated in a recent study:

> The growing role of strategic airpower and the vital importance of Middle Eastern oil had transformed British policy in Asia. For over a century, British policy in the Gulf had largely been shaped by the strategic interests of her Indian Empire. This was no longer the case.... By 1947, the tables had been turned – Britain's strategic interests in the Gulf and Middle East had become a major factor in her South Asia policy.[7]

Only on one point was Wavell in complete agreement with Linlithgow (and Churchill): that the British position in India depended on the goodwill of the Muslims and could be salvaged by the cooperation of Jinnah's Muslim League Party.

Wavell was convinced that the leaders of the Congress Party would not cooperate with Britain on defence matters as rulers of an independent India. His distrust of this party, which he considered the fountain of all mischief, he expressed in a letter to the King as follows:

> I can never entirely rid my mind of the recollections that in 1942 at almost the most critical period of the war in India, when I was endeavouring as Commander-in-Chief to secure India with very inadequate resources against Japanese invasion, the supporters of the Congress [Party] made a deliberate effort to paralyse my communications to the eastern front by widespread sabotage and rioting.[8]

In the same letter, he cautioned: 'The loyalty of the police and the Indian Army in face of a really serious challenge to British rule is problematic.'[9]

Wavell had been shocked that, on the fall of Singapore in 1942, so many Indian officers, who had sworn allegiance to the King Emperor, as well as thousands of soldiers of his Army, had so easily switched sides to join the Japanese, much to the acclaim of the nationalists of the Congress Party in India. Subhash Chandra Bose had arrived in Singapore, in early 1943, dispatched by the Germans from Europe by submarine, as recounted in Chapter 5. Bose's charismatic personality, energy and organizing ability made themselves immediately felt amongst the 60,000 Indian prisoners of war in Japanese hands and amongst the Indian residents in the region who pledged him support and money. His call 'Dilli Chalo' (on to Delhi), after the cry of the Meerut mutineers of 1857, enthused the prisoners, and despite strict British censorship, began to find echo in India. Whereas the British Military Intelligence put the figure of the officers and men of the British Indian Army who joined Bose to form the Indian National Army (INA) at 20,000, Bose's officers later claimed their strength was nearly 50,000. At the beginning, British Military Intelligence underestimated and belittled Bose's movement, but later admitted that the soldiers who had changed sides had been deeply affected by Bose's 'inspiring and courageous leadership'. They fought the British Indian Army bravely and regarded themselves as 'liberators of their motherland'. Moreover, 'there was substantial popular support from the public in India for the INA'.[10]

Even more shocking to Wavell had been the defection of some soldiers belonging to the forward units of the Indian Army to Bose's Indian National Army (INA) and to the Japanese in the fighting in Burma. Churchill blamed the sudden expansion of the Indian Army and the intake of Hindu recruits for this state of affairs. There was no point, he pointed out, in having an army 'that might shoot us in the back'.[11] The fact was that with the modernization of warfare and with the introduction of tanks, aeroplanes and other mechanized instruments of war, higher standards of education had become necessary among the rank and file, and educated Indians of all communities were more nationalistic. What part racialism might have played in switching loyalties, now that for the first time British and Indian officers in such large numbers were thrown together, is discussed later.

✳

Wavell's apprehensions on taking over as viceroy could not be ascribed to pessimism or defeatism, and were confirmed when mutinies took place in several branches of the armed forces within a couple of years. Indian naval ratings first mutinied in strength in the port of Bombay in early 1946, an insurrection that soon spread to other ports such as Karachi and engulfed other services as well.

The naval mutiny is said to have been provoked by the behaviour of the commanding officer of HMIS *Talwar* (a shore signals school in Bombay) who commonly called his men 'black buggars' or 'coolie bastards' and by the refusal of the commanding officer, Bombay, to replace him. The mutiny quickly spread to other ships in the port; over 7000 sailors joined in, and some of the warships involved threatened to fire at British barracks and at the bastions of the European community on the Bombay seafront, such as the Yacht Club and the Taj Mahal Hotel. In Karachi port a two-hour duel took place between the shore batteries and a Royal Indian Navy sloop,

HMIS *Hindustan*, before its crew surrendered. The unrest was not confined to the Indian Navy. The personnel of the Royal Indian Air Force at Madras, Karachi, Poona, Allahabad and Delhi, the Royal Indian Army Signals Corps at Jabalpur and other towns and 1600 Royal Electrical and Mechanical Engineers at Madras also revolted. In all these units, better educated Indians were to be found.

The naval mutiny in Bombay was suppressed after over 200 persons, mostly demonstrators in Bombay city who had joined them, were shot and over 1000 injured. The fact that it spread like wildfire showed that the bullying by a few British officers could not be the only cause, and that the disaffection was part of a deeper malaise. Could, under these circumstances, the British rely on the loyalty of the officers of the Indian Army to suppress a renewed mass agitation or an armed struggle by the nationalists? According to the newly released documents, neither the Joint Intelligence Committee in London nor the officials in Delhi thought so by 1946. Field Marshal Claude Auchinleck, who had replaced Wavell as commander-in-chief, was to record in a top-secret appreciation: 'It is no use shutting one's eye to the fact that any Indian soldier worth his salt is a Nationalist though that does not mean...that he is anti-British.' And added that: 'Wholesale defections and disintegration of the Indian Army was [sic] possible.'[12]

Wavell's judgement of the capabilities of Indian leaders also influenced his assessment of their value as Britain's future partners. Except for Vallabhbhai Patel, whom he considered 'the most forceful character among them' and 'more of a man...though communal',[13] Wavell had little time for the others. Maulana Azad, he noted, was a 'gentleman but against Gandhi like a rabbit faced with a stoat'; Ghaffar Khan 'stupid and stubborn'; and Gandhiji 'shrewd but devious and malevolent'. Nehru was 'sincere and intelligent and personally courageous but unbalanced', according to Wavell's opinion of the future prime minister. The epithets he used for Jinnah were: 'unhappy', 'arbitrary', 'self-centred', 'lonely', 'but straighter and more sincere', which apparently did not disqualify him in the same sense as they did the Congress Party leaders.[14]

Some officers of the Indian Army, while recounting their exploits of chivalry in the Middle East and Burma, told me that they were surprised how racist the British were, though they shrugged this off as 'one of those things'. So, when writing this book, it became necessary to explore a little further if racism had indeed played a part in creating mutual Anglo–Indian antipathy in the British Indian Army. Fears about the loyalty of this Army, perhaps more than any other factor, shook the foundations of the Raj.

Major General Udey Chand Dube, now in his nineties, is probably the oldest King's Commissioned Officer alive in India today. Commissioned from the British Military Academy at Sandhurst in 1928, he is still fit. David Niven, the famous actor, was his roommate at the renowned British War College and John Hunt, who led the team that climbed Mount Everest, and Mohammad Ayub Khan, who became the president of Pakistan, were his contemporaries there. When asked whether he ever faced racial discrimination in the Army, Major General Dube replied as follows.

After Sandhurst he was attached for a period to the Black Watch, a British regiment, in which he found absolutely no discrimination. But after he joined the Gurkha Regiment of the Indian Army, he found some. For example, on guest nights, when the local British community members, including ladies, were invited, Indian officers were separated and had to take their meals in the card room or the billiard room. One of his colleagues, Captain Mohammad Ali, he recalled, lost his commission for being 'politically minded', or 'maybe because he had married an English girl'. His British colleagues at times made snide remarks about Indian officers. Some British officers tried to create friction between the Indian officers to keep them apart.

Major General Dube then said: 'During the fighting in the Buthigong jungles in Burma, while bullets were flying from all sides, some Indian officers bumped off those British colleagues who they considered bullies', thereby suggesting that some Indian officers at least had been strongly affected by real or imagined racialism or anti-Indian sentiments of certain British officers. Dube also said that 'Wavell and [his successor] Mountbatten must have heard of these incidents'. He then stated: 'I must not give you the impression that these problems prevented us, the Indian and the British, from fighting together against the enemy; but facts are facts.'

General Stan Menzes has mentioned in his book* only one case known to him when a British CO was shot. Another Indian major general gave the following picture: 'By 1941 the majority of Indian officers serving in units would have been under ECOs (Emergency Commissioned Officers, i.e., those commissioned during the war) and they did not suffer so greatly at the hands of the "Koi Hais", as we regulars did pre-war. Most British officers would have been by 1942 uninhibited by colonial prejudices. It was the pre-war British Officer who was the enemy...I cannot imagine an Indian officer killing his superior officer just to settle a racial grudge! Can you?'[15]

D.K. Palit was commissioned into the Indian Army in 1938 in the Baluch Regiment. He had spent his earlier years in England and was a keen polo player. He observes: 'There was almost no social contact between British and Indian officers in the army...I was never asked by my commanding officer, my second in command or my company commander for a meal or a cup of tea in his [sic] house. There was just no contact even though the one army fought the same enemy and carried the same weapons. But we never mixed.'[16] Khushwant Singh, the acclaimed writer, who has been an admirer of England all his life, has said: 'If they [the British] ever made any friends, it was in a benign attitude towards their servants. Most of them hated this country when they were here.'[17]

Lord Mountbatten, in one of his earliest weekly top-secret reports to the secretary of state in April 1947, states that he had to address the governors of British provinces, after he heard some English ladies talking offensively about his Indian guests at a reception at the Viceroy's House, requiring them to absolutely ensure that such practices ceased forthwith. How much of such behaviour was the result of British hatred of people who were on the verge of snatching away from them the brightest jewel in the British Crown and how much pure racism is difficult to say. What, however, was clear was that an overwhelming majority of Englishmen in India by this time

---

* *Fidelity and Honour: The Indian Army from the Seventeenth to the Twenty-first Century* (Penguin, New Delhi, 1993, p. 357).

considered the Congress Party and the Hindus generally their enemy and the Muslims their friend. 'The immense gulf between the Hindu religion and mentality and ours and the Moslem is the real core of all our troubles in India,'[18] wrote Wavell in his diary.

There have been changes in the British perception of Indian Muslims from one century to another – 'humours turning with chimes and principles with times'. Up to the 1857 Mutiny, as recounted in Chapter 3, the Muslim had been Britain's enemy number one. That year, Sir Henry Rawlinson, a member of the India Council in London, had spoken of the 'seething, fermenting, festering mass of Muslim hostility in India'.[19] But for much of the twentieth century the Muslim was Britain's friend. Sir Olaf Caroe (once the governor of NWFP) rationalized that the Muslim had better absorbed Western values and was more dependable than the Hindu in India. Western opinion again turned against the Muslims in the twenty-first century after the Al-Qaida terrorist attacks on the World Trade Center towers in New York and the Pentagon in Washington on 11 September 2001.

*

There were other reasons for Wavell's view that the game was up. When he took up his post in 1943, famine was raging in Bengal. Over three million people died. Wavell wired to Leopold Amery a few months after assuming the viceroyalty:

> Bengal famine was one of the greatest disasters that has befallen any people under British rule and damage to our reputation here…is incalculable.[20]

The situation was obviously not at all 'trim', as Linlithgow had imagined.

There had been several famines in the 1930s, which clearly indicated the growing weakness of the administrative machinery and the impoverishment of the masses, because famines occur as much from faulty management of food stocks as from their scarcity. Essential services such as the police, posts and telegraphs, railways, courts of justice and land tax collection were impeccably maintained till the end of British rule. But there was minimal capital expenditure on developing the economic infrastructure after the First World War. Agriculture was the main source of revenue, but there was no construction of new canals and dams for irrigation or roads to carry produce. The expansion of industries was not encouraged to preserve markets for British goods. Revenue from raw material exports was depressed in the 1930s because of worldwide recession. There was hardly any middle class to yield income-tax. The inevitable periodic jacking up of the tax on land to meet the rising civil and military budgets was the main cause of increasing poverty and rural indebtedness. For fifty years before independence (in August 1947), the per capita income in real terms in India had been rising only at 0.6 per cent per annum, whereas the increase in population was well over 3 per cent annually. A splendid new capital had indeed been built and British officials continued to live extraordinarily comfortably, with the governors of provinces maintaining summer retreats in the hills matching Scottish castles. But, by the end of the Second World War, there were neither the funds, nor the forces, nor the confidence – despite the brave words of Churchill and the British Tories – to sustain British rule in India.

By 1944 a possible solution to the problem Britain faced had taken shape in Wavell's mind. He believed that one way to retain the military base in the subcontinent, as Britain bowed out, would be to build up the ambitious Jinnah and, with his cooperation, to withdraw the British forces from the Congress Party-dominated parts of India into the Muslim-majority provinces. These territories would include the strategic northwest of India – and the port of Karachi – as they were the most suitable areas to counter any Soviet expansionist designs. Pakistan would become a *dominion* in the British Empire, while the rest of India would be left to its own devices, indeed, its potential for mischief neutralized by the Anglo–Pak alliance. This objective was achievable, considering the close cooperation his predecessor, Linlithgow, had developed with Jinnah during the war and keeping in view the promises the latter had made with respect to cooperation on defence matters.

But Wavell felt that there was no point in consulting London, since Churchill was dead set against any move on India. He therefore began methodically and quietly to create the realities on the ground for the fulfilment of his objective at a later date. The first task he saw in this context was to build up Mohammad Ali Jinnah.

The position of the Muslim League in India did not appear as comfortable to Wavell as Linlithgow had pronounced it to be at the time of his departure. In the east, the Muslim League Government in Bengal had fallen because of internecine quarrels and the Muslim League chief minister in Assam had to come to an arrangement with the Congress Party in order to survive. With regard to the west, Wavell noted in his diary: 'The Sind Government seems to be revolting from League control, the NWFP (Muslim League) Government [is] likely to fall [and it fell in 1945] and the Unionists (the anti-Jinnah coalition) Ministry in the Punjab [is] consolidating itself.'[21] This last development was the most galling to the viceroy, for, without the Punjab fully in Jinnah's grip, Wavell could not possibly proceed with his plans to detach northwest India from the rest of the country.

Linlithgow had been able to block the loyalist premier of the Punjab, Sikandar Hayat Khan, from opposing Jinnah on the wider Indian scene, but had been unable to supplant Sikandar Hayat Khan's Unionist coalition of Muslims, Hindus and Sikhs with a Jinnahite government. And even after Sikandar Hayat Khan's death in 1941, the old Unionist coalition under Khizar Hayat Khan Tiwana continued to hold. The NWFP, another crucial province for the creation of Pakistan, was also outside Jinnah's control. Indeed, the 'Hindu Congress Party' was in power in this totally Muslim province – 'a bastard situation', as Lord Hastings Ismay, Mountbatten's chief of staff, was to describe it.[22] But this was largely because of the traditional Pushtoon antipathy to foreign rule: once the British departed, they could be expected to turn against the control of the plainsmen from Hindustan. It was the Punjab that held the key to Pakistan. How was Jinnah's supremacy to be established there?

In the eight British provinces, where the Congress Party Governments had resigned at the beginning of the war, namely, the

United Provinces, the Central Provinces, Orissa, Bihar, Bombay, Madras, Assam and the NWFP, British governors continued to rule. In all these provinces, and particularly in the United Provinces, the Muslim League strength was rising and rising fast. In the Muslim-minority provinces, the slogan 'Islam in danger' worked. It did not work in the Muslim-majority provinces, such as the Punjab or the NWFP, where it was the Muslims who ran the governments and dominated political life.

The general attitude to the growing communalism in the United Provinces and the other British-ruled provinces was one of laissez-faire and certainly not of crushing it with an iron hand.

Then, an event took place that provided Wavell the ideal opportunity to move Jinnah to the forefront in the Punjab. Gandhiji, still behind bars, had been impatient to stem the growing communalism, and had tried to contact Jinnah, in vain, from jail. After he was released on grounds of ill health at Wavell's behest in mid-1944, the Mahatma decided to call on Jinnah. Their much-publicized meetings over several days took place in Jinnah's villa on Bombay's fashionable Malabar Hill. Hoping to curb the growing Hindu–Muslim cleavage, Gandhiji offered to appease Jinnah by promising to persuade the Congress Party to agree to district-wise referendums in the British provinces claimed by Jinnah and give these districts the option to opt out of India, with the proviso, that this opting out should take place only after the British quit India. Jinnah was emphatic that Gandhiji's proposal would mutilate the boundaries of the Punjab, Bengal and Assam provinces, which he claimed in their entirety for Pakistan, thereby leaving the Muslims, as he put it, with 'no more than a husk'. And, under Gandhiji's scheme, even this truncated Pakistan was to be delayed till the British departed from India, with no statutory guarantee that it would be fulfilled. 'This offer made to me is an insult to our intelligence', Jinnah told a representative of the *London News Chronicle*.

There was an episode during the talks that Hector Bolitho, Jinnah's biographer, has recorded as follows:

One day when Mahatma Gandhi went to see the Quaid-i-Azam ['the great leader'] they ended their arguments and talked, simply, of their daily life. They were weary a little like exhausted boxers, finding relief in their parting handshake. Jinnah mentioned that, among his ills, one of his feet was troubled with a nervous rash. The Mahatma sank to the floor and insisted on removing Jinnah's shoes and socks. The scene of Jinnah in his immaculate clothes, and Gandhi, robed in bare simplicity is at first amusing, and then touching. The Mahatma held the troubled foot in his hands and said, "I know what will heal you. I shall send it tomorrow morning." Next day, a little box of clay mixture arrived. Jinnah did not use it, but he thanked Gandhi when he came that evening, for one more talk, and told him that the medicine had already relieved the pain.[23]

Jinnah had exhibited exemplary manners, but Gandhiji's gesture made no difference to his course. Indeed, Gandhiji's attempt to reach out to Jinnah had the opposite effect of that intended. It convinced anti-Jinnah Muslims that partition in one way or the other was coming and therefore to oppose Jinnah was futile and attracted many opportunist Muslim leaders and job seekers to the Muslim League. Side by side, it reinforced the views of those in the League who believed that fanning communalism was the best way to pressurize the Mahatma. 'This meeting must surely blast Gandhi's reputation as a leader', wrote the viceroy that night in his diary.[24]

This was not the only result that flowed from this meeting. To Wavell, Gandhiji had, willy-nilly, accepted the principle of Pakistan, whatever the differences on its area and the timing of its coming into being. So, taking courage in both hands – for he had been warned not to take any initiative on his own in India – he wired directly to the great man:

I think the failure of the Gandhi–Jinnah talks has created a favourable moment for a move by HMG...[25]

Wavell argued that the British administrative machinery had become too weak to control nationalists' pressure and that prolonging British rule by repression would not be acceptable to the British public or to world opinion. He sought permission to return home for consultations, which he felt would help in working out a fresh

British initiative. To convince Churchill, however, was not that simple. The prime minister had no intention of presiding over a reform packet for India. Wavell's request was turned down, with Churchill wiring back: 'These very large problems require to be considered at leisure and best of all in victorious peace.'[26] Although rebuffed, Wavell persevered and, after five months and many more telegrams, was summoned home in early 1945.

Wavell reached London on 23 March 1945, about a month and a half before the German surrender and the end of the war in Europe. The bonhomie engendered by the Yalta Conference between the British and Americans on the one hand and the Russians on the other had begun to flounder on the differences on the future government of Poland. In April 1945 Stalin accused the British and US generals of reaching an agreement with the Germans in neutral Switzerland that would 'permit Anglo–American troops to advance to the east and the Anglo–Americans in return would ensure milder peace terms for Germany'.[27] This charge infuriated the US president, Roosevelt, who, in a telegram to Stalin, termed it 'a vile representation of my action or those [sic] of my trusted subordinates'.[28] In the Middle East too the first chill of the Cold War became apparent in Anglo–Soviet relations, as Moscow tried to prize Azerbaijan away from Persia. Stalin's announcement that the USSR's production of oil was insufficient for its purpose further exacerbated British anxiety about a possible Soviet push towards the oilfields of the Persian Gulf and even into Afghanistan.

The concern that the British military felt about future Soviet intentions emerges clearly from a top-secret report on 'the Security of India and the Indian Ocean', prepared by the Post-Hostilities Planning Staff of the War Cabinet on Churchill's orders. This report, which has been alluded to in Chapter 1, states: 'The USSR is the only major power which would be capable of seriously threatening our interests in India and the Indian Ocean area by 1955–1960.' The report also points out: 'It is of paramount importance that India should not secede from the Empire or remain neutral in war.' The strategic importance of India, according to this report's analysis, were attributed to the following factors:

(1) "Its value as a base" from where forces "would be suitably placed for deployment within the Indian Ocean area and in the Middle East and the Far East";

(2) "its position in relation to our air and sea communications; from the UK and the Middle East to Australia and the Far East"; and

(3) the contribution which India is "capable of making to the war effort of the British Empire in consequence of its large reserve manpower (part of which is of high fighting quality)".

The report notes that: 'Soviet oilfields in the Caucasus would be vulnerable to attacks from airfields in (northwest) India' since the 'sea communications in the Persian Gulf and in the Arabian Sea carry a major portion of the oil produced in the Middle East and are therefore of great strategic value'. The report then hinted at the possibility of detaching a part of India to achieve British objectives:

We must ensure that whatever constitutional changes occur, we retain the right to station military strategic reserves in India.... There might be political objections to stationing the strategic reserve in India proper after she has been granted Dominion Status.... Central Headquarters India have suggested Baluchistan as an alternative to India proper, on the ground that it may be relatively easy to exclude this territory from the Dominion of India.

The report also touched upon the role of the USA: 'In the event of Soviet aggression early support from the US is essential to the security of our interests.' It suggested how this support could be secured: 'A World Organization might well result in the USA assuming definite military responsibility in the Indian Ocean area despite the fact that she has few direct interests there.' However, it added: 'It would be necessary to ensure that the USA would not regard participation in regional defence measures as a pretext for intervention in questions involving the relationship between Great Britain and India.' The seeds of some form of partition of India and setting up of multinational defence arrangements – CENTO – can be discerned in this report as also the British anxiety to keep India away from the influence of its main partner, the USA.[29]

The records do not show that Wavell was associated in any way with this assessment. However, his view that Britain's prime interest in India was strategic because of its usefulness as a military base, transit point and contributor of fighting manpower, was exactly the same as in the report. Only on one point did his views differ: Whereas the report envisaged the possibility of the continuation of British control over India till 1955, Wavell had no such hope.

Wavell's most important meeting in London was with Churchill, which was held on 29 March 1945. A record of this meeting is unavailable. But one can get some idea of what was discussed from a cryptic entry made by the viceroy in his diary that night:

> The PM then launched into a long jeremiad about India which lasted for about forty minutes. He seems to favour partition of India into Pakistan, Hindustan and Princestan.[30]

On whether there was any talk on how such a goal was to be achieved, the viceroy's diary is silent.

Wavell's talks with the members of the India Committee of the War Cabinet, headed by Clement Attlee, were spread over two months. They revolved round his proposal to hold a conference of Indian leaders to discuss the formation of a politically representative executive council that would contain an equal number of 'caste Hindus and Muslims' and would function with minimum interference from the viceroy. Further, Wavell felt that before the conference was called, those Congress Party leaders still in jail should be released. The War Cabinet finally agreed to the proposal but it was understood that Jinnah's assent to the composition of the proposed executive council was a prerequisite. Initially, Churchill hesitated to take the plunge but later yielded after he was assured that he need have no fears that a government in India would result from the proposal and, indeed, the conference was destined to fail.[31]

184 ⅠⅠ THE SHADOW OF THE GREAT GAME

Despite these assurances, Churchill may not have given his consent to such experiments but for the necessity to trump pressure mounting once again from across the Atlantic. While Wavell was holding consultations in London, the British foreign secretary, Sir Anthony Eden, had travelled to the USA in April 1945 to attend the San Francisco conference to launch the United Nations. Taking advantage of this visit, the Americans decided once more to tackle the British on India. Both the US secretary of state, Edward R. Stettinius, and the assistant secretary of state, Joseph Grew, spoke to Eden on the necessity for constitutional advance in India. The gist of the conversations was recorded by Grew (on 17 May 1945) as follows:

> I had an opportunity to say [to Eden] that I thought that Mr Stettinius had already spoken to him of our feeling that our prestige in the Far East would be greatly improved whenever a solution to the problem of India is found and that we must always reckon with the future development of "Asia for the Asiatics Movement". I added that progressive steps in India would tend to offset the strengthening of such a movement. Mr Eden made no comment except to say that he did not believe that the Indian problem would be settled as long as Gandhi lived.[32]

Despite Eden's stiff response, Britain, within a few days, was able to inform the Americans that arrangements had been made to set free the members of the Congress Working Committee (kept in detention since 1942) and that Lord Wavell had been authorized to make a fresh proposal to the Indians. Churchill had successfully trumped Roosevelt's pressure tactics for granting self-government to India after the fall of Singapore by playing the Muslim (or the Pakistan) card through the Cripps mission. A Hindu–Muslim disagreement in a conference as proposed by Wavell would help to again quieten down the Americans.

The Americans had continued their 'friendly pressure' on the British for granting self-government to India in accordance with the policy laid down by the president, as described in Chapter 4. In July 1944, John G. Winant, the US ambassador to the UK, on instructions from Washington, informed London 'that a satisfactory solution of the Indian problem should contribute much to the successful prosecution of the war in the Far East and is of great importance to the future peace of the world'.[33] However, Churchill ignored the advice. But in November 1944 the Americans got an opportunity to hit back.

Drew Pearson, the well-known journalist, published a piece alleging that Ambassador William Phillips, the special representative of the US president to India, had sent the following report:

(1) The morale of the Indian Army (which he termed a "purely mercenary force") was low;

(2) Britain had no intention to play much of a role in the war against Japan; and

(3) Churchill did not wish to apply the Atlantic Charter to India.[34]

This report made Churchill see red. Despite numerous urgent representations made by the British ambassador, Lord Halifax, that the White House or the State Department deny the report, the Americans refused to oblige, President Roosevelt concurring with the acting secretary of state that 'we share in general the view expressed in the Ambassador's letter'.[35]

★

The conference of Indian leaders called by Wavell on 25 June 1945 was a charade from the beginning to the end. Delegates from all the major parties, the representatives of the Sikhs and the Scheduled Castes and premiers of British provinces present and former – including the Congress Party premiers who had resigned in 1939 – were invited to meet the viceroy in the Viceregal Lodge in the Raj's summer capital of Simla, up in the Himalayas. It would transport the Indian leaders from the sweltering heat of the Indian plains in summer, some from jails, to a climate approximating summer in Scotland or Gstaad in Switzerland, amongst hillsides covered by pine, oak and deodar trees, with spectacular views of snow-clad mountains to the north. In Simla they would either walk to the

Viceroy's Lodge or be carried there in a rickshaw, for no car except that of the viceroy was permitted on the roads of this hill station. The rickshaw was a light wooden contraption with a double seat suspended over two wheels, which was pulled and pushed by five men with the help of poles attached to its front and rear. The lodge itself was a replica of a Scottish castle with towers and gabled windows, surrounded by sloping lawns, gravelled paths and miles of hedges of English summer flowers. Gandhiji also came to Simla, but did not attend the conference; Nehru was not invited because he did not fall within any of the categories for participation designated by Wavell. It was Jinnah, in his London suits, who was the star.

The conference failed as it was planned to fail, because Wavell refused to veto Jinnah's pretensions to represent *all* the Muslims of India. According to Durga Dass, a journalist of great integrity, Jinnah told him in the lift of the Cecil Hotel, Simla (towards the end of the conference) that he had been assured by friends in England, through a member of the Viceroy's Executive Council, that 'if he remained firm on the demand [of exclusively representing the Muslims and thus breaking the conference] he would get Pakistan'.[36] One of the two secretaries of the Simla Conference has written: 'Hossain Imam, who attended the conference in his capacity as the leader of the Muslim League Party in the Council of States, stopped me on my way to the Cecil Hotel and said that a member of the Viceroy's Executive Council was advising Jinnah to stand firm.'[37] These British counsels to Jinnah were merely by way of abundant caution, because Jinnah was already playing the British game. He used the Simla Conference to make a long statement, arguing fully the case for Pakistan and highlighting Hindu–Muslim differences, which provided enough material to London to pass on to the Americans. According to the US State Department secret documents, Wavell's officers briefed the American Commissariat in Delhi on eight separate occasions during and after the conference.

Providing parity to the Muslims in the envisaged Viceroy's Executive Council could be understood as ensuring a safeguard for a minority. But sustaining Jinnah's claim as the sole spokesman of all the Muslims of India, when in both the Punjab and the NWFP, ministries of Muslims opposed to Jinnah were in office and commanded majorities in the legislatures, demonstrated that the British aim was not to instal a new government in India but something different. Wavell had before him the top-secret and personal telegram sent by Sir Bertrand James Glancy, the governor of the Punjab, dated 3 July 1945, stating: 'Jinnah's claim to nominate all Muslims appears to me in light of League's meagre hold on Muslim-majority Provinces, to be outrageously unreasonable. If he is given three nominations out of, say, five Muslim seats he should account himself [sic] fortunate indeed.'[38] And, on the same day, the governor of Bengal, Lord Richard Casey (who later became the foreign minister of Australia) warned Wavell in a top-secret, personal message that Khwaja Nizam-ud-din (the ex-Muslim League Bengal premier) had informed him that 'he believed Jinnah would accept a Punjabi Muslim who is neither a member of the Congress nor of [the] League'.[39]

Wavell knew all along that Jinnah would stick to his guns, a stand that would be unacceptable to the Congress Party. He also knew that London would never agree to overrule Jinnah's demand, however absurd it may be; or let the Congress Party enter his 'cabinet', without the countervailing presence of the Muslim League in it. Therefore, 'enacting' the Simla Conference had no other purpose except to build up Jinnah against his Muslim rivals in the Punjab and to head off renewed American pressure for Indian self-government. And in this, Wavell succeeded brilliantly. The results of Simla were recorded by the Punjab governor as follows: 'Since Jinnah succeeded by his intransigence in wrecking the Simla Conference his stock has been standing very high with his followers and with a large section of the Muslim population. He has openly come out that the [coming] election will show an overwhelming verdict in favour of Pakistan. The uninformed Muslim would be told that the question he is called on to answer at the polls is – Are you a true believer or an infidel or a traitor? Against this slogan the Unionists have no spectacular battle cry.'[40]

Glancy then warned: 'If Pakistan becomes an imminent reality we shall be heading straight for bloodshed on a wide scale.'[41]

H.V. Hodson, the former reforms commissioner and main adviser to the viceroy, concurs with Glancy: 'Mr Jinnah's demonstration of imperious strength at the Simla Conference was a shot in the arm for the League and a serious blow for its Muslim opponents especially in the Punjab...Lord Wavell's sudden abandonment of his plan [to set up a representative executive council] was a decisive move that made the partition of India inevitable.... To twist Mr Jinnah's arm, it is clear, was not part of the plan that he had so laboriously agreed with His Majesty's Government.'[42]

After Simla, Muslims with political ambitions, including those from other Muslim formations, began to switch sides to the League in large numbers, though, in the Punjab, Tiwana held his ground. Soon after the conference, the secretary of state, Leopold Amery, in a personal telegram to the viceroy, congratulated him: 'The Congress Party, after all by coming into the Conference, abandoned their claim that they are only people to take over from us.'[43] The same Amery who, in 1940, had warned Linlithgow of the dangers of Pakistan, had by now become an enthusiastic supporter of the partition of India. A Britain greatly weakened by the war needed allies in the subcontinent to help it to resist Soviet pressure in the fresh *chukker* of the Great Game, which was about to begin. For the British to listen to warnings of massacres and blood baths would be similar to the Americans denying support to the Mujaheedins against the Soviets in Afghanistan some forty years later, despite the ever-present danger of fuelling Islamic fundamentalism.

★

Two unexpected developments took place soon after the breakdown of the Simla Conference that gave a jolt to the British in India. First, Churchill's Conservative Party lost the general elections and a Labour Party Government, with Clement Attlee as prime minister, took office on 23 July 1945. This was a defeat for Churchill at the very moment of his triumph and attested to the changing mood of the British public against war and the Empire, which the new government could not possibly ignore. The second was the dropping of atom bombs by the United States on Hiroshima and Nagasaki that brought about the unconditional surrender of Japan on 15 August 1945. This military feat increased America's confidence to follow its own agenda and, among other things, to insist on the application of the Atlantic

Charter to European dependencies in Asia and see them freed from European control. Attlee frankly admits in his autobiography that Britain could not continue to hold on to India because of 'American pressure against Empire'.[44]

The trumpet for the British retreat was sounding from another quarter as well. John Maynard Keynes, the economist, warned the Labour Cabinet members soon after they assumed power that the British debt had risen to £3000 million. He also pointed out that 'the expenditure which is wholly responsible for our financial difficulties is the 2000 million pounds on policing and administering the Empire', a situation that another commentator described as one of the most outstanding examples of strategic overextension in history. Keynes concluded that 'British financial independence from the US (so dear to some Labourites of the day) was impossible without substantial cuts in future spending'.[45] And the harsh reality was that India could no more help to recoup the losses. British exports to India had declined from £83 million in 1930 to less than £40 million by the start of the great war (in 1939). The downfall was the result of competition from American and Japanese goods.

Attlee, whatever his reservations about the Congress Party and its leaders, was anxious to retain, if possible, the goodwill of a future independent Hindustan, which even if India was partitioned, would emerge as one of the largest nations in the world, abutting a still-unsettled China and resource-rich South-east Asia. He and Sir Stafford Cripps also felt it in their bones that, if judiciously handled, Jawaharlal Nehru, the Harrowian, could be won over into some kind of a partnership. On his visits to England, they found that he shared the same Fabian ideals they themselves had been influenced by and they understood his anger at the beginning of the war as directed against Neville Chamberlain's 'reactionary' government rather than at England as such. Had he not, in 1940, said that England's difficulties should not be India's opportunities, even though sometimes his actions did not match his words? And had he not maintained a channel of communication with Attlee and Cripps through the Labourite Krishna Menon, in London? They believed that Nehru's 'tireless energy' could be diverted into 'constructive channels' and his 'delusions' curbed if he was saddled with responsibility. And whatever the viceroy's views about him, they were unwilling to quarrel with a man with whose help they hoped to possibly reconstruct British–Hindustani relations.

On the other hand, after the Labour Government took over power, Wavell became more assertive on his policy in favour of Jinnah and the Muslim League, probably believing that with Churchill dislodged, the Labour Government might 'mishandle' the India situation. For example, he wrote in his diary on 6 August 1945: 'I know nothing of the new Secretary of State [Frederick William] Pethick-Lawrence. I fear he may have fixed ideas derived from Congress Party contacts.'[46] On 20 August he alerted his new masters as follows: 'HMG must be most cautious in any immediate announcement [on India] they wish to make. It is easy to say that the Muslims cannot be allowed to hold up the settlement; but they are too large a proportion of the population to be bypassed or coerced without very grave danger.'[47] And when summoned to London for a policy review by the cabinet, he spoke as follows:

> There was no possibility of a compromise between the Muslim League and the Congress (Party) and we...have to come down on the side of one or the other.... It was most unlikely that Mr Jinnah would now enter into discussions without a previous guarantee of acceptance in principle of a Pakistan. While it was possible to overestimate the importance of any individual political leader [his] own judgment [was] that Jinnah spoke for 99 per cent of the Muslim population of India in their apprehensions of Hindu domination.... Before further progress could be made, we should face up to the root cause which was the problem of Pakistan.[48]

Wavell further clarified his views in a note for the cabinet's consideration (on 31 August 1945). In this note, he stated: 'The draft declaration of 1942 [the Cripps offer] proceeded on the assumption that partition in the last resort provided solution of the Hindu–Muslim question.' But, in 1945, the Cripps offer would not any more be acceptable to Jinnah because the Muslim majorities in the Punjab and Bengal were too slim and he could not be sure whether these two provinces would definitely vote for Pakistan. 'If a plebiscite was held of the whole population, the Punjab would quite possibly not vote for Pakistan.' Further, Jinnah would not welcome the idea of a Constituent Assembly as envisaged in the Cripps offer at the end of hostilities, unless Pakistan was accepted in principle. Wavell then called attention to the fact that since no agreement between the parties was likely to be reached, 'the nature of the secession safeguard...to the Muslim majority' may have to be the acceptance by HMG of the Pakistan scheme. However, Wavell put in a rider that not all the territories demanded by Jinnah could be conceded because the Punjab and Bengal would need to be divided: for the entire Punjab to go to Pakistan would be totally unacceptable to the Sikhs and to award the Hindu-majority Calcutta and West Bengal to Pakistan would be patently unfair to the Hindus.[49]

It becomes obvious from the foregoing discussion that Wavell was relentlessly pursuing the policy he had had in his mind soon after he became viceroy. It is also noteworthy that while Labour ministers in their public pronouncements and briefings to the Americans were singing the tune of a united India, they were seriously contemplating the least controversial way of dividing the country. And all these events occurred *two years before* India's independence and subsequent partition and long before Lord Louis Mountbatten, who is generally blamed for partition and the Punjab bloodbath that followed partition, appeared on the scene.

While in London, Wavell, on 31 August 1945, called on Churchill. According to Wavell's account: 'He warned me that the anchor [himself] was now gone and I was on a lee shore with rash pilots.... His final remark, as I closed the door of the lift was: "keep a bit of India."'[50]

Britain's position at this stage could be summarized as follows:

(1) The British military was emphatic on the value of retaining its base for defensive and offensive action against the USSR in any future dispensation in the subcontinent;

(2) Wavell was quite clear that this objective could only be achieved through partition – keeping a bit of India – because the Congress Party after independence would not cooperate with Britain on military and strategic matters; and

(3) while Labour leaders did not agree with Wavell that all was lost with the Congress Party, Attlee was, nonetheless, ready to support the division of India as long as the responsibility could not be attributed to Britain.

Significantly, Gilbert Laithwaite, the former private secretary of Lord Linlithgow and a strong supporter of Jinnah, was appointed the secretary of the India Committee of the British Cabinet and Lord Ismay, the alter ego of Churchill during the war, became a senior member of the British Cabinet Secretariat. It was the latter who provided the liaison between Attlee and the British chiefs of staff.

*

Elections in India to the Central and Provincial Legislatures had been announced for the winter of 1945. These elections were to be held on the basis of the franchise as hitherto, i.e., only 14 per cent of the population voting, with separate electorates for the Muslims. It is amazing that the Congress Party did not object to such a low franchise in an election that would be considered by the rest of the world as a sort of referendum on the question of India's division. It was also announced that, after the elections, a constitution-making body would be convened and, in the meantime, an executive council having the support of the main Indian parties would be formed to help run the government and 'to enable India to play her full part of working out a new World Order'.[51] The last formulation was expected to make the scheme attractive to Nehru, who, Cripps and Attlee knew was waiting breathlessly like a runner at the start of a race to enter office and win laurels for India in the international arena.

*

Subhash Chandra Bose was believed to have been killed in an air accident in Formosa in 1945, soon after the British forces reconquered Rangoon. However, the trial of the three INA officers – one Hindu, one Muslim and one Sikh – at the Red Fort in Delhi

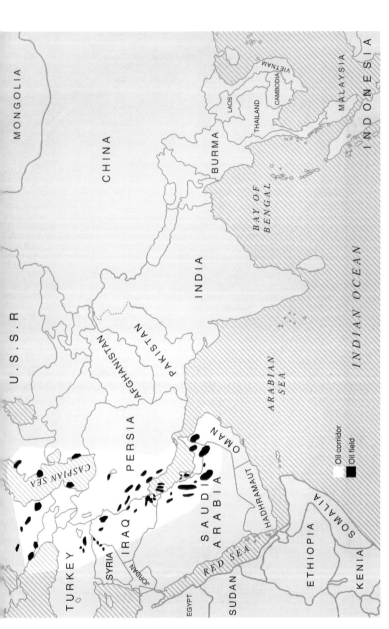

The (oil) *wells of power* around the Persian Gulf.

(*Note*: Borders depicted on the map are notional. The map is neither accurate nor drawn to scale; it is merely indicative of the geographical area.) (*Courtesy: India Today.*)

Lord Linlithgow, viceroy of India from April 1936 to September 1943 on a picnic.
(*Courtesy*: Nehru Memorial Museum and Library, New Delhi.)

The US president, Franklin Delano Roosevelt, and the British prime minister, Winston Churchill (both seated) among others. Standing behind Roosevelt is General George Marshall, the US secretary of state at the time of India's independence.
(*Courtesy*: US Embassy, New Delhi.)

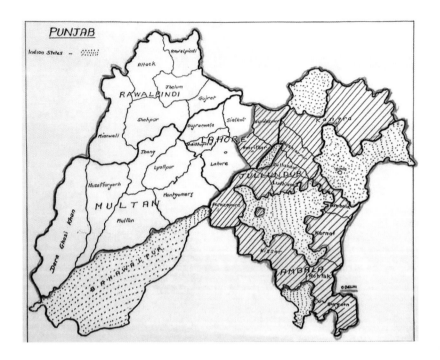

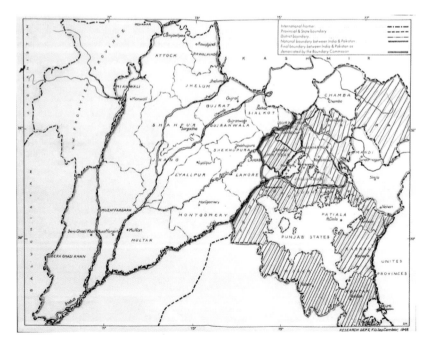

Top: Lord Wavell's proposed demarcation line for the Punjab of February 1946.

Bottom: Sir Cyril Radcliffe's award of August 1947 for the same province.

e maps are neither accurate nor drawn to scale; they are merely indicative.) (*Courtesy*: Transfer of power documents.)

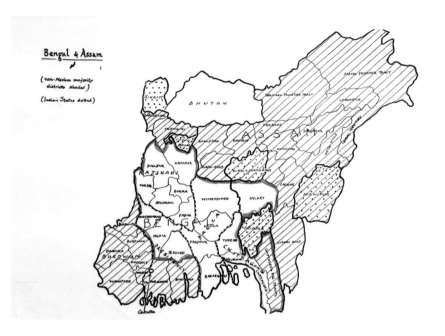

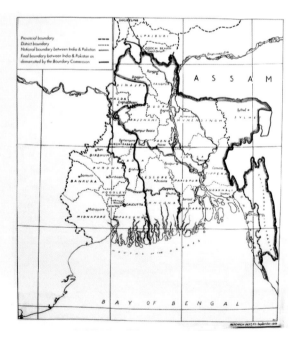

Top: Lord Wavell's proposed division of Bengal and Assam of February 1946.
Bottom: Sir Cyril Radcliffe's award of August 1947 for the same two provinces.
(The maps are neither accurate nor drawn to scale; they are merely indicative.) (*Courtesy*: Transfer of power documen

for treason in 1946 excited so much emotion around the country that, after being sentenced, these officers had to be pardoned and the trials of the others more or less abandoned. The rebellion in the British Indian armed forces soon erupted and many nationalists felt that the moment to 'do or die' was now, when the British were exhausted after the war and demoralized in India, a moment more opportune than the one Gandhiji had chosen in 1942. 'Our struggle was gradually affecting the Indian Army...there would have been a fight, many of us would have died, but there would have been far less bloodshed than in 1947', claimed one of the leaders of the naval mutiny.[52] The Intelligence Bureau's view was that communal disorders were an antidote to the agitation taking an anti-British course. Conversely, the launching of a full-blown revolution by the nationalists might have been an antidote to Jinnah's threats of starting a civil war and may have possibly headed off his flashing of the sword – in the form of the historic 'direct action' – a few months later.

While the new Labour Party ministers cogitated on the next step, in India, Wavell launched a frontal attack to make them accept the principle of partition and foreclose the issue. On 6 November 1945 he sent a top-secret memorandum to the secretary of state:

We are now faced in India with a situation of great difficulty and danger.... The Congress leaders intend to provoke or pave the way for mass disorder...counting on the INA as a spearhead of the revolt. They would suborn the Indian Army if they could, and hope that their threats will impair the loyalty and efficiency of the Police.... They have been encouraged by events in French Indo–China and Indonesia which they are watching carefully, and a good deal may depend upon what happens there and in Syria and Palestine.... There is no doubt about the growth of Hindu enthusiasm for the Congress.... The British members of the ICS [Indian Civil Service] and IP [Indian Police] are dispirited and discontented...while the Indian subordinates on whom the administration so largely depends are naturally reluctant to make enemies of the future masters of India.[53]

He followed up this cannonade with another telegram on 27 December 1945, recommending that Britain should base itself on the following two principles:

(1) If Muslims insist on self-determination in genuinely Muslim areas this must be conceded; and
(2) on the other hand there can be no question of compelling large non-Muslim populations to remain in Pakistan against their will.[54]

★

Jinnah, meanwhile, was working independently to achieve the recognition of the principle of Pakistan. Woodrow Wyatt, a Labour Member of Parliament, records that Jinnah told him emphatically on 8 January 1946 that he 'will not take part in any Interim Government without a prior declaration accepting the principle of Pakistan, though he would not ask at that stage for any discussion or commitment on details'. Jinnah then added: 'Hindus would accept it [Pakistan] as it would give them three-quarters of India, which is more than they have ever had before.'[55]

The Congress Party Working Committee in its resolution of September 1945, while forcefully reiterating its demand for independence and unity, had, nevertheless, declared that 'it cannot think in terms of compelling the people in any territorial unit to remain in [the] Indian Union against their declared and established will'. This rider in regard to the right of secession was roundly attacked at the All-India Congress Committee and not passed. But it gave an indication to the Muslim League (and the British) that the Congress Party's objections to some sort of partition could be overcome by further manoeuvring and by applying pressure. The Congress Party's preoccupation with appearing to uphold lofty principles more than once led to their being hoist by their own petard. In any case, the Congress Party leaders did not threaten to revolt.

On 29 January 1946, the secretary of state in London finally reacted to Wavell's messages by sending the following telegram: 'It would help me to know when I may expect to receive your recommendations as regards definition of genuinely Muslim areas if we are compelled to give a decision on this.'[56] It was in response to this telegram that Wavell, on 6/7 February 1946, forwarded the blueprint of the future Pakistan, which was implemented almost to the letter when India attained independence eighteen months later. This was one of the most important communications sent by any viceroy of India ever since the inception of that office, though ignored by most historians:

(1) If compelled to indicate demarcation of genuinely Moslem areas I recommend that we should include:
   (a) Sind, North-West Frontier Province, British Baluchistan, and Rawalpindi, Multan and Lahore Divisions of Punjab, less Amritsar and Gurdaspur districts.
   (b) In Bengal, the Chittagong and Dacca Divisions, the Rajshahi division (less Jalpaiguri and Darjeeling), the Nadia, Murshidabad and Jessore districts of Presidency division; and in Assam the Sylhet district.

(2) In the Punjab the only Moslem-majority district that would not go into Pakistan under this demarcation is Gurdaspur (51 per cent Moslem). Gurdaspur must go with Amritsar for geographical reasons and Amritsar being sacred city of Sikhs must stay out of Pakistan...

(5) We should make it clear in any announcement that this is only an indication of areas to which in HMG's view the Moslems can advance a reasonable claim, modifications in boundary might be negotiated and no doubt the interests of Sikhs in particular would be carefully considered in such negotiations. Some such saving clause is indicated by importance of preventing immediate violence by Sikhs.

(6) In Bengal the three Moslem-majority districts of Presidency division must I think be included in Pakistan, though this brings frontier across the Ganges. The demarcation includes in Pakistan all Moslem-majority districts and no Hindu-majority districts.

(7) There is no case, consistent with the principle suggested in [the] breakdown plan, for including Calcutta in Pakistan.

The Moslems will probably try to negotiate for its being made a free port. If negotiations fail Eastern Bengal's prospects as a separate autonomous State will be seriously affected. But Moslems, if they insist on Pakistan, must face up to this problem.[57]

About two years after leaving India, Wavell addressed the Royal Central Asia Society in London (June 1949):

There are two main material factors in the revolutionary change that has come over the strategical face of Asia. One is air power, the other is oil.... Oil, which is the source of air power, concerns very deeply that part of Asia with which this society deals, since the principal known oil reserves of the world lie in the Persian Gulf. The next great struggle for world power, if it takes place, may well be for the control of these oil reserves. It may centre on Western Asia, the Persian Gulf, the approaches to India.... This may be the battleground both of the material struggle for oil and air bases, and of the spiritual struggle of at least three great creeds – Christianity, Islam, Communism – and of the political theories of democracy and totalitarianism. In such a struggle the base of the Western Powers must surely be in the Middle East...[58]

He did not, of course, even hint that he had played a part in laying the foundation of a state that would help buttress the British military position in the Middle East.

Notes and References

1. See Wavell, *The Viceroy's Journal* (Oxford University Press, London, 1977, p. 463).
2. Patrick French, *Liberty or Death: India's Journey to Independence and Division* (HarperCollins, London, 1995, p. 173).
3. Wavell, op. cit., p. 111.

4. French, op. cit., p. 171.
5. Wavell, op. cit., p. 24.
6. Penderel Moon, *The British Conquest and Dominion of India*, Vol. 2 (India Research Press, Delhi, 1999, p. 1129).
7. C. Dasgupta, *War and Diplomacy in Kashmir: 1947–1948* (Sage, New Delhi, 2002, p. 18).
8. Wavell, op. cit., p. 499.
9. Ibid.
10. TOP VI, p. 532, dated 13 August 1945.
11. Penderel Moon, op. cit., p. 1127.
12. TOP VII, S. No. 286.
13. Wavell, op. cit., p. 245 and TOP VII, S. No. 641, Appendix.
14. Ibid.
15. From a letter to me from Ms Talbot Rice, military researcher, London, dated 17 August 2001. (She withheld the name of the officer.)
16. Trevor Royle, *The Last Days of the Raj* (John Murray, London, 1997, p. 269).
17. Ibid., p. 271.
18. Wavell, op. cit., p. 271.
19. Henry Rawlinson, *England and Russia* (John Murray, London, 1875, pp. 279–80).
20. TOP IV, S. Nos. 706–07.
21. Wavell, op. cit., pp. 185–86.
22. Alan Campbell-Johnson, *Mission with Mountbatten* (Atheneum, New York, 1986, p. 54).
23. Hector Bolitho, *Jinnah* (John Murray, London, 1954, p. 25).
24. Wavell, op. cit., p. 91.
25. Ibid., p. 99.
26. TOP V, S. No. 111.
27. Winston Churchill, *Memories of the Second World War: Triumph and Tragedy* (Cassell & Co., London, 1950, pp. 105–06).
28. Ibid., pp. 107–08.
29. All extracts from Post-Hostilities Planning Staff report dated 19 May 1945, top secret PHP (45) 15 (O) [Oriental and Indian Collection (OIC), British Library, London].
30. Wavell, op. cit., p. 120.
31. Penderel Moon, op. cit., p. 1137.

32. US FR 1945, Vol. VI, p. 251.
33. US FR 1944, Vol. V, p. 240.
34. US FR 1943, Vol. IV, pp. 220–22.
35. US FR 1944, Vol. V, p. 242.
36. Durga Dass, *India from Curzon to Nehru and After* (HarperCollins India, New Delhi, 2000, p. 216).
37. V.P. Menon, *Transfer of Power in India* (Longman Green, London, 1957, p. 241).
38. TOP V, S. No. 565.
39. Ibid., S. No. 566.
40. TOP VI, S. No. 29.
41. Ibid.
42. H.V. Hodson, *The Great Divide: Britain-India-Pakistan* (Oxford University Press edition, Delhi, 2000, p. 127).
43. TOP V, S. No. 598.
44. Clement Attlee, *A Prime Minister Remembers* (Heinemann, London, 1961).
45. TOP VI, S. Nos. 484 and 486.
46. Wavell, op. cit., p. 161.
47. TOP VI, S. No. 47.
48. Ibid., S. No. 78.
49. Ibid., S. No. 82.
50. Wavell, op. cit., p. 168.
51. TOP VI, S. No. 99, Annexure II.
52. C.R. Das, quoted in Minoo Masani, *Our India* (Oxford University Press, Delhi, 1953, p. 126).
53. TOP VI, S. No. 194.
54. Ibid., S. No. 316.
55. TOP IV, S. No. 323, Enclosure.
56. TOP VI, S. No. 387.
57. Ibid., S. No. 406.
58. Quoted in Olaf Caroe, *Wells of Power* (Macmillan, London, 1951, p. 184).

8

Attlee's 'Smoke Screens'

*L*ORD WAVELL'S RECOMMENDATION THAT HMG MAKE AN AWARD TO divide India was thoroughly unwelcome to Prime Minister Attlee. Alan Campbell-Johnson, Mountbatten's press attaché, once told me: 'Attlee was decisive, but supersensitive to the charge of dividing India, especially in the face of the US Government's view that the partition of India may give a fillip to the leftist forces in the subcontinent.' Further, such an award would mean a clean break with the Congress Party, which the British Labour Party leaders were anxious to avoid. Attlee broadly agreed with the thrust of Wavell's policy to create the smaller Pakistan to safeguard British strategic purposes but wanted this done, if possible, with the assent or at least the acquiescence of the Congress Party. It is important to bear in mind that Attlee was throughout his own secretary of state.

Attlee, later in life, admitted: 'You might have got a united settlement at the beginning of the 1930s',[1] thereby implying that, in his view, a united India was no longer possible by 1946. As deputy prime minister and chairman of the India Committee in Churchill's War Cabinet from 1942 to 1945, he was fully aware of the steps that had been taken by Britain on India's partition, though the matter was kept locked in a closet. The British secretary of state, Leopold Amery, had written to the viceroy, Linlithgow, in 1942 (as recounted in Chapter 4) that Attlee was facing pressure from his party to adopt a more liberal stance on India, meaning that if left to himself, he might have been more helpful to the Conservative point of view on India. Lord Listowel (William Hare), who was the secretary of state at the time of India's independence, told a London audience in 1967: 'Attlee was much more conservative on India than is generally believed.'[2]

This does not mean that Attlee was unsympathetic to Indian aspirations, as Churchill was. In 1947 he helped to strengthen India by permitting Mountbatten, despite protests by Lord Listowel and the India Office, to stampede the Indian princes to accede to India that prevented their vast territories from breaking away. Against the objections of the chiefs of general staff, he handed over the Andaman and Nicobar Islands, situated in the Bay of Bengal, to India. This acquisition increased India's reach into South-east Asia. He wanted not only a Pakistan that could assist British policy in the Middle East, but also an India that would cooperate with and assist Britain in South-east Asia. For him, while two 'Indias' were desirable from the point of view of British strategy, more than two – a 'Balkanization' – as hoped for by the Tories, would be counterproductive.

Dean Acheson, the US secretary of state, has noted in his memoirs: 'Attlee was apt at operating behind a smoke screen.'[3] Attlee now deployed this talent to the full to achieve two contradictory objectives: to secure the partition of India and also maintain good relations with the future 'Hindustan'. In November 1945, Sir Stafford Cripps, who was Attlee's pointsman on India and acquainted with Jawaharlal Nehru, got in touch with him. Nehru's response was instantaneous and warm: 'Many things that have been done during the past few years [meaning the Cripps Mission of 1942] have hurt me...but at no time did I doubt that you had the cause of India at heart.' He promised: 'We shall do our utmost to avoid conflict and to restrain the hotheads'.[4] Cripps was delighted. Attlee's greatest anxiety was that a full-blooded revolt would be launched by the nationalists in India, as predicted by Wavell, which the British had scant means at their disposal to suppress. Such a revolt might result in loss of control over the situation, bringing ignominy to Britain in the eyes of the world, particularly in the US.

The winter of 1945–46 was a winter of discontent for Britain in India. The disciplinary trial of the officers of Bose's Indian National

Army had backfired and raised public feelings against the Raj. There were mutinies in the Royal Indian Navy, Royal Air Force, the Royal Signals Corps and the Engineers and uncertainty about the loyalty of the Indian Army, as recounted in Chapter 7. Famine stalked the land, the morale of the civil services and the police was crumbling and Britain at home was facing a severe financial crunch. On 12 December 1945 Cripps replied to Nehru: 'I am so glad you are convinced as I am, that we must do our utmost to restrain the use of force on either side and that we must concentrate on it [the problem's solution] by reason.' He then artfully posed the question: 'If you were in the Viceroy's place what line of action would you lay down to be followed after the elections?... Let me have an off-the-record answer to that!'[5]

The question appears to have tickled Nehru's ego and he replied to Cripps in a letter that contained over 3500 words on 27 January 1946. It is not clear from the historical records whether he consulted any of his colleagues before doing so. The main points of the letter are as follows:

(1) The British Government should declare in the clearest terms possible that they accept the independence of India.

(2) The constitution of a free India should be determined by India's elected representatives without any interference from the British side.

(3) The British Government should not encourage any division of India, the matter being left to the people of India themselves to be decided. The ideal would be a loose Indian federation with safeguards to protect the minority interests and in which powers, except for the defence, external affairs, communications and currency are left to the federating unit.

(4) Even if the inhabitants of any territorial unit wished to opt out this would only be done after a plebiscite and they would not carry with them inhabitants within the same unit who did not wish to opt out. *The crux of the Pakistan issue is that* [of] *a Pakistan consisting of only part of Punjab and part of Bengal or no separation at all* [italics added].

(5) In the event of separation, defence should still remain common.

(6) Since the North-West Frontier Province is unlikely to vote for separation, Pakistan is an impossibility.

(7) Vote for the Muslim League in the election is no vote for Pakistan, it is only a vote for the organization which represents a certain solidarity of Indian Muslims.

(8) The League agitation is on the surface and firm actions can defeat it.

(9) Some Princely States may be encouraged not to join the Indian Union if there is a Pakistan, only the larger states, probably a dozen, could survive as independent federal units, the others must be absorbed in the Provinces or amalgamate together to form big enough federal units with the same democratic liberties and forms of administration as in the Provinces...

(10) An increasing number of young men and women are convinced that only a big struggle can produce something worthwhile – this was the threat.[6]

Nehru had promised a negotiated and peaceful solution. This immensely relieved both Attlee and Cripps. Nehru had also mentioned the possibility of 'separation', though in guarded language. More evidence of the Congress Party's flexible attitude on this aspect reached London on 10 January 1946. Woodrow Wyatt, the Labour Party MP, reported via the viceroy that in a four-hour discussion he had with him, 'Nehru conceded that the British might have to declare for [sic] Pakistan but said there must be a plebiscite in border districts...so that solid blocks of Hindu territory were not included [in] Pakistan'.[7]

The viceroy had already cut out the non-Muslim areas from Jinnah's territorial claims. The crucial question for the British was: Could the Congress Party now be induced to agree to a smaller, 'truncated' Pakistan? Nehru's letter, holding out an olive branch, confirmed their own belief that the need of the hour was to keep talking to the Indians and even saddle them with real responsibility to squeeze out all confrontationist tendencies from them. In any case, it was an effort worth a try, but certainly not, Attlee felt, with Wavell negotiating with Gandhiji and Nehru, considering the deep distrust that existed between him and them. He therefore decided to send out Cripps with a team of cabinet ministers to New Delhi to explore matters further on the spot.

On 27 February 1946 the secretary of state for India wired to the viceroy as follows:

> We do not feel able to take a decision on your proposal [on Pakistan] until the ground has been tested by the first stage of conversations and we shall have to take time to consider our course.... Failing agreement amongst Indians some other means of settling the Pakistan issue must be found.[8]

The cabinet ministers selected to accompany Cripps included Lord Pethick-Lawrence, the secretary of state for India (an elderly Quaker, who soon came to be called 'pathetic' Lawrence because of the somewhat loose assertion of his authority) and A.V. Alexander the First Lord of the Admiralty ('a working class Labour stalwart with no experience of India...who found politicians dressed in dhotis "baffling and tricky" '). Cripps, greatly encouraged by Nehru's letter, was brimming with confidence to secure a settlement.

Wavell failed to grasp that Attlee's idea might have been to arrive at the same solution that he had suggested, but to be achieved in a way that would place the responsibility for partition squarely on Indian shoulders. He feared that his new masters may ignore Britain's long-term strategic interests in the region. Thus, on 3 March 1946, he shot back:

> The first, most important is [the] Pakistan issue. It is essential that HMG should have some policy on this.... They may decide that the unity of India is of such importance that they will in no circumstances allow a complete partition of India and discount the adverse effect this will have on Muslims not only in India but in other parts of the world and [are] prepared to face the consequences [that might include] civil war in India and enmity in other Muslim countries.[9]

The decision, he insisted, would affect not only India but also other parts of the world and requested that the precise areas to go to Pakistan should be worked out by the Cabinet Mission before leaving London.

In Wavell's dispatches, appeasement of the Muslim League in India has been throughout justified on the ground that ignoring Jinnah's demands in India would hurt the British position amongst the Muslims of the Middle East. The British were indeed anxious to retain the goodwill of the Arabs at a time when they were committed to permitting Jewish immigration into Palestine. But appeasing Jinnah was not quite relevant for this purpose, because there was no special sympathy for Jinnah or his movement in Muslim countries. Indeed, many people in these countries saw Jinnah as a British puppet. In the Middle East at that time, feelings of anti-colonialism, nationalism and socialism were stronger than those of the Islamic brotherhood. The Palestinians were fighting the Jews to prevent their land from being occupied on the basis of nationalism and not on communal considerations. The secular Baath party of Lebanon, which was to spread to Syria and Iraq, and later the phenomenon of 'Nasserism' in Egypt, attempted to adopt socialism and nationalism as their planks, essentially to create an ideological platform other than one based on Islam, on which people of other faiths could join Muslims in their struggle against foreign domination. In reality, Britain's main concern was the USSR, i.e., about finding partners for the Great Game to block Soviet influence in the oil-rich Middle East.

Afghanistan was so hostile to Pakistan that it was the only country in the world to vote against the latter's admission to the United Nations. There was no contact between Jinnah and Saudi Arabia. The Saudi royal family saw Muslim regimes that espoused secularism as a threat to their kingdom and to themselves. Mohammad Mossadeq, the prime minister of Iran, who nationalized oil, was moved by a secular impulse. Iran turned pro-Pakistan after the British and the Americans helped to build up the Pakistan–Iran axis under the umbrella of the anti-Soviet Baghdad Pact and the CENTO Pact.

★

Attlee was unwilling to show his hand to the viceroy. 'You should discuss and explore all possible alternatives without proceeding upon any fixed or rigid preconceived plan', he instructed the Cabinet Mission and the viceroy on 17 March 1946 and laid down three cardinal points to be followed:

(1) Constitutional protection for the minorities.
(2) Provision for the defence of India and the Indian Ocean area.
(3) The freedom to the princely states to make whatever arrangements they wished after British withdrawal.[10]

Just two days earlier, i.e., on 15 March 1946, in a debate held in the House of Commons on the Cabinet Mission's visit to India, Attlee had declared: 'What form of Government was to replace the present regime was for India to decide.' He then bowled a smooth googly: 'We are mindful of the rights of the minorities, on the other hand we cannot allow a minority to place a veto on the advance of the majority.'[11]. This was a dodge because the veto given to the Muslim minority on constitutional developments, embodied in Britain's Declaration of 8 August 1940, was not to be revoked in the forthcoming talks and Jinnah's intransigence remained the bedrock of British negotiating strength. However, Attlee's statements prepared the ground for a friendly reception of the Cabinet Mission by the Congress Party. They also satisfied the Congress Party sympathizers in his Labour Party.

The results of the provincial elections had, meanwhile, come in. Even though the Muslim League emerged as the largest Muslim grouping, it made a poor showing in the Muslim-majority British provinces that had been earmarked by Wavell, either in whole or in part, for Pakistan. In the vital NWFP, with a 95 per cent Muslim population, the Congress Party was returned to power. In the Punjab, another crucial province if Pakistan were to be realized, a large proportion of the Muslims continued to side with the Unionists, who again formed a coalition government with the help of the Sikhs and Hindu groupings. In Assam a non-Muslim-majority province, contiguous with Burma, which was claimed by Jinnah, the Congress

Party once more emerged victorious. In only two British provinces (Bengal and Sind), out of the five claimed by Jinnah for Pakistan (besides British Baluchistan), could the Muslim League form governments. In Sind, the governor's intervention was needed since the League and the opposition had equal numbers in the legislature. All the impressive gains of the Muslim League were made in the six Muslim-minority provinces (5 per cent to 15 per cent of the population) that had been earmarked by Wavell for 'Hindustan', namely, the United Provinces, Bihar, the Central Provinces, Bombay, Madras and Orissa, even though in each of them the Congress Party was returned with overwhelming majorities.

All these developments served to confirm once again the prognosis that the Pakistan idea was catching on amongst the Muslims of the Muslim-minority provinces, where the cry of 'Islam in danger' could be raised, but not in the Muslim-majority areas, where the Muslims already exercised political dominance. The League's campaign in the election had been strongly communal, the students of the Aligarh Muslim University in the United Provinces in their speeches to Muslim villagers invoking the martyrdom of Imam Hussain, the grandson of the Prophet Mohammad, and making out that in the new Congress (Hindu) Raj cows will be tethered to their mosques. Other such devices were also used to whip up communal frenzy. The success of the Muslim League in Muslim-minority provinces can also be attributed to the fact that no one explained to the Muslims in these provinces that if Pakistan was achieved they would be excluded from it. Even the educated Muslims failed to think through the Pakistan idea. As one writer has noted: 'It stood for them as some sort of general salvation from Hindu domination and symbolized an Islamic revival in India.'[12]

★

Britain's stated *raison d'être* for supporting Jinnah's position was 'to protect' the minorities. But then what about the thirty million Muslims who were to be left out of Pakistan? Was not the selective concern for the Muslims of India not so much to protect them as to use a portion of them to realize Britain's strategic goals? And how was the two-nation theory that Muslims could not coexist with people of other faiths within the same country to be squared with leaving these millions to do exactly that? Notwithstanding all these unanswered and inconvenient questions, confidential papers prepared for the Cabinet Mission indicate that Wavell's plan for the truncated Pakistan had caught the British imagination and had become HMG's goal, even though in public pronouncements, they continued to chant the mantra of unity. For example, on 13 March 1946, Francis Turnbull, assistant secretary in the India Office, London, suggested to the secretary of state in a note (also sent to Sir Stafford Cripps) on how to get the scheme for partition through:

> Mr Gandhi has frowned upon a truncated Pakistan.... If the [Cabinet] Mission can avoid a discussion with Mr Gandhi in the opening stages there may be advantage.... If there is any hope of compromise, it is likely to be best worked out with [Maulana] Azad and Nehru.... If Mr Gandhi has not committed himself (at the beginning) he may be affected by the views of his supporters if they are sufficiently unanimous.[13]

The Cabinet Mission landed in Delhi in the middle of March 1946 when English summer flowers in gardens and the blue jacaranda and orange *gulmohar* trees on the roads were in bloom. But within a month the heat would set in, the flowers would wilt and the houses and offices of Indian politicians that were not airconditioned would become furnaces. New Delhi was built by Sir Edwin Lutyens as a winter capital to which officialdom descended for a few months from salubrious Simla. The square low white bungalows surrounded by large lawns recalled transient Persian or Mughal tent encampments set amidst gardens, though here the dwellings were of brick and mortar. This garden city was dominated by the massive red stone Viceroy's House, the Imperial Secretariat with its two wings facing each other and, at a slightly lower level, the immense colonnaded rotunda of the Legislative Assembly. Eyeing these structures, when being built in 1919, M. Clemencau (the French PM, who led his country to victory in the First World War) had quipped: 'What magnificent ruins they would make.'

The heat did not bother Sir Stafford but old Pethick-Lawrence and A.V. Alexander suffered, with the latter, after a while, hardly venturing out of the airconditioned comforts of the Viceroy's House. Despite all his enthusiasm, Cripps could not keep up the pace for more than a couple of months. And it was from the end of May, when Cripps fell ill, that Wavell was able to impose his agenda on Pethick-Lawrence.

By 11 April 1946, Cripps had worked out a plan, on which the Cabinet Mission and the viceroy sought Prime Minister Attlee's instructions:

> There appears to us two possible bases of agreement, the first a unitary India with a loose federation at the Centre charged primarily with control of Defence and Foreign affairs (Scheme A). The second based upon a divided India and the smaller Pakistan – [as in Wavell's blueprint of 6/7 February 1946] – (Scheme B).[14]

Attlee's response was immediate. On 13 April 1946 he wired back as follows:

> You may work for an agreement on the basis of Scheme B (Pakistan) if it seems to be the only chance of an agreed settlement. I send you in Paragraphs 2 to 7 the views of the Chiefs of Staff for your information and for the use at discussions.

The views of the chiefs of staff were as follows:

(2) An agreement involving a loose all-India federation is far better than Scheme B. We recognize however that this may be impossible of achievement. The alternative of Scheme B (Pakistan) in spite of the disadvantages listed below is better than no agreement at all as this would lead to widespread chaos.

(3) The disadvantages of Scheme B (partition) are as follows: Pakistan lies across the two entrances to India from Peshawar to the sea in the west and from the Himalayas to the sea

to the east. In her hands would lie the responsibility to bar or open the road into Hindustan. Air bases from which India can be attacked lie in Soviet Central Asia and in Western China. The easiest and quickest routes to the large cities of India from these bases lie over the territories of Pakistan, both in the West and East of India. Similarly the air bases from which countermeasures can be taken lie mainly in Pakistan. It can therefore be said that the territory of Pakistan is vital to the defence of India as a whole.

(4) Scheme B would destroy the homogeneity of the Indian Army, which is now strong and well equipped and is charged with the defence of all India. There would evolve the forces of Pakistan, the forces of Hindustan and the forces of the many Indian States; each weak, each with its own standards of training, its own scale of equipment and its own tactical ideas. Even if all were acting in common for the defence of India, cooperation would be far from easy unless all acknowledged a central directing authority.

(5) To operate effectively the communications of Hindustan and Pakistan must supplement each other as they were designed to do. Again, central control is essential.

(6) In Pakistan there is almost no industrial development, Karachi is at the end of a long and vulnerable railway, and Chittagong is in a similarly exposed position. To fight a war Pakistan must rely on Hindustan for producing a part of the warlike stores required and for importing and transporting the rest. Without a central authority this would not be possible.

(7) In the case of Pakistan (west) it seems likely that she would tend to identify her interests more with the Muslim lands of Central Asia, weak, unstable, and exposed though they may be, then [sic] with Hindustan. This might well lead to Pakistan being involved in wars not properly of vital importance to Hindustan, nor to India as a whole. Or she might through fear engendered by her own weakness uncover the vitals of India by not resisting on the natural battleground of the hills of the Indian frontier.[15]

Attlee's instructions suggest that in accepting the division of India, he wanted to act from behind a smoke screen. It appears incongruous that the chiefs of staff's support for the creation of Pakistan contained in Paragraph 2 should be at such absolute variance with their own strong opposition to it as contained in Paragraphs 3 to 7 of their report. We get a whiff of what happened at the chiefs of staff's meeting that was hurriedly summoned by Attlee on 12 April 1946 from its verbatim record. At this meeting Field Marshal Francis Alanbrooke, supporting the Pakistan scheme, told the gathering:

Pakistan...was in fact militarily unsound but as chaos would probably take place in India if this scheme, which was *a political one* [italics added] was not put into effect...[16]

The mention of the political factor by Alanbrooke discloses Attlee's hand. It suggests that the field marshal had been briefed by the government to support the creation of Pakistan on the ground of avoiding chaos in the subcontinent. Thus, Attlee could take shelter behind 'military advice' for agreeing to the division of India.

It is incongruous that Attlee should be so worried about the immediate possibility of disturbances erupting in India if Jinnah were not appeased that he should remain virtually unconcerned about the serious long-term threat to India from partition as sketched out by the chiefs of staff. Attlee had been consistently discounting Wavell's warnings of a violent revolt in India, but did not hesitate to make it his justification for this decision. In any case, Jinnah could not possibly set the Ganges on fire if Attlee had the Congress Party on his side. The key to Attlee's manoeuvres lay simply in obtaining the chief of staff's support for partitioning India, despite the chiefs' true opinions.

★

The 'three wise men', after lengthy consultations with the Indian politicians and the viceroy, produced, on 16 May 1946, a plan for British withdrawal from India. Immediately, an Interim Government would be set up, with the leaders of the political parties replacing the nominated members in the Viceroy's Executive Council. Elections would be held for a Constituent Assembly that would eventually draw up the constitution of the country. There would be an all-India Union Government and a legislature consisting of the British provinces to deal only with foreign affairs, defence and communications, the rest of the powers vesting in autonomous provinces. The Centre would be a weak one.

As per the new plan, the legislators in the proposed Constituent Assembly would be representing one of the three following groups:

(a) The six provinces with non-Muslim majorities excluding Assam, i.e., Madras, Bombay, Orissa, the Central Provinces, Bihar and the United Provinces;

(b) the Muslim-majority areas in the northwest: the Punjab, the North West Frontier Province, Sind and Baluchistan; and

(c) Bengal and Assam.

The legislators belonging to the last two groups and (which included all the British provinces demanded by Jinnah for Pakistan) would draw up the constitutions of their respective groups. The provinces would have no choice but to join the groups in which they had been placed. As soon as the elections for the Constituent Assembly were over (scheduled for July 1946), the legislators of all the three groups would come together to begin drafting the all-India constitution.

The plan provided that, after ten years, the constituents of groups (b) and (c) would have the option of opting out of the Union on the basis of majority votes cast by their group legislators and could form an independent state or states, the individual provinces having no say in the matter. The incantations in the preamble of the plan rejected the division of India but left a large loophole for the creation of Pakistan, even larger than the one proposed by Wavell to London earlier that year.

Woodrow Wyatt in his article (*Spectator*, 13 August 1997) reveals how he convinced Jinnah, who was suspicious about the plan since it rejected the idea of a sovereign independent Pakistan 'in the immediate', to accept it:

...I put to him that...though the statement announcing the Plan ruled out Pakistan, it was the first step on the road to it.... I spoke at length. When I finished his face lit up. He hit the table with his hand: "That's it. You've got it."[17]

Wyatt was referring to the option for groups (b) and (c) to opt out after ten years. Jinnah never concealed the fact that he saw the plan as the first step in his journey towards the full-fledged Pakistan he had been demanding. In fact, he announced at a Muslim League public meeting in Bombay soon after the Cabinet Mission's departure: 'The Plan had conceded Pakistan.'

The Sikh leader Baldev Singh was quick to inform Attlee that the Muslim League had accepted the plan with the main object of opting out and establishing an independent, sovereign state. Baldev Singh pointed out that the Sikhs in the Punjab would be especially vulnerable. So indeed would be the Pathans of the NWFP, who were with the Congress Party. In the east, Assam, which had a non-Muslim majority (30 per cent Christian) and a Congress Party Government as well as the non-Muslims of the metropolitan city of Calcutta, were being placed in the 'nascent eastern Pakistan autonomous group' with no guarantee that the all-India federation would survive and that they would not one day find themselves in Pakistan. Indeed, a delayed action bomb was being put in place, which would eventually go off and result in the British provinces of groups (b) and (c) breaking away from the proposed federation and chaos and violence ensuing in the meantime.

If the Muslim League's past policies were any guide, it would provoke communal violence against minorities in groups (b) and (c) to unite the Muslims in them behind the call for Pakistan and quitting the federation after the ten-year period. In case there was retaliatory communal violence in other parts of India, as was likely, this would only inflame the Muslims in the 'nascent Pakistani autonomous groups' against the minority communities in them, establishing a pattern of escalating violence. The Centre, paralysed as a result of serious divisions between the Congress and Muslim League ministers and, in any case with limited authority, would be helpless in controlling the situation. During partition in 1947, massive violence and large-scale killing were confined to the Punjab. Under the Cabinet Mission plan, there was a danger of a much larger area getting engulfed in violence over a period of ten years with unpredictable consequences.

Some felt, or hoped that, once an all-India federation was launched, a momentum for unity would be generated. But the situation, as it was developing, made this problematic.

What about the princely states comprising one-third of India? Under the plan, all of them, big and small, would become legally independent and would be free to make their own arrangements. Such a provision led to the dicey question: How could the bigger princely states, that might seek independence, be prevented from breaking away, when the Central Cabinet would be a house divided against itself on the issue? The British chiefs of staff, in a memorandum issued as late as 7 July 1947 (referred to in Chapter 1), envisaged the availability of transit rights for British military aircraft in a few princely states. Thus, they foresaw the possibility of some large states (such as Hyderabad in the Deccan plateau situated on the air route between the British garrisons in the Middle East and South-east Asia) becoming independent. Travancore state, on the southwestern coast of India, was trying to attract foreign companies to exploit its thorium deposits and also to become independent. So also Kashmir on the Afghan–Sinkiang border.

And how could the overwhelming majority – the middling and small states – survive without any arrangements for support from the Centre? Lying interspersed with British Indian territories and dependent on them for communications, roads and railways, power, water for irrigation and so many other services, they would be easy targets for forced absorption by neighbouring Congress Party- or Muslim League-run provinces, resulting in mayhem. Would not Manipur and Tripura states – situated on the Burmese border and cut off from the 'Hindustan' provinces by Muslim League-dominated group (c) provinces and severely underpopulated – get settled by Bengali Muslims and forcibly incorporated into East Pakistan?

★

214 || THE SHADOW OF THE GREAT GAME

At this stage, the Congress Party leaders were urged by some nationalists to renew the Quit India movement, this time using violent means. Certainly, circumstances were now more propitious for revolt than in 1942, when, in the middle of the war, Britain had the will, the forces in India and the support of international opinion to quash any rebellion. However, the Congress leaders turned away from this option. They feared the unpredictability of such an attempted solution, which would require them to establish their control over not only the whole of British India but also the princely states, many of which possessed armed forces. The realization that they had made a tactical mistake in choosing confrontation rather than cooperation with Britain at the beginning of the war also made them cautious. There was yet another factor. The flattering attention being paid by Attlee and Cripps to the Congress leaders made them complacent. Vallabhbhai Patel and Jawaharlal Nehru failed to foresee that their restraint could provide an opportunity to the Muslim League to launch 'direct' or violent action in order to exert pressure for the acceptance of its own point of view. And this is precisely what happened.

To the Congress Party the most objectionable part of the plan was the possibility of groups (b) and (c) breaking away from the federation and forming a separate state or states. On the other hand, they were attracted by the plan's proposal to set up an Interim Government with immediate effect. By assuming the reins of power in the Interim Government and by establishing a majority in the proposed Constituent Assembly, they hoped somehow to be able to muddle through and achieve a united India. Therefore, instead of rejecting the plan, they resorted to a half-baked legalistic stratagem to reserve their position on its long-term arrangements and accepted its short-term provisions. This stratagem was that since Britain had always insisted on the 'provincial option', there could be no other interpretation to the plan than that the provinces placed in the (b) and (c) groups obviously had the option under it to join or not to join these groups. If the Congress-dominated NWFP and Assam stood out of groups (b) and (c), any possibility of these groups quitting the federation in order to form Pakistan after ten years would disappear.

The Congress interpretation of the grouping scheme was contrary to the Cabinet Mission's intentions. In fact, the grouping scheme, as Wavell put it, 'was the keystone of the whole edifice'. However, the Attlee Government was so keen to saddle Nehru and Patel with responsibility in the Interim Government, that it allowed preparations for the formation of such a government and the elections to the Constituent Assembly to go forward, turning a Nelson's eye to the Congress Party's self-serving interpretation of the grouping provision in the plan and to Wavell's warning that the cabinet members were not playing straight with Jinnah. In fact, none of the three was playing straight with each other: not the Congress Party as stated above; not Jinnah, who was eyeing the plan, tongue in cheek; and not the British, making a show of doing one thing and doing the other.

It is inconceivable that Attlee did not appreciate the disastrous potential of his Cabinet Mission scheme. In my view the plan was essentially conceived as a smoke screen to achieve the following objectives of Attlee's policy:

- First, by inducting Nehru and Patel into the Interim Government to prevent the possibility of the Congress Party organizing a revolt in India and side by side to placate Nehru and Patel.
- Second, to whittle down Jinnah's rising demands by placing on record the disadvantages of the Pakistan scheme, so that, at a later date, he could be browbeaten to accept the smaller or "truncated" Pakistan.
- Third, to create the impression in the USA and amongst the ranks of his own Labour Party that he was doing his utmost to maintain the unity of India.

★

Dean Acheson, the US secretary of state, was keenly following developments in India. He was impressed by Britain's efforts to work for Indian unity, little realizing that a loophole had been left for partition of the country. He wired the US chargé d'affaires in

New Delhi: 'Assam and NWFP...have little economic importance and their strategic significance would in any event enable Indian Union Government through defence and foreign affairs to concern itself with developments there.'[18] In fact, Assam's economic wealth, in the form of tea, oil and timber, was not inconsiderable; and one may well ask: how would the Union Government impose its fiat on the NWFP and Assam, as Acheson proposed, when there would be fundamental differences between the Congress Party and Muslim League ministers on each other's foreign and defence policy goals?

In those days, the Americans' understanding of India was extremely limited. To take an extreme example, John Foster Dulles, President Dwight Eisenhower's secretary of state, had to be disabused by Walter Lippmann, during a conversation on SEATO as late as in 1955, that Gurkha troops were *not* Pakistanis.

'Look Walter', Dulles said, 'I've got to get some real fighting men into the south of Asia. The only Asians who can really fight are the Pakistanis. That's why we need them in the Alliance. We could never get along without the Gurkas.' 'But Foster', Lippmann replied, 'the Gurkas aren't Pakistanis, they're Indians'. (Actually, Gurkhas are of Nepalese origin.) 'Well', responded Dulles, 'they may not be Pakistanis but they're Moslems.' 'No I'm afraid they're not Moslems either; they're Hindus', Lippmann pointed out.[19]

Ignorance about India was the reason why the Americans came to rely substantially on British advice on questions concerning the subcontinent after its independence.

Wavell, whom Atlee did not take into confidence on higher policy, was alarmed at the turn of events; Jinnah even more so. What if the Constituent Assembly, in which the Congress Party would be in a majority, turned itself into a sovereign body and declared independence with or without British acquiescence? Would the Attlee Government have the requisite will or the means to oppose such a move, especially now that the US appeared to be lending support to the Congress Party? Jinnah's political base was far from secure; the governments in the NWFP and the Punjab were in control of Muslim politicians not belonging to the Muslim League; British commercial interests might incline towards the larger and richer Hindustan; and Wavell's friends, such as Churchill, had gone. Jinnah could by no means be certain that in case he instigated his supporters to revolt, the Muslim officers in the British Indian Army would desert and join him rather than remain loyal to the Army command structure, which was still dominated by British officers. The advantage he had built up during the war, when the British really needed him, appeared to be slipping away. The last straw on the camel's back would be a *rapprochement* between the British and the Congress Party.

The upshot of all this was that Jinnah, who had agreed to the Cabinet Mission plan, decided to repudiate it. On 6 July 1946 Nehru had announced to the press in Bombay that the Congress was committed to nothing beyond entering the proposed Constituent Assembly, a statement that provided Jinnah with a *casus belli*, although he himself had been equally provocative, boasting that the Cabinet Mission plan had opened the gates for achieving Pakistan. However, before turning to the solution that Jinnah worked out to salvage his position, it would be necessary to consider Wavell's recipe to block the Congress Party.

On 30 May 1946, after the Cabinet Mission plan had run into difficulties, Wavell submitted a memorandum to the mission, which, *inter alia*, made the following points:

> It is going to be almost impossible to obtain Hindu–Muslim cooperation.... We should try and secure an orderly withdrawal but not necessarily from all India, certainly not from all India at once.... We must at all costs avoid becoming embroiled with both Hindu and Muslim at once.... We should hand over the Hindu Provinces [the Congress-ruled ones] by agreement and as peacefully as possible to Hindu rule, withdrawing our troops, officials and nationals in an orderly manner [into Muslim-majority provinces] and should at the same time support the Muslim Provinces of India against Hindu domination and assist them to work out their own constitution. We should make it quite clear to the Congress [Party] that it would result in the division of India.... This might compel them [the Congress] to come to terms with the Muslim League, i.e., agree to partition.[20]

As for the Indian princely states, he noted:

Kashmir, Baluchistan and the Punjab states would remain within the British sphere of influence in the northwest; Sikkim, Bhutan, Cooch Behar and Manipur, etc., in the northeast...rulers of Hyderabad would undoubtedly remain within the British orbit.[21]

Wavell continued:

It is not suggested that this arrangement should be a permanency...that would amount to a Northern Ireland in India. We should endeavour to bring about union on the best terms possible, and then withdraw altogether.[22] [The last line appears to have been added for the record in deference to Britain's public posture of working for a united India.]

As to the Interim Government, Wavell's memorandum stated:

To give control of all India to a government in which Muslims refused to take part would be very dangerous. It would be likely to lead to grave disorders in the Punjab and Bengal and would be injurious to our whole position in the Muslim world. There is also sure to be in an Interim Government controlled by the Congress a continuous attempt to sap British authority in every possible way. A real coalition government might avoid this, as the Muslims...would not wish British influence to lessen or [be] removed.[23]

Wavell ended by advising that if it proved difficult 'to hold together the Interim Government or the Constituent Assembly', it would be best to fall back on his plan, which he termed 'the Breakdown Plan'.

✫

Field Marshal Claude Auchinleck, the commander-in-chief of the British forces in India, had been asked to report on the repercussions of 'the inclusion of Pakistan in the British Commonwealth [i.e., of remaining linked with the British defence system] while leaving

Hindustan to its own devices and [for Britain] to undertake no responsibility for its defence'. Auchinleck's comments (dated 16 May 1946) were considered by the Cabinet Mission in Delhi on 31 May together along with Wavell's memorandum. Auchinleck dealt with the issue under two heads:

(1) Influence of a British-controlled Pakistan on Hindustan.
(2) The problem of defence of Pakistan.

On (1) the report, *inter alia*, observed:

In theory it might appear that Pakistan under British influence could act as a check to the hostile potentialities of an independent Hindustan. However: it is very doubtful if Pakistan would have the necessary resources in raw materials, industrial production, manpower, and above all requisite space to enable it to become a base for warlike operations against a Hindustan, supported and equipped by a hostile power such as Russia.... It would most certainly not be adequate as a base for operations on a grand scale. As atomic energy develops and weapons of all sorts whether on the sea, on the land, or in the air, improve, depth in defence and adequate space for dispersion...must become increasingly essential in war.... It follows, therefore, that Pakistan, whether it has two zones or the northwest India zone only, will not provide the means by which the British Commonwealth can hope to influence or coerce an independent Hindustan and keep it free of hostile foreign influence so as to ensure the security of our communications through the Indian Ocean area.[24]

On (2) the report stated:

Assuming that it [Pakistan] will absorb or at any rate dominate Kashmir, Pakistan cannot be seriously threatened from the North [Sinkiang] protected as it is by the Himalayas...Pakistan would however be open to attack by land on a large scale from the northwest [Afghanistan] and the southeast [India].[25]

Auchinleck expressed the positive aspect of the creation of Pakistan (as a prospective partner in the Great Game) as follows:

Because here we have Pakistan as a sovereign Muslim State controlling its own destinies, whereas before the real power was Britain, a non-Muslim State and, therefore disliked, suspected and feared by Afghanistan and also Russia. This change of affinities may, it is true, ease the problem of defence of Pakistan's western frontiers.[26]

Auchinleck's conclusion was, however, unambiguous:

If we desire to maintain our power to move freely by sea and air in the Indian Ocean area, which I consider essential to the continued existence of the British Commonwealth, we can do so only by keeping in being a united India which will be a willing member of the Commonwealth, ready to share in its defence to the limit of her resources.[27]

Auchinleck's view that partition would not be of much help to Britain militarily was at odds with Wavell's ideas. Thus, Wavell strongly challenged the commander-in-chief's view at the meeting of the Cabinet Delegation at which Auchinleck was present (but Cripps was absent because of his illness). The record reads:

His Excellency the Viceroy said he did not feel that there were final grounds for rejecting the possibility that we might remain in North-East and North-West India [the proposed Pakistan] for an indefinite period. He was not entirely in agreement with the Commander-in-Chief that Pakistan as part of the Empire receiving British support would be strategically incapable of being defended and of no military advantage to the Empire.[28]

This statement gives away the game. Attlee held the same view with minor reservations, but was unwilling to reveal his hand. To do so would have made it difficult for him to create the circumstances that might have persuaded Nehru and company to give up the northwest, if not the northeast, *of their own volition.* The chiefs of staff in London were also getting impatient with the prime minister's apparent dithering. General Lord Ismay, who had been Churchill's right-hand man during the war and, under Attlee, a member of the Cabinet Secretariat with the duty to liaise with the chiefs of staff, wrote to the PM:

The fact remains however that should India so elect (independence) the chances of obtaining even our minimum requirements are remote, since the Indians will possibly be just as suspicious and jealous of their new-found sovereignty as Egyptians have been.... The Chiefs of Staff do not know what, if anything, can be done to influence the course of events...[29]

Attlee continued to hold his cards close to his chest and to concentrate on wooing the Indian leaders.

With Stafford Cripps laid up, Wavell was able to persuade a harassed secretary of state and Alexander to forward his 'Breakdown Plan' to Attlee. This plan proposed the British evacuation from the Congress Party-controlled provinces to those areas he had marked out for Pakistan. This was done on 3 June 1946. Pethick-Lawrence took the precaution to add that Cripps, from his sick bed, considered the Wavell Plan unworkable. Attlee, who preferred to catch flies with honey instead of vinegar, was bound to find Wavell's approach distasteful. However, he armed himself with the views of the chiefs of staff before replying: 'A Policy of withdrawal into Pakistan' in the way proposed (by Wavell) 'was unacceptable on military grounds', the chiefs opined.[30] Attlee, in his reply to Pethick-Lawrence on 6 June 1946, rejected Wavell's proposal: 'We ourselves get the impression that Muslims and Congress are not anxious to push matters to a certain crisis and that there might be advantage in a short delay'; i.e., the Cabinet Mission might as well return to London.[31]

Wavell's plan depended on London's consent, which was not forthcoming. Jinnah's plan, on the other hand, did not depend on anybody's writ, except the fanaticism that his subordinates could whip up amongst his followers and the prowess of the Muslim

National Guard that had been created. His plan envisaged violence and more violence to intimidate the British Labour Government and the Congress Party leaders.

On 27 July 1946, in Bombay, the Muslim League passed a resolution, revoking its decision to support the Cabinet Mission plan. On this day, Jinnah announced that the League should 'bid goodbye to constitutional methods and take "direct action"'. He added: 'Today we have forged a pistol and are in a position to use it.' Expressing doubts about the British Government's will to adhere to their commitments, he addressed the gathering thus:

> Only the League's direct action could prevent the Congress from hijacking the Constituent Assembly on the basis of its majority, turn it into a sovereign body and attempt a de facto takeover of power.[32]

The sixteenth day of August 1946 was earmarked as 'Direct Action Day'. On this day, Muslims were enjoined to observe a hartal and to organize meetings to explain and propagate the new League resolution. Bengal was the only major Muslim-majority province under the League's control; Calcutta, its capital, was a major city from which Jinnah could effectively make his point, and Huseyn Suhrawardy, its premier, was the League's most unscrupulous leader, who was well suited to launch Jinnah's campaign.

★

The violence that the Muslim League unleashed in Calcutta on 16 August 1946 was a measure of Jinnah's desperation. He wanted to make the point that the Muslim League could not be ignored. Much has been written about the 'great Calcutta killings', in which about 5000 people belonging to both communities were killed and over 20,000 injured. (Here the picture is presented as it appears in British official documents.)

On 22 August 1946, the governor of Bengal, Sir Frederick Burrows, sent a long report to Wavell and Pethick-Lawrence, which amongst other things, says:

The Muslim League meeting at the Ochterlony Monument began at 4 p.m. [on 16 August] though processions of Muslims from all parts of Calcutta had started assembling soon after the midday prayers...the number attending the meeting...about 100,000.... The Chief Minister (Suhrawardy) made a Laodicean speech, of which his audience naturally remembered the hot passages more clearly than the cold. The Central Intelligence Officer and a reliable reporter deputed by the military authorities agree on one most mischievous statement (not reported at all by the Calcutta Police). The version in the former's report is: "He (Suhrawardy) had seen to police and military arrangements who [sic] would not interfere." The version in the latter is "He had been able to restrain the military and police...." The impression an uneducated audience would form of such a statement by the Home Minister (the Chief Minister also held the law and order portfolio) must have been that it was an open invitation to disorder; and in fact many of the listeners started attacking Hindus and looting Hindu shops as soon as they left the meeting.... Short of a direct order from me, there was no way of preventing the Chief Minister from visiting the control room whenever he liked; and I was not prepared to give such an order, as it would clearly have indicated complete lack of faith in him.... I can honestly say that parts of the city on Saturday (17 August) morning were as bad as anything I saw when I was with the Guards on the Somme [Somme, in France, was the scene of a fierce battle between the British and the German armies in July 1916 during the First World War].[33]

Though not mentioned in the governor's report, the British brigadier in charge of law and order in Calcutta, J.P.C. Makinlay, 'had ordered his troops confined to barracks for the day, leaving the city naked for the mobs'.[34]

An English resident of Calcutta sent a report (now in the British archives) on the riots:

It is the unanimous decision of all that the Mohammedans struck the first blow and took many lives before the latter (Hindus) were ready. I can quote the statement of an American Consul who watched the main meeting held in Calcutta from an apartment situated atop the highest building in the city. The movement of lorries carrying the League flags and filled with supporters containing piles of bayonets and sticks as well as stones could be seen from above while they could not be seen from the street level. The horror of the next four days is now known throughout the country.[35]

After the Hindus, reinforced by the Sikhs, who plied all the taxis of Calcutta, struck back, Suhrawardy sought Gandhiji's help. The Mahatma rushed to Calcutta. His threat to fast unto death, unless the killings stopped, had an immediate therapeutic effect. And the storm died down. However, its poison spread to Bihar, which was next door, where the Hindus took the offensive to a much wider area.

Burrows concluded his long report to the viceroy by justifying his stand: 'It was a programme between the rival armies of the Calcutta underworld.... My special responsibility for law and order is not a "discretionary" matter. I had always to consider the susceptibilities of my Ministry.' [36]

The British archives contain a copy of the Muslim League's proclamation for 'Direct Action Day', published on 13 August 1946, which was forwarded to London and to New Delhi from the governor's office. This document leaves little doubt that the governor had received advance notice of the League's intentions. It reads like some Al Qaida abracadabra of more than half a century later. The last paragraph of the League's proclamation states:

It was in Ramzan that the Quran was revealed. It was in Ramzan that the permission for Jehad was granted by Allah. It was in Ramzan that the Battle of Badr, the first open conflict between Islam and Heathenism, was fought and won by 313 Muslims (against 900 in A.D. 634) and again it was in Ramzan that 10,000 Muslims under the Holy Prophet conquered Mecca (in A.D. 630) and established the kingdom of Heaven and commonwealth of Islam in Arabia. The Muslim League is fortunate that it is starting its action in this holy month.[37]

Jinnah was never held responsible by the viceroy for the Calcutta killings. On the contrary, after his visit to Calcutta, Wavell, on 28 August 1946, in his telegram to the secretary of state, exonerated the Muslim League by noting:

Both sides had made preparations, which may or may not have been defensive.[38]

He dismissed Suhrawardy's speech of 16 August as 'foolish'. The lesson Wavell drew from the entire episode was that the Muslim League should be persuaded to enter the Interim Government. In order to enable him to accomplish this, he wanted a definite decision to be handed down by London in favour of Jinnah's position on groupings in the Cabinet Mission plan, namely, that the NWFP and Assam not be given the option to keep out of groups (b) and (c), respectively, before their group constitutions were drawn up.

Thus, Wavell tried to take advantage of the Calcutta killings to implement his own policy. The impact of Calcutta massacres on the ongoing constitutional negotiations will be discussed in the following chapter. But, in any event, the killings enabled Jinnah to convincingly reinforce his contention abroad that Muslims and Hindus could not be expected to coexist in the same country. The question whether they could, in fact, be separated into two distinct compartments in the subcontinent, an equally pertinent question, was swept under the carpet.

Wrote N.P.A. Smith, the director of the Intelligence Bureau, in a memorandum to the viceroy a little later:

Grave communal disorder must not disturb us into action [sic] which would reintroduce anti-British agitation. The latter may produce an inordinately dangerous situation and lead us nowhere. The former is a natural, if ghastly, process tending in its own way to the solution of the Indian problem.[39]

This report was forwarded to London by the viceroy, suggesting that he approved of the director's views.

Notes and References

1. Transfer of Power (TOP) X, S. No. 194.
2. John Grigg (ed.), *Nehru Memorial Lectures: 1966–91* (Oxford University Press, New Delhi, 1991, p. 139).
3. Dean Acheson, *Present at the Creation: My Years at the State Department* (W.W. Norton, New York, 1969, p. 483).
4. CAB/127/143, 75800, Nehru to Cripps, Public Records Office, London.
5. Ibid., Cripps to Nehru.
6. Ibid., Nehru to Cripps.
7. TOP VI, S. No. 796, Para 7.
8. Ibid., S. No. 472.
9. Ibid., S. No. 491.
10. Ibid., S. No. 507.
11. Attlee in the House of Commons, 15 March 1945. Quoted by V.P. Menon, *Transfer of Power in India* (Longman Green, London, 1957, pp. 234–35).
12. Anita Inder Singh, cited in Patrick French, *Liberty or Death: India's Journey to Independence and Division* (HarperCollins, London, 1995, p. 226).
13. Francis Turnbull, CHF, 127/128, Public Records Office London.
14. TOP VII, S. No. 86.
15. Ibid., S. No. 105.
16. Minutes of COS meeting of 12 April 1946, Para 6 (OIC, British Library, London).
17. Quoted in *The Asian Age*, New Delhi, 14 August 1997.
18. US FR 1946, Vol. V, p. 97.
19. Dennis Kux, *Disenchanted Allies* (Oxford University Press, Karachi, 2001, p. 72).
20. TOP VII, S. No. 407.
21. Ibid.
22. Ibid.
23. Ibid.
24. Claude Auchinleck's top-secret note on the strategic implications of Pakistan, GHQ, Delhi, 16 May 1946.
25. Ibid.
26. Ibid.

27. Ibid.
28. TOP VII, S. No. 415, Para 7.
29. COS 1046/8, Para 2 of Lord Ismay's top-secret minute to Attlee, 30 August 1946.
30. TOP VII, S. No. 509, Para 25 of COS Cabinet Papers, 12 June 1946.
31. TOP VII, S. No. 495, Para 9.
32. See V.P. Menon, op. cit., pp. 234–35.
33. TOP VIII, S. No. 197, Paras 7, 8, 9 and 14 (2).
34. M.J. Akbar, *Nehru* (Viking, London, 1981, p. 382).
35. File in Indian Office Records (IOR), L/WS/1/1030, p. 127.
36. TOP VIII, S. No. 197.
37. Ibid., enclosure, Para 6.
38. TOP VIII, S. No. 206, Wavell's report to secretary of state, 28 August 1946.
39. TOP IX, S. No. 304, enclosure.

9

Nehru in the Saddle

On 2 September 1946, Attlee and Cripps succeeded in saddling Jawaharlal Nehru with responsibility. He was made the vice-president of the Viceroy's Executive Council in the Interim Government. The Muslim League did not join it. This council came to be popularly called the 'cabinet' and its vice-president, 'prime minister'. It created a thrill of success amongst the nationalists. Jawaharlal Nehru kept the foreign affairs portfolio with him; Sardar Patel became the home minister.

To Jinnah, this development was ominous; it might have enabled the Congress Party to consolidate its hold on the levers of power as the British power faded. It could not be called a cabinet, he told the press. 'You cannot turn a donkey into an elephant by calling it an elephant.' To some Englishmen it was a deal: in exchange for keeping its followers in check, the Congress Party was given responsibility for a large tranche of the Government of India. The director of the Intelligence Bureau, N.P.A. Smith, looked ahead:

> As I have said for some months, Pakistan is likely to come from "Congresstan" [the acceptance of office by Congress Party].[1]

Attlee would have concurred with Smith's forecast.

On 30 August 1946, Dean Acheson, the assistant secretary of state in the State Department, Washington, exactly on the other side of the globe from Delhi, advised the new president, Harry S. Truman, on developments in India as follows:

The new Cabinet would be composed of outstanding leaders of the principal Indian political party together with representative leaders of certain minority groups. The British plan likewise calls for the convening of a Constituent Assembly in the immediate future which will have authority to complete severance of India from the Empire and Commonwealth if the Indians so desire. Although the second most important Indian political party [the Muslim League] has refused to participate thus far in these developments, it is believed that the new Government will be representative of at least 80 per cent of the Indian people.

It is anticipated that one of the first acts of the new Government will be to request the exchange of fully accredited diplomatic representation between India and the United States.

While the Viceroy will continue legally to have the power of veto until the new constitution comes into effect, we feel that representative Indian leaders capable of speaking in the name of the great majority of the Indian people will now be in effective de facto control of the affairs of India. In view of the violent repercussions which would probably follow a decision by the Viceroy to act contrary to the advice of his new Cabinet on any important issue...we should without hesitation agree to receive an Indian Ambassador and to send an American Ambassador to India.

I should appreciate receiving your views on the subject in order that we may act with a minimum of delay in case the new government would like to have such an exchange effected.[2]

Truman approved of this memorandum on 2 September 1946.

The British Government was not too pleased with the American move. When the American chargé d'affaires informed Sir Paul Patrick of the India Office, London, on 9 September 1946, of his government's readiness to appoint an ambassador to India, Patrick replied:

It would give a certain prestige to Interim Government [and] make Muslims more conciliatory to Congress following this direct evidence that US Government considers Interim Government respectable enough for an exchange of Ambassadors.... US willingness to establish direct diplomatic relations with India might encourage Nehru to take decisions in foreign policy which would meet with British disapproval. Technically Interim Government comes under Government of India, where it will remain until a new Indian constitution is formulated. Therefore, there might still be "Whitehall interference" in decisions of Interim Government, but British Government would make every effort to avoid such interference. Nevertheless subject might be raised by questions in Parliament as to decisions and activities of Interim Government.[3]

When a crisis arose soon after with regard to the convening of the Constituent Assembly and the possibility of the resignation of the Nehru Government loomed large, the British ambassador to the US, Lord Inverchapel (Sir Archibald Kerr), could not help taking a dig at the Americans in a telegram to London: 'To all intent and purposes they [the US] have given HMG a hostage by their possibly premature assumption of full diplomatic relations with the Interim Government, the dissolution of which could leave their faces very red.'[4] Whatever its reservations, the Attlee Government did not hesitate to give its consent to the US proposal. And Henry Grady, a professional diplomat and an assistant undersecretary in the US State Department, was named the ambassador to India. (India followed suit by sending to Washington Asaf Ali, a Congressman of the Muslim faith, who had never visited the USA and whose wife Aruna was a rabid leftist.)

According to the US archives, the first message that Jawaharlal Nehru as 'prime minister' addressed to the US Government was on 20 September 1946. It reads as follows: 'In view of very serious food situation in India which is being aggravated by delay in arrival of promised allotment due to shipping strikes in America, would earnestly request you and through you the labour leaders to permit and arrange for earliest dispatch of food ships to India.'[5] There is no recognition in this message of the United States' policy to support Nehru's Interim Government and the Congress Party position vis-à-vis the Muslim League.

Wavell had bitterly opposed the formation of an executive council without including the representatives of the Muslim League in it. But he had been overruled by London. On 27 August 1946, he made a last desperate attempt to induce Gandhiji and Nehru to accept the Cabinet Mission's grouping formula without reservation. Without such acceptance, he argued, the League was unwilling to enter the Viceroy's Executive Council, which may mean more communal riots. Gandhiji and Nehru rejected Wavell's plea on the ground that Jinnah had to first enter the Constituent Assembly. Attlee was adamant that, whatever the dispute over the Constituent Assembly, the formation of the Interim Government should go through; he wanted a 'Congresstan'. Wavell's entry in his diary on 29 August 1946 reads: 'I had an almost panic-stricken telegram from the Secretary of State to do nothing rash with the Congress',[6] and on 30 August 1946, he noted: 'I had another panic-stricken cable...S of S asking me on no account to do or say anything that might occasion a breach with Congress.'[7] To the last cable, he replied that he would form the government on 2 September 1946, but that 'he did not think a single party government could control India for long without serious trouble arising'. Wavell's view of his secretary of state was not particularly charitable. 'Without Commonwealth backbone', was what Wavell wrote about his secretary of state in his diary.

The Calcutta killings had hastened the Congress leaders' decision to enter the Interim Government. Short of taking up arms, getting into the driver's seat that was being offered appeared to them their best bet. The British invitation to form the Interim Government and the prospect of the early summoning of the Constituent Assembly, in which they held a majority, gave them the feel that they might be able to muddle through to establish a united, free India. Cripps' companionability during his long stay in Delhi, as part of the Cabinet Mission, had encouraged their hopes to the extent of their becoming complacent. Even the down-to-earth Sardar Patel appears to have succumbed. He wrote to a friend on 2 June 1946: 'His [Jinnah's] main demand of Pakistan is buried forever.'[8]

Later, while speaking to a representative of the *Bombay Chronicle* newspaper, on 2 August 1946, Patel compared Pakistan 'to a deflated cycle tube'.[9]

If Nehru was excited by the prospect of acquiring, with British help, the means and the wherewithal to remould India to his heart's desire, Patel's change of heart towards Britain had a political purpose. He had opposed a violent upheaval against British power in 1946, helped to pacify the naval mutineers in Bombay and cooperated with Cripps in the hope of mollifying the British. He had come to feel that the nationalists could not possibly fight Britain and Jinnah at the same time and that the British, who were on their way out, were a better option than the Muslim League, whose fortunes were on the rise. Patel wanted to do exactly what Jinnah feared, that is, to get hold of the levers controlling the executive and constitution-making powers and, with Britain looking the other way, make a united free India a *fait accompli*.

★

A little before he was sacked in early 1947, N.P.A. Smith, the powerful director of the Intelligence Bureau, submitted a note to Wavell. This note gives a flavour of the easy relationship that Patel could establish with his English subordinates, even with those who knew that he wanted them to go, as Smith did:

> I told him [Sardar Patel]...that any attempt to force the Muslim would result, through the disintegration of the police and Army, in the loss of NW India. His reply was that, if I thought that generosity would placate the Muslim Oliver Twist, I did not understand either the Muslim mind or the situation. With which statement I am tempted to agree.[10]

Wavell, who diliked the Congress Party leaders, described the Sardar as follows: 'Patel is more like a leader than any of them, and might become the easiest to do business with.'[11] Whether or not Patel would have succeeded in winning over Britain by merely demonstrating goodwill is problematic. Britain would not so easily give up on Jinnah, who alone could deliver them the strategic prize in the form of northwest India. Moreover, Nehru, as foreign minister, had adopted a stance that was the least likely to lull the British mistrust of the Congress Party. Even so, Patel did succeed, in early 1947, through his intermediary, the reforms commissioner to the viceroy, in limiting the area of India that would secede and, particularly, in preventing the princely states from breaking away.

Wavell's gloom, after the Attlee Government had decided to induct the Congress Party into the Interim Government without the Muslim League, is reflected in an entry in his diary on 20 August 1946:

> Ian Scott usually cheerful and optimistic was very depressing in a talk I had with him out riding this morning. Both he and George [Abell] now seem to be convinced that our only course is to get out of India as soon as possible and leave her to her fate, which will be civil war.[12] [Scott was the deputy private secretary to the viceroy and Abell private secretary to the viceroy.]

It was in this frame of mind that Wavell revived his 'Breakdown Plan', which he had submitted to the Cabinet Mission on 30 May 1946, without any result. This plan would, in one stroke, sweep away the Cabinet Mission's proposed Nehru Government, the Constituent Assembly, and indeed the whole structure raised by the Cabinet Mission. This plan would also permit Britain to maintain its hold on the strategic areas of both the northeast and northwest in the immediate future, while retreating from the rest of British India, and would force the Congress Party to accept Pakistan as a *fait accompli*. On 10 August 1946, he had put down, in a note, the following ingredients of his plan, which concluded with the remark: '[The] Muslim League would presumably welcome the Plan':

(1) Britain would hand over Congress-majority provinces, i.e., Bombay, Madras, Orissa, Central Provinces, Bihar and United Provinces to the Congress Working Committee.

(2) Present constitution and control would be maintained in the NWFP, Punjab, Sind, Bengal, Assam, the Chief

Commissioner's Province of Delhi and the Agency of British Baluchistan (all except Delhi being claimed for Pakistan).

(3) HMG will undertake responsibility for defence of NW and NE India, and will, by agreement, assist Hindustan in external defence, if desired.

(4) The exercise of Paramountcy over the [Princely] States that lie within the boundaries of Hindustan will be relinquished by the Crown. Paramountcy will continue with those States which lie within the boundaries of NW and NE India still remaining under British control.[13]

A detailed plan of action was then drawn up on the basis of this note, with some amendments made in order to cloak the latent Pakistan scheme in it. The plan was to be put into effect as soon as there was a breakdown in the negotiations, and when Nehru and company tried to either unilaterally declare independence or launch a massive agitation.

While forwarding his plan to London, Wavell added a few comments: 'On administrative grounds we could not govern the whole of India for more than a year and half from now' and 'in most provinces they [the constitutional powers of the governor] can now only be enforced to a limited degree by persuasion and bluff.'[14] He also emphasized that a government at the Centre, exclusively in the hands of the Congress Party, and any attempt to run the Constituent Assembly without the Muslim League, would result in serious Hindu–Muslim clashes. He highlighted the Calcutta tragedy as an example of what could happen. He added that it would be impossible to maintain the integrity of the Army if the main political parties were to instigate communal war.

Wavell's plan was received with shock and dismay in London. Attlee's reaction can be summed up in his following comment: 'While it is reasonable for the Viceroy to want to have a breakdown plan, it is unreasonable of him to expect us to envisage failure'[15] (i.e., failure of his own policy, unrevealed to the viceroy). Rebuffed, Wavell, nevertheless, persevered: 'We shall be without power to control events within eighteen months and delay would increase dependence on the hostile Congress Party.' He argued: 'Our present position in India was analogous to that of a military force compelled to withdraw in the face of superior numbers.... As a military commander [he knew] something about retreats.'[16] Wavell then tried to sweeten the pill for Whitehall:

My proposals do provide for British control of the vulnerable North-Western and North-Eastern frontiers of India for a certain period.[17]

Attlee was in favour of partitioning India but with the Congress Party's concurrence and not by way of an award. Whereas several British historians and political analysts have criticized Attlee's India policy as one of appeasing the Congress Party, the fact is that, by creating 'Congresstan', he not only succeeded, the following year, admittedly under a different viceroy, in placing the responsibility for the partition of India squarely on Indian shoulders, but also in inducing the Congress Party to accept independence as a British dominion (i.e., as a member of the British Commonwealth).

The nationalists' only hope of accomplishing their goal of a united India was if they could hold the reins of government firmly in their hands and exclude Jinnah from entering it. This would encourage those Muslim leaders, opposed to Jinnah, to come to the forefront and thus weaken his hold over the Muslims. Wavell understood this, but had failed to obtain HMG's support to block the Congress Party. He now turned to achieving his goal through his 'prime minister', Nehru! Wavell did not like Nehru – Harrow boys were not supposed to act so emotional – nor could he switch on charm from one minute to another as his successor (Louis Mountbatten) and indeed even his predecessor (Linlithgow) could, though he did gift Nehru, in jail (in 1943), the anthology of poems he had compiled, titled *Other Men's Flowers*.

As soon as Nehru was sworn in as 'prime minister' on 2 September 1946, Wavell started to press him to invite the Muslim League to enter the Interim Government 'in the interest of communal peace and harmony', a sentiment that he knew was so dear to the staunchly secular Nehru. The record shows that he spoke to Nehru on 11, 16, 26 and 27 September on this subject, but that Nehru stood firm, demanding that Jinnah first enter the Constituent Assembly to prove his acceptance of the Cabinet Mission plan; in other words, of a unitary solution. But then on 2 October 1946, unexpectedly, Nehru threw in the towel and gave an answer to Wavell that could be interpreted as his acquiescence with the viceroy approaching Jinnah on this subject. 'Well this man [Wavell] had been pestering me to start talks with Jinnah. A few days ago I told him in sheer exasperation that if he was so keen to talk to Mr Jinnah he could do so. The next morning he [Wavell] started negotiations with Jinnah', Nehru told Sudhir Ghose, a young confidant of Gandhiji. 'Why did you not tell the Viceroy that if he was going to interfere with your responsibility he could have your resignation?' asked Ghose. In this context, Ghose has written: 'Nehru looked tired, worried and unhappy and replied, "Well, I have told you all I know about it".'[18] Wavell's version of the incident is as follows: 'N [Nehru]...tried to minimize the danger of communal trouble (in case the League was kept out) and said that the police could easily suppress it. I firmly disabused him of this idea. In the end, he said: "If you want to see Jinnah I can't prevent you."'[19]

H.V. Hodson, the former reforms commissioner to the viceroy, notes:

> Had they [the Congress leaders] threatened to resign rather than take in the Muslim League until it had accepted the Cabinet Mission Plan and agreed to take part in the Constituent Assembly, they would have forced the Viceroy either to abandon his negotiations with Mr Jinnah or to substitute the League for the Congress in office, or to return to a nominated quasi-official government.[20]

As it happened, Wavell invited the Muslim League to join the Viceroy's Executive Council without either insisting that its members agree to enter the Constituent Assembly or even to call off their 'direct action' campaign.

The League's entry into the Interim Government signified a great victory for Jinnah and the viceroy and a major debacle for the Congress Party. Jinnah and his party leaders had been taken into the government without compromising his stand: the League could now proceed to sabotage the working of the Nehru Government from the inside and once again prove that the parting of ways maybe the best for all. This indeed they successfully accomplished within a few months after their men, led by Liaqat Ali Khan, entered the Viceroy's Executive Council. Liaqat Ali Khan was given the finance portfolio; Jinnah did not join.

A couple of months earlier, on 29 July 1946, Sardar Patel had written to D.P. Mishra, the senior Congress leader in the Central Provinces, as follows:

> He [Nehru] often acts with child-like innocence.... He has done many things recently which [have] caused us great embarrassment...[his] acts of emotional insanity...put tremendous strain on us to set matters right. But, in spite of his innocent indiscretions, he [has] unparalleled enthusiasm and a burning passion for freedom which makes him restless and drives him to a pitch of impatience where he forgets himself.[21]

Wavell's contention that a coalition government would prevent communal violence proved totally wrong; the Muslim League's entry into the government merely emboldened this party to increase political pressure by organizing riots. In the Noakhali and Tripura districts of East Bengal, 'direct action' was launched in November 1946 after the formation of the coalition government. 'There was evidence that this was an organized operation and not a spontaneous combustion of individual communal hatred,'[22] has written a British observer, who was close to the scene. Gandhiji roamed the affected countryside on foot, which had a calming effect. Then the Hindus in the neighbouring Bihar province once again retaliated and terrible massacres followed, Nehru wanting the ravaging Hindu mobs to be bombed. The riots were finally quelled by the Army. Irrespective of the extent of the suffering caused to the people, Jinnah's point had again been made for all to observe in England, India and elsewhere: Hindus and Muslims were best separated.

★

With the installation of the Muslim League ministers in the Delhi Secretariat, senior civil servants started to get communally divided, and the nucleus of a Pakistan civil service began to form. Liaqat Ali Khan, the finance minister, in his first budget imposed a tax of 25 per cent on all profits over £1200 (roughly translated to the present rate of exchange) on capital gains. Congress ministers protested that the finance minister's aim was to dissipate public confidence in the government. Those who were hit by the tax were businessmen, who, by and large, financed the nationalists.

Despite serious internal problems, Nehru devoted an extraordinary amount of time to foreign affairs. He took a keen interest in the Indian initiatives in the UN on apartheid and decolonization, set afoot plans to organize a meeting of Asian leaders in Delhi by the following summer under the slogan 'Asia for the Asians' and established diplomatic ties with a number of countries, selecting the ambassadors and even their staff himself.

The Indian delegation to the UN General Assembly of September–December 1946 was headed by Nehru's sister, Vijayalakshmi Pandit. The activism displayed by the delegation burst like fireworks over the assembly, heralding the entry of a new star on the international horizon. Vijayalakshmi's success in bringing the apartheid issue before the assembly despite stiff opposition from the British and the European powers on the grounds that this was an internal matter of South Africa, a sovereign state, was hailed in India as a great diplomatic victory. It raised India's profile with the subject people of Africa and Asia. However, the most important issue that faced India at that time was negotiations for its own emergence as an independent and united country and not apartheid, however heinous and despicable that system might have been. South Africa was an old ally of Britain and that was not the most appropriate moment to raise this issue at the UN and embarrass Britain. (India's entry into the UN, with a lot of fanfare, was in contrast to that of China to the same body many years later. The Chinese delegation had been forbidden by Beijing, during the first few years, from taking any initiatives in the General Assembly or from appearing to be in the forefront of events.)

Soon after the General Assembly session ended, a Reuters news item appeared in the Indian press that John Foster Dulles (the future secretary of state of the USA), who had been a delegate at the UN that year, had alleged at a dinner speech (at the National Publishers' Association) that communists appeared to be exercising influence over India's Interim Government. Nehru, in an official statement to the press, rebutted the allegation, expressing his surprise and also regret if the report was correct. Before the matter snowballed further, General George Marshall, the new US secretary of state, just returned from China, intervened. He asked the US chargé d'affaires, George Merrell, in Delhi to hand over to Nehru in person a clarification that Dulles' speech was completely unofficial and that the US Government had no such misconceptions about Indian policy. Marshall also stated: 'Dulles may have obtained the impression from talking to some Indian delegates at the General Assembly.' Marshall informed Merrell for his own background: 'We are hoping to let Dulles have a more complete picture of Indian situation.'[23] It was revealed later that Dulles had formed his impression after talking to Krishna Menon, a member of the Indian delegation. As the years went by, the UN became a fertile forum for the origination of misunderstandings between India and other countries, chiefly Western ones, but on this first occasion in 1946 the Americans had acted swiftly to avoid rancour.

Soon after Nehru took over the reins of the Interim Government, Lord Ismay wrote to Prime Minister Attlee on 20 September 1946: 'The Chiefs of Staff...would like to suggest for your consideration...the necessity to do everything possible to retain India within the Commonwealth'[24] (i.e., within the British defence orbit). On 8 September 1946, the British chiefs of staff had submitted a report entitled 'The Strategic Value of India to the British Commonwealth'. This report basically reiterated the earlier comments that the manpower and territory of India were indispensable for the defence of the British Commonwealth. The main points made in the report may be summarized as follows:

(1) No potentially hostile power should be permitted to establish bases in the Indian Ocean area.
(2) The oil from the Persian Gulf is essential to the British Commonwealth and its safe passage must be ensured.

(3) If India became dominated by Russia with powerful air forces...we should have to abandon our command of the Persian Gulf and the northern Indian Ocean routes.

(4) India is an essential link in our Imperial strategic plan.

(5) [India is also important] because with the coming of atomic warfare there is increased necessity for space and India has this space.

(6) For the Commonwealth to undertake military operations on a large scale in the Far East, India is the only suitable base.

(7) From a military point of view, one of India's most important assets is an almost inexhaustible supply of manpower.

(8) [Britain should] not give up Andaman and Nicobar Islands which should be developed as an outpost to Burma and Malay [which were still then under British rule].[25]

A few days after the service chiefs' assessment was finalized, Field Marshal Auchinleck alerted General Rupert Mayne in London that 'from a note he had received from Pt. [Pandit] Nehru on the question of Indian troops overseas he anticipated that an early demand for their withdrawal from outside India would be made'.[26] At that time Indian forces were stationed in Iraq, Burma, Malay, Hong Kong and Japan and provided the bulk of the administrative organization in South-east Asia Command (SEAC). This information put the chiefs of staff in London in difficulty. Pethick-Lawrence wired Wavell on 26 September 1946: 'Demand of your Interim Government for the withdrawal to India of all the Indian forces outside India...would result practically in a breakdown in Southeast Asia Command and a very serious situation in the Middle East'. He also endorsed the chiefs of staff's recommendation that every effort be made 'to dissuade the Interim Government from pressing such a demand'.[27] Nehru's orders to pull back troops remained in force.

In September 1946, Nehru sent Krishna Menon to meet Vyacheslav Molotov, the Soviet foreign minister. Menon handed over to Molotov a letter from Nehru and conveyed India's earnest desire to establish friendly relations with the USSR. Menon stepped beyond his brief. He also explored the possibility of the Soviets sending a team of military experts to India. This initiative did not meet with the approval of Patel and some other Congress Party leaders. The British were still responsible for the policies followed by the Interim Government; but Nehru did not consult them. India Office, at this stage, attempted to warn (or 'educate') the chiefs of staff about the realities of the Indian scene. On 31 October 1946 the permanent undersecretary at the India Office, Sir David Monteath, wrote to Major General Sir Leslie Hollis, chief staff officer to the minister of defence, as follows:

I must emphasize that it would be unwise to place reliance on the prospect of India as a whole being willing to remain in the British Commonwealth. I say "as a whole" because if India were to split up into two or more parts, Muslim areas and the [Princely] States would probably be anxious to remain in the Commonwealth...Pt. Nehru's speeches on the policy of the new Interim Government since he took office have all emphasized their intention in the field of foreign policy, to maintain an independent attitude and to avoid becoming involved with any major bloc [which was bound to affect military collaboration with India].[28]

The views of the India Office can be gleaned from the following draft paper it submitted to the cabinet:

It should be noted that the advantages which Chiefs of Staff expect to get from having India within the Commonwealth [meaning defence cooperation under its umbrella] are not obtained in fact unless India is a *willing and cooperative member* [italics in the original].... India may prove to be a very unreliable and elusive ally.... There is a strong tradition of pacifism in Hindu India of which Mr Gandhi is only an exemplary.... In time of war she is likely to maintain neutrality.[29]

The British Foreign Office also took alarm. In a joint memorandum with the India Office, it expressed concern to the cabinet on India's foreign policy during the period of the Interim Government. The memorandum states: 'Many of the leaders of the Congress Party, and Pt. Nehru in particular, have well-defined views on this intriguing brand of administration, with a lack of experience in the field, and an impatience to carry out ideas formed in conditions of irresponsibility...without regard for [their] wider implications.' The memorandum continues: 'In the UN General Assembly of 1946 (that started in September) clashes between the British and the Indians had already occurred on the question of apartheid in South Africa and on colonial matters in the UN Trusteeship Council. India might offer public support to the Indonesians against the Dutch and to Vietnam against the French. It should not be forgotten that the independence movement in Burma, Malay and Ceylon might equally be supported by Indian political leaders and India might demand the return of Portuguese and French possessions.'[30]

On British interests in the Middle East, the memo observes:

> The magnitude and character of the interest of HMG on the Arab shore of the Persian Gulf (referring mainly to the protection of oil supplies and development of oil resources and air and sea communications of increasing strategic importance as Russian pressure on Persia becomes intensified) make it necessary that the charge of these interests should be *in reliable hands* [italics added] and under HMG's direct control. We must not risk any Indian interference with our essential interests in the area.[31]

What were to be these 'reliable hands' if India would not play the Great Game?

The British Government appointed Sir Terence Shone as the high commissioner in Delhi. He reached India on 19 November 1946. The first reports of the high commissioner confirmed the worst fears of Whitehall on the direction that the new government's foreign policy was taking. He highlighted the strong concern in the Congress Party circles with regard to the French action in Indo–China and on the nationalists' view that 'Asia was for the Asians'. He also reported that Indians were generally 'underestimating' the communist strength and the Soviet machinations in Asia. It was Shone who first warned Whitehall that 'the Congress Party was planning to draft a constitution that would provide for an independent sovereign republic'. This would mean the end of the British hope to coordinate defence and foreign policies with an independent India under the umbrella of the British Commonwealth, as they did with Australia, Canada and South Africa.

All these developments were a far cry from the British Foreign Office expectations on foreign policy that an independent India would pursue. A memorandum prepared by the Foreign Office earlier in the year (1946) had stated:

> India will continue to be dependent upon the United Kingdom for defence, and will follow the United Kingdom's lead on all major issues of foreign policy…India is likely to become more conscious of herself as the centre of a zone…and may be expected in practice to devote equally close attention to her Eastern as to her Western and Northern neighbours…. A self-governing India within the Commonwealth may well wish to take the lead in Asia and to assume a more important role than China…India will probably take an ever-increasing interest in the welfare of her nationals living outside India…India's foreign policy will be conducted chiefly in terms of her dealings with her smaller neighbours. Fundamentally, her overriding interest…should be strategic, a concern that the small countries on her perimeter should be "buffer States", areas which must not be allowed to fall into the hands of any hostile or potentially hostile Power: but it seems somewhat rash to assert that strategic considerations will necessarily be the decisive factor in determining Indian policy.[32]

That the British Foreign Office view was getting through to the Labour Government foreign secretary, Ernest Bevin, a former trade union leader and powerful member of Attlee's Government is clear from his statement to the Labour Party conference at Margate after the partition plan had been announced in June 1947 to the effect that this would help to strengthen the British position in the Middle East.

★

As soon as he had formed his government, Nehru began planning a visit to the North West Frontier Province, which came under his charge as minister of external affairs. The NWFP was divided into two parts, the settled districts and the tribal belt area. In the former, which included cities such as Peshawar, the Pathans had been brought under direct British administration. In the latter, lay mountain tracts along the border with Afghanistan, which were inhabited by nomadic Pathan tribes. These areas were controlled indirectly by a 'carrot-and-stick policy' – the carrot being in the form of large annual subsidies* to the tribal Maliks or leaders and the stick being in the form of punitive expeditions by British forces to quell sedition or rebellion or raids in the settled areas for loot. The British maintained a cadre of officers with great knowledge of the tribal people and their leaders who, as political agents, were posted in the tribal belt to deal with them.

The NWFP and Baluchistan (to its south) were brought under British control in 1880 after the second Afghan war, when certain Afghan tribal areas were wrested from Afghanistan, which brought British-controlled territories to within 50 miles of Kabul. Thereafter, in 1893 the Indo–Afghan frontier was drawn up. This move served to divide the major Afghan tribes and bring impenetrable rugged Afghan territory under British control. Kabul never accepted this boundary, called the Durand line. These tribes remained a permanent thorn in the British flesh, requiring over ten thousand troops to be posted in the area to control them.

'As long as your government is strong and in peace, you will be able to keep them quiet by a strong hand, but if any time a foreign enemy appears on the boundaries of India these frontier tribes will be your worst enemies',[33] was the warning given by Abd-ur Rehman, the Amir of Kabul, to Lord Lansdowne (George Granville), the viceroy of India.

Fixing the Indo–Afghan border, however, yielded one advantage. It calmed the Russian anxiety that Britain would continue to extend its territory further west, i.e., towards Russia, and cooled the Great

---

* Rs 30 million annually, equivalent to Rs 1500 million at present or about $30 million dollars.

Game. Under the Anglo–Russian convention of 1907, Afghanistan became a buffer between the two mightiest empires in Asia, its boundary recognized by each other though not by Afghanistan. (The Durand line has not been recognized by Afghanistan to this day.) The northwest frontier, stretching from the Pamirs in the north to the Arabian Sea to the south, was by far the most important of the land boundaries of India. It was the only land frontier from which India could be invaded in strength because further north and east the wall of the high Himalayas (abode of snow) stretched from Afghanistan to Burma. Over thirty major invasions had taken place from this direction over the last two thousand-odd years.

The Pathan was always trying to break out from whatever political control that he may have been subjected to and had made allies with those who were trying to unseat the British, i.e., the Congress Party. The NWFP was 95 per cent Muslim, where the communal division could not be exploited, as in other parts of the country. In fact, after Jinnah rejuvenated the Muslim League from 1937 onwards, the Pathans saw him and his party as stooges of the British. As explained in Chapter 3, Gandhiji had offered the Congress Party's support to the Khilafat Movement. This move helped to endear the Congress Party to the Pathan frontier tribes. From the 1930s, as agitation against the British for self-rule intensified all over India under Mahatma Gandhi's leadership, many Pathan tribes, under the leadership of Khan Abdul Ghaffar Khan, popularly called the 'Frontier Gandhi', saw the possibility of overthrowing the British. In the 1936 general election held under the 1935 Act, which had granted considerable provincial autonomy, the Congress Party beat the Muslim League hands down all over the NWFP.

The Congress Ministry in the NWFP resigned in October 1939 in pursuance of the party's policy of non-cooperation with the British war effort. This situation created a power vacuum in the region. Soon after, i.e., in early 1940, Jinnah announced his scheme for the creation of a separate independent Islamic state in the subcontinent at British withdrawal. This announcement offered the Pathans the choice between India and an Islamic state and introduced a communal factor in the province's politics. Even so, in the general elections of 1945, which were primarily fought on the issue of

Pakistan, the Congress Party won thirty seats as against seventeen captured by the Muslim League. Consequently, a Congress Ministry headed by Dr Khan Sahib was returned to power once again. A former doctor in the British Indian Army, he was strongly opposed to mixing religion with politics. He had an English wife.

★

In March 1946, Wavell posted Sir Olaf Caroe, a highly knowledgeable officer on frontier affairs (whom we have already met in Chapter 1), as governor of the NWFP. Caroe was a strategic thinker like his chief. His first concern was to preserve the NWFP's half-a-century-old defence connection with Britain, so that the 'lengthening shadows from the north' (of Russia), as he put it, did not reach the 'wells of power' (the oil wells of the Persian Gulf) nor cast a shadow over Afghanistan. He preferred an independent entity in the northwest of India, which would remain linked to Britain and from where London could also influence events in Afghanistan. The Post-Hostilities Staff of Churchill's cabinet in 1945 had envisaged the possibility of detaching Baluchistan to maintain military bases there, in Quetta, the area of the Bolan Pass, and along the sea coast near the entry to the Persian Gulf. Why could not the same be done with the NWFP? The alternative was that the area be placed in the new Islamic state whose leaders would be more cooperative with Britain on matters of mutual defence against Soviet designs than those of the Indian National Congress Party.

If Caroe did use his political and intelligence officers to sway the tribes, many of whose leaders he personally knew, to back the Muslim League in 1946, as claimed by the Khan brothers and their supporters, he was greatly helped in this activity by the developing situation. As the Pathans became aware that the British were leaving, their wariness started to turn against those whose rule would follow. The Muslim League, in the circumstances, was able to make out that, after the British went, it would not be the Khans but non-Muslims from the plains of India who would rule over them. And the Pathans were least interested in the substitution of the British Raj by a Hindu Raj. The fact that all this propaganda had not, by

1946, appreciably swayed the Pathans is clear from the results of the elections for the Constituent Assembly held in July that year. In these elections, the Indian National Congress Party bagged three of the four seats allotted to the province.

The Congress Party for its part was banking on frustrating the Pakistan scheme by denying the NWFP to Jinnah. When Nehru, who held the charge of tribal affairs, decided to visit the NWFP, Patel and Maulana Azad, the Congress Party president, advised him against doing so. Patel and Azad wanted Ghaffar Khan, Dr Khan Sahib, the chief minister of the province, and their Pathan supporters, to handle the situation. But Nehru, with memories of the hero's welcome he had received on his last visit to the NWFP in 1935, did not heed their advice. His natural optimism, the belief that the Pathans were with the Congress Party for ideological reasons and his inclination to discount the power of religion over people led him to grossly misjudge the situation. General Frederick Roberts' advice (given in the nineteenth century) that the 'less they see us, less they will dislike us', would be anathema to him. How could someone as concerned with the welfare and uplift of the tribes as himself not be popular with them?

As he landed in Peshawar, he was greeted by a large and unfriendly crowd, for which demonstration, rightly or wrongly, Ghaffar Khan publicly blamed the governor and his officers. The next day, at Wazirstan, Miranshah and Razmak, Nehru received an extremely hostile reception. This was the territory dominated by the important Mahsud tribe. According to the resident of Wazirstan, K.C. Packmans: 'Pt. Nehru completely lost all dignity and his temper and commenced shouting at the Jirga [tribal assembly].'[34] Caroe's report to Wavell said: 'What they [the tribal leaders] particularly disliked was talk of a regime of love coupled with an arrogant loss of temper.'[35] However, a few Mahsud tribesmen did meet and welcome the Indian leader. On the following days, for his other visits, notwithstanding warnings of hostile demonstrations, Nehru decided to make the journey by road. On the way back from the Khyber Pass, which is in Afridi territory, stones were hurled at his car at Landikotal and the Khyber Rifles escort had to open fire to disperse the mob. At Malakand, the stone throwing bruised Nehru's ear and chin and injured Ghaffar Khan and the chief minister. Again firing had to be resorted to in order to stop the attack, which could have cost Nehru his life. However, at Sardaryah, Ghaffar Khan's 'ashram', the Congress Party supporters rallied in large numbers and kept the Muslim League tribesmen at bay.

B.M. Segal, a former resident of Mardan in the NWFP and now over ninety years old, lives in Delhi. He told me that on his way back from the disastrous trip to Malakand, Nehru stopped to have refreshments at his house. While there, Nehru decided to make an unscheduled trip to meet the Baloch tribe, who welcomed him with open arms. Segal, by this episode, sought to convey that only in those areas on Nehru's predetermined schedule could the authorities organize hostile demonstrations. Segal, however, admitted that the tide was gradually turning against the Congress Party and was swinging in favour of Pathan independence or Pakistan. The tide, however, he felt, would not have risen sufficiently to sweep away the Congress' hold on the tribes and the rest of the NWFP in the ten months more that the British stayed on in India.

Caroe reported to Wavell on 23 October 1946 on Nehru's visit: 'All these demonstrations were organized by the [Muslim] League.... As soon as it became known that Nehru was coming to the frontier the League decided to intensify the propaganda among the tribes and the Mullah of Manki went on a tour in the Malakand protected area and in Jamrud in Khyber, the tour being timed just to precede Nehru's arrival. There is no doubt that at those meetings a good deal of fanaticism was stirred up...'[36] The governor justified his own inaction to prevent the above propaganda as follows:

> Given the fact that Nehru's tour was obviously intended to push the Congress cause, it would have been wrong to put active restraint against the League's propagandists going into tribal territory.... Roughly the position is that we have told the tribes that for the time being, power is with Nehru and the tribes have told Nehru that they will have none of him...[to Caroe] Nehru's visit more than anything else made partition inevitable.[37]

When Nehru met Caroe before flying back to Delhi, he complained against the political agents in Khyber and Malakand for their partisan behaviour. (The viceroy, despite Caroe's protests, later instituted an investigation to probe the behaviour of Sheikh Mahbub, the political agent of Malakand.) Nehru advised Caroe that the stranglehold of the Maliks over the tribes should be broken and education, democracy and economic development should be encouraged in tribal areas. Caroe replied as follows: 'If he [Nehru] had gone round by himself quietly and without losing his temper and told the tribes that he was their guest he would have been politely received.'[38] To Wavell, he wrote: 'This politician of worldwide repute is entirely without any element of statesmanship and that matters such as timing, adjustment, a quiet approach and a decision after weighing a great issue are beyond his ken. He showed courage, but it was better described as bravado with something feminine in its composition.'[39] Nehru, by nature, was not a vindictive man. When he started to pressurize the viceroy to remove Caroe, it was only to change the policy of dependence on the Maliks and not because Caroe had lectured him.

Nehru showed great personal courage during this trip. Caroe's assessment that Nehru's visit decisively helped the cause of Pakistan was not true. (The story of how the NWFP became a part of Pakistan is taken up in the next chapter.) Soon after Nehru's visit, Wavell himself went to the NWFP. There, he assured a tribal Jirga that after the British withdrawal their territories would be returned to them. This was seen as a stratagem to mobilize opinion in favour of a fresh election in the NWFP in order to bypass the elected representatives of the province who were willing to take part in the All-India Constituent Assembly.

*

The formation of the Interim Government had been an important development, but the summoning of the Constituent Assembly that would write the constitution of a free India was being delayed. For Jinnah to relent on the plan he had so assiduously negotiated with the Cabinet Mission and now agree that the provinces placed in groups (b) and (c) be given the option to join these groups or not, as the Congress Party wanted, would be akin to committing political hara-kiri. Such a step would dash all hopes of achieving, through the Cabinet Mission plan, after the ten-year period, the goal of Pakistan. Further, once it became known that the British had stopped supporting his intransigence, Jinnah's constituency would shrink, particularly in the Muslim-majority provinces of the Punjab, Sind and the NWFP, where the cry of 'Islam in danger' evoked little response and amongst Bengali Muslims for whom the call of the *quam* (universal Islamic fraternity) was muted by inherent Bengali nationalism. A crucial question was: why had the Congress Party gone along with a plan that placed the pro-Congress NWFP and Assam in the 'nascent' Pakistan groups? From a letter Patel wrote to Cripps (quoted later in this chapter) it would appear that Cripps, in his anxiety to rope in the Congress leaders into the Viceroy's Executive Council, had given them some verbal reassurances to the effect that the 'provincial option' idea would be respected. However, in view of the Congress Party's leaders imprecision in negotiating and, at that moment, their impatience to get into the saddle, nothing can be said for certain.

Wavell had advised London that the Constituent Assembly could not be summoned till the HMG had clarified the Cabinet Mission's intention about the affiliation of provinces in groups (b) and (c) since the constitution would have to be drafted accordingly. However, Attlee and Cripps were not ready at this stage to give a clarification on this disputed matter because it would perforce have to be in favour of Jinnah's contention, which might provoke the Congress Party to resign from the Interim Government. Such a development would wreck their policy to continue to soften Nehru and Patel by allowing them to exercise real power in the Interim Government. Even more importantly, the resentment against continued British rule in India was rising, as detailed in Chapter 7. It was therefore absolutely necessary to keep the Congress Party leaders as part of the Interim Government in order to curb their potential for mischief from the outside.

★

Elections had been completed in July 1946 for the 296 assembly seats assigned to the British Indian provinces. The Muslim League had won an impressive seventy-three seats, out of the seventy-eight allotted exclusively to the Muslims under the prevalent 'separate electorates' system. But, nevertheless, the assembly would be dominated by the Congress Party. Even if the ninety-three representatives of the Indian princely states joined the Muslim League, the Congress Party would still have a majority. (The precise method of electing the ninety-three representatives from the princely states had not by then been settled.)

On 18 November 1946, George Abell, the private secretary to the viceroy, met Liaqat Ali Khan, Jinnah's second in command, and reported his views on the summoning of the Constituent Assembly to Wavell as follows: 'When I explained to him that the Viceroy could not continue to give assistance to the Muslim League point of view indefinitely', Liaqat Ali Khan was quite blunt in his response: 'The League could not possibly enter the Constituent Assembly unless HMG themselves guarantee what they said about the group constitutions.' Abell adds: 'From what Liaqat said the League could not afford to let the communal feeling in the country die down. They require this communal feeling as a proof of their case for Pakistan.'[40]

On the other hand, the pressure by the Congress Party leaders and behind the scenes by the Americans, for the long overdue summoning of the Constituent Assembly, could not be indefinitely ignored. Consequently, the opening of the assembly was fixed for 9 December 1946. In the circumstances, Attlee had to take the risk of giving a clarification on the grouping provision but thought it might be best to discuss the issue in a conference before making his official statement and thus soften the blow for the Congress Party as far as possible. The upshot was that he invited the Congress and the Muslim League leaders as well as Baldev Singh, to represent the Sikhs, to London for a conference from 2 to 6 December 1946, just before the scheduled opening of the Constituent Assembly. Patel argued vehemently against participating in this conference after realizing what its real aim was and he himself refused to go.

The conference could not reconcile the irreconcilable even though an effort was made to fudge the disputed issue by proposing that the Constituent Assembly, after the Muslim League had entered it, might refer this matter to the Federal Court. Jinnah smartly shot down this suggestion by stating that no one could better clarify the issue than the authors of the plan themselves. The British clarification on the grouping controversy given on 6 December said:

> The Cabinet Mission had throughout maintained the view that decisions of sections in the absence of agreement to the contrary, be taken by simple majority vote of representatives of the sections (and not by majority votes of representatives of individual provinces)...[41]

The British statement created a great furore in India, which has been reflected in a letter written by Patel to Cripps on 15 December 1946; however, the Nehru Cabinet did not resign from the Viceroy's Executive Council:

> I do not know whether there is realization of the amount of mischief that has been done by the statement [of 6 December]...the sense of faith and confidence about the sincerity of Britain that was created by our settlement is fast being dissipated.... What can we do to satisfy the Sikhs who have admittedly been unjustly treated. If they [the Muslim League] frame the constitution of [non-Muslim] Assam in such a way as to make Assam's opting out [separating from Bengal] impossible what is the remedy in your statement? All of us feel that there has been a betrayal...[42]

Nehru's frustration was apparent from the fact that immediately on his return from London, on the day of the opening of the Constituent Assembly, i.e., on 9 December, he introduced a resolution, which included a declaration that on achieving independence India would become an 'Independent Sovereign Republic'. The resolution was called 'the Objectives Resolution', which he described as 'an oath, which we mean to keep'. It began as follows:

> This Constituent Assembly declares its firm and solemn resolve to proclaim India as an Independent Sovereign Republic and to draw up for her future governance a constitution...

Penderel Moon's understatement on this development catches the official British reaction: 'This was not a very tactful move in the absence of the representatives of two important parties, the League and the Princes, both of whom might be expected to say something on the subject.'[43] The powerful British establishment in India, still manning all the senior posts in the civil services and armed forces and already hostile to the Congress – 'the Hindu Party', the enemy – interpreted this resolution as a slap on the face of the Empire. In England, it led to a further warming of British sentiment towards the Muslim League and Jinnah. The British are the most practical and pragmatic of people. Yet, as said in *Hamlet*: 'Give me that man that is not passion's slave.' The romance of the Empire had entered the British soul. Since the nationalists had opted for a negotiated solution (instead of a combative one) from 1946 onwards, the key lay in tempering the British wrench from Empire. That Nehru's move was not properly thought out or coordinated with the other Congress Party leaders is clear from the fact that three weeks later, V.P. Menon, the reforms commissioner, discussed with Patel a different course i.e., the possibility of India becoming independent as a dominion.

This discussion marked an important development. It helped in moulding the course of the Congress Party's future policy. Menon argued with Patel that in a divided India

...the Central Government would be strong, united and effective, i.e., able to withstand the centrifugal tendencies all too apparent at the moment and enable the Constituent Assembly to frame a truly democratic constitution unhampered by any communal considerations.... If we agree to partition Jinnah obviously could not ask for those portions of the Punjab, Bengal and Assam which were predominantly non-Muslim on the same principle that he was advocating for the communal division of India. Jinnah's intransigence had the support of a large section of British opinion and, even more important, the sympathy of most of the British officers in India who still occupied the top positions in the civil departments in the capital and in the provinces and headed the armed forces. These Britishers had it in their power to create endless trouble at the time of the transfer of power if India declared itself a republic and left the British Commonwealth. The hostility of the British element could be mitigated and opinion in Britain turned, if India accepted Dominion Status to begin with. The nationalists were not in control of the whole of India, i.e., over the...Princely States, one-third of the total territory that had still to be integrated. India remaining a Dominion would also be an assurance to the Princes who had a history of past association with the British Crown. This would make negotiations with them that much easier.[44]

Patel was particularly struck by Menon's emphasis on the necessity of having a strong Central Government. Menon further noted: 'Like the great statesman that he was, he assured me that if power could be transferred at once on the basis of Dominion Status, he for one would use his influence to see that the Congress accepted it.'[45]

A note on the discussion between Patel and Menon was sent to the secretary of state, with Wavell's concurrence. Pethick-Lawrence did not react because of his feeling 'that in view of the unequivocal demand of the Congress [Party] for complete independence, there was no ground for assuming that Congress will accept a transfer of power on the basis of Dominion Status'. Wavell's successor, Lord Louis Mountbatten, saw or was shown Menon's note on the above conversation with Patel before he set out for India.

★

There was another factor playing on the mind of British officials, particularly 'India hands', who, because of their firsthand knowledge of the country exercised considerable influence on Britain's policy. This was their genuine belief that India may not last as one unit as an independent state, whereas Pakistan, because of the unifying force of Islam, would prove a more viable option. A top-secret appreciation, prepared in the Commonwealth Relations Office (soon after it replaced the India Office) for the British Cabinet, gives an insight into British apprehensions about India. Though prepared after India became independent, the view in this appreciation had not obviously developed overnight. Such views influenced British policy makers not to put all their eggs in the Indian basket. The appreciation (a fairly long one) was circulated in Whitehall. Its crux is as follows:

...financially, industrially and from the point of view of manpower and general material resources India was stronger than Pakistan. But that India had no real background on which to build and unite a nation, there being no real affinity between its North and South, the existence of disruptive elements like the Sikhs and the likelihood of the Communists, with their own agenda, growing in numbers and influence.[46]

On the other hand, the appreciation states that Pakistan, although weak in financial and material resources but comfortable in food and manpower,

...has a definite background, Islam, on which to build up a nation and to unite the people...and has less to fear from internal disruptive forces than the Government of India, and less to fear from secessionist tendencies.[47]

There was, however, no unanimity in the British Cabinet on this perception. Some ministers, such as Ernest Bevin (the foreign secretary) and Philip Noel-Baker (appointed the secretary of state for Commonwealth relations), were more influenced by officials who held such views. Sir Strafford Cripps was optimistic about the future of India. Attlee, after the Congress Party agreed to the creation of Pakistan, worked with the next viceroy, Lord Mountbatten, to strengthen India and prevent its Balkanization.

History has proved the above assessment wrong. The authors ignored the importance of deep roots that bind a people together despite their differences and gave too much importance to a revealed religion to hold a country together. In fact, it was Islamic Pakistan that broke with the secession from it of Bangladesh in 1971, whereas the apparently polyglot India survived many serious internal and external challenges.

★

The US State Department had kept mum while the Cabinet Mission was in Delhi. The US chargé d'affaires, George Merrell, advised that neither the British nor the Indians were eager for US intervention. He quoted Major Wilson Wyatt of the Cabinet Delegation as exclaiming (on seeing a Reuters news item that Washington favoured submitting the Pakistan question to international arbitration): 'What? Are they going to interfere now?'[48] On the Indian attitude, in a subsequent telegram, Merrell pointed out: 'Our Govt. – through various official channels – "oversold" itself to Indians. Rightly or wrongly many of them gained the impression that the US was going to "liberate" them from British rule. When this hope was not realized Indians were bitterly disappointed and...began to class the US with Britain as an Imperialist Power.'[49]

The State Department became active after President Harry S. Truman accepted Dean Acheson's recommendation for the appointment of an American ambassador to the Interim Government in December 1946. It then made several efforts to intervene in order to break the constitutional deadlock and support a unitary solution for India. Acheson had been impressed by what Sir Girja Shanker Bajpai, the Indian agent general in Washington, had told him on 8 November 1946:

> Any constitution which would come out of the Constituent Assembly in India would create a relationship between the Government of India and the Government of Great Britain more attenuate [sic] than that of such Dominions as Canada, Australia and New Zealand and more in the nature of Eire [Ireland]. Therefore there would be factors which would result in the Indian Government not leaning heavily upon Great Britain for advice or guidance...while Nehru would not wish to be put in a position of choosing between close relationships with the

western powers and with the Soviet Union, nevertheless, the facts were such that ultimately he must choose. In the light of these conditions an American Ambassador might exercise very considerable influence in the direction of friendly or helpful advice – in fact rather more so than might be possible in countries which we might consider more important and whose constitutional structure and foreign policies were more settled.[50]

There is, however, no record of any Indian effort to carry forward thereafter a dialogue to identify mutual interests or to work with the USA. Asaf Ali, the first Indian ambassador who went over to Washington in February 1947, did not have the experience or the talent for such a task. When Asaf Ali first called on the secretary of state, General George Marshall recorded his surprise that 'the Ambassador made no reference to unity on which his predecessor Bajpai had laid so much stress or on orderly democratic government', especially after he (Marshall) had given him a lead by stating that the US aim in China 'was first unity and second a reasonably democratic system of government'. Marshall was baffled when, instead, Asaf Ali talked of 'India's indebtedness to the stand the British had taken on Indian independence'.[51]

On 30 November 1946 Dean Acheson instructed Waldemar Gallman, the US chargé d'affaires in the UK, to convey to the British authorities the administration's view in advance of the London conference between the British and Indian leaders that was to begin on 2 December 1946. This view was as follows:

Any halt in the constitutional process there [in India] may cause widespread chaos similar [in] China which would last for many years and would have worldwide repercussions…[the] US looks forward [to] mutual advantageous economic relations with stable powerful *united* [italics added] India.[52]

Acheson also instructed Gallman to remain in touch with Jinnah and Nehru in London. Acheson followed these instructions up by addressing a press conference in Washington on 3 December 1946. In this conference, he said: '[The] US awaits with deep concern the outcome of the current talks in London.' On his instructions to contact the Indian leaders, Gallman was smartly sidetracked by the India Office. He wired back that, according to British officers, the leaders had 'an extremely tight schedule...that this is (exclusively) "Prime Minister's Party"...and existing tension may cause Nehru, Jinnah or both to interpret whatever is said by [the] Embassy as US interference or taking sides'.[53]

★

After the failure of the London conference, Pethick-Lawrence wired its results to the foreign secretary, Ernest Bevin, then in the US, for briefing the Americans:

> It is not possible to induce Nehru to modify in any way Congress position as it was already known to us.... If voting is by majorities of representatives of each province (as Nehru insists) grouping constitutions will probably not be formed because of objections by Assam and NWFP.... Fair opportunity to secure the formation of groups is vital to secure Muslim League cooperation and was an essential part of Mission's proposal.... If therefore [the] US concur in our interpretation of the statement of 16 May 1946 it might be very helpful if a US representative in Delhi were to make approach to Congress leaders...I should be grateful to learn what are reactions of the State Department.[54]

Acheson thereupon wired Merrell on 11 December 1946 to speak to Nehru as follows:

> When you see Nehru, suggest you stress...recent expressions of US interest in Indian political impasse and dispel any Indian belief US actions inspired at instance Brit. Although the limited powers of Union Centre in British Plan are open to honest and objective criticism...US historical experience in federalism indicates...Central Government initially with limited powers gradually acquired...additional authority which it must have to meet problems of the federal union [e.g., over NWFP and Assam,

which were border states, because defence was a federal subject].... Congress attitude at this point would rest on reciprocal understanding by Muslim League to work loyally within framework [of] Indian federal union subject only to reopening constitutional issues after ten years of experiment.[55]

Merrell reported Nehru's reaction to Acheson on 14 December 1946 as follows: 'The Congress realized thoroughly the necessity of starting union with weak centre.... But League members had announced publicly that they joined Cabinet in order to fight. Now they were saying privately that if they entered Constituent Assembly it would be with purpose of wrecking it...Nehru blamed London for throwing spanner into works by encouraging Jinnah in his intransigence by their statement of 6 December 1946 after the London conference.'[56]

On 19 December the State Department instructed Merrell to

...inform Jinnah and Liaqat Ali Khan or both, our doubt that Congress attitude re. Provincial groupings can be modified unless accompanied by public declaration or other tangible evidence of Muslim League willingness to cooperate loyally within framework of Indian federal union to be established in accordance with Cabinet Mission Plan...necessary safeguards can never be achieved unless the concept of union itself is generally accepted by the principal parties.[57]

On the approach to Liaqat Ali Khan, Merrell wired back on 27 December 1946 that Jinnah's deputy had argued that the Congress had not accepted the British Government's statement of 6 December 1946 on groupings, a fundamental point of the Cabinet Mission plan. Liaqat had then gone on to refer to 'communal warfare' in Bihar in which he claimed 30,000 Muslims had been killed, not 5000 as officially declared. Liaqat Ali Khan then said: 'If chaos developed in India, [the] USSR would move in.'[58] Thus, he tried to broadly hint that the Muslim League would be willing to cooperate with the West on strategic issues, believing that this stand was more likely to influence the Americans than any arguments on the merits of the case. Merrell followed this two days later by cabling that Liaqat had confirmed that Jinnah could not be persuaded to offer assurances of any sort until such time as Congress accepted the British grouping plan. The US State Department then chased Jinnah to Karachi, where the American vice-consul, Joseph S. Spark, was able to catch up with him. 'Tell your government...for God's sake not to be chloroformed by meaningless Congress gestures for purely propaganda effect' was the Quaid-i-Azam's response.*[59]

The Muslim League had been exploring the US attitude by sending delegations to that country. M.A.H. Isfahani, a prominent Calcutta businessman close to Jinnah (and soon to be appointed Pakistan's first ambassador to the US) after one such visit in November 1946, wrote to Jinnah: 'I have learnt that sweet words and first impressions count a lot with Americans' and advised Jinnah that the *Time-Life* South Asia correspondent should be cultivated.[60] The previous summer *Time* had put Jinnah on its cover and, in a three-page article, described the political rise of Jinnah as 'a story of lust for power, a story that twists and turns like a bullock-cart track in the hills'. In this context, Dennis Kux has commented: 'If the State Department was cool towards the idea of Pakistan, some US media commentary was positively hostile.'[61]

On 7 February 1947, the Congress Party and minority members of the Interim Government presented the viceroy a petition demanding the resignation of the Muslim League representatives from that body. Their argument was that, despite the fact that the Congress Party had (on 6 February 1947) accepted the grouping formula as contained in the British declaration of 6 December 1946, Jinnah (on 31 January 1947) had refused to enter the Constituent Assembly, terming the aforementioned declaration a 'dishonest trick'. The fact was that the Congress Party had not accepted the 6 December formula unreservedly, which had enabled Jinnah to cry foul. But the Muslim League's strong words could suggest that, during his stay

---

* Quaid-i-Azam means 'great leader', the title used for Jinnah.

in London after the conference, Jinnah had received assurances that continued intransigence was in order.

★

The US again stepped in on 11 February 1947. On that day, General Marshall, the new secretary of state, instructed the US chargé d'affaires in London as follows:

If you have opportunity we hope you will endeavor to ascertain whether or not Brit are disposed to instruct Viceroy dismiss Muslim League Ministers from the Council [and] whether they are planning to bring pressure on princes to reach definitely agreement with Congress.[62]

Before the American chargé d'affaires could deliver this pointed démarche, the British ambassador in Washington called on Marshall on 20 February 1947 and handed over to him the statement that Attlee was going to make on India in the House of Commons the same day, which would change the entire format of the negotiations.

Attlee's statement of 20 February 1947 fixed 'not later than June 1948' as final for British departure from India:

Should it appear that...a constitution will not have been worked out by a fully representative Assembly before the time mentioned [June 1948], HMG will have to consider to whom the powers of the Central Government in British India should be handed over, on the due date, whether as a whole to some form of Central Government of British India or in some areas to the existing Provincial governments or in such other way as may seem most reasonable and in the best interests of the Indian people...[as far as the princely states were concerned] HMG's powers and obligations under Paramountcy would not be handed over to any government of British India [and thus they would be free to make independent arrangements, even declare independence].[63]

Attlee also announced the replacement of Wavell by Mountbatten as the viceroy of India.

The foregoing statement was momentous in the sense that it had fixed the date for British departure from India. Considering the vital role the man on the spot played in the British dispensation, the change of viceroy was also a major development. However, on the main issue of a united versus a divided India, the old British policy was to continue. If the Muslim League did not join the Constituent Assembly, it would not become 'fully representative' and the constitution that it would work out would not be applicable to the whole of India but only to those parts the representatives of which had taken part in the assembly's proceedings. Thus, Indian unity remained, as ever since 1940, a hostage to Jinnah's agreement to it; in reality, dependent on British discretion. This was because, as Linlithgow had pointed out to Zetland way back: 'He [Jinnah] represents a minority that can only hold its own with our assurance.'

Since everyone knew that Jinnah would never yield, especially so after this latest British pronouncement, Attlee's statement of 20 February was once again a recipe for the creation of Pakistan presented in yet another form. And the only questions that really remained as far as the British were concerned were: Which areas of India were to be ceded to Pakistan and what was to be done with the princely states?

Mountbatten was being sent out to use his well-known charm and negotiating skills to get the Congress Party to agree to partition, especially the secession from India of the strategic North West Frontier Province – a Muslim-inhabited province, but in Congress Party hands. And to get Jinnah's agreement to the 'truncated' Pakistan that Wavell had recommended the previous year.

Wavell wired Pethick-Lawrence on 26 February 1947 the Indian political parties' reactions to HMG's statement: 'The Congress welcome the fixing of date and hope that the statement means that if they did not get an agreement with the Muslim League, they can establish a strong unitary government based not on the Cabinet Mission's Plan [that envisaged a weak Centre] but on their own estimates of India's requirement.' The Muslim League reaction was, Wavell said, 'based on the assumption that if the League refused to

NEHRU IN THE SADDLE Ⅱ 263

cooperate with the Constituent Assembly, they will receive not the small Pakistan but the large Pakistan'. Wavell then added: 'It may turn out all right.'[64] Although Wavell was being dismissed from the viceroyalty, his policy was emerging triumphant!

★

Khaliq-uz-Zaman, the number three in the Muslim League hierarchy, has written in his memoirs: 'This [Attlee's] statement gave great relief to the League as it had no intention of entering the Constituent Assembly or framing the Central Constitution, thus keeping the door open for the partition of India...' He added: 'Strange as it may seem Pt. Jawaharlal Nehru characterized the statement as wise and courageous.'[65]

The British gave the following slant to Attlee's announcement of 20 February 1947 when their ambassador called on Secretary Marshall the same day:

The statement is designed to avoid on the one hand a commitment to create Pakistan [which would encourage the League to be obstructive], and on the other hand any indication that we should, whatever happens, hand over to one authority only [and encourage the Congress Party to be uncompromising].[66]

The Americans' impulse continued to be to resist a possible fragmentation of India, as discernible from Acheson's wire to the American Embassy in London dated 4 April 1947:

Our political and economic interest in that part of the world would best be served by the continued integrity of India.[67]

Acheson sent this message in the context of reports regarding purported plans of the Hyderabad (princely) state to establish a 'direct relation' with the British and presumably maintain a status completely separate from that of the rest of India. 'We are assuming', he added, 'that the British Government would not lend encouragement to [such plans]...a separatist move by Hyderabad may be a prelude to a fragmentation process which might have far-reaching effects on any plan for *ultimate Indian unity*' [italics added].[68]

Before Mountbatten arrived to replace Wavell on 22 March 1947, the Congress Party Working Committee had adopted a resolution (on 8 March) with far-reaching implications. The resolution accepted

a division of Punjab into two provinces so that the predominantly Muslim part may be separated from the predominantly non-Muslim part.

Many Congress Party leaders had convinced themselves that since the North West Frontier Province was in their hands, the division of the Punjab (or even the attachment of Sind to the Muslim areas of the Punjab) would merely result in a predominantly Muslim enclave within the boundaries of India, which could not last forever. However, by accepting the division of the Punjab they had impliedly accepted the principle of the division of India on the basis of Jinnah's two-nation theory. If the Congress Party was willing for the aforementioned principle to be applied to the Punjab, why not elsewhere? Indeed, Nehru wrote to Wavell on 9 March 1947, while forwarding the Congress Party resolution, in a covering letter that:

This principle [of communal division in the Punjab] would, of course, apply to Bengal also.[69]

Patel's experience in the Interim Government – and perhaps the talk (or talks) he had had with V.P. Menon – had brought home to him that it was absolutely important for India's future to have a strong Centre, even if some parts of the country had to be 'amputated'.

The US chargé d'affaires in India, George Merrell, analysing the Congress Party's resolution to the State Department, wired on 22 April 1947:

The Congress efforts to make Pakistan as unattractive as possible – by demanding partition of the Punjab and Bengal – Congress leaders have in effect abandoned the tenets which they supported for so many years in their campaign for united India. They have also agreed by implication [to] Mr Jinnah's allegation that Hindus and Muslims cannot live together, a charge which in the past Congress has – quite rightly I believe – denied.[70]

Marshall and Acheson were soon to realize that their hopes of a united India had been dashed. It is worth noting that the Indian nationalists never exploited the potential of US support in favour of a unitary solution. They did not realize the growing influence of American policy on Britain, as Jinnah did. The Americans, ultimately, not only reconciled themselves to the formation of Pakistan but also, some years later, developed a defence partnership with this strategically located new state. Without partition, Indo–US relations might not have plunged to the extent they did during the Cold War era. The division not only removed the adversarial factor in Anglo–US relations because of their differences on policy towards India (which has been discussed in Chapter 6) but also increased British influence over US policy in South Asia.

If there were misgivings in certain British quarters on the wisdom of dividing India, the performance of the nationalists in the Interim Government helped to dispel them. The passage of the resolution in the Congress Party-dominated Constituent Assembly on India's intention to leave the Commonwealth was a shock to the British. It signalled the foreclosing of the hoped-for continued cooperation of the Indian armed forces in Commonwealth (Empire) defence. Then, the foreign policy pursued by Jawaharlal Nehru created apprehensions that unless a part of India was detached – a part on which they could rely – Indian independence might prove an unmitigated strategic disaster for England. In any case, the assessment of the director of the Intelligence Bureau (quoted at the beginning of this chapter) that 'Pakistan is likely to come from "Congresstan" [the acceptance of office by the Congress Party]', had proved prophetic.

Notes and References

1. TOP IX, p. 304, enclosure.
2. US FR 1946, Vol. V, pp. 92–93.
3. Ibid., pp. 93–94.
4. TOP IX, S. No. 69.
5. US FR 1946, Vol. V, p. 94.
6. Wavell, *The Viceroy's Journal* (Oxford University Press, London, 1977, p. 343).
7. Ibid.
8. Patel, *Collected Works*, Vol. X (Government of India, New Delhi, p. 230).
9. Ibid., p. 257.
10. TOP IX, p. 304, enclosure.
11. Wavell, op. cit., p. 315.
12. Ibid., p. 336.
13. Ibid., p. 330.
14. TOP VIII, p. 286.
15. TOP IX, p. 35 (Attlee's undated note).
16. TOP VIII, p. 501 (Paras 3, 8 and 11).
17. Ibid.
18. Sudhir Ghose, *Gandhiji's Emissary* (First Cresset, London, 1967, pp. 25–26).
19. Wavell, op. cit., p. 349.
20. H.V. Hodson, *The Great Divide: Britain-India-Pakistan* (Oxford University Press edition, Delhi, 2000, p. 173).
21. Patel, op. cit., Vol. X, pp. 252–53.
22. Hodson, op. cit., p. 180.
23. US FR 1947, Vol. III, p. 139.
24. TOP IX, p. 224, annexure, dated 30 August 1946.
25. COS (46) 229 (O), appendix (OIC, British Library, London).
26. Private telegram from Auchinleck to Mayne, No. 270087/CGS, dated 14 September 1946.
27. TOP VIII, p. 371.
28. Ibid., p 537.
29. TOP IX, p. 338, enclosure, Para 7 (ii).
30. TOP VIII, p. 228.

31. Ibid.
32. Foreign Office files (1946), p. 479.
33. Stanley Wolpert, *Roots of Confrontation in South Asia* (Oxford University Press, London, 1982, p. 67).
34. R/3/1/92, File No. 243/8/99 (43–46), Packmans to Caroe (OIC, British Library, London).
35. Ibid., DO No. 911–16, Caroe to viceroy, 23 October 1946, Paras 3, 6, 12 and 15.
36. Ibid.
37. Ibid.
38. Ibid.
39. Ibid.
40. TOP IX, p. 49, para 6.
41. Ibid., p 166.
42. Patel, op. cit., Vol. X, S. No. 367, 15 December 1946.
43. Sir Penderel Moon, *The British Conquest and Dominion of India*, Vol. 2 (India Research Press, Delhi, 1999, p. 1162).
44. V.P. Menon, *Transfer of Power in India* (Longman Green, London, 1957, pp. 358–59).
45. Ibid., p. 359.
46. MBI/D/241 (Broadland Archives, University of Southampton).
47. Ibid.
48. US FR, 1946, Vol. V, p. 87.
49. Ibid., p. 91.
50. Ibid., p. 97.
51. Ibid., p. 98.
52. Ibid., p. 99.
53. Ibid., pp. 103–04.
54. TOP IX, p. 170.
55. US FR 1946, Vol. V, pp. 103–04.
56. Ibid., p. 105.
57. Ibid., p. 106.
58. Ibid., pp. 106–09.
59. US FR 1947, Vol. III, pp. 137–38.
60. *Correspondence M.A. Jinnah–Isfahani: 1936–48* (Karachi Royal Book Co., Karachi, 1976).

61. Dennis Kux, *Disenchanted Allies* (Oxford University Press, Delhi, 2001, p. 8).
62. US FR 1947, Vol. III, p. 141.
63. TOP IX, p. 438.
64. Ibid., p. 469.
65. Khaliq-uz-Zaman, *Pathway to Pakistan* (Longman Green, London, 1961, p. 375).
66. US FR 1947, Vol. III, p. 143, Para 4.
67. Ibid., pp. 151–52.
68. Ibid.
69. TOP, Vol. IX, p. 511, Para 4.
70. US FR, Vol. III, pp. 152–54.

10

Mountbatten's Counsellor

REAR ADMIRAL EARL LOUIS MOUNTBATTEN OF BURMA REACHED DELHI on 22 March 1947. He had been the supreme commander of the South-east Asia Command and had taken the surrender of the Japanese forces in Burma, Malay, Indo–China, Indonesia and Singapore. He had been appointed supreme commander by Prime Minister Winston Churchill over the heads of several senior British service officers. Churchill considered him an outstandingly innovative and positive leader who, with the force of his personality, could match the aplomb of General Douglas MacArthur, 'the American Caesar', and Generalissimo Chiang Kai-shek. In South-east Asia, he showed a capacity to get on with people of every race and to comprehend 'the vitality of Asian nationalism'.

He had won his spurs as the chief of Combined Operations, a new formation, set up in 1941, 'to organize raids of ever-increasing intensity across the Channel combining Naval [*sic*], Army and Air Force, the main object being to prepare for [the] invasion of France'.[1] Churchill had himself briefed him: 'Your whole attention is to be concentrated on offensive action.'[2] The post gave him an opportunity to deploy his innovative talents and unconventional ideas to the full. As chief of Combined Operations, he soon started to sit with the other three chiefs in the top military echelon that conducted the war. This position enabled him to rub shoulders with top British and American brass, including US Generals George Marshall and Dwight

Eisenhower, who both liked him; in fact, more than his English seniors who considered it wrong that a mere naval commodore in rank should receive so much attention.

Mountbatten was a cousin of the King Emperor George VI and married, in July 1922, one of the richest heiresses in England, Edwina Ashley, who was considered one of the most sought-after girls in London for her 'fierce brilliance and elegance'.[3] Her grandfather, Sir Ernest Cassel, a Jewish banker, had emigrated from Germany to London at the end of the nineteenth century and had become a close friend of King Edward VII. He had left behind a fortune of £7.5 million, together with Brook House, his London residence, and £30,000 a year, to his sister for life and then to Edwina, his favourite granddaughter, who also got the lion's share of the residue of £2.3 million. So this was also an alliance in which royal blood on one side balanced a great fortune on the other. The young couple's lifestyle in London's merry 1920s was, what would be called today, that of jetsetters. For their honeymoon they travelled to the United States, Mountbatten taking an instant delight 'in the brash, vibrant, enthusiastic society of New York'.[4] In Hollywood they were entertained at the houses of major stars, including Charles Chaplin, and found time to even make a film. Mountbatten noted in his diary on 18 October 1922: 'It was fascinating work. Edwina and I are "lovers" in it.'[5]

Mountbatten's pay at this time was £310 a year and his income from dividends provided an additional £300.[6] His father, Admiral Prince Louis of Battenberg, a migrant from the principality of Hesse on the river Rhine in Germany, had been a naval officer during his entire career and was by no means rich. He had migrated to England because of his passion to serve in the Royal Navy, the greatest navy in the world at that time. The English Battenbergs made up for their modest means by the importance of their connections not only with the British royal family but also with most of the royal houses of Europe. Czar Alexander II of Russia had married a sister of Mountbatten's grandfather; a daughter of Empress Victoria had married into the Hesse family and it was through her that the future viceroy was a great-grandson of the British Queen. His own sister was married to the king of Sweden. According to his biographer,

Philip Ziegler: 'The genealogy which he worked out enumerated the channels that divided him from Emperor Charlemagne and the intricate web of cousinship which bound him many times over to the Wellesbachs and the Romanovs, the Hapsburgs and Hohenzollerns.'[7] At his birth, Queen Victoria had insisted on adding her husband's name, Albert, to his others, which lengthened to Louis Francis Albert Victor Nicholas Battenberg. The Earldom, the Garter and other honours came his way, as his career progressed and made him one of the most decorated Englishmen of that era.

Neither his high connections nor his wife's wealth detracted Mountbatten from his utter devotion to his career in the Royal Navy, earning from one of his colleagues the sobriquet 'an undersexed workaholic'.[8] He was determined one day to head the British Navy, a post that his father Admiral Battenberg had held and from which, at the beginning of the First World War, he was allowed to resign by Churchill, the then secretary of the Navy, because of his German birth. It was during the First World War that the family anglicized its name to Mountbatten.

Whatever else, Louis Mountbatten, nicknamed Dickie, did not lack gumption and showmanship. In May 1941, when HMS *Kelly*, the destroyer he was commanding, received direct hits from German Junker bombers off the coast of Crete and started to capsize, he believed that he ought to be the last to leave the ship. 'I left it a bit late...', he recounted to his daughter, Patricia. 'Then I started swallowing water. I knew I would be finished, if I couldn't stop this. So I put my left hand over my mouth and nose and held them shut. Then I thought my lungs would burst. Finally, I began to see daylight and suddenly shot out of the water like a cork released.'[9] According to the crew, as soon as Mountbatten found a raft to hold on to, he rallied others who had survived and were on other rafts to call for three cheers as the *Kelly* finally went down. 'Mi Lord' was always popular amongst the crew much more so than amongst his senior officers, who felt that he was not averse to taking short cuts to further his career.

Churchill harboured a life-long guilt for not standing up to defend Mountbatten's father. In 1941, after he lost *Kelly*, Churchill, through Harry Hopkins, President Roosevelt's troubleshooter, had the 'dashing and well-connected young sailor'[10] invited on a lecture tour to the United States to recount British naval exploits against the Germans 'to make propaganda and cultivate useful contacts'.[11] Lady Edwina accompanied him on a goodwill tour to thank the American Red Cross for all its help. According to Ziegler: 'His tour of the United States turned into a triumphal progress. Everywhere he was feted by the rich and the powerful.'[12] Thrice he dined at the White House, on the first occasion talking to the president till 1 a.m. 'He has done more than anyone else to instil and to encourage American admiration for Britain', observed a commentator.[13] 'Mountbatten has been really useful to our Navy people', the president himself wrote to Churchill.[14] It was while he was still on his American tour that Churchill recalled him to be groomed to become the chief of Combined Operations.

India was not a totally new country to Mountbatten. He had first visited it on a lengthy trip as companion to the Prince of Wales (later King Edward VIII) in 1921 and had noticed both the Indian animosity towards the British and also his British compatriots' pleasant lifestyle in India – polo, pig-sticking, hunting and shooting (he shot his first tiger on this trip, of which then there were 40,000 in the Indian jungles), the pageants, the ballroom dancing as well as the merry making in the courts of the Indian princes. No one could have then imagined that the end of Empire was only a little more than a quarter century away. It was while on this trip that he got engaged to Edwina Ashley in Delhi. She had wangled an invitation from the viceroy, Lord Reading (Rufus Issacs) and the vicereine, to be their guest. On appointment as the supreme commander of the South-east Asia Command (SEAC), Mountbatten was in India once again. The HQ of the SEAC was first located in Delhi, before he shifted it to Kandy, the hill station in Ceylon (now Sri Lanka).

Attlee and Cripps also thought highly of Mountbatten. 'He was an extremely lively exciting personality,' wrote Attlee. 'He had an extraordinary faculty for getting on with all kinds of people.... He was also blessed with a very unusual wife'.[15] Cripps admired him for his qualities of leadership that he himself lacked. It is said that it was Cripps who, in March 1946, manipulated a visit for Jawaharlal Nehru to South-east Asia and to be the guest of the Mountbattens in Singapore. Nehru had never received such friendly treatment from any other British official and fell under his spell. It was also here that Nehru first discovered Lady Edwina, indeed rescued her, after she had got knocked down to the ground in a melee of enthusiastic Singaporeans at a reception.

This background is important for an understanding of Mountbatten's impact on the Indian political scene. On the one side were his high royal connections, the confidence reposed in him by both Churchill and Attlee and his handsome and, in a way, flamboyant presence. On the other was his utter lack of lordliness or stiffness in dealing with his Indian interlocutors, showing no hesitation to stoop to conquer. These qualities had an immediate effect on the Indians. And so did his wife: by her indefatigable capacity to undertake tours to refugee camps and hospitals, day in and day out, a wealthy grand lady, she cared for the poor and shared their suffering and misery.

Mountbatten had not been sent out to India in 1947 to persuade the Indian leaders to accept the partition of the country. That had already been agreed to in principle. What he had been sent out to do was to:

(1) Fix responsibility for the division of India squarely on Indian shoulders;

(2) persuade the Congress Party leaders to abandon their demand for the inclusion of the North West Frontier Province in India (thereby clearing the way for this strategic area to be placed in Pakistan's hands) and for Jinnah to forego his claim for the whole of the Punjab, Bengal and Assam (to make partition palatable to the nationalists); and

(3) ensure that, after independence, India would remain a member of the British Commonwealth – Jinnah's Pakistan was expected to do so anyway.

General Lord Hastings Ismay, who had been Churchill's chief of staff during the war, came out as chief of staff to Mountbatten. In the 1930s he had initially served in the North West Frontier Province and later as military secretary to the viceroy, Lord Willingdon (Freeman Freeman-Thomas). Lord Ismay was acquainted with Churchill's policy on India as well as with Attlee's views on the country. Although Churchill's and Mountbatten's views on India were dissimilar, this did not make any difference to Ismay's loyally serving Mountbatten. Indeed, Ismay was a friend of Mountbatten, who sometimes asked him to intervene in order to soothe his quarrels with Edwina. Ismay had acquired great influence in the British establishment because of his discreet and unassuming nature. He has left behind hardly any personal papers or diaries on the principle that public servants involved in the highest secrets of state should keep their mouths sealed. His natural inclination was to side with the Muslims in India and one of the duties assigned to him was to keep in touch with Jinnah. On the other hand, he cooperated fully with Mountbatten to consolidate India after the agreement on partition was announced. Differences arose between Mountbatten and Ismay only after partition, because the latter felt that the former was playing too pronounced a role as governor-general of India and might get identified with the policies of India as against those of Pakistan.

To any Indian leader he met for the first time, Mountbatten told Ismay, 'I...started off with my usual lecture on a strong Union of India'. This opening was no doubt to establish his credentials as one opposed to partition. 'I was determined', he emphasized 'that so far as possible the decision whether to have partition or not should rest on the shoulders of the Indian peoples themselves and that the accusation against Britain having divided the country should thus be avoided.'[16] He was equally determined to keep India within the Commonwealth. This was not only because he had been directed by Attlee to do so but also because of his own strong personal convictions. Mountbatten believed that for Britain 'to continue to play a major role in the post-war world, the old Empire should be transformed into a multiracial and worldwide association of free nations remaining linked to Britain through the membership in the Commonwealth'.[17]

*

After being named viceroy, Mountbatten did not wait to get to India before embarking on his mission. He contacted Krishna Menon, Jawaharlal Nehru's confidant and main interlocutor with the Labour Party leaders in London. The following sentence in a letter Krishna Menon wrote to Mountbatten a little later gives us a glimpse into what the two discussed:

> When I first submitted to you ideas on what may be done and we had talks in London last March, the one thing we both thought fundamental was that in any partition which I put forward (i.e., suggest to Nehru) as necessary to a solution, the outer line of India must remain intact – all secession must be subject to it.[18]

Krishna Menon was here reflecting the views of the Congress Working Committee resolution of 6 March 1947 that proceeded on the assumption that as long as the North West Frontier Province remained with India, a Pakistan consisting of western Punjab locked inside the boundaries of India would prove harmless and would, most probably, be only a temporary phenomenon. Krishna Menon also told Mountbatten that, in view of the Constituent Assembly's resolution of January 1947, India's membership in the Commonwealth appeared to be a non-starter. In London Mountbatten had seen the note by V.P. Menon (no relation of Krishna Menon), the reforms commissioner to the viceroy, on his talks with Vallabhbhai Patel at the end of 1946. This note suggested that Patel may agree to accept a Pakistan of the truncated variety and independence on a dominion status basis – if power was transferred to Indian hands immediately. But Mountbatten did not pay much attention to this note in view of Krishna Menon's above advice.

On his arrival in Delhi on 22 March 1947, Mountbatten found that the Asia Relations Conference organized by Nehru was to begin the next day and the 'prime minister' was engrossed in it. Nehru had been planning for this conference ever since he had become the minister for external affairs in the Interim Government in September 1946. Non-official representatives of all shades of opinion in the countries of Asia (plus Egypt) were invited to the conference. All views were represented; thus, the delegates could listen to both the Kuomintang and the Chinese communists as well as to the representatives of the Arab League and the Hebrew University. 'An amazing success from every point of view. I think we can definitely call it the beginning of a new era in Asian history',[19] declared Nehru. Actually, nothing came of the Asian Relations Organization set up by the conference and no participating country acted on the resolution to set up national units of this organization or academies of Asian studies. There was not even a second session of the Asia Relations Conference, though one may perhaps discern its influence in the origins of the Asian–African Conference held in Bandung, Indonesia, in 1955.

Neither the problems of law and order nor his 'prime minister's' preoccupation with the Asia Relations Conference prevented Mountbatten from straightaway launching – working at an average of twelve hours a day – on a series of meetings with Indian leaders. He had written to Gandhiji on the very day of his arrival to come and see him. Gandhiji had promptly returned to Delhi from riot-torn Bihar and saw Mountbatten on 31 March 1947 and every day thereafter, except one, till 4 April.

Mountbatten's tactics, with Lady Mountbatten joining in, was not to enter into any serious negotiations with him but just to humour him by lending a patient ear to all that he had to say. No vicereine before her had tried to woo Gandhiji. A photograph that showed the Mahatma's hand resting on her shoulder was the butt of much adverse comment in England. Mountbatten knew that Gandhiji's endorsement of whatever agreement he reached with Nehru and Patel would be vital. 'No one listens to me any more; I am crying in the wilderness', he had been complaining. Well, this viceroy had all the time for him that he wished.

Gandhiji was, however, not willing to be totally sidelined in the coming negotiations. During the second meeting on 1 April, he told

Mountbatten that 'the Indian problem could be solved if Mr Jinnah were to form a new Interim Government and the Viceroy eventually handed over power to him. Under it, the new Cabinet would be named entirely by Jinnah who could have all Muslim League representatives if he so liked. The Congress Party, with their majority in the Legislative Assembly, would guarantee to cooperate fairly and sincerely with such an administration. However if Jinnah rejected the offer, it was to be made *mutatis mutandis* to the Congress Party.'[20]

Mountbatten was not willing to be waylaid by such a proposal, whether or not it made any sense. He countered by asserting that he could have nothing to do with it unless Gandhiji had obtained the full backing of the Congress Party's Working Committee, knowing fully well that for Nehru and Patel to agree to step down at this stage and take the risk of installing Muslim League rule in India was a non-starter. And, indeed, on 11 April 1947, Gandhiji wrote to him that 'he had been unable to obtain the agreement of the leading members of the Congress'.[21]

★

Gandhiji, in fact, was making this offer some twenty years too late. If, in 1928, he had offered Jinnah the Congress Party's presidency, instead of to the younger Nehru, Jinnah – an old Congress Party stalwart, at heart no fundamentalist, and hungry for attention – might have grasped it and not thrown himself into the British lap. He was a more intelligent and a more disciplined negotiator than the others. Once he accepted a brief, his professional barrister's pride and ego would drive him to win at all costs, irrespective of other considerations. If he could have been persuaded to lead the Congress Party, the division of India could perhaps have been avoided, as there was no other Muslim leader to unite the Muslims for a separate state.

Gandhiji continued to meet Mountbatten on and off, without coordinating his views with the other Congress leaders. These approaches were skilfully used by Mountbatten to obtain information from him on the latest thinking amongst the Congress leaders and to brief himself on the internecine differences among them.

Mountbatten first met Jinnah on 5 April and their conversations continued every day from 7 to 10 April. Jinnah demanded that power be handed over, province by province, with the provinces themselves choosing how they would form themselves into groups, and 'those with a Muslim majority forming a new State'. He threatened that 'an attempt to maintain the unity of India would lead the Muslim League to resort to armed force to resist it'.[22] Mountbatten argued that, logically, the same principle would have to be applied to areas of Bengal and the Punjab, where non-Muslims made up nearly half of the population, and, as a result, these two provinces would be partitioned. It was on 10 April that Mountbatten finally brought Jinnah to his knees, proving once more that his strength lay in direct proportion to the support he received from the British. 'I do not care how little you give me as long as you give it to me completely', he said. And then: 'I do not wish to make any improper suggestion to you but you must realize that the new Pakistan is almost certain to ask for Dominion Status within the British Empire.'[23]

On another occasion, according to the viceroy's report, Jinnah pleaded:

All the Muslims have been loyal to the British from the beginning, supplied a high proportion of the army which fought in both wars, none of our leaders has ever had to go to prison for disloyalty, not one member of the Muslim League was present in the Constituent Assembly when the Resolution for an Independent Sovereign Republic was passed.[24]

Jinnah had yielded on all the three points of interest to Mountbatten: He was accepting a truncated Pakistan; he was giving his assent to membership of the Commonwealth; and he was willing to be recruited as an ally in the Great Game on the British side – even though he continued to raise certain issues till the end, such as an independent Bengal, the joint control of Calcutta and even a corridor to link West Pakistan and East Pakistan.

★

When Mountbatten first met Patel, surprisingly, they did not focus on the nitty-gritty, though he was the leader most likely to be helpful in persuading the Congress Party to accept partition and the continued Commonwealth link. Even later, he mostly used V.P. Menon as a 'go-between' in the negotiations with Patel. Had he sensed the growing rift between Nehru and Patel and was careful not to burn his boats with his frontman, Jawaharlal?

The Nawab of Bhopal, the chancellor of the Chamber of Princes, asked the viceroy whether groups of princely states could be granted dominion status, i.e., become independent. Mountbatten gave him no encouragement. Bhopal then complained that some major princes had broken away from him and joined the Constituent Assembly to please the Congress Party. As things turned out, Bhopal soon lost the chancellorship of the Chamber of Princes and was replaced by the Maharaja of Patiala, the premier Sikh prince: Bhopal's pro-Pakistan feelings had alienated the other princes. Mountbatten, from the start, showed great confidence and a deft touch in handling the princes, giving himself only the last three weeks of his viceroyalty to make them accede to his will.

C.H. Bhabha, the member for works, mines and power, told the viceroy: 'He was no politician but a businessman, who would not give a seat on the Board of his least important Company to most other members of the Interim Cabinet.'[25] Mountbatten would not have included this remark in his top-secret report if he was not inclined to agree with it, though, in public, he showed the greatest degree of deference to his ministers.

Nehru was the first Indian leader whom Mountbatten had seen. This was just two days after his arrival, on 24 March. Nehru started by saying: 'Economic problems were by far the most serious of all those which faced India.'[26] When Mountbatten succeeded in focusing his attention on the question before them, that of the transfer of power, Nehru bluntly replied: 'For psychological and emotional reasons India cannot remain in the Commonwealth.'[27] Mountbatten, in his report to London, says: 'It was not until 8 April (after several meetings in between) that I asked Pt. Nehru outright what his solution would be for the transfer of power if he was in my place' (shades of Cripps!). Nehru replied, according to Mountbatten, that 'it would not be right to impose any form of constitutional conditions on any community which was in a majority in a specific area'.[28] Mountbatten took this reply to mean that Nehru was agreeable not only to non-Muslim parts of the Punjab and Bengal being given a free choice but also to all of the British provinces including those which were with the Congress Party, such as the NWFP.

It was after these conversations that Mountbatten's staff, headed by Lord Ismay, started to draw up a plan for British withdrawal. To them it was inherent in Attlee's statement of 20 February 1947 that freedom of choice be accorded to the British provinces (and to the princely states). They assumed that both Jinnah and Nehru accepted this. Therefore, under their plan, the elected members to the assembly of each and every British province (including those under the Congress Party control) were given a free choice about future affiliation to the All-India Constituent Assembly or to a second Constituent Assembly or assemblies that they might constitute; this included the freedom to declare independence. The freedom of choice given to the British provinces would apply equally to the Indian princes who would be enabled to affiliate their territories in any manner they wished, or to choose independence.

The NWFP, a wholly Muslim province, could not be detached from India as long as its representatives to the All-India Constituent Assembly supported its affiliation to India. The way to bypass them would be to decree another election there, despite one held just a few months back and ask the electorate to vote directly on the province's future. The Ismay–Mountbatten plan, therefore, provided for an election once again in the NWFP, the justification being that freedom to become independent had not been a choice in the last election. Now that the creation of Pakistan was on the cards, it was hoped that joining a Muslim state or choosing independence might persuade the Pathans to turn away from the Congress Party.

✸

Sir Olaf Caroe, the most knowledgeable British expert on Pathan and tribal affairs, took over as governor of the NWFP the previous year. The Muslim League had already begun an agitation against the incumbent Congress Party Government led by Dr Khan Sahib, who like his stepbrother, Khan Abdul Ghaffar Khan, was totally opposed to Muslim separatism in India. He took strong measures against the Muslim League's agitation, employed pressure tactics and jailed thousands of its supporters.

On the very day that Mountbatten arrived in Delhi (22 March 1947), he received a long letter from Governor Caroe advising him on the unsettled situation in the province. The governor squarely laid the blame for the Muslim League's agitation on Dr Khan Sahib's 'repressive measures' and advised that the only way to pacify the province was to hold another election in it, and to ensure it was fair, dismiss the Khan Sahib Government and hand over direct control over the administration to the governor under Section 93 of the Constitution. He pressed for the same policy at the Governors' Conference that Mountbatten called in the middle of April 1947, saying that the Congress Party would be trounced if a fresh election were held. Jinnah too requested the viceroy to impose governor's rule and to hold an election in the province.

Mountbatten turned down the request for the dismissal of a duly elected government, but agreed to explore, with Nehru, the possibility of directly consulting the people on the province's future. Mountbatten privately told Caroe that Nehru, Ghaffar Khan and Dr Khan Sahib were all baying for his blood and, indeed, Nehru had made a formal proposal for his dismissal. Mountbatten hinted that he might try to strike a deal with them by agreeing to replace Caroe and leave the Khan Sahib ministry in place, provided they agreed to a referendum in the province. Mountbatten felt that a referendum was needed in the province, which would mean the same thing as an election, but the change of word would provide an excuse for Nehru and his party colleagues to climb down.

'Operation Frontier' was launched by Mountbatten on 18 April 1947. According to the viceroy's report, Nehru 'forcefully rejected' the idea of an election in the NWFP but 'did agree in principle that it would be desirable to obtain the views of the people before the final turnover of power was effected'.[29] Having gained this important point, the viceroy next sent for Dr Khan Sahib. The Pathan accused the governor to his face of indulging in 'partiality, non-cooperation and interference'. Mountbatten then decided to visit the province on 28 and 29 April 1947. On his arrival in Peshawar, a huge crowd of over 50,000 had assembled, shouting 'Mountbatten ki jai' (victory to Mountbatten) and 'Pakistan zindabad' (long live Pakistan). When Dr Khan Sahib told him that Jinnah had no control whatsoever over the Muslim League in the NWFP, Mountbatten asked: 'Who then controls it?' Promptly came the Khan's reply: 'His Excellency the Governor, of course and his officials; their one object is to turn my Ministry out of power.'[30] Whatever Dr Khan Sahib's view, the large demonstration in Peshawar and the strong anti-Congress showing in the tribal belt, when Mountbatten visited that area, enabled him to argue 'that it would certainly be necessary to know whether they [the Congress Party] still had a mandate from the people before the decision would be taken as to who was to inherit the Province at the transfer of power'.

Meanwhile, the Muslim League agitation and 'direct action' had started to take their toll, communalizing the situation in the NWFP as the Sikhs and Hindus in towns came under attack. The viceroy's report mentions certain areas such as Dera Ismail Khan, Bannu and Tank, where 'property amounting to millions of rupees was damaged and bitter hatred was laid [sic] by massacres, forcible conversions and atrocities'.[31]

Towards the end of April Mountbatten was able to convince Nehru to accept a referendum in the NWFP on the simple issue of 'Pakistan or the new India' instead of a fresh election. Records the viceroy: 'Pt. Nehru accepted the proposal saying that the organization running the election should be controlled by me, so as to ensure impartiality.'[32]

Thus, in the case of the NWFP, the Congress Party departed from the procedure to be followed in all other British provinces for ascertaining their affiliation to India or Pakistan. The Congress leaders agreed that the elected representatives of the NWFP, sitting in the Constituent Assembly, who had the responsibility of deciding the future of the province, could be bypassed. In so doing, they had taken a big risk with their plans to frustrate the creation of Pakistan by denying the Muslim League the NWFP. The hope that the Congress Party would win a referendum if the Pathans were not given the option of independence influenced their judgement. This was the situation in the NWFP as Ismay prepared to leave for London, on 2 May 1947, with the Ismay–Mountbatten plan on India's future.

After Husyen Suhrawardy (the premier of Bengal) and Jinnah realized that a divided Bengal would deprive them of the opportunity of ruling from Calcutta, the second city of the British Empire, they had started to lobby Mountbatten and the Congress Party legislators of Bengal for a united independent Bengal. Admittedly, Bengal had a distinct culture and the Bangla language was spoken by all communities. Then also, Britain had a special stake in Calcutta. It was the hub of British commercial interests in India and housed the headquarters of most British enterprises in the country. Tea from British-owned tea gardens in Assam and Darjeeling was tasted and packed there and exported from its major port. British-owned jute mills were all in West (non-Muslim) Bengal around Calcutta, whereas the fibre was grown in East Bengal, which was to go to Pakistan. If it became independent, and was ruled by the League, Bengal would continue to depend upon Britain.

Calcutta also enjoyed the Raj's flavour more distinctly than any other city in India. Some of its streets resembled those in the city of London around Threadneedle Street; Chowringhee was fashioned after Piccadilly with the vast open space of the Maidan on one side. The marble Victoria Memorial, a huge domed edifice in classical style, dominated the Maidan. The Royal Turf Club was nearby and numerous sports and social clubs dotted the shaded streets in the English quarters of the town. The Bengal Club still prohibited Indian membership. Before the massive influx of refugees from East Pakistan, Calcutta was not the overswollen and dirty city that it became later. Under the Ismay–Mountbatten plan, a provision was made for an independent Bengal if its legislators so decided.

Similarly, in the Punjab, efforts had started for a united province, which, would surely land in Pakistan's hands. Baldev Singh, the Sikh minister of defence, has recounted how, during the December 1946 conference in London, Jinnah approached him and stated:

> Baldev Singh! You see this matchbox. Even if Pakistan of this size is offered to me, I will accept it. But it is here that I need your collaboration. If you persuade the Sikhs to join hands with the Muslim League, we will have a glorious Pakistan, the gates of which will be near about Delhi if not in Delhi itself.[33]

Approaches were also made to win over Master Tara Singh, the most important Sikh leader, who was naturally concerned about the fate of his co-religionists spread over the fertile irrigated lands of West Punjab and those living in the former capital of Sikh power, Lahore, which would go to Pakistan if the Punjab were divided.

Originally, the Sikhs had simply been a religious sect of Hindus that sought to purge the most objectionable features of Hindu society, such as the caste system and an attitude that placed too much emphasis on individualizing and neglecting social responsibility. By the end of the seventeenth century, the Sikhs had become a militant community with a distinct identity. This transformation was the result of the proselytizing zeal of, and persecution by, the Mughal emperor, Aurangzeb. Most of the Sikhs were farmers who belonged to the same Jat tribe as the Hindus and the Muslims of the Punjab did. In the nineteenth century, under the illustrious Maharaja Ranjit Singh, the Sikhs had established their rule all over the Punjab and up to the Khyber Pass and had acquired an awe-inspiring reputation as warriors.

The Sikhs were greatly alarmed at the possibility of the formation of Pakistan, in which case, the whole of the Punjab might slip under Muslim rule. The 'Akalis' (or immortals) originally constituted a famous regiment in Ranjit Singh's army. In the twentieth century, a militant Sikh political party gave itself the name Akali Dal and started a struggle against the government-sponsored priests of Sikh shrines, including the holiest of all, the Golden Temple at Amritsar. In the process, the Akalis turned hostile towards the British authorities. On the other hand, the Sikhs formed a large segment of the British Indian Army and many of their families received pensions from the government. During Gandhiji's Quit India movement in 1942, only a handful of Akalis had taken part, most remaining aloof. In times of trouble, a minority community, such as theirs, could be expected to look towards the British power for protection. British officials, including the expert on the Sikhs, Major John Mclaughlin 'Billy' Short ('settle the Sikhs and you settle India', he used to say) had worked assiduously, during the war years, to win over the Sikhs to the British cause and together to arrange for a Muslim–Sikh *rapprochement* in the Punjab to keep the province united. 'A Unionist–Akali Alliance was likely to prevent the division of the province between two sovereign States and lead to an offer of special rights and privileges which would make them feel that their community had a more glorious future as part of Pakistan, supported by the combined might of Muslims and Sikhs, than an insignificant fragment of Hindu India',[34] observed a British civil servant, who, as deputy commissioner in their holy city of Amritsar, was expected to remain in close touch with the Sikh leaders.

The Unionist Party's coalition ministry of Muslims, Sikhs and Hindus in the Punjab had resigned in March 1947. After Attlee's statement of 20 February, it had become obvious that partition was coming, which led many Punjabi Muslims to shift their allegiance to the Muslim League from the Unionist Party. This shift, in turn, led to the resignation, in March 1947, of Khizar Hayat Khan Tiwana's coalition ministry, which had governed the Punjab for about a decade. Thereafter, communal tension mounted in the province and Master Tara Singh, brandishing his sword, raised the slogan: 'Pakistan murdabad' (death to Pakistan). The carnage of March 1947 in the villages around Rawalpindi, followed by large-scale killings and pillaging in other places and in Lahore, brought home to the Sikhs the danger that the community faced as a result of the division of India. The Sikhs' instinct for survival as a united community, combined with the ruthless leadership of Master Tara Singh, led them to certain decisions: to evacuate their fertile agricultural lands in the Punjab, calculated to go to Pakistan, regardless of the material losses to be suffered in the process and to withdraw in *jathas* or 'formations' into areas to the east that were to remain in India and after reaching these areas they resolved to 'cleanse' the Muslims from them and occupy their lands and homes. The Sikhs ultimately lost more agricultural property in the 'exchange', but the less well-organized Muslims lost more lives. The Hindus, prominent in the economic life of the province, hung on to their properties and businesses in Lahore and other towns in West Punjab till it was too late and suffered heavily.

All these events took place *after* the partition plan became known. The riots in the Punjab raised communal tensions in the NWFP (lying to its west) and in Sind (to its south) giving a boost to communal forces there and helping the Muslim League in these Muslim provinces.

During the period between 16 April and 2 May 1947, the withdrawal plan was drafted and redrafted by Lord Ismay and his colleagues at least a dozen times. According to Mountbatten's report, its broad outlines were shown to Nehru and Jinnah by Sir Eric Mieville, the viceroy's principal secretary. Both the leaders gave their approval to this plan, but, in fact, the points shown to Nehru gave him no idea of the full scheme.

On 2 May 1947, Lord Ismay left for London with the plan and, on 6 May, wired back that the preliminary reactions back home had been favourable. Mountbatten now embarked on the second phase of his task, i.e., to tackle Nehru on India's adherence to the Commonwealth.

The Ismay plan had made no mention of India's affiliation to the British Commonwealth. After hearing from Nehru and Krishna Menon that India would leave the Commonwealth, Mountbatten had decided to take up this issue after he had achieved the first two of his three objectives. The Commonwealth issue was no small matter for Britain or for Mountbatten's own reputation. King George VI, his cousin and sovereign, had expressed to him the wish, during his farewell call on him, to keep India, if possible, in the British Commonwealth. If independent India remained a member of the British Commonwealth, it would prove that its leaders had accepted partition of their own free will. If this was not so, why would India continue to remain in the British Commonwealth?

This factor was particularly important in the context of the US opposition to partition.

Such an outcome was also necessary to avoid a Conservative backlash against the Indian Independence Bill when it would be introduced in the British Parliament and to head off opposition generally in Britain on the ground that the Labour Party was 'throwing away India'. The White dominions of the British Commonwealth, particularly South Africa and Australia, were sceptical about the British Labour Party's policies. Jan Smuts, the prime minister of South Africa, had written to Attlee on 16 February 1947:

> British retirement now would in effect give sovereignty to Congress India. Surely the Muslim position in India and the Middle East and the British interests generally would make this a very undesirable development.... Strategically and ideologically as well as Imperial considerations point to the Muslims as the better choice if a choice is forced on Britain by the course of events.[35]

If India abandoned the British Commonwealth, such sentiments against Attlee's Government would be strengthened.

To accomplish his task, Mountbatten recruited Krishna Menon. There were three reasons for his doing so. The first was because Menon genuinely believed that if the British Commonwealth remained a force in the post-war world, it would prevent the establishment of American hegemony over the newly emerging countries. In a long talk Menon had with Mountbatten on 20 April 1947, he had said that 'the object of US policy was [to create] an economic, political and military vacuum in India which America would fill'.[36] In the correspondence he carried on with Mountbatten that summer, in one of his letters, he wrote: 'Public opinion is putting the brakes on Mr Bevin [the foreign secretary] and the surrender to the dollar. The resistance to American domination is fortunately mounting high in Labour ranks, although the incapacity to alter social habits combined with administrative muddles tend to retain the dollar grip and to confuse domestic and foreign policies.'[37] About a month earlier, in a handwritten letter to Mountbatten, he had noted:

Perhaps you noticed that the Americans are going to help us to fight for our independence, according to Ambassador [Henry] Grady [the US envoy to India]. Independence from whom, it does not say? Some people take time to grow up![38]

The second solid reason why the viceroy could count upon Menon was the latter's anxiety to get Mountbatten's help to become the Indian high commissioner to the UK after independence. Nearer the day of independence, there is a record of a cosy exchange on this issue between the viceroy and Menon: 'Perhaps you would consider whether it is necessary to ask JN to make up his mind [on the appointment]', penned Krishna Menon.[39] To this, Mountbatten replied: 'The next time I see JN I will ask what he is proposing to do.'[40]

The most crucial reason was Menon's close links with Nehru. Mountbatten explained to the secretary of state the reasons for his keeping in close contact with Menon, who was quite a controversial figure even amongst the leftists in London, as follows:

He [Krishna Menon] was a close friend of Pt. Nehru...I would ask him to tell me what was in Pt. Nehru's mind. He would keep me informed of the background of what was going on in Congress circles generally: I would recruit his assistance to "put over" any points which I find too delicate to handle myself and at all events to prepare the ground for me.[41]

Mountbatten decided to raise the Commonwealth issue with Nehru in the cool heights of the Himalayas. He invited him and Krishna Menon to be his guests from 7 May 1947, at the Retreat, the viceroy's hideaway in Mashobra above Simla – a very English cottage with rafters, chintz-covered sofas, water colours on the walls and dahlias and hollylocks in the garden. In Simla, however, it was the other Menon, V.P., who emerged the hero, and in a startling week, settled this matter – and not only this, but also of the partition of India.

Even though V.P. Menon was the viceroy's reforms commissioner, he had not been consulted during the formulation of the Mountbatten–Ismay plan. According to Mountbatten's press adviser, Alan Campbell-

Field Marshal Lord Archibald Wavell, viceroy of India from September 1943 to March 1947, writing his journal.
(*Courtesy*: Nehru Memorial Museum and Library, New Delhi.)

US envoys in pre-independence India.
Top row: Colonel Louis Johnson and Louis Phillips.
Bottom row: Henry F. Grady and George Merrell.
(*Courtesy*: US Embassy, New Delhi.)

Sardar Vallabhbhai Patel and Maulana Abul Kalam Azad at Simla (June 1945).
(*Courtesy*: Nehru Memorial Museum and Library, New Delhi.)

Clement Attlee (with a pipe in his hand), prime minister of Great Britain,
with Sir Stafford Cripps, his pointsman for dealing with Indian nationalists.
(Author's collection.)

Sir Olaf Caroe (ICS), the governor of the North West Frontier Province from September 1946 to July 1947.
(Author's collection.)

Lord Mountbatten of Burma, viceroy of India at the time of independence and thereafter governor-general till June 1948.
(Author's collection.)

The Frontier Gandhi, Khan Abdul Ghaffar Khan, in 1947.
(*Courtesy*: Nehru Memorial Museum and Library, New Delhi.)

Jawaharlal Nehru and Lady Edwina Mountbatten at The Retreat, Simla, 1948.
The author is standing behind Lady Mountbatten.
(Author's collection.)

Johnson,[42] Ismay advised against involving any Indian in the process. V.P. had his own well-considered views on what should be done. He was aware that the Congress leaders' priority was for early independence and they were willing to make concessions – including territorial – to get it. For their part, the British were determined to ensure that India remained in the Commonwealth and were willing to yield a great deal for such an outcome. V.P. Menon's contacts with Sardar Patel since 1946 had convinced him that the Congress Party's Working Committee would come round to accept the secession of West Punjab, Sind, Baluchistan and East Bengal, as also the Sylhet district from Assam. The only major problem would be posed by the NWFP, where the Congress Party held the majority in the Provincial Legislature.

V.P. Menon had no direct contact with Jinnah, but from his British colleagues on the viceroy's staff, he was aware that, whatever his bluster, Jinnah was reconciled to accepting a cut in the territory he had asked for, for Pakistan. Had Jinnah not told Wavell in November 1946: '[The] British should give him his own bit of territory, however small it might be?'[43] And had he not told Mountbatten, on 10 April 1947: 'I do not care how little you give me as long as you give it to me completely?'[44] Jinnah had also promised the British that Pakistan would remain in the Commonwealth. So, the outline of a deal was discernible to V.P. Menon:

(1) Partition of India on the Wavell plan, i.e., the smaller Pakistan;
(2) an immediate transfer of power;
(3) since (2) could only be done by amending the Act of 1935 that was in force (rather than wait for the labours of the Constituent Assembly or Assemblies to be completed) this procedure would *ipso facto* mean the two successor states would become independent as British dominions and as part of the Commonwealth, whatever was decided by their respective Constituent Assemblies ultimately; and
(4) to make India accept the amputation of the NWFP and Baluchistan from its territory, Mountbatten to give a verbal assurance to Patel that he would persuade the princes to

accede to one or the other dominion and oppose any princely state from trying to become independent. (Such an assurance would mean 90 per cent of the territories of princely states would go to India and more than compensate it for the territory lost to Pakistan.)

V.P. Menon hailed from the erstwhile princely state of Cochin (in present-day Kerala) on the southwestern coast of India. He had risen from the clerical rank in the Viceroy's Reforms Commissioner's Office. He did not belong to the Indian Civil Service (ICS), the elite cadre that administered India. A prince who met him for the first time in a lift in the Savoy Hotel, London, during the Second Round Table Conference in 1931, described him 'as having an air of authority even though he was clutching a bulky portfolio in his arms, no doubt files for the senior British officers of Viceroy Lord Irwin's staff'.[45] Short, slightly hunched, his lower lip hanging out, he looked the typical diffident babu.*

It was V.P. Menon who put forward the formula used as the basis for India's constitutional independence. Later, as secretary of the newly created Ministry of (Princely) States he arranged – under the ministership of Sardar Patel and with Mountbatten's help – for the princes to accede to the dominion of India before the date of Indian independence. The following year (1948) he played a central role in the total absorption of the princely states into the country (or 'mediatization' as Mountbatten would call it after the pattern followed in the case of German principalities in the nineteenth century). During 1946–48, he stood out as an innovative tactician, a brilliant draftsman and a highly successful negotiator and was probably the ablest Indian civil servant produced during the British Raj. After May 1947 he became the closest adviser of the Mountbattens, who, in conversations later, always acknowledged his crucial role. Most historians, with the exception of H.V. Hodson, who was once his boss, have tended to ignore him. A loyal public

---

* In the northern and western parts of India 'babu' means a lowly clerk. In Bengal it is equivalent to the French 'monsieur' though not quite to the English 'gentleman'.

servant of the Raj, V.P. was also an Indian patriot who, by 1946, had come to the conclusion that, on the basis of the realities that had developed on the ground and taking into account the Congress Party leaders' incapacity to handle the situation, unless they agreed to cut their losses, India could be Balkanized further with disastrous consequences.

V.P. Menon got an opportunity to explain his alternative strategy to the viceroy only when he was taken to Simla in the second week of May 1947. He found the viceroy listening to him with the greatest attention. Mountbatten was particularly struck by the possibility of the Congress Party agreeing to partition and accepting dominion status (and thus remaining in the Commonwealth) if power was transferred forthwith. He also agreed with V.P. Menon that it might be better for the country to be divided, with two strong governments taking over the reigns from the British with their boundaries already decided. This move would be less dangerous than for numerous entities to emerge, and possibly triggering off a free-for-all. If that happened, the country would drift into anarchy and damage British prestige the world over. Mountbatten, taking a quick decision, asked V.P. Menon to discuss his ideas with Nehru who was staying in the same house and seek out his reactions. (By this time, Mountbatten and Nehru had moved from the Retreat to the Viceroy's Lodge in Simla.) V.P. Menon did raise the issue with Nehru on 9 May 1947 and found the future prime minister not unresponsive.

*

In Simla 10 and 11 May 1947 were days of high drama. The plan sent to London on 2 May was received back, with HMG's approval, on 10 May, without any real major amendments, except that its language had further diluted the concept of Indian unity. That night Mountbatten gave it to Nehru to get his reaction. This step was against the advice of his staff, who felt it should be shown to all the parties or to none at all. Mountbatten maintained that he did so on a 'hunch' and this 'hunch' saved his viceroyalty from failure. However, it is doubtful whether Mountbatten would have had his famous 'hunch' to take Nehru into confidence, if he did not also have a 'hunch' that V.P. Menon's plan was the better solution to secure all his three objectives in one go.

The Ismay plan had a bewildering impact on Nehru. He stayed awake till 4 a.m. and the next morning the viceroy received a handwritten note, later followed by a longer typewritten one, rejecting the plan in the most emphatic terms. To Nehru his acquiescence in splitting the Punjab and Bengal did not imply casting away the geographical and historical oneness of India. The concept of India having full continuity as conceived by the creation of the Constituent Assembly from which the Muslim-majority areas might be shed, but to which most princely states would adhere, was one thing. To give the various parts of the country the initial option of independence – creating numerous potential successor states and then their combining to form one, two or more dominions – was quite another. Nehru wrote that the plan would Balkanize India, lead to a breakdown of the central authority, provoke civil conflict and greatly demoralize (by making headless) the Army, the police and the civil services. Working under pressure, Nehru had produced possibly the most persuasive letter he ever wrote. Mountbatten immediately understood that the Congress Party would not accept his plan, even though adopting Nehru's ideas may not, in practice, result in too different a result from his own plan.

To the British, Indian unity may have appeared to be their own creation, but India, with the Himalayas in the north and with the seas washing its shores to the south, had throughout recorded history been one distinct socio-cultural entity. Its people now wanted a 'nation-state' on the basis of political unity as the Germans and the Italians had achieved in the nineteenth century, even if some parts remained separated.

It was characteristic of Mountbatten that 'in a moment of calamity his thought was not how to muffle the difficulties with compromises or procrastination but to find an alternative course to recapture the initiative and succeed'.[46] Moreover, Mountbatten now had a fallback position. From one moment to another, he jettisoned his plan and adopted V.P. Menon's ideas and informed London accordingly. This move was carried out with such alacrity that it has been suggested that the first plan was shown to Nehru to browbeat him to accept the second. This was not so. But nothing focuses the mind more than the prospect of impending disaster and Nehru, who had been dreaming of Asian unity and of salvaging the colonial peoples from the Empire, was brought down to earth to the imminent danger facing his own country. The Ismay plan, therefore, did contribute to his accepting partition beyond the amputation of the Punjab and Bengal and agreeing to independence on a dominion status basis.

★

Mountbatten's sudden shift caused tremors in London but the viceroy was confident that if he could persuade the Indian leaders to agree to the 'truncated' Pakistan, which would include the NWFP, and to accept independence on a dominion status basis, Attlee would agree to the new plan. He wired to Ismay on 11 May 1947 to explain the plus points of the new plan as follows:

(1) The terrific worldwide enhancement of British prestige;
(2) The completion of the framework of world strategy from the point of view of Empire defence;
(3) An early termination of present responsibility especially in the field of law and order; and
(4) A further strengthening of Indo–British relations.[47]

The advantages that would accrue would be

(1) because the Indian parties themselves would agree to the settlement (partition) and remain in the Commonwealth;
(2) because the creation of an entity separate from India in the strategic north-west of the subcontinent that would cooperate with Britain on strategic matters would plug the hole in Empire defences resulting from the British withdrawal from India;
(3) because Britain would be absolved of all administrative responsibility of dealing with the coming upheaval in the Punjab and elsewhere; and

(4)   because India, despite being divided, would remain on good
      terms with Britain.

'I had only two or three hours in which to prepare an alternative
draft plan and I sat to work on it at once', wrote V.P. Menon. 'The
Viceroy was anxious to show the draft to Nehru and to ascertain
his reactions before he left Simla that evening and I had barely got
the draft into shape when Sir Eric Mieville came and took it away
to the Viceroy. That night I dined at [the] Viceregal Lodge. I found
that Lord Mountbatten had completely regained his buoyant spirits
and good cheer.'[48]

Lord Mountbatten was summoned back to the UK to explain
his U-turn. Upon reaching London, he immediately went into a
meeting with the British Cabinet. He explained that the possibility
of the Indian parties willingly accepting partition and the transfer
of power on a dominion status basis, which would mean India
remaining in the British Commonwealth, was an entirely new and
very significant development. He emphasized that to secure the
Congress Party's agreement, power would have to be transferred
immediately. There would be no fresh election in the Congress-run
provinces. In the NWFP, however, even though this province had
joined the Constituent Assembly, he declared that he would negotiate
for a referendum (not an election) to decide anew whether it wanted
to join India or Pakistan. The withdrawal of the option to the British
provinces, including the NWFP, to choose independence, would of
course apply to the possibility of Bengal becoming independent.

The procedure for ascertaining the wishes of British Baluchistan
through a more democratic system, as insisted upon by the Congress
Party by a vote in the Shahi Jirga (Royal Assembly), would be
explored, even though this change would not alter anything in reality.
The armed forces would be divided according to territorial
recruitment. A Boundary Commission would finalize the precise
boundaries between India and Pakistan on the basis of the agreement
on division. With regard to the princely states, nothing more needed
to be stated except that British paramountcy would lapse.

The point about India accepting dominion status as a basis for
independence was enthusiastically received by the cabinet. Doubts

were, however, expressed on foreclosing Bengal's option to become independent, but this was not insisted upon. For Bengal to remain under Muslim League rule might confer some advantages to British enterprises in the immediate future, but the essential requisite for Britain was to remove the strategic NWFP from Congress control. Attlee, as usual, was decisive. The draft of the India Independence Bill based on the new plan, he said, would be ready in six weeks after 3 June, the date on which the plan was to be announced.

The next step was to obtain the approval of the leaders of the opposition, including Winston Churchill. Churchill was unhappy that Mountbatten had accepted the viceroyalty. Churchill had built him up to serve and uphold the old Empire, least expecting him to agree to go out to dismantle it. Mountbatten described to me in 1973 how his meeting with Churchill had gone. (This meeting must have been on 20 or 21 May because, according to the record, when he saw him on 22 May under Attlee's instructions, Churchill gave him a letter approving the plan.)

Churchill was at the time in bed with a severe cold and Mountbatten was shown to his bedroom. 'As soon as he saw me come through the door he turned away to face the other side without acknowledging my presence', Mountbatten recounted. He pulled up a chair and sat down without saying a word. After a few minutes of absolute silence, Churchill growled: 'I know why you have come to see me.' Mountbatten said that he then enquired about his cold. There was silence again; and then another growl: 'Keep them as Dominions and in the Commonwealth at least.' Mountbatten replied at once: 'This is exactly what I have been able to do.' This response had a therapeutic effect on Churchill, who turned, the cold forgotten, to listen to him with attention. Mountbatten then recounted to him how he had been able to obtain the separation of Pakistan from Hindustan and yet keep them both as dominions and in the Commonwealth. Churchill was moved. 'He thanked me with moistened eyes and promised to support the India Independence Bill in the House of Commons if it adhered to what I had reported to him.'

When Mountbatten saw Churchill again on 22 May, he mentioned that, before he had left Delhi, he had secured the assurance of the

Congress Party to his new plan in writing. He, however, pointed out that he had not yet managed to get Jinnah's assent, though he had no doubt that he (Jinnah) would ultimately accept it. Churchill's reply is quoted in Mountbatten's report. 'It is a matter of life and death for Pakistan to accept this offer with both hands. By god! He [Jinnah] is one man who cannot do without British help.'[49] And Churchill pointedly asked Mountbatten to pass on this advice from him to Jinnah.

Churchill, a few months earlier, had condemned, in Parliament, the formation of the Constituent Assembly, calling the Indian legislators in it 'men of straw of whom in a few years no trace will remain'. He also lambasted the Labour Government for its India policy: 'Many have defended Britain against her foes. None can defend her against herself; but, at least, let us not add by shameful flight, by a premature scuttle; at least let us not add to the pangs of sorrow so many of us feel – the taint and smear of shame.' However, after the plan was announced on 3 June, he spoke in the House of Commons thus: 'These are matters about which it is difficult to form decided opinions now, but if the hopes that are enshrined in the Declaration should be borne out, great credit will indeed be due to the Viceroy, and not only to the Viceroy but [also] to the Prime Minister who advised the British Government to appoint him'.[50]

When Mountbatten met Churchill on 22 May 1947, the latter had given him a letter for Attlee approving the Mountbatten–Attlee plan based on 'an effective acceptance of Dominion status for the several parts of a divided India....' This letter suggests that he was under the impression that dominion status had been accepted by India and Pakistan as a permanent feature. Further, the letter suggests that Churchill was expecting more dominions, not merely two, to emerge from the Indian Empire – the larger princely states most likely. Mountbatten next met Churchill at the reception in Buckingham Palace for Princess Elizabeth's (the future Queen) wedding in November 1947. Churchill hurled angry words at him suggesting that his former protégé had led him up the garden path. Then Churchill turned and walked away in full view of the assembled guests. He refused to talk to Mountbatten for many years thereafter.

Notes and References

1. Philip Ziegler, *Mountbatten* (Collins, London, 1985, p. 156).
2. Ibid.
3. Ibid., p. 66.
4. Ibid., p. 71.
5. Ibid., Mountbatten's diary, 18 October 1922.
6. Financial year ending 5 April 1920, Broadland Archives (BA), p. 10.
7. Ziegler, op. cit., p. 21.
8. Patrick French, *Liberty or Death: India's Journey to Independence and Division* (HarperCollins, London, 1995, p. 284), based on an interview with Alan Campbell-Johnson in 1946.
9. Ziegler, op. cit., p. 144, based on Lady Mountbatten's Papers, 10 June 1941.
10. Ibid., p. 149.
11. Rear Admiral A.M. Peters to H. Hardinge, RA GVI (PS) (Navy), pp. 53–78, 21 June 1941.
12. Ziegler, op. cit., p. 150.
13. British ambassador's letter, 27 October 1941, BA, p. 116.
14. Francis Lowenheim *et al* (eds.), *Roosevelt and Churchill: Their Secret Wartime Correspondence* (De Capo Press, New York, 1975, p. 162).
15. Clement Attlee, *A Prime Minister Remembers* (Heinemann, London, 1961, pp. 209–10).
16. Report on 'The Last Viceroyalty', Part A, Para 94 (OIC, British Library, London).
17. In conversation with me in 1958.
18. Krishna Menon to Mountbatten, MBI/104, 14 June 1947, Hartley Library, University of Southampton.
19. S. Gopal, *Nehru* (Oxford University Press, Delhi, 2003, p. 345).
20. Report on 'The Last Viceroyalty', Part A, Para 11 (OIC, British Library, London).
21. Ibid., Para 14.
22. Ibid., Para 19.
23. Ibid., Para 26.
24. Ibid., Part B, Para 152.
25. Ibid., Part A, Para 41.
26. Ibid., Para 28.

27. Ibid., Para 31.
28. Ibid., Para 34.
29. Ibid., Part B, Para 46.
30. Ibid., Para 49.
31. Ibid., Para 54.
32. Ibid., Para 62.
33. Baldev Singh to Nehru, *Nehru Papers* (Nehru Memorial Museum and Library, New Delhi, 19 September 1955).
34. Penderel Moon, *Divide and Quit* (Oxford University Press, London, 1998 edition, p. 33).
35. IOR/L/Part/10/77 (409), p. 303.
36. MBI/E 104, 16 July 1947, Hartley Library, University of Southampton.
37. Ibid., 18 July 1947, pp. 6–7.
38. Ibid., 10 June 1947, p. 2.
39. MBI/E 104, 16 July 1947 and 18 July 1947, Hartley Library, University of Southampton.
40. Ibid., 23 July 1947.
41. Report on 'The Last Viceroyalty', Part B, p. 123 (OIC, British Library, London).
42. Alan Campbell-Johnson in a conversation with me.
43. V.P. Menon, *Transfer of Power in India* (Longman Green, London, 1957, p. 323).
44. Report on 'The Last Viceroyalty', Part A, Para 26 (OIC, British Library, London).
45. As told by the late Raja of Sarila to me.
46. H.V. Hodson, *The Great Divide: Britain-India-Pakistan* (Oxford University Press edition, Delhi, 2000, p. 308).
47. TOP X, p. 409.
48. V.P. Menon, op. cit., p. 365.
49. Report on 'The Last Viceroyalty', Part C, Para 56 (OIC, British Library, London).
50. Quoted from V.P. Menon, op. cit., p. 378.

11

The End Game of Empire

MOUNTBATTEN HAD NOW IN HIS POCKET THE REVISED INSTRUCTIONS from Attlee for the final round of negotiations with the Indian leaders. He returned to Delhi barely two days before the British withdrawal plan was to be announced on 3 June 1947 to the world. The most serious issue that remained to be tied up was the future of the NWFP. As long as this remained uncertain, the future of Pakistan and the whole plan would continue to hang in the balance.*

Gandhiji, since his return from the riot–torn areas of eastern India to Delhi on 24 May 1947, had been speaking against partition, and influencing public opinion against it. Mountbatten saw him on 2 June. His report on his talk with Gandhiji says: 'My relief may, therefore, well be imagined when I saw him entering the room with his fingers on his lips indicating that it was his day of silence. "I am sorry I can't speak", he scribbled on a note paper. His waggishness had not deserted him in calamity. His second sentence read: "But

---

* Sir Olaf Caroe, while reviewing H.V. Hodson's book *The Great Divide* in the 1960s, says: 'The fate of the 3 June "Menon" Partition plan hung on a resolution of the North-West Frontier problem. So long as the Khan Brothers (owing allegiance to the Congress Party) ruled the frontier, Jinnah could not claim leadership of Muslim India, and it was impossible for even a moth-eaten Pakistan to emerge. It followed that all Congress efforts were to preserve, and all League efforts to upset, the Khan Brothers in Peshawar' (offprint available in the Caroe papers IORL, MSS Eur F 203/1).

I know you too do not want me to break my silence." He then wrote another chit to say that Abdul Ghaffar Khan had asked him to convey to him to remove the governor of NWFP (Sir Olaf Caroe). I do not know whether he (Ghaffar Khan) is right or wrong. He is truthful. If it can be done decorously you should do it'.[1]

It had been agreed between Mountbatten and Nehru before he left for London that the problem of the NWFP would be tackled after an agreement on all the other points had been reached. Even so it was essential that the Congress Party gave its agreement in principle to a referendum in the NWFP before 3 June. While talks in London were going on, Abdul Ghaffar Khan had started propaganda in favour of a 'Pathan national province',[2] i.e., for a Pathanistan or Pakhtoonistan as a separate independent state. What had happened was that, as the Muslim League propaganda intensified that the Khan brothers were about to deliver the Pathans into the hands of the Hindus of the plains of India, the Frontier Congress Party men decided that the best way to beat this Muslim League line of approach was for them to demand an independent Pathan state. This, they felt, would also appeal to tribal leaders such as the Fakir of Ipi.

As Mountbatten landed in Delhi, the Congress Party, according to his report, made to him 'the request to allow the NWFP referendum to include a third choice – for independence'. Mountbatten took up this request with Nehru on 3 June, just before the Indian leaders were scheduled to meet him to approve the plan. Mountbatten argued that 'the Muslim League would never accept it'. Further, 'it had been at Pt. Nehru's own request and in order to avoid "Balkanization" that the option for independence in the case of Bengal and other provinces had been removed. I expressed surprise that he should have raised this point at this stage, all the more since he admitted that the NWFP could not stand on its own.'[3] It was at this meeting that Mountbatten played two cards he had kept up his sleeve. First, he told Nehru that he intended to remove Caroe; this gesture would appease the Congress Party. And second, that he would assist with the integration of the Indian princely states to the dominions. The second gesture was a significant one, and V.P. Menon was dispatched to Sardar Patel to explain its significance.

Nehru explained to his colleagues that if they did not yield on the referendum, Mountbatten, having committed himself on it to the British Cabinet, would have to resign and that would be harmful as he could be counted upon to help them during the crucial period before British withdrawal.[4] There was no time to get Dr Khan Sahib's agreement to the referendum before the meeting of the leaders on the plan that very morning.

Mountbatten saw Khan Sahib on 5 June 1947. Mountbatten told him that he was helpless in the matter as 'the independence option had been excluded for all Provinces at the express request of the Congress Party to avoid "Balkanization"'. Mountbatten also pointed out to Khan Sahib that a province of three million people, which received considerable subventions from the Centre, could not stand alone. He said that the referendum would be supervised by military officers under his auspices.[5] If he wanted the NWFP to join India, why not through the referendum?

Though Khan Sahib could not argue back because his peers had blocked the possibility of Pathan independence, he decided to fight the referendum on the slogan that a vote for his party would give them Pakhtoonistan. But in this quest also he was blocked, this time by the Frontier Gandhi, Khan Abdul Ghaffar Khan, who decided that his party would not take part in the referendum. Mohammed Yunus, the nephew of the Frontier Gandhi, told me that Ghaffar Khan made this decision for two reasons. First, in a referendum, unlike in an election, there could be no provision that the votes of those who had cast them with fraudulent means would be discounted and he feared massive abuse by the Muslim League supporters, as, for example, the same voter casting his vote several times (which Yunus claimed actually happened.) Secondly, the Frontier Gandhi feared massive violence and blood-letting between the two Pathan groups and he was absolutely bent upon avoiding violence. 'Gandhiji's pacifism had entered his soul', said Yunus. 'The referendum would go forward without any interference by the followers of Khan Abdul Ghaffar Khan', Gandhiji assured Mountbatten through a letter on 29 June 1947.[6]

★

Dr Khan Sahib and many others in the NWFP and India considered the above stance of the Frontier Gandhi, to which Nehru and Patel acquiesced, a big mistake if they indeed wished to scuttle Pakistan. Dr Khan Sahib believed that no great revolution could be brought about without the spilling of blood and wanted to take part in the referendum, matching violence with violence, if necessary. He was confident of winning.

The referendum was held in July. Caroe had left Peshawar by then, replaced by General Robert Lockhart as governor. The Congress Party leaders were instructing their followers to be peaceful and abstain from voting, reported Lockhart to Mountbatten. The results declared on 20 July 1947 showed that out of a total electorate of 572,798, 289,244 or 50.49 per cent had voted for Pakistan. The results suggested that Dr Khan Sahib's assessment that, had his party participated in the referendum, India had a good chance of winning it and blocking Pakistan, might have been correct. Less than three lakh people decided the fate of the NWFP. The last bastion from which the defence of a united India could be organized was evacuated without a fight.

The tribes were divided: some, like the Afridis around Khyber, siding with the League, but many others remaining with Dr Khan Sahib. Lockhart's last report to Mountbatten on 12 July 1947 said:

Pakhtoonistan is being vigorously advocated and the idea, I think, proving attractive to many Pathans. Rumours and reports of the Fakir of Ipi flow in details [Ipi wanted to proclaim himself the Amir of Wazirstan]...the revival of talks (commentaries) on the Kabul radio and articles in the Afghan press...is also disturbing.[7]

These were now matters to be dealt with by Jinnah: the Indian leaders had washed their hands off the frontier. A vague bitterness was to linger in the minds of the pro-Congress Party Pathans that the party's high command had betrayed them.

*

In Baluchistan the vote was cast by the members of the Tribal Jirga (Assembly) and the members of the Quetta Municipality, as sketched out in the Ismay plan. No way to work out a more democratic procedure, as demanded by Nehru at Simla in May 1947, could be found. The result was predictable.

Sir Olaf Caroe was sacrificed by Mountbatten to get the Congress Party to accept a referendum in the NWFP. In fact, his views were more complex than presumed by Indian leaders. It is worth touching upon these views since they have some bearing on the situation that developed in the NWFP and Afghanistan later. Caroe believed that the real challenge to Britain (and the West) from the Soviet Union would come via Afghanistan, which he called 'the uncertain vestibule', while talking to the American diplomat Ely E. Palmer (see Chapter 1). This challenge, he felt, could best be faced if Britain retained control of the Indian frontier from the Pamirs to the Arabian sea, after India's independence; that is, control over northern Kashmir, the NWFP and Baluchistan – all territories west of the Indus river. Caroe believed that Britain had not only the expertise to control the warring tribes in the area but also, through its military presence close to Afghanistan, to influence Afghan policy, which the Indian Muslims (i.e., the Pakistanis) would be unable to do, not the least because of limited financial resources. He was not for Britain getting enmeshed in the communal problems of India by supporting the Muslims there in order to safeguard its vital interests in the eastern Middle East. Instead, he wanted Britain to work for the independence and separation of these territories from India and continue to maintain direct relations with their tribal chiefs and people in order to protect its interests. (The other view was that an independent NWFP linked to Baluchistan, Chitral and the 'Gilgit Agency', if it managed its own foreign relations, might become the target of foreign intrigue.)

Caroe's view, to an extent, proved prophetic. The Soviets did ultimately move south through 'this uncertain vestibule' in the late 1970s. Pakistan could never influence Afghan policy and, when in the 1990s, it tried to do so by exporting Islamic fundamentalism to Afghanistan, it got badly mauled by the Arab terrorists it had recruited to help in the enterprise. In 2000–01 the US established its presence in the NWFP to control the Pathans (and the Pakistanis) on the two sides of the Durand line.

As late as 22 May 1947, Caroe continued to advocate a separate Pathan state. In a telegram to the acting viceroy, Sir John Colville (while Mountbatten was finalizing the brief on the referendum in the NWFP with Attlee in London), he wrote

> my Ministry and Abdul Ghaffar Khan have started propaganda on a theme which I advised them to take up some months ago: that of a Pathan national Province under a coalition if possible, and making its own alliances as may suit it. When I put it to them then, they professed what amounted to fury at the mere suggestion. There is a good deal in the theme itself, and the appeal is a far more constructive one than that of Islam in danger. The switchover has probably come too late, but to my mind it is a strength, and not a weakness, that Pathanistan cannot subsist financially or otherwise on its own legs. The weakness is that the Pathans have hitherto been too divided among themselves to set up a stable State, and where they have ruled they have ruled as conquerors of alien populations. They themselves had always been in a state of anarchy right through history until we came and put them in order. [Afghanistan is not really a Pathan State at all.][8]

As soon as a firm decision not to permit an option for the NWFP to become independent was taken, Caroe immediately fell in line with government policy. He then, in his retirement, concentrated on the second best alternative, that of tying Pakistan firmly to the West. No other old India hand did more 'to sell' Pakistan to the Americans on the basis that it was the West's best defence prop in the region. (Some of his efforts have been referred to in Chapter 1.) His bestselling book, *The Wells of Power*, is built around the same theme.

Despite the growing turmoil in the NWFP as a result of the agitation by the Muslim League against the Congress Party rule there, Mountbatten continued to refuse Jinnah's request to sack Dr Khan Sahib's Government and impose governor's rule before the referendum there. It was Muslim Pathan pitted against Muslim Pathan, though this was not an unusual situation for the Pathans as history can show. B.M Segal, who has been referred to in Chapter 9, told me that, by May 1947, it was clear to the small minority community of Sikhs and Hindus that they would have to move out whatever the province's future. The only Pathan in whom they had confidence was Dr Khan Sahib. The Frontier Gandhi, according to Segal, was so concerned with avoiding bloodshed amongst his race that he was ever willing to turn the other cheek to the aggressor. (It was in memory of Khan Sahib that the evacuees from the frontier had the Khan Market in Delhi built some time later.)

The few effective Pathan political leaders who existed were with the Congress Party. Jinnah therefore tapped people other than Pathans or politicians to reinforce his position in the tribal belt. Iskander Mirza, a Bengali Muslim nobleman, was a member of the Indian Political Service that managed relations with the tribes of the NWFP. In 1947 he was serving as joint secretary in the Ministry of Defence in New Delhi. He was an outstanding officer who had spent most of his career in the NWFP. (In the 1950s, he was to become the president of Pakistan.) Jinnah had first met him in 1943, introduced by Liaqat Ai Khan. He now sent for him and spoke as follows, according to his son, Humayun Mirza:

> While he intended to continue with his negotiations with vigour, he felt it prudent to be prepared for the worst.... He asked Iskander Mirza to resign from the Government of India and return to the tribal territories he knew so well. There he was to start a Jihad (Holy War)...urging him to take this extraordinary step to preserve the interests of the Muslims of India. Jinnah's request stunned Iskander Mirza.... He knew that if the tribes were persuaded to rise in revolt, there would be considerable bloodshed as a result of raids on border villages in the settled areas.... Yet...he could not refuse Jinnah...so he told Jinnah that money would be needed to undertake this immense task, particularly if it involved inciting the tribesmen in Wazirstan, Tirah and the Mohand country.... When asked how much, Iskander Mirza estimated one crore of rupees [equivalent to Rs 50 crore at the end of the twentieth century]...Iskander Mirza was given Rs 20,000 for immediate expenses and told that

the Nawab of Bhopal would provide the rest. As for cover, he would be told of it at the right time.⁹

Humayun says that after some time (he does not say when) 'Jinnah informed him that Pakistan had been won and there was no longer any need for a Jihad'.

Iskander Mirza's expertise with tribal affairs came in handy to Pakistan, when as defence secretary in the new state, he helped to organize the tribal *lashkar* (militia) that invaded Kashmir a few months later.

★

On his return from London, Mountbatten found Jinnah in a rebellious mood. He continued to oppose the division of Bengal and to press for the province to be given the option to choose independence. On 22 May, 'in an interview with Reuters correspondent', records Mountbatten, 'Jinnah had gone even further, stating that he would resist to the last the partition of Bengal and the Punjab and demanding a corridor between East and West Pakistan'.¹⁰ (The corridor would presumably pass through Delhi, the old Mughal capital; the Muslim princely state of Rampur; Lucknow, the former capital of the Shia Muslim state of Oudh; and Patna the capital of Bihar, the old domain of the Afghan Sher Shah Suri.) These demands may have been the reason why Mountbatten armed himself with Churchill's message, when he saw him that day, to discipline Jinnah. Jinnah finally yielded on Bengal, the corridor forgotten, but he pressed for six months of joint control of Calcutta. When Mountbatten sought Patel's view on this topic through V.P. Menon, arguing that it might help in avoiding trouble in the city during partition, Patel replied: 'Not even for six hours.'¹¹

On 3 June Nehru, Jinnah and Baldev Singh (for the Sikhs) gave their formal assent to the plan – Jinnah merely by a nod. The same evening Indian independence and partition were announced to the world from Delhi and London.

The following day Mountbatten requested Gandhiji to see him again. 'I told him that although many newspapers had christened it "the Mountbatten plan", they should have really christened it "the Gandhi plan" since all the salient ingredients – such as leaving the choice of their future to the Indian people themselves, avoiding coercion, and transferring power as soon as possible – were suggested by him.' And Mountbatten knew from Gandhiji's statements in the earlier days that 'he had not been averse to Dominion Status'.[12] Pyare Lal, Gandhiji's secretary, has written that Mountbatten put his case to the Mahatma with a skill, persuasiveness and flair for salesmanship which the author of *How to Win Friends and Influence People* might well have envied. The same evening Gandhiji told his prayer meeting: 'The British Government is not responsible for partition. The Viceroy had no hand in it.... If both of us, Hindus and Muslims, cannot agree on anything else then the Viceroy is left with no choice.'[13]

Gandhiji's intervention in the All-India Congress Committee on 14 June was decisive in persuading the party to accept the 3 June plan:

The Congress was opposed to Pakistan.... Yet he had come before the All-India Congress Committee to urge the acceptance of the Resolution on India's division. Certain decisions, however unpalatable they might be, had to be taken.[14]

Govind Ballabh Pant had moved the resolution. He put the situation before the committee in stark terms: 'The choice today was between accepting the 3 June Plan or committing suicide.' Patel said: 'Had they accepted it (the Cabinet Mission plan of 16 May 1946) the whole of India would have gone the Pakistan way. Today they had 75 per cent to 80 per cent of India which they could develop and make strong according to their genius. The League could develop the rest of the country.' The Muslims in the Congress Party and members of the Hindu minorities to be placed in Pakistan opposed the resolution. In an impassioned speech Purshotamdas Tandon forecast: 'The Plan would benefit neither the Hindus nor the Muslims. The Hindus in Pakistan would live in fear and the Muslims in India would do the same'. The resolution was carried by one hundred and fifty-seven votes, with twenty-nine to thirty-two members abstaining.[15]

The die was cast.

It was Patel who first grasped the dangers to India of continued confrontation with Britain. This opened the door for the creation of the smaller (Wavell's) Pakistan and the amalgamation of the princely states with India. Nehru, for whom Linlithgow had no time at all, Wavell considered charming but unbalanced and other Britishers found supercilious, according to Mountbatten, proved 'indispensable' in the final Indo–British negotiations. Many of his English interlocutors found it hard to stomach his vanity. But, all in all, this old Harrowian found Englishmen more congenial and was less stuck up with them, than with other foreigners, Western or Eastern. (Did not Zhou En Lai, the Chinese premier, remark in Bandung in 1955 how arrogant he found Nehru?)

Soon after Nehru became prime minister of India, George McGhee, the US assistant secretary of state, prepared a note on him for President Harry S. Truman. In this note, among other things, he touched upon this aspect:

> The effects of Nehru's high-caste Hindu background were reinforced by his education in the aristocratic tradition of the English public school and university thirty-odd years ago. It is significant that his closest British friends are found among the nobility and the intelligentsia. Occasional overtones of disdain creep into Nehru's dealings with the British Labour Government and, politics apart, it would be reasonable to assume that he would find a closer kinship with a Churchill than an Attlee... he cannot find in his heart sincere appreciation of our efforts during and immediately after the war to persuade the British to accept their fate in India...[16]
>
> Heavily weighted as they are against us, we should bear in mind that many of these biases also operated against the British and that Nehru's attitude towards the UK is still replete with inconsistencies and contradictions. Nonetheless Nehru has reached an accommodation with the British generally satisfactory to both sides.[17]

It was soon after the announcement on partition that the foreign secretary in the British Cabinet, Ernest Bevin, stated at the Labour

Party Annual Conference in Margate in England that 'the British withdrawal from India will help to consolidate Britain in [the] Middle East'. Pakistan was to become the lynchpin in British defence plans for the Middle East and the Indian Ocean area, as is clear from the British chiefs' report dated 7 July 1947 (quoted in Chapter 1).

★

How was the Soviet Union reacting to the goings-on in India? On 25 March 1947 the British ambassador to the USSR met Stalin and briefed him on the subject. Stalin, reported the ambassador, 'agreed that India was a difficult question. He said that Russia was not interfering and that they wished success to Great Britain in the enterprise she had started in India.'[18] The Soviet press was less circumspect. 'The British Plan for the partition of India', wrote I. Petrov in the Red Star of 31 July 1947, 'by artificially separating the industrial from the agricultural areas, sought to disrupt the economic life and this will result in weakening the political economy of India.'[19]

Further evidence of Soviet views was provided by a lecture on 4 June 1947 by Yuri Zhukov, a member of the Academy of Sciences and one of the recent Soviet participants in the Inter-Asian Conference held in New Delhi in March 1947. Referring to Attlee's offer of dominion status, he said, 'although overdue, it was even now aimed at postponing the grant of independence'. Zhukov opined: 'In view of the successful post-war struggle for independence of the "colonial" peoples in North East Asia and of the development of a working class movement in India, Britain had been compelled to find a new form of relationship to cover continued domination of India by British capitalists.... The Labour Government had promised independence "knowing they could turn it into a fiction. Although British forces were being nominally removed, the principalities were being turned into British bases whence British domination of India would be maintained by force.... Indian parties and leaders, all...from the bourgeoisie, feared their own exploited working class and preferred the maintenance of close ties with Britain.... The essence of the Ghandi [Gandhi] programme is to keep the people disarmed and to retard progress".' The Pakistan scheme is said to have been inspired 'by the British as a means of dividing and ruling, while placing Britain's main hopes upon Pakistan'. Nevertheless, Zhukov said: 'The Moslem League was somewhat more progressive than Congress.'

Zhukov then explained how the Indian communists saw the matter, views that he probably heard from them during his visit to Delhi. 'The Indian Communist Party wished to see the country divided into independent States', Zhukov observed, 'with the right of self-determination and social and cultural development, economic unity, and the right to join or remain outside an all-India Union. This was the only correct way to grant true independence to different communities.'[20] They obviously saw greater opportunities if India was Balkanized.

✲

Meanwhile, Jinnah had started to woo the Americans. After seeing him on 2 May 1947, Raymond A. Hare of the US State Department reported to his headquarters that Jinnah had told him that the 'establishment of Pakistan is essential to prevent "Hindu Imperialism" from spreading into Middle East; Muslim countries would stand together against possible Russian aggression and would look to us for assistance'.[21] Nehru had expressed a different view to Henry Grady, the US ambassador in India. Nehru had told him, as reported by Grady to the State Department on 9 July 1947, that 'India's foreign policy is based on a desire to avoid involvement with any particular bloc'. The ambassador further reported that Nehru made the following points:

(1) While there was some fear in India of US economic penetration, India would want US...capital goods;

(2) While USSR in the past had held considerable attraction for Indians, internal troubles now are such that interest in USSR had declined;

(3) Indian economy would probably tend to follow the trend of British economy under socialist government.... Certain large industries would probably be nationalized; and

(4) India was opposed to Afghanistan's efforts to claim the Pathan-inhabited NWFP.[22]

A measure of American caution towards establishing ties with Pakistan is apparent from the telegram sent by the secretary of state to the US Embassy in Delhi dated 20 June 1947, a fortnight after the announcement for partition had been made. A Reuters dispatch had quoted the US consul in Karachi saying that an American Embassy would be established in Karachi, which was earmarked to become the capital of Pakistan. George Marshall thereupon stressed 'the need to avoid premature indication of any US intention regarding establishment of additional Diplomatic Missions in India (that is, in Karachi) or that the question is engaging the attention of US authority this time'.[23]

The US attitude towards the princely states of India is plain from the secretary of state's telegram, dated 16 July 1947, warning the US Consulate at Madras about an enquiry from the Travancore state whether the US Government was interested in its strategic minerals. (Travancore had thorium.) The telegram states: 'Direct and formal correspondence should be avoided (with officials of Indian princely states) since it definitely encourages US Government giving support to moves by certain Indian States to assert their independence from rest of India.... Such correspondence inconsistent with standing instructions.... We do not wish to take any action that might interfere with the sound objectives of avoiding further balkanization of India.'[24]

At a discussion in the State Department on 16 December 1947, US Ambassador Grady had this to say on the British attitude to the US Mission in Delhi:

The British have been friendly but have made no attempt to consult with us on common problems or to ask our advice. Neither [Terence] Shone [the UK high commissioner in Delhi] nor Mountbatten think of us in any way as partners...on more than one occasion Mountbatten has warned Nehru against dollar imperialism...[25]

★

Unlike Wavell, Mountbatten scrupulously avoided any reference in his reports or minutes, which are available for examination, to British strategic considerations. Instead, he used Ismay's flying trips to London for consultations with the civil and military authorities to handle this matter. Mountbatten's role in detaching the NWFP from the Congress Party's control shows that he was fully cooperating, under Ismay's watchful eye, to promote British post-war defence strategy in the region. Kashmir's adherence to Pakistan was considered a foregone conclusion by the entire British establishment. However, there was one very important difference from the earlier Churchillian policy. Having acquired Britain's minimum strategic requirements in the subcontinent through the creation of Pakistan, the British Labour Government did its best to consolidate the India that remained.

The period immediately after the Indian acceptance of the partition plan was a high watermark in Indo–British reconciliation. The Andaman and Nicobar Islands in the Indian Ocean were left with India. This was done despite the demands of the British military chiefs to retain them as bases to guard the sea lanes in the Indian Ocean and despite the Pakistani claim to them on the ground that they would provide a connecting sea link between its eastern and western wings. Since India was to be a dominion in the British Commonwealth, Attlee, on the viceroy's advice, saw no need for these islands to be detached from, or to raise a controversy over them with, India. Mountbatten and Attlee knew that India's status as a dominion was temporary and its adherence to the Commonwealth by no means certain. The islands, not having been part of the 'Menonite' trade-off, India could do very little, if they were retained under British control. Their handing over was, therefore, a gesture of British friendship to India, reflecting their desire to cooperate on strategic matters relating to South-east Asia and encourage India to adhere to the Commonwealth. It was an attempt to open a new chapter in Indo–British relations – once the essential business of partition had been accepted.

Similarly, HMG accepted the Indian demand that it should inherit the Indian seat at the United Nations, and that Pakistan as a new entity should apply for membership of the world organization.

★

The most important service rendered by the Attlee Government, and particularly by Lord Mountbatten, to India, was to persuade their allies, the princes, to accede to the Indian dominion, before they withdrew on 15 August 1947. The value of this service has not been fully recognized, because the operation went through so smoothly. The princely states occupied nearly one-third of the British Indian Empire; the territory involved was vast. There were problems, of course: Jammu and Kashmir, Hyderabad and Junagadh. But imagine the situation if there were ten or more Kashmirs and Hyderabads to contend with, as was quite possible considering that Jinnah was offering Hindu rulers of Hindu-majority states attractive terms to accede to Pakistan and several Hindu princes were on the verge of doing so. Sardar Patel provided the support and V.P. Menon the staff work during the negotiations with the princes, but it was Mountbatten, who, with a mixture of courtesy, panache and menace, actually roped them in.

The princely states were autonomous, but subject to British overlordship or 'paramountcy', as it was called. Until 1947, British policy towards the princely states, announced in 1942, was that on British departure, 'paramountcy' would lapse and the states – big or small – would become free agents. No provision was made as to how thereafter the relationship between them and the Centre would be regulated.

Princely states, by and large, lay interspersed with British provinces and depended for communications, currency, electric power, water for irrigation, imports and exports and other related matters on them, and for security on the Central Government. Out of the 350* princely states only five or six could hope to survive as independent entities. The others – about 50, 500 to 5000 square miles in area, the rest not more than 25 to 200 square miles in size – were too small to survive without the backing of the Central Government. In a demi-official letter marked 'very secret', dated 30 November 1943, Sir Francis Wylie, secretary of the Political Department, while

---

* This figure does not include the 200-odd states controlling a village or two, which, through a quirk of history, in Kathiawad (Gujarat) were left out from absorption in the British provinces or other states.

answering a query from Sir Arther Lothian, the resident in Hyderabad, lifts slightly the veil around British policy towards the majority of the princes. Sir Francis wrote: 'It is realized that they may ultimately be overthrown, perhaps violently,' but it was 'very high policy to let the situation drift for the time being'.[26]

In order to leave the door open for some of the bigger states to become independent, the fate of the overwhelming majority was to be left in the lurch. The policy had the support of Field Marshal Lord Wavell who had taken over as viceroy in September 1943. The British chiefs of staff took the independence of some princely states as a foregone conclusion. Those that remain independent could provide air transit facilities to British aircraft going eastwards. They had particularly in mind the airport in the large state of Hyderabad in peninsular India.

In 1947 this policy changed. In his letter of instructions to the viceroy, Prime Minister Attlee had said: 'It is of course important that the Indian States should adjust their relations with the authorities to whom it is intended to hand over power in British India...but HMG do not intend to hand over power and obligations under paramountcy to any successor State.'[27] This modification of the earlier policy had left the door open for the viceroy to work out a new relationship between the princely states and the successor dominions. 'Accordingly', reported Mountbatten, 'for India a standard Instrument of Accession was drafted to be put before the rulers for them to accede and hand over control to the Central Government on three subjects only – Foreign Affairs, Defence and Communications.... Sardar Patel had made it clear...only if I could offer the promise of accession by all or very nearly all of the States – the "full basket"... – before 15th August, would it be possible for him to persuade the Congress to abide by this limitation of subjects.'[28] That this was part of the wider deal struck with the Congress Party, on the lines proposed by V.P. Menon mentioned earlier, is apparent from Sardar Patel's statement in the Constituent Assembly in July 1949:

In exchange for Indian acceptance of partition, Britain had agreed to withdraw not only within two months but [also] not to interfere in the question of Indian States.[29]

'So far as Pakistan was concerned, Mr Jinnah...insisted on dealing with each State separately.... This', reported the viceroy, 'seemed reasonable in view of the fact that [the] only States which appeared likely to accede to Pakistan were Kalat, Kherpur, Bahawalpur, Chitral, Dir, Swat and possibly Kashmir.'[30] (Kalat, Chitral, Dir and Swat were small principalities in the mountainous tribal belt of the North West Frontier Province, between Afghanistan and Kashmir.)

'Operation Princes' was launched by Mountbatten on 25 July 1947, at a meeting of the Chamber of Princes.* The chamber had been brought into being in 1921 as a deliberative, consultative and advisory body to function under the presidency of the viceroy. Its formation was a further step in the evolution of British policy initiated after the Mutiny in 1857 to turn potential enemies into potential friends, indeed, into pillars of the Raj. After the Mutiny, the British had signed treaties or given guarantees to all those rulers and chiefs whose territories had not been annexed and incorporated into British India till then.** They promised to respect the autonomy

---

* The chamber comprised 108 rulers who were members in their own right plus twelve additional members elected by the rulers of the smaller stares. The Nizam of Hyderabad and the Maharaja of Mysore stood aloof from this chamber.
** Who were these rulers? Most of the rulers belonged to the old warrior clans who had survived the Turkish onslaught of the twelfth century by relocating themselves in deserts, forests and hilly areas. [Until the tenth century India was a distinct socio-cultural-religious entity in which the warrior clans ruled (and defended) the country under a centripetal polity. This system was wrecked by the Islamic invasions.] The Muslim rulers were those who had emerged from the satrapies of the crumbling Mughal Empire in the eighteenth century. (The British had conquered most of India by defeating Muslim rulers and annexing the territories they ruled. A few made alliances with the conquerors and survived. One amongst these was the Nizam of Hyderabad.) The Maratha rulers were the scions of the Maratha commanders, who in the eighteenth century from their redoubts in the Western Ghats, had conquered all of Central India from the weakening Mughals and clashed with the advancing British. The Marhatta ruler at Poona was removed but his commanders were left to rule large territories in Central India under British paramountcy. The Sikh states were founded after the collapse of Sikh power in the Punjab in mid-nineteenth century. This happened on the death of the powerful Sikh ruler, Ranjit Singh, based in Lahore. Much of the Punjab was annexed, but some areas were left to be ruled by Sikh princes under British paramountcy. The Dogra Rajput ruler of Jammu and Kashmir was recognized by the British about the same time. From 1935 onwards he permitted a force, commanded by British officers, to be stationed in his Northern Territories bordering Sinkiang.

of their domains as long as these rulers remained loyal to the King. Indeed, every effort was made to build up the importance of the princes. It was hoped that the chamber would help them coordinate policies among themselves – and with the viceroy – on the changing political scene in India.

The British expectations about the princes reached their zenith with the promulgation of the All-India Federation Act of 1935, as explained in Chapter 2. One-third of the Lower House of the Central Legislature was to be filled by the nominees of the princes who, if they could work unitedly and coordinate their policies with the conservative elected leaders, could dominate the federation. However, the princes dithered to join the federation because of the fear that their participation in a legislature with elected representatives might increase pressure for elective government in their own territories. Overdependence upon the British had rendered them incapable of thinking for themselves, individually or collectively, or taking any meaningful political initiatives. It was after the war started and the idea of the All-India Federation shelved, that the policy – that paramountcy over the rulers would lapse at British departure – was announced.

The meeting of the Chamber of Princes on 25 July 1947 was its last. I, standing in for my father, was a witness to Mountbatten's performance at this meeting. The viceroy appeared on the podium in the white uniform of an English admiral with an imposing array of civil and military decorations. For a moment, in the hushed silence, he stood still, very upright, but slightly moving his head to the left and to the right in perfect showmanship. Then he started to address the gathering in a loud and clear voice: 'Your Highnesses and gentlemen...', he began. Speaking extempore Mountbatten made two points: First, that the princes were being provided with a political offer that was not likely to be repeated, as, under the proposed Instrument of Accession, they were conceding rights (on foreign affairs, defence and communications), which they had never enjoyed anyway; and, second, that after 15 August he would no longer be in a position to mediate on their behalf as the representative of the King Emperor with the Government of India. He succeeded in creating the impression that he was a friend who was trying to help the princes and his bearing and enthusiasm were infectious. The speech was followed by a question-and-answer session. The questions showed that the dramatic shift of British policy towards the states was not grasped by most who were present. An amusing scene then took place. The diwan of Bhavnagar said that since his ruler was abroad, he could not obtain instructions on whether to sign the Instrument of Accession or not. Mountbatten immediately picked up a glass paperweight from the rostrum and said: 'I will look into my crystal [ball] and give you the answer.' There was pin-drop silence while he looked at the glass for several seconds and then announced: 'I see that His Highness asks you to sign the Instrument of Accession.' Mountbatten's reply brought the house down. Alan Campbell-Johnson in his diary records: '...it was wise to strike a humorous note as being the best method of penetrating what seemed to be quite a high proportion of thick skulls.'[31]

In the days that followed, an overwhelming number of states acceded to India. The princes' euphoria that on British withdrawal they would become independent to do what they willed evaporated very fast. 'Without entering into some kind of an organic relationship with the Central Government Your Highnesses would be totally exposed to the Congress Party-inspired agitations with no help to come as until now from the Reserved Crown Police under the Political Department', warned the Maharaja of Nawanagar. Most signed up. 'But there were some "sluggards"', noted Mountbatten. 'Apart from Hyderabad and Kashmir (and Junagadh), the states which gave the most trouble were Travancore, Indore, Bhopal, Rampur, Jodhpur and Baroda.'[32]

Bhopal state, situated in Central India, was the largest Muslim-ruled state after Hyderabad. Its ruler, Nawab Hamidullah Khan, with some neighbouring Hindu princes, did not attend the 25 July meeting of the Chamber of Princes, saying that they were being invited like the Oyster to attend the tea party with the Walrus and the Carpenter. Rulers of Jammu and Kashmir and Travancore-Cochin were also not present. The former had not been invited. (The Nizam of Hyderabad never attended the chamber believing that he could not be placed at par with the other princes.) Hamidullah, by 1947, had fully entered the Pakistani camp and was busy persuading his Hindu princely friends whose territories lay between Bhopal and the western wing of Pakistan, such as Indore, Baroda and the Rajasthan states, not to accede to the Indian dominion. Mountbatten records in his report:

A serious effect which Jodhpur's defection from New Delhi would have been to open up opportunities for contiguous States such as Jaisalmer, Udaipur and Jaipur to accede to Pakistan through the contiguity provided by Jodhpur.[33]

Mountbatten then describes how he frustrated Bhopal's plans:

The young Maharaja of Jodhpur was next taken to see Mr Jinnah in the presence of the Nawab of Bhopal and Sir Mohd. Zafrullah Khan, the latter's Adviser (who became the first Foreign Minister of Pakistan).

Mr Jinnah offered the Maharaja the use of Karachi as a free port, free import of arms, jurisdiction over the railways which ran between Jodhpur and Hyderabad in Sind and a large supply of grain for famine-threatened districts in the State – all on condition that Jodhpur would declare its independence on 15 August and subsequently join Pakistan.[34]

What Jodhpur told me in 1948 contained the following nugget: 'After explaining the offer Jinnah pushed across the table a blank paper with his signature on it asking me to fill in our other terms for acceding to Pakistan. Expecting trouble from the Congress-wallas after independence I was frankly tempted. But the heir-apparent of Jaisalmer who was with me suggested we consult my mother, the Dowager Maharani, and the Sardars (the feudal lords) at Jodhpur. So I thanked Mr Jinnah for his offer and said we would think about it and then return. As soon as I said this Jinnah pulled away rather brusquely the blank paper with his signature that I held in my fingers.'

Mountbatten's report goes on: 'A family Council attended by some headmen (feudal lords) was held in Jodhpur on 5th August whereat the majority was against joining Pakistan. The Maharaja however still thought that Mr Jinnah's offer was the best and telegraphed to the Nawab of Bhopal saying that he would meet him to fix up details in Delhi on 11th August. On 7th August the Maharaja of Jodhpur left for Baroda to persuade the Gaekwad (of Baroda) not to sign the Instrument of Accession. The same day a telegram was sent to the Maharaja saying that I wanted to see him at once.... It was apparent that Sardar Patel (the Home Minister) was prepared to go to any lengths to prevent this from materializing. Sardar Patel agreed that Jodhpur should continue to allow his Rajputs to carry and import arms without restrictions...[Patel] also understook to provide food for their famine-stricken districts...and finally [assured] that he would give the highest priority for the building of railway from Jodhpur to a port in Kutch (in western India).'[35] On these terms – and no doubt on account of the viceroy's pressure – young Hanwant Singh gave in.*

Mountbatten then turned his attention to other wayward princes. 'Indore (a Maratha prince), another of Bhopal's friends, refused to come and see me', reported Mountbatten. 'I got hold of the Maharaja Gaekwad of Baroda and Maharaja of Kolhapur and asked them to collect other Maratha rulers and fly down and bring the Maharaja of Indore back with them.' When Indore eventually agreed to show up in Delhi on 5 August, Mountbatten told him 'that he had shown a lamentable lack of sense of responsibility towards his people apart from discourtesy which he had shown to the Crown Representative.... The Maharaja handed me a long letter that argued that my policy was against the one announced by the British Government in Parliament'.[36] He went back to his state without signing the Instrument

---

* 'During my absence from my office for a moment', says Mountbatten, 'the young Maharaja pulled out a revolver concealed in a pen and told Mr V.P. Menon, the Secretary for Indian States, that he would shoot him down like a dog if he failed the starving people of Jodhpur.'[37] This was not the last of Hanwant Singh's histrionics. During the first elections held in Jodhpur after its integration with India, he sponsored thirty-five of his own nominees as candidates who all won, defeating in the process Jaya Narain Vyas, the chief leader of the Congress Party in Rajasthan. He, however, did not live to savour his brilliant triumph, as he died in a crash of his private monoplane the same afternoon.

of Accession. But he sent it to the States Ministry by ordinary post to reach on 15 August 1947. The Maharaja of Baroda subsequently told the viceroy that the prime minister of Indore, a British ex-police officer called Ralph Albert Horton (together with Bhopal), was behind his recalcitrance.

Mountbatten, according to his report, spent hours reasoning with Bhopal because 'he was his friend and did not want his dynasty destroyed by bringing upon himself riots and trouble in the State'. Bhopal confided in him that 'he had been promised high positions in Pakistan, possibly as Governor and even as an eventual successor to Mr Jinnah as Governor-General'. When Bhopal finally gave in, he stipulated that his accession to India be kept secret for ten days after India's independence. Mountbatten persuaded Patel to accept this stipulation.[38] Bhopal possibly wanted to avoid queering his pitch for the high appointment in Pakistan he expected to be made immediately after 14 August. But would not Jinnah, even if he gave him a high post, denounce him as soon as his secretive accession to India became known? Anyway, Hamidullah waited for the appointment for ten days, in vain.

Hamidullah's tragedy was that, faced with the loss of his beloved Bhopal, he turned in panic to the protection of Muslim separatists, forgetting his family's integration into India and his ancestors' and his own tolerant rule over his subjects of all faiths, plus his high standing in the country. And once again became the rootless wanderer his forefathers had been in Central Asia two hundred years ago, before they settled in Central India. Faced with the same dire prospect of losing their kingdoms, his Hindu brother princes, even the direst of diehards such as Panna and Dholpur, who detested the Congress Party like the plague, nevertheless, remained irrevocably tied to their old country. And their children, after a time, were able to make the adjustments, so that Panna's son was elected a Member of Parliament in the 1970s and his grandson, a Member of the Legislative Assembly of the federated unit of Madhya Pradesh in the 1980s. The daughter-in-law of Dholpur became the minister of state for external affairs and, in 2000, the chief minister of Rajasthan.

Nehru and Sheikh Abdullah had no time for Maharaja Hari Singh of Kashmir, who left his state to settle down in Bombay after

Abdullah formed the government in Kashmir. However, Karan Singh, his heir, became the Sadr-i-Riyasat or governor of Jammu and Kashmir and later a minister in Indira Gandhi's Government and yet later the Indian ambassador to the United States of America.

The alleged misdemeanours of Maharaja Bhupinder Singh of Patiala were recorded in the bestseller *Maharaja* by Dewan Jermani Dass (Allied, New Delhi, 1970). His grandson, Captain Amrinder Singh, in 2002, became the popular chief minister of the most prosperous state of India, Punjab. In the wars fought by India, in 1965 and 1971, there were sons of two former rulers in the Indian Army: Colonel Bhawani Singh of Jaipur and Brigadier Sukhjeet Singh of Kapurthala. Both were awarded Mahavir Chakras for valour in action.

Travancore (in the present-day Kerala state) on the southwestern coast of India had declared its intention to become independent before the meeting of the Chamber of Princes on 25 July 1947. As mentioned earlier, Travancore had thorium deposits, which could be utilized for producing nuclear energy. Travancore was the first place anywhere in India to introduce universal primary education and had, as far back as 1930, opened temples to the untouchables. Travancore was also the first to start the manufacture of aluminium and the building of sea vessels. Sir C.P. Ramaswamy Iyer, the all-powerful prime minister of the state, felt Travancore was so much more advanced than other areas of India – both British and princely – that joining the rest would set it back. Loyal to his king, he also feared accession might prove to be the thin end of the wedge for the maharaja's elimination. Travancore had entered into negotiations with a British company to exploit its thorium deposits and tried to contact the American consul in Madras to explore US recognition for its independence. As stated earlier, the US secretary of state forbade the US consul to establish any contact with the state. This step no doubt dampened the enthusiasm of those in England who hoped that Travancore might emerge as a dominion in its own right.

Mountbatten had to adopt a firmer line to discipline Ramaswamy Iyer. The viceroy reported: 'He, Sir C.P., sought to prove that Mahatma Gandhi...was a most dangerous semi-repressed sex maniac...and that if he insisted on backing the unstable Nehru against the realistic Patel it would break up the Congress Party within two years...and said he was not prepared to ally himself with so unreliable a dominion.'[39] Admittedly, his sentiments were more like those of a repressed opposition leader in the country rather than those of a traitor. 'When arguments did not seem to work I told him', says Mountbatten, 'that it was reported that Seth [R.K.] Dalmia (the richest industrialist in India at that time and a supporter of the Congress Party) had that morning paid Rs 5 lakh into the Travancore Congress Party funds in anticipation of starting internal trouble in the State after 15th August.'[40] The viceroy subsequently reported: 'Shortly after his return to his State (from Delhi) at the end of July he (Sir C.P.) was assaulted with a bill-hook and very nearly killed. The State Peoples' Organization turned the heat full on and Travancore immediately gave in. The Maharaja telegraphed his acceptance of the Instrument of Accession to me personally and Sir C.P. Ramaswamy Iyer's friends asked Sardar Patel to call off the State Peoples' movement.'[41]

Travancore's collapse persuaded those princes who had by then not made up their minds to accede to the future Indian dominion. This development enabled Mountbatten to present the 'full basket' he had promised Patel – except, of course, for Hyderabad, Junagadh and Kashmir. The last mentioned, London expected to join Pakistan. And the same Mountbatten, who had so assiduously worked to attach the princely states to India, frustrated Indian efforts to absorb Kashmir into India. How all this happened is the subject of the next chapter.

Before an Indian sunset there is often a glow that bathes the landscape in a mellow light. Princely India experienced such a radiance, before darkness descended upon it. Mountbatten's biographer, with typical economy, describes this spectacle: 'It was to be almost the last fine flourish of princely India; processions of pompous elephants; palatial splendour; the traditional diversions of the rulers – tiger shooting in Gwalior; fishing in Mysore; and celebrated grouse of Bikaner. Nor were humbler pursuits despised; at Ootacommand: "Golf course lovely. They cut a tree down to make it easier for me." It was a world which he had helped to destroy; but the inevitability of its passing made its attractions no less seductive.'[42]

The Mountbattens visited the Maratha princes of Baroda and Gwalior; Mysore; Travancore and Cochin; Kapurthala, the Sikh State (where the old maharaja asked the guests to raise a toast to Lord and Lady Willingdon); Bhopal, who had opposed him; and Jaipur, Jodhpur, Udaipur, Bikaner and Bundi in Rajputana. At the last place, young Maharaja Bahadur Singh performed the 'tiger trick'. His Excellency bagged a tiger literally between gimlets and luncheon – ten minutes' drive to the machan, five minutes on it and five minutes for the inevitable photograph with the dead beast at the shikari's feet. I can vouchsafe the Bundi 'tiger trick' having been in attendance as ADC.

No rancour was noticeable during the viceregal tour about the events of July and August 1947. Did this tour help to smoothen the princes's path to oblivion? One prince was heard to say three months after independence: 'What nonsense the British are going. The Viceroy was at the annual Bikaner shoot.'

Fraternizing with Indians had stopped after the Great Mutiny of 1857. Social intercourse, except with the princely order and some selected Indians, did not exist, even between British and Indian officers in the Army. Indians were unwelcome in train compartments occupied by Britishers even when they held valid tickets. British clubs excluded Indians. Indians dismounted from their ponies or other conveyances to salute the 'Sahib' if they happened to cross one on the road. That Harcourt Butler, the governor of the United Provinces, sent a bottle of champagne to the jail cell of Motilal Nehru, Jawaharlal's father, on his first night in prison for participating in Gandhiji's civil disobedience, in remembrance of the many drinks they had together, was an exception that proved the rule.

There were many causes for this attitude, by all accounts very strong till the Second World War. In the seventeenth and eighteenth centuries, the struggle had been between the British and Indian forces of not dissimilar strength, and equality in battle breeds mutual respect, even fraternity. By the nineteenth century, one side had achieved absolute ascendancy in industry, science, arms and organization, and the Indians were pushed into an inferior position. Weakness is what weakness does. The impression of India as a rich country with an ancient civilization that had remained fixed in the European mind for so long was destroyed, and with it respect for India and Indians. Further, the onerous challenges of a worldwide empire required British belief in their own superiority and pre-eminence. This resulted in slogans like the 'white man's burden'. Christian missionaries who entered India in the nineteenth century were sustained by donors back home and it was only natural for them to project the worst possible picture of those to be redeemed, so as to obtain funds. And sex, the great equalizer, lost its humanizing influence, as faster ships made it possible to bring out British wives to India.* To protect them too the race card had to be played to the full.**

The Mountbattens made it a rule that no less than 50 per cent of those invited to their garden parties, lunches and dinners should be Indians, when until then few, if any, Indians had been invited to such functions. He took an Indian aide-de-camp – the first ever appointed. 'These measures were not popular among certain class of Europeans', he reported. 'This was made clear when my younger daughter (Lady Pamela) standing near two English ladies to whom she had not been introduced, heard one say to the other: "It makes me sick to see this house full of dirty Indians."'[43]

In 1947, 50 per cent of the senior civil services, 60 per cent of police officers, and all posts above lieutenant colonel in the Army, were held by Britishers (K.M. Cariappa was made brigadier, the first

---

* Sir Kenneth Fitze, ICS, when appointed political secretary to the Government of India, had to leave his Anglo-Indian wife back in England. His colleagues in Simla and Delhi would not accept her.
** A British historian has written: 'A company's servant of the Mutiny days, Charles Raikes, while bluntly asserting that the British "should legislate and govern India as the superior race", added with some provision: "Whenever that superiority ceases, our right to remain in India terminates also." A century later the concept of racial superiority, though employed by Hitler, had become outmoded, and in addition the undoubted advantage that the British had once enjoyed over Indians in scientific knowledge, technical skill and political organization had greatly diminished as Indians from the Mutiny onwards steadily acquired the know-how that they had previously lacked. One noteworthy, but not often mentioned, example of change was the ending of the superiority of British to Indian troops, which had been a factor in the Company's original conquest of India. By 1943 Indian Divisions, in the opinion of Field Marshal Sir William Slim, were among the best in the world.... Thus, Charles Raikes, if he had still been alive, would probably have felt obliged to admit that on his own premises the time had come for British withdrawal.'[44]

Indian to reach that rank, that year). The Indian National Congress Party, having taken the lead against British rule, was seen by them as an enemy and the Muslim League and Pakistan a friend. At the bottom was the frustration at losing the most precious jewel of the Empire as well as their employment, security, good salaries and status. Some of the British anger also got rubbed off on Mountbatten. 'He lost India of course', was the common refrain heard against him in Britain from Brighton to Newscastle.

> ...to identify him [Mountbatten] with the British Government or with the British people generally is entirely wrong. I know that the great body of British opinion, both official and non-official shares our view of Mountbatten...he has definitely sided with India (against Pakistan)...

wrote Sir Francis Mudie to a friend in Lucknow soon after independence. Mudie had been home secretary in the Government of India and then governor of Sind before independence. He opted for service in Pakistan. He went on:

> The facts of the situation are that Pakistan is situated between hostile – a very hostile – India on the one side and...an expansionist and unscrupulous Russia [on the other]. As long as the relations between Pakistan and Britain are good and Pakistan remains in the Commonwealth an attack by Russia – and also I am inclined to believe an attack by India – on Pakistan brings in the UK and the USA on Pakistan's side. If these conditions do not hold then Pakistan stands alone and sooner or later will be swallowed by India or more probably partitioned as Poland was. I can assure you that the feeling in Britain is strongly pro-Pakistan, whatever Mountbatten and Cripps may do, and that it is growing so. I know this from the letters I receive from home.[45]

The views of British officers in the Army were reported by Sir Arthur Smith, the deputy C-in-C and the chief of the General Staff of the Indian Army in his periodical top-secret and personal report for August 1947 to the chiefs of staff in London as follows:

I will try and summarize what I believe to be the views of thinking senior officers here.... Events of the last two months have shown clearly that Congress (the Hindu) cannot be trusted. Congress have [*sic*] proved themselves dishonest, corrupt, conceited, inefficient and without any decent morals.... You can appreciate that it is not easy to keep the balance and be impartial. I suppose nearly every British officer who has opted to stay on would prefer to go to Pakistan than the new India...I fear that India will get more and more inefficient and become a second Persia.... Their only hope is a change of outlook but there is no sign of such anyhow at present.

One more example of the Hindu outlook. Pakistan wanted General [Walter Joseph] Cawthorn [who was serving with the Pakistani Army] to help their delegation at the forthcoming Canberra conference on the Japanese Peace Treaty, India refused...to show the world their self-sufficiency and independence, and so they are sending an Indian Brigadier from Japan.[46]

No wonder then, that so many British officers, military and civilian, who opted to serve in Pakistan, did their utmost to help that country against India on the problems left unresolved at independence, the most important of them being the question of the affiliation of the princely state of Jammu and Kashmir.

In splitting the Indian Army, Mountbatten had to ignore the view of his commander-in-chief, Field Marshal Auchinleck, who had throughout held the view that it would be more difficult to influence Indian defence policy once the Army was divided and joint British Command over it removed. But he had no answer to the old questions: How could the Indian Army help Britain if Indian leaders would withhold from cooperating? And how could Pakistan help Britain in the Great Game unless it had its own independent force?

The date for the withdrawal of the British forces proved a contentious issue. Auchinleck opposed early withdrawal, whereas Mountbatten argued that if these forces were retained, it would be 'tantamount to an admission that we did not trust them (the new Dominions)'.[47] Field Marshal Bernard Montgomery visited India at this time and Mountbatten used him to make Auchinleck accept the inevitable. Philip Ziegler writes: 'The Viceregal servants wore Mountbatten's personal insignia "M of B" (Mountbatten of Burma) set within the Garter. For Montgomery of Alamein also Member of the Order of the Garter, "B" on the guests' servants' uniforms was changed to "A". Montgomery of Alamein was delighted. "M of B" then persuaded "M of A" to make Auchinleck accept the splitting of the Indian Army. Not only was the Army divided within two months but [also] British forces were ordered to evacuate as soon as transport was available. "Magnificent", wired Cripps to Mountbatten, "we have been thinking of you hour by hour".'[48]

V.P. Menon's counsel came to Lord Mountbatten's aid once again at the time of independence. And it was this counsel, Mountbatten told me, that made possible the joyous and tumultuous celebrations of Independence Day in India 'that helped so much to bury past Indian animosity to Britain'. The Boundary Commission under Justice Lord Cyril Radcliffe of England was to pronounce its award before 15 August 1947. Menon's counsel was simple: Postpone the announcement of this award till after independence. The award was bound to fall short of the expectations of one or other side or both, said V.P., and create explosive frustrations within the two countries as well as suspicion of British intentions, which would mar the celebrations. The excuse then contrived for delaying the announcement of the verdict was to put it in a safe on receipt and to say that it was received from Lord Radcliffe on 13 August, after the viceroy had left for Karachi to take part in the Pakistan Independence Day celebrations there on 14 August.

The emotional celebrations in the streets of Delhi, with Lord and Lady Mountbatten joining the crowds, added enormously to British prestige in the world. That night, 10,000 invitees participated in the reception in the Mughal Gardens in the former Viceroy's House. Shanker Pillai, the cartoonist, captured the atmosphere of the changed era in a cartoon with the caption: 'Water flowed like champagne at Government House.' Free India had imposed prohibition at official receptions. It is another matter that Indians and Pakistanis celebrated their independence not knowing where exactly their boundaries would be: the Punjab holocaust had begun and the war in Kashmir that renewed Indo–British differences was a couple of months away.

Notes and References

1. Report on 'The Last Viceroyalty', March–August 1947, Part C, Paras 78–79 (OIC, British Library, London).
2. TOP X, S. No. 512 (L/P&J/5/224 F 45).
3. Report on 'The Last Viceroyalty', Part C, Para 87 (OIC, British Library, London).
4. S. Gopal, *Nehru* (Oxford University Press, Delhi, 2003, p. 357).
5. Report on 'The Last Viceroyalty', Part D, Para 60 (OIC, British Library, London).
6. Ibid., Para 71.
7. TOP XII, S. No. 394.
8. TOP X, S. No. 512 (L/P&J/5/224 F 45).
9. Humayun Mirza, *From Plassey to Pakistan* (Rowman & Littlefield Publishers, Oxford, UK, 1999, pp. 151–52).
10. Report on 'The Last Viceroyalty', Part C, Para 61 (OIC, British Library, London).
11. Ibid., Para 28.
12. Ibid., Paras 105–06.
13. V. P. Menon, *Transfer of Power in India* (Longman Green, London, 1957, p. 382).
14. Ibid., p. 386.
15. Ibid., p. 386.
16. Note by McGhee, State Department Paper 611, 91/11–350, 3 November 1950.
17. Ibid.
18. FO, File No. 6567, 31 June 1947, telegram from the ambassador, Sir M. Patterson.
19. FO, File No. 905, pp. 4189 ff.
20. Ibid.
21. US FR 1947, Vol. III, pp. 154–55.
22. Ibid., pp. 160–61.
23. Ibid., pp. 156–57.
24. Ibid., pp. 162–63.
25. Ibid., pp. 177–78.
26. Wylie to Lothian, Letter No. F 148, p. 143, Para 3, 30 November 1943.
27. TOP IX, S. No. 543.

28. Report on 'The Last Viceroyalty', Part E, Para 68 (OIC, British Library, London).
29. Philip Ziegler, *Mountbatten* (Collins, London, 1985, p. 405).
30. Report on 'The Last Viceroyalty', Part E, Para 69 (OIC, British Library, London).
31. Alan Campbell-Johnson, *Mission with Mountbatten* (New Age Publishers, Delhi, 1994, diary entry dated 25 July 1947, p. 142).
32. Report on 'The Last Viceroyalty', Part F, Para 12 (OIC, British Library, London).
33. Ibid., Para 36.
34. Ibid., Para 33.
35. Ibid., Para 36.
36. Ibid., Paras 16–24.
37. Ibid., Para 37.
38. Ibid., Paras 25–27.
39. Ibid., Part E, Para 73.
40. Ibid., Para 75.
41. Ibid., Para 13.
42. Ziegler, op. cit., p. 459.
43. Report on 'The Last Viceroyalty', Part A, Para 112 (OIC, British Library, London).
44. Sir Penderel Moon, *The British Conquest and Dominion of India*, Vol. 2 (India Research Press, Delhi, 1999, p. 1187).
45. See Khaliq-uz-Zaman, *Pathway to Pakistan* (Longman Green, London, 1961, p. 392).
46. File L/WS/1/1107, IOR, London, dated 12 August 1947, pp. 242–44.
47. Report on 'The Last Viceroyalty', Part D, Para 99 (OIC, British Library, London).
48. Ziegler, op. cit., p. 391.

12

The Kashmir Imbroglio I: Gilgit and Poonch

ON 25 OCTOBER 1947, ANSWERING JAWAHARLAL NEHRU'S COMPLAINT about Pakistan's tribal-led invasion of the princely state of Jammu and Kashmir (J&K), Attlee replied evasively: 'The future relations of this State with Pakistan and India have obviously, from the beginning, presented a problem of difficulty, the merits of which I do not think it incumbent of me to discuss.'[1] However, Britain's policy on J&K was made explicit by the secretary of state for Commonwealth relations in an internal top-secret policy directive to the British high commissioners in Delhi and Karachi on 31 October 1947, five days after Kashmir had acceded to India:

> It would have been *natural* for Kashmir to *eventually* accede to Pakistan *on agreed terms* [italics added].[2]

This was the pith of British policy on J&K: the state had to go to Pakistan but with India's agreement, as was done with the NWFP. (The compromise could be the partition of the state or India receiving compensation in some other way; for example, British support to India on Hyderabad.) This did not happen: war ensued. However, the two areas of the state that Britain had absolutely marked out for Pakistan – one in the context of Britain's world strategy and the other to ensure Pakistan's security – were successfully kept out of

Indian control and so they remain even after more than fifty-five years. These were the Northern Areas of the state along the Chinese and Soviet frontiers and the strip of territory in the west with a common border with Pakistani Punjab.

The Northern Areas consisted of the Gilgit Agency, with its dependencies of Hunza and Nagar and the principalities of Swat and Chitral* at the northern end of the Durand line, the de facto boundary between Pakistan and Afghanistan. Lying to the north and east of the NWFP, the Gilgit Agency stretched to the Chinese province of Sinkiang ('the new dominion') and only a narrow strip of Afghan territory separated it from the Soviet Union. It was of no less strategic importance in British calculations than the NWFP, which Mountbatten had worked so assiduously to place in Pakistan's hands. It may be recalled that, on 27 May 1947, speaking to Ely E. Palmer, the US diplomat in Afghanistan, Sir Olaf Caroe had drawn the American's attention to the possibility of Soviet penetration of this area when mentioning the desirability of the establishment of Pakistan. Ever since Lord Archibald Wavell formulated the partition plan, the British expectation was that northern Kashmir would remain under their influence either as part of an independent state or as a part of Pakistan.

Sinkiang, in the mid-1940s, had become a sort of 'no man's land', full of tension. The Kuomintang Government's authority over this province was crumbling. Mao Ze Dong's Red Army, which, at that time, was believed to be closely allied to Soviet Russia, was expected to enter Sinkiang shortly and, according to the British and American consuls in that province, a Soviet invasion too was imminent. The British believed – and rightly too – that if India acquired Gilgit, it would not permit any anti-Soviet moves to be made from there. On the other hand, Jinnah had already agreed to cooperate with Britain on matters of defence.

---

* The ruler of Chitral, in the nineteenth century, had accepted a 'tributary relationship' with the Maharaja of J&K and this move was confirmed in 1914 by Britain. On 6 October 1947 the Chitral ruler formally repudiated all ties with J&K, and, on 2 November 1947, formally acceded to Pakistan.

In 1935, the administrative and defence responsibilities of this northern frontier had been transferred by the Maharaja of Kashmir to the British Government of India under a sixty-year lease. As the result of the civil war in China became uncertain, the viceroy had prevailed upon him to do so in the interests of the security of the Empire. The region was administered by the Political Department from Delhi in the same way as agencies in the NWFP, such as Malakand or Khyber, with political officers stationed there reporting to the viceroy through Peshawar. A carefully chosen force capable of rapid movement in mountainous territory, and controlled by British officers (called the Gilgit Scouts), provided the muscle to the administration.

Fifteen days before independence, i.e., on 1 August 1947, the Gilgit lease was receded by Delhi to the Maharaja of J&K and Lieutenant-Colonel Roger Bacon, the British political agent, handed over the area to Brigadier Ghansara Singh, the newly arrived state's governor sent from Srinagar. According to V.P. Menon, 'the Kashmir authorities did not have the resources, including financial, to hold Gilgit which was cut off from Srinagar during winters.... In view of the lapse of paramountcy the retrocession was probably inevitable; but the fact remains that no sooner was Gilgit handed over to the Maharaja than it came under the mercy of Pakistan [through the NWFP)]'.[3]

The British officers of the Gilgit Scouts, Major William Alexander Brown and Captain A.S. Mathieson, remained to serve the Maharaja of J&K as contract officers, though they continued to report to, and receive instructions from, the political agent, Khyber, based in Peshawar, which, after 14 August 1947, had become part of Pakistan. Brown and Mathieson had had to swear an oath of allegiance to the maharaja on the 'Holy Book'. According to the historian Alistair Lamb: 'In fact they knew as the story has it that the book which they held in their hand, while swearing, was actually the *Shorter Oxford English Dictionary,* suitably wrapped in opaque cloth.'[4] The new *wazir* or governor occupied his official residence 'in the grandeur of impotence'; it was Brown and Mathieson who held the keys to power in Gilgit. Lieutenant-Colonel Bacon, on transfer from Gilgit, was given the Khyber post. This ensured perfect coordination between the Gilgit Scouts and Peshawar. According to the *Bulletin of Military Historical Society of Great Britain*: 'The broad post-partition plan had been discussed by [Major] Brown and the Colonel [Bacon] in June [1947].' And after Mathieson arrived (in Gilgit), as second in command, 'the two British Officers refined contingency measures, should the Maharaja take his State over to India'.[5]

In such a situation, whatever the fate of the rest of J&K, delivering Gilgit to Pakistan was fairly straightforward. This was accomplished on the night of 31 October 1947, apparently according to the already worked-out plan. As soon as Maharaja Hari Singh acceded to India, Brown got the Gilgit Scouts to surround the Residency and, after a short gun battle in which he lost a scout, he imprisoned Governor Ghansara Singh. Peshawar was then informed by Brown about the accession of Gilgit to Pakistan. On 2 November the major raised the Pakistani flag at his headquarters and informed the force that they now served the government in Karachi (then the capital of Pakistan). Brown and Mathieson had opted for service in Pakistan on the maharaja signing the Instrument of Accession in favour of India. Since Gilgit by this act had become a part of India, properly, they should have made an immediate request for release from their appointments. Their staying on and the action they took were political in nature.

★

Brown described his action as a 'coup d'état'. Alistair Lamb has written three books during the last fifteen years on J&K, imaginatively upholding the Pakistani point of view. He says:

Brown was certainly not acting as a party to a British conspiracy.... There existed, however, a small number of British soldiers and officials who, in a private capacity as friends of Pakistan, encouraged Brown and Mathieson to be in Gilgit on the eve of the Transfer of Power. Moreover, what happened subsequently came as no surprise to someone like Colonel Bacon...[who] certainly acted as a liaison between Major Brown in Gilgit and the Government of Pakistan, and in this respect he may have contributed significantly to the success of Gilgit coup d'état.

Colonel Bacon, however, in no way represented the policy of the British Government in London.... Neither [Colonel] Bacon...nor indeed [Colonel] Iskandar Mirza, Defence Secretary to Government of Pakistan, [was] particularly unhappy when they heard about what was going on.[6]

Sir George Cunningham, the new governor of the NWFP, 'on hearing of Brown's coup in Gilgit instructed him and his colleague Mathieson...to restore order'.[7] Cunningham totally ignored the fact that J&K, of which Gilgit was a part, had acceded to India. Nor did the King in England frown upon the coup. An entry in the 1948 *London Gazette* reads: 'The King has been graciously pleased on the occasion of the celebration of His Majesty's Birthday to give orders for the following appointments to the Most Exalted Order of the British Empire: "Brown, Major (Acting) William Alexander, Special List (ex-Indian Army)".' The abovementioned *Military Bulletin*, which cites the above award, thereafter states: 'No further details are available from official sources for what might have been recorded as a somewhat equivocal award.'

Soon Major Aslam Khan, once the deputy to Major Khurshid Anwar (one of the Pakistan Army officers who had helped to organize and lead the Pakistani tribal invasion of Kashmir) arrived to take over control of Gilgit. Apparently, there was some resistance from a few chiefs at the transfer to Pakistan and, in fact, a republic called 'Gilgit-Astore' had been proclaimed in the interregnum. However, Aslam Khan was able to suppress this movement and the republic of 'Gilgit-Astore' sank without a trace.

Says Lamb:

Pakistan would retain a direct territorial contact with China to be of immense geo-political significance in years to come. India would not acquire the direct territorial contact either with Afghanistan or with the NWFP and thus miss the consequent opportunities for intrigues with Pathans both in and outside Pakistan to the detriment of that country's integrity. It was a failure of India which would unquestionably contribute towards the survival of West Pakistan in future years.[8]

Throughout the Kashmir war, right from 22 October 1947 to 1 January 1949 (when a ceasefire was proclaimed that left Gilgit in Pakistan's hands), Britain successfully ensured that Pakistan's occupation of this region was not disturbed. After Mountbatten's mediatory role and the direct talks between Nehru and Liaqat Ali Khan collapsed, the Indian Cabinet girded up its loins for a full-scale war. However, Mountbatten was able to persuade Nehru that alongside preparations for military action he should seek the help of the United Nations. He argued 'that the UN would promptly direct Pakistan to withdraw the raiders, which would make war unnecessary'.[9] And Nehru believed him. Nor did the Indian prime minister anticipate how far the Security Council would come in the way of India's military options. But that is a different matter; the military threat to Gilgit had been removed.

Alarm about Indian military moves against Gilgit was sounded in late 1948. On 1 November, Indian tanks crossed the Himalayan range through the 3500-metre-high Zojila Pass. Never before had tanks been used at such heights anywhere in the world. This crossing opened the passage to Ladakh in the east and via Kargil, Skardu and the Indus Valley to Gilgit in the north. General Sir Douglas Gracey, the commander-in-chief of the Pakistan Army, in a briefing in Karachi a few months earlier, had analysed the dangers of an Indian push towards the northwest as follows:

> It would have placed [sic] the Indian army to reach the boundaries of the Pakistani State of Chitral and Swat (west of Gilgit) and establish a physical link with the leaders of the anti-Pakistan movement for independent Pathanistan.... It would have opened the opportunity also for a pincers movement against Pakistan by India and Afghanistan, the latter having shown a suspicious interest in the Pathan movement.[10]

The Zojila crossing was a false alarm. The Indians had crossed the Himalayas to save Leh, the capital of Ladakh, from being occupied by Pakistan. In mid-February 1948, a Pakistan Army column had started to move from Gilgit towards Ladakh, with Leh as its target.

This column had been halted for six months at Skardu, where the maharaja's forces put up stiff resistance. But, by September, it was marching again up the Indus. It must be noted that since most Ladakhis were (and are) Buddhists, it cannot be argued that 'the tribesmen' were wanting to liberate Muslims there.

✫

How the Gilgit issue together with the rest of the state of J&K was tackled at the United Nations is for the next chapter. Suffice it to highlight here the reasons the British gave to the Americans why they wanted Gilgit to go to Pakistan. Matters came to a head in August 1948 after the United Nations Commission for India and Pakistan (UNCIP) proposed the withdrawal of Pakistani troops that had entered Kashmir (which would include Pakistani withdrawal from Gilgit also). This proposal was against British policy. However, the Americans continued to support a Pakistani withdrawal on the ground that the state's accession to India could not be questioned until India lost the proposed plebiscite. It was at that stage that Ernest Bevin, the British foreign secretary, decided to talk frankly to George Marshall, the American secretary of state. Bevin spoke to Marshall on 27 October 1948 when the two were present in Paris for the UN General Assembly meeting. After observing 'that Nehru since he was a Kashmiri Hindu was very emotional and intransigent on the subject', Bevin added:

> The main issue was who would control the main artery leading into Central Asia. The Indian proposals would leave that in their hands...[11]

Bevin had let the cat out of the bag: that the issue concerning Gilgit was strategic and not one of the legality or the presence or otherwise of the Pakistani forces there. The 'main artery' into Central Asia that Bevin had referred to was the British-built track from Gilgit to Kashgar in Sinkiang, via the 4709-metre-high Mintaka Pass, across the mighty Karakoram range. (This artery had been an important link for them with their Consulate General in Kashgar, which maintained a British presence north of the Karakoram.)

From the internal telegrams exchanged between the State Department in Washington and the US delegation to the UN in Paris, it is evident that Bevin failed to carry the Americans along.

Simple cease-fire order (as the British were insisting on) without provisions for truce and plebiscite *would imply sanctioning of Pakistani troops* [italics added] and would not only be inconsistent with provisions of SC (Security Council) and UNCIP approach but would [also] be highly unacceptable to GOI (Government of India).[12]

wired back Washington to its delegation in Paris on 11 November 1948.

Accordingly, the US delegate to the UN, John Foster Dulles, on 20 November 1948, told Sir Alexander Cadogan, the British delegate to the UN: 'Difficulties involved in immediate cease-fire remain substantial without overall political settlement and in the light of India's claim to this area [Gilgit].'[13]

Let us now for a moment look at India's policy towards Gilgit. Nehru first briefed Mountbatten on J&K through a note on 17 June 1947: 'The State consists of roughly 3 parts: Kashmir Proper, Jammu and Ladakh [Baltistan, Skardu and Kargil].' The note altogether omitted to describe Gilgit as a part of the state. Such a document coming from the future prime minister could have created the impression in London that the Indian leaders had ceased to consider Gilgit as a part of J&K (possibly because of the lease). It could have emboldened those planning Brown's 'coup'. However, on 25 October 1947, after Pakistan attempted to seize J&K through the tribal invasion, Nehru wrote to Attlee as follows:

Kashmir's northern frontiers, as you are aware, run in common with those of three countries, Afghanistan, the USSR and China.

Security of Kashmir...is vital to security of India especially since part of the northern boundary of Kashmir and India is common. Helping Kashmir, therefore, is an obligation of national interest of India.[14]

Yet, some four months later, i.e., on 20 February 1948, the prime minister wrote to Krishna Menon, the Indian high commissioner in the UK, as follows:

Even Mountbatten "has hinted at partition of Kashmir", Jammu for India and the rest including lovely Vale of Kashmir to Pakistan. This is totally unacceptable to us.... Although if the worst comes to the worst I am prepared to accept *Poonch* and *Gilgit* being partitioned off [italics added].[15]

Lord Mountbatten was anxious to settle the Kashmir dispute before he relinquished the governor-generalship in June 1948. At his behest, V.P. Menon and Sir Gopalaswamy Ayangar, the minister without portfolio, drew up a plan for the partition of the state, complete with maps (which left Gilgit to Pakistan). It is difficult to believe that the Indian ministers remained ignorant of this exercise. Nothing came of it but the proposal was not kept confidential. V.P. Menon, on 23 July 1948, told the chargé d'affaires of the US Embassy in Delhi that the 'Government of India will accept settlement based on accession of Mirpur, Poonch, Muzaffarabad and Gilgit to Pakistan'.[16] Such a statement cut the ground from under the US's stand that to leave the occupied areas in Pakistan's control 'would be highly unacceptable to GOI'.

★

Josef Korbel was a member of the UNCIP, which visited Delhi in July 1948. He has written that Sir Girja Shanker Bajpai, secretary-general of the Indian Ministry of Foreign Affairs, while talking to UNCIP members on 13 July 1948, sought the withdrawal of the Pakistani forces from J&K (which would include Gilgit) before all else and said '...the sands of time are running out. If the problem is not resolved by reason, the sword will find the solution'.[17] This was in line with India's complaint to the Security Council. However, Korbel goes on to say that, a few days later, the Indian prime minister told him: 'He would not be opposed to the idea of dividing the country between India and Pakistan.'[18] This meant leaving Gilgit to Pakistan. Lars Blinkenberg, a Danish diplomat, has recorded that:

On 20 August [1948], Nehru in a separate letter to the UNCIP Chairman stated "that the authority over the region (the Northern Areas) as a whole has not been challenged or disturbed, except by roving bands of hostile or, in some places, by irregulars or by Pakistani troops...we desire that after Pakistani troops and irregulars have withdrawn from the territory, the responsibility for the administration of the evacuated areas should revert to the Government of Kashmir and that for defence to us.... We must be free to maintain garrisons at selected points in this area".[19]

The chairman, in his reply, fudged the issue: 'The question raised in your letter could be considered in the implementation of the Resolution.'[20] However, the question was never pressed diligently afterwards.

✶

On 4 November 1948, a Pakistan Air Force Dakota on a supply-dropping flight to Gilgit was attacked by Indian planes. As a result the Pakistani Cabinet decided that fighter escorts would be provided for supply-dropping missions to Gilgit that was cut off in the winter from Pakistan. Whitehall was worried that if this was done, India may then try to take on the Pakistan Air Force and attack airfields in Pakistan. After consulting the UK high commissioner in Delhi, Air Marshal Thomas Elmherst, the chief of the Indian Air Force, then called on the prime minister and held an hour-long discussion on the subject with him. During this discussion, he succeeded in persuading Nehru to ignore the Pakistani aircraft supply-dropping missions to Gilgit. Besides abandoning the simplest way to cut off

Gilgit from Pakistan in the coming winter months, this decision amounted to recognizing Pakistan's presence in the Northern Areas. It may be noted that no offensive was ever planned by India to regain Gilgit. Admittedly, the Army had constraints in reaching the Northern Areas during 1948 but the matter was never raised at any cabinet or Joint Defence Committee meeting.

In view of the erratic positions adopted by India on Gilgit, it is not surprising that the UNCIP proposals of Augtust 1948 were amended by interested parties in Pakistan's favour, so that the Pakistani vacation of Gilgit (and other occupied areas) did not remain unconditional. India failed to exploit the US support for its juridical position in Kashmir; indeed, it made statements that undermined the favourable stand taken by the Americans.

After India accepted, in December 1948, a ceasefire on UNCIP terms that left Gilgit in Pakistani control, the US dropped its insistence on a Pakistani withdrawal from Gilgit. The US State Department had sought the opinion of John Hall Paxton, its consul in Tihwa in Sinkiang, on the feelings of the Muslims there on the issue. The consul replied that the Sinkiang Muslims felt closer affinities with the Muslims than the Hindus of the subcontinent. He also reported that most of the trade between India and Sinkiang was in the hands of Muslims.[21] This information also possibly persuaded the US to accept the status quo.

*

The other area of J&K that Britain definitely wanted to go Pakistan, as mentioned at the beginning of the chapter, was the western strip of territory from Naushera to Muzaffarabad lying along Pakistani Punjab. The reason why Britain felt this area had to go to Pakistan is best told in the words of General Douglas Gracey, the British commander-in-chief of the Pakistan Army:

> Its [this area's] going to India would [mean facing] "the Indian Army on the long Pakistan border within 30 miles of the strategic railway leading from Peshawar through West Punjab to Lahore".... Occupation of Bhimber and Mirpur [two important

places in that area] will give India the strategic advantage of...sitting on our doorsteps, threatening the Jhelum bridge which is so vital for us. It will also give them control of the Mangla Headworks placing the irrigation in Jhelum and other districts at their mercy.... Furthermore, loss of Muzaffarabad-Kohala [a strategically located place] would have the most far-reaching effect on the security of Pakistan. It would enable the Indian Army to secure the rear gateway to Pakistan through which it can march in at any time it wishes.... It will encourage subversive elements such as Khan Abdul Ghaffar Khan and his party, [the Fakir of] Ipi and [those in] Afghanistan. If Pakistan is not to face another serious refugee problem...if civilian and military morale is not to be affected to a dangerous extent; and if subversive political forces are not to be encouraged and let loose in Pakistan itself it is imperative that the Indian Army is not allowed to advance beyond the general line Uri-Poonch-Naoshera.[22]

To make Pakistan a confident and willing member of the British team, it had to be made to feel secure.

Unlike Gilgit, India and Pakistan fought for over a year to take control of this belt along the Pakistani part of Punjab. This matter presented a very complicated diplomatic tangle. Before we proceed to deal with this story, let us take a quick look at J&K's topography, its relevant past and the events leading to the crisis and subsequent war.

Nearly the size of France, the state extended from the subcontinental plains to the Pamirs. Three great mountain ranges ran across it, east to west, and their spurs, north to south, cut up the vast area into different segments, so that people of different racial stocks and different cultures, who spoke different languages and professed different faiths, were found in this patchwork.

The Karakoram range separated the state from Central Asia. This range contained glaciers larger than any seen beyond the Poles and massive mountains – K2 (8610 metres), the second tallest peak in the world, and a host of other giants over 7600 metres. The Himalayan range ran through its middle, with the massif of the Nanga Parbat (8126 metres) at its western extremity. The Pir Panjal range separated these highlands from the southern foothills, where the Dogra stronghold of Jammu was situated.

The Kashmir Valley, or Kashmir Proper, was situated in the western reaches of the mountains with the ancient city of Srinagar, on the Dal Lake. The valley occupied less than 10 per cent of the total area of the state though it contained well over half the state's population of about four million. The only all-weather road from this isolated and beautiful valley ran along the Jhelum river to the west towards Pakistan. From Srinagar to Jammu there existed a fair-weather road through the Banihal Pass (2700 metres), closed during winter.

The Northern Areas were inhabited by Shia Muslims including Ismalias; eastern Ladakh along Tibet, with Leh as its capital, by Lamaistic Buddhists; Jammu province by Dogras and other Hindus; and its western strip, along Pakistan, by Sunni Muslims of the same stock as the Punjabi Muslims across the border. The Kashmir Valley had 80 per cent Sunni Muslims, the rest being Sikhs and Kashmiri Pandits (the last, because of their talents, having spread to occupy important posts throughout India). The valley enjoyed a distinct cultural identity (Kashmiriyat), the main characteristic of which was a tolerant form of Islam – thanks to the Sufis who had proselytized there in the Middle Ages and to its relative isolation. Or was it because rare is the union of beauty and purity?

Till the fourteenth century, the Kashmir Valley and some of the areas of the present state were ruled by a series of Buddhist and Hindu dynasties, which later were supplanted by Muslim rulers. In the sixteenth century, Akbar the Great started to spend the summer months in Srinagar. Towards the end of the eighteenth century, the area passed into the grasp of the Afghans, from whom the Sikh king, Ranjit Singh, wrested it in 1819.

The origin of the state dated from 1846. After the British defeated the Sikhs decisively and annexed the Punjab that year, they handed over the mountainous territory to the north of the Punjab to Gulab Singh, the Dogra chieftain of Jammu – for a monetary consideration. Gulab Singh and his generals extended Dogra sovereignty up to the Pamirs and Tibet. They united and held together this fragmentary land, the maharaja providing the focal point and a certain razzmatazz. The British were content to let the Dogras enlarge the territories of the

Empire up to Central Asia, cost free. As the Russians started moving southwards in the 1860s and the Great Game began, the viceroy assumed greater control over the territory by stationing political agents in it. In the 1880s the British built the track from Gilgit to Kashgar in Sinkiang via the Mintaka Pass in the Karakoram, referred to earlier. Kashmir became even more important for Britain after the Bolsheviks took hold of Russia in the 1920s and started to penetrate frontiers 'with the invisible force of ideology', sending communist agents and literature into India. They used the unfrequented Kashmir passes, including the 5575-metre-high Karakoram Pass on the track from Leh to Yarkand.* Agents of both sides used Kashmir rather than the more exposed routes via Afghanistan. Colonel F.M. Bailey, on his famous mission to Tashkent in 1918, left via Kashmir.

Till March 1947, it was expected that the rulers of some of the bigger princely states, such as J&K, might choose independence and remain associated with Britain, particularly in the vital sphere of defence. However, as indicated in the last chapter, British policy in April 1947 suddenly changed, and the princely states were advised to accede to one or the other dominion. As soon as the agreement on partition was reached, Lord Mountbatten himself, on 17 June 1947, travelled to Srinagar to discuss the future of this strategically placed area with the ruler, Maharaja Hari Singh. They were old acquaintances, having served together as aides-de-camp to the Prince of Wales (later King Edward VIII) during his fairly lengthy tour of India in 1921. Mountbatten broached the subject with the maharaja, during a car drive, with Hari Singh at the wheel of his Bentley. Mountbatten told me many years later:

> I explained to HH [His Highness] that his choice was between acceding to India or Pakistan and made it clear that I had

---

* Both the towns, Kashgar and Yarkand in Sinkiang, lay on the old silk route between Europe and China.

assurances from the Indian leaders that if he acceded to Pakistan they would not take it amiss.

According to V.P. Menon: 'These assurances had been given by Sardar Patel, the Home Minister, himself.'[23]* H.V. Hodson, who was given permission to see the Mountbatten papers that are still unavailable to others, has written that the viceroy also told Hari Singh not to take a decision till the Pakistan Constituent Assembly had been convened.[24] While briefing Jinnah on 1 November 1947, at Lahore, Mountbatten maintained that he had advised the maharaja 'to ascertain the will of the people and then accede to the Dominion of the people's choice'.[25]

The loss of the option of independence came as a shock to Hari Singh. He withdrew like an oyster into his shell, avoiding thereby further discussions with the viceroy. He probably felt that his friend wanted him to join Pakistan. This he was absolutely unwilling to do. It would outrage his entire Dogra base and could lead to his elimination by the Muslim fanatics gathering in Pakistan. If he acceded to India he risked alienating a large section of his Muslim subjects. Besides, there was no safety for him in India either. Sheikh Abdullah, the leader of the National Conference – then the strongest party in the Kashmir Valley – posed a major threat to his throne and Dogra rule, against which Abdullah and his followers had been agitating since the 1930s. The fact that Abdullah's party was allied to the Indian National Congress and that he himself was admired by Nehru presented a double danger. Hari Singh had been compelled to take the future prime minister into custody in 1946 when he had tried to enter Kashmir to agitate for Abdullah's release from prison. The fact that a majority of the 80 per cent of the Muslims of the Kashmir

---

* Before the 'basket of princes' promised by Mountbatten had been delivered to him, which happened around 15 August 1947, Patel was more flexible on Kashmir. The viceroy was helping to place in the Indian dominion an area spread over 500,000 square miles with a population of 86.5 million, comprising the princely states. Patel was more concerned with them and also in obtaining Mountbatten's help to discourage the Nizam of Hyderabad from seeking independence for his state. It was after Pakistan tried to seize J&K by force through a barbaric attack that Patel became the most indefatigable crusader against Pakistan on Kashmir.

Valley acknowledged Abdullah as their leader excited Nehru greatly. Here was a Muslim leader who rejected Jinnah's two-nation theory; who would serve as a bridge between Kashmir and India; who would help to make his ancestral home a symbol of Indian secularism. Karan Singh, Hari Singh's heir apparent, has observed:

> I suspect that in his heart of hearts my father still did not believe that the British would actually leave.... Independence could perhaps have been an attractive proposition but to carry that off would have required careful preparation and prolonged negotiations and diplomatic ability.... Instead of taking advantage of Mountbatten's visit to discuss the whole situation meaningfully and trying to arrive at a rational decision, he first sent the Viceroy out on a prolonged fishing trip to Thricker (where Mountbatten shocked our staff by sun-bathing in the nude) and then – having fixed a meeting just before his departure – got out of it on the plea that he had suddenly developed a severe attack of colic.... Thus the last real chance of working out a viable political settlement was lost.[26]

Mountbatten reached out to the maharaja again at the time of India's independence. Lord Ismay visited Srinagar on a 'holiday' during the Independence Day celebrations in India and met him there. According to Philip Ziegler, he applied pressure on the maharaja. When Ismay referred to the Muslim population of Kashmir, the maharaja replied that the Kashmir Valley's Muslims (where two-thirds of the Muslims of Kashmir lived) were very different from the Punjabi Muslims. 'All he would talk about was Polo in Cheltenham in 1935 [Ismay was then military secretary to the viceroy, Lord Willingdon] and the prospect of his colt in the Indian Derby.'[27]

The Maharaja of Kashmir had not been invited to the last meeting of the Chamber of Princes on 25 July 1947, in which Mountbatten launched his operation to rope in the princes (see Chapter 11 for details). V.P. Menon, who was the secretary dealing with the princely states, has written: 'If truth be told I for one had simply no time to think of Kashmir',[28] an amazing statement from a live wire like him, unless Mountbatten, whose closest adviser he was, had infected him with his apathy for building up an India–Kashmir connection.

In his personal report to the secretary of state (of July 1947), while enumerating the states that might join Pakistan, Mountbatten mentioned 'the possibility of Kashmir joining Pakistan'.[29] This report was sent after he had seen Hari Singh. On 10 October 1947, Mountbatten saw the diwan of Kashmir and told him that while there was no legal objection to Kashmir acceding to India, if it did so against the wishes of the majority of the population, such a step would not only mean immense trouble for Kashmir but might also lead to trouble for the dominion of India. Whatever the future of Kashmir, a plebiscite must be the first step. Mountbatten, while reporting the above to London, said that he had informed Nehru and Patel of the discussions 'and they both accepted what I had said'.[30]

Jinnah and the Muslim League from the very start believed that J&K should come to them and that Britain would assist them in this acquisition, if for no other reason, then for strategic considerations. The acquisition of Kashmir was the least that the Muslim League could expect after having been handed out a 'moth-eaten' and truncated Pakistan, one-fifth the size of India. The Kashmiris of the western belt of the state were of the same stock and faith as the Punjabi Muslims. Admittedly, those of the valley were different, less communal and under the political spell of Abdullah. But, in the end, they were likely to harken to the call of Islam. There was the security angle also, as explained earlier in General Gracey's words. It is a matter of speculation whether it ever occurred to Jinnah that the acquisition of the Northern Areas might one day help Pakistan develop ties with China.

Jinnah had commissioned an architect to design a house for himself in the Kashmir Valley. The matter seemed straightforward. Srinagar was just 135 miles from the Pakistan border. The only proper all-weather road into it was from Pakistan. If Pakistan could seize Srinagar in a lightning strike, no help could possibly reach the maharaja from anywhere. But there were constraints.

The first was the British attitude. Although London favoured Kashmir's attachment to Pakistan, it wished this 'on agreed terms' with India. Therefore, if the Pakistanis wished to jump the gun, they evidently could not take HMG into confidence. There is, however, some circumstantial evidence that certain people in the Commonwealth Relations Office (CRO) were aware of Pakistan's designs, the principal staff officer to the secretary of state, General Geoffrey Scoones (an ardent supporter of Pakistan), as we shall see, amongst them. The matter had to be kept hush-hush, especially from Mountbatten in Delhi, whom Jinnah did not trust.

Secondly, the situation in the valley – Kashmir 'Proper' – was not promising for Pakistan. There, the National Conference led by Sheikh Abdullah had the upper hand over the Muslim Conference allied to the Muslim League. According to a report of the British resident, W.P. Webb, Agha Shaukat Ali of the Muslim Conference had threatened 'direct action' in Kashmir in 1946 but 'failed to unite the warring factions of the Muslim Conference proving there was no communal feeling'.[31] This was the main reason why Jinnah had hummed and hawed over a plebiscite when one under UN auspices was suggested to him by Mountbatten on 1 November 1947 in Lahore. On the other hand, a forcible seizure – a daring display of dash – might break Abdullah's spell on the valley's Muslims.

Even in the west, along the Punjab border, there was no massive spontaneous revolt against the maharaja to justify an incursion by Pakistan to save the Muslims. According to H.V. Hodson, the trouble that broke out in Poonch was 'sporadic for most part' and there was 'some evidence of Pakistan taking part'. He says: 'The above was nothing surprising or pretentious in view of Punjab happenings.... To justify action (by Pakistan) in Kashmir on the above basis would be incorrect.'[32] The reports of Webb, the British resident in J&K, and of the British commander-in-chief of the Kashmir State Forces, General Victor Scott, confirm Hodson's assessment. According to Webb, 'relations between Hindus and Muslims began to grow uneasy and in some areas strained as communal violence flared up in the plains around the State. Kashmir remained free from communal disturbances. The unease was more confined to Jammu and along the frontier areas adjoining Pathan Tribal Agencies'.[33] General Scott reported in September 1947 that: 'The State troops had escorted one lakh Muslims through Jammu territory on their way to Pakistan and an equal number of Sikhs and Hindus going the other way',[34] signifying that the communal situation in J&K was totally different from that in the Punjab. Lars Blinkenberg, the Danish diplomat, has pointed out: 'The Maharaja with Mehr Chand Mahajan [his prime minister] toured the western part of Jammu from 18 to 23 October 1947. The local revolt in the areas of Poonch and Jammu made out by Pakistan was therefore not sufficiently powerful to obstruct the Maharaja's circulation.'[35]

The most formidable obstacle in Pakistan's path was Maharaja Hari Singh. He had absolutely no desire to accede to Pakistan. It was no secret to Jinnah that the replacement of Pandit Ram Chandar Kak as the prime minister of J&K by Mahajan in the middle of September 1947 signified that Hari Singh had decided to accede to India. The Pandit detested Sheikh Abdullah like his master and had kept playing a diplomatic game with Pakistan to counterbalance the Abdullah–Nehru pressure. For his part, Kak hoped to work for J&K's independence with guarantees from both India and Pakistan to uphold the same.* His hopes were dashed as a result of the change in British policy in April 1947 that the princely states should accede to one or the other dominion. In July 1947, Mountbatten had introduced Kak to Jinnah in Delhi to discuss the possibility of J&K's accession to Pakistan and Jinnah had sent his private secretary to Srinagar on a long sojourn to keep in touch with the situation there. After Kak's fall, despite the existence of a Standstill Agreement

---

* The British resident in J&K had reported from Srinagar on 1 November 1946: 'I am inclined to think that the Maharaja and Kak [prime minister of J&K from 1945 onwards] are seriously considering the possibility of Kashmir not joining the...(Indian) Union if it is formed.... The Maharaja's attitude is, I suspect, that once Paramountcy disappears Kashmir will have to stand on its own feet, and that the question of loyalty to the British Government will not arise and that Kashmir will be free to ally herself with any Power – not excluding Russia – if she chooses.'

between Pakistan and J&K, Pakistan started to pressurize the state, starting with an economic blockade.

★

Meanwhile, the matter of the state's accession to India was being delayed only because of Prime Minister Nehru's insistence that the maharaja hand over power to Sheikh Abdullah and instal a fully representative government before any further step could be contemplated. Hari Singh was unwilling to do so. On 27 September 1947, Nehru wrote to Sardar Patel, who was keeping in touch with the maharaja, as follows:

> I understand that the Pakistan strategy is to infiltrate into Kashmir now and to take some big action as soon as Kashmir is more or less isolated because of the coming winter.... It becomes important therefore that the Maharaja should make friends with the National Conference so that there may be this popular support against Pakistan.... Once the State accedes to India it will become very difficult for Pakistan to invade it officially or unofficially without coming into conflict with the Indian Union.... It seems to me urgently necessary therefore that the accession to the Indian Union should take place early.[36]

Patel wrote to Hari Singh on 2 October:

> I need hardly say how pleased we all are at the general amnesty which your Highness has proclaimed [meaning the release of Sheikh Abdullah]. I have no doubt that this would rally round you the men who might otherwise have been a thorn in your side. I can assure Your Highness of abiding sympathy with you in your difficulties nor need I hide the instinctive response I feel for ensuring the safety and integrity of your State.... In the meantime I am expediting as much as possible the link-up of the State with the Indian Dominion by means of telegraph, telephone, wireless and radio.[37]

350 II The Shadow of the Great Game

Time was obviously running out for Jinnah. To avoid an open conflict with India, pro-Muslim League tribesmen from the frontier areas (Masoods, Afridis and Hazzaras) would be used as proxies, enticed with the promise of loot and more. They would be recruited by Pakistani officers of the old Indian Political Service who had a vast knowledge of the tribes and armed and transported by Pakistan and led by Pakistani officers. (We have seen, in Chapter 11, the confidence Jinnah and Liaqat Ali reposed in some senior Muslim members of the Political Service in the episode related by Humayun Mirza, the son of Iskander Mirza; the father was at this time the defence secretary in the Pakistan Government.)

Mohammed Yunus, the nephew of Khan Abdul Ghaffar Khan, the Frontier Gandhi, has narrated an interesting anecdote in his memoirs. Yunus recounts that one day his uncle received a message from George Cunningham, governor of the NWFP, that one way to rehabilitate himself with Jinnah would be for Ghaffar Khan to lead a tribal *lashkar* (militia) into Kashmir. Yunus says that he passed on this information to Pandit Brij Kishen Mohan, the teacher of Yuvraj Karan Singh, who conveyed it to his mother, the maharani. According to Yunus, the maharaja sent for him to get more details but Prime Minister Kak convinced Hari Singh that Yunus was acting for the Congress Party and was trying to frighten him into acceding to India, apart from releasing and making up with Sheikh Abdullah. Much later, when I enquired from Dr Karan Singh about the veracity of this episode, he replied (on 13 December 2002) as follows:

I do recollect that such a message was in fact passed on to Pt. Brij Kishen Mohan and then to my mother who mentioned it to my father. If I remember correctly Yunus and one of his cousins did call upon my father at the Gulab Bhawan although I am not sure what transpired at the meeting.

Colonel (later major general) Akbar Khan of the Pakistan Army has described in his book how the 'tribal operation' was planned under the direct supervision of Prime Minister Liaqat Ali Khan. Akbar Khan was the military member of the Liberation Committee. He has written in his book:

Upon my seeking a clarification of our military objective, the Prime Minister said that all he wanted was to keep the fight going for three months which would be enough time to achieve our political objective by negotiations and other means.[38]

Did Liaqat Ali Khan expect that Pakistan's occupation of the Kashmir Valley would force India to accept a settlement in J&K, satisfactory to Pakistan, under British aegis?

It is not my purpose to follow the course of the war in any detail. The Pakistani attempt to seize Srinagar failed. The Dogra commander of the J&K Forces, Rajindar Singh,* held back the tribal hordes (the first attack was by about 5000 tribesmen) for three days at the entrance of the valley, till he was killed. Then two days were lost by the invaders in pillage and rapine in Baramullah, at the entrance of the valley. Moreover, according to one source, 'the rapidity with which Indians flew into Srinagar was outside Jinnah's calculations'.[39] For carrying out this operation, almost all the commercial planes flying in India were commandeered.

On 14 November 1947 Akbar Khan found himself in Uri, 100 kilometres on the road to Srinagar with the tribesmen retreating from the valley after their clash with the Indian forces at the gates of Srinagar at Shelatang. They had suffered 600 casualties. He was attempting to reason with them not to abandon the battle:

Some had held out hope of cooperating. Some had even got into their lorries and started towards the enemy, but then changed their minds and turned back.... At 9 p.m. the taillights of the last departing vehicle disappeared in the distance. Taking stock of what was left, I discovered that in the rush my Staff Officer,

---

* Rajindar Singh was the first Indian to be awarded the Mahavir Chakra (posthumously) after India's independence.

Captain Taskin-ud-din and the wireless set had also gone. Barring about a dozen people, nothing remained. The volunteers, the tribesmen, and other Pathans, had all gone.... My mission had ended in complete failure....

But I did not think I could go back yet. I had already, as it were, burnt my boats behind me by adopting the name of General Tariq. I had no pretensions to that great name but I felt it would provide an inspiration, as well as conceal my identity. Tariq, twelve centuries earlier, upon landing on the coast of Spain, had burnt his boats, and when told that it was unwise to have abandoned their only means of going back to their own country had replied, in the words of [Mohammad] Iqbal: "Every country is our country because it is our God's country."[40]

Akbar Khan continues:

In India, in the absence of homogeneity, a penetration in any direction can result in...separation of different units geographically as well as morally because there is no basic unity among the Shudras (low castes), Brahmins, Sikhs, Hindus and Muslims who will follow their own different interests. At present, and for a long time to come, India is in the same position as she was centuries ago, exposed to disintegration in emergencies.[41]

This analysis has to be juxtaposed with what V.P. Menon has written:

Personally when I recommended to the Government of India the acceptance of accession of the Maharaja of Kashmir, I had in mind one consideration and one consideration alone, viz., that the invasion of Kashmir by the raiders was a great threat to the integrity of India. Ever since the times of Mahmud Ghazni, that is to say, for nearly eight centuries...India had been subjected to periodical invasions from the north-west.... And within less than ten weeks of the establishment of the new State of Pakistan,

V.P. Menon:
Mountbatten's counsellor.
(*Courtesy*: Rani Govind Singh.)

The areas in grey show the princely states that covered more than a third
of the British Indian Empire.
(*Note*: Borders depicted on the map are notional. The map is neither accurate nor
drawn to scale; it is merely indicative of the geographical area) (*Courtesy: India Today.*)

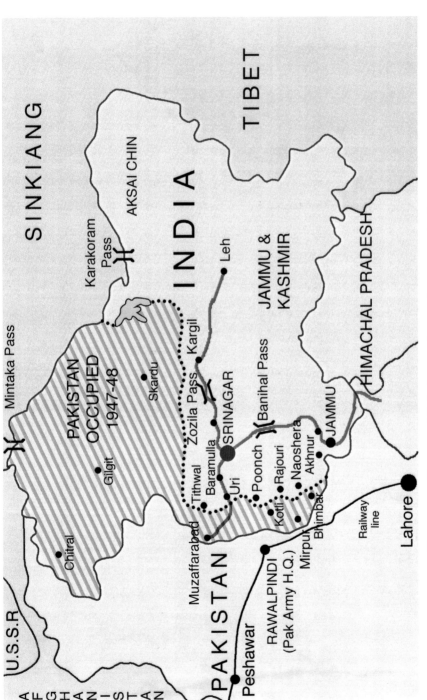

The contours of Jammu and Kashmir state after ceasefire was agreed to between India and Pakistan in January 1949.

(*Note:* Borders depicted on the map are notional. The map is neither accurate nor drawn to scale;

A tiger shoot in Bundi, Rajasthan, May 1948. (The author is behind Lord and Lady Mountbatten.) (Author's collection.)

Major Alexander Brown, head of the Gilgit Scouts, who unfurled the Pakistani flag over northern Kashmir on 2 November 1947. He was awarded the OBE in 1948. (Author's collection.)

Mohammad Ali Jinnah at the governor-general's house in Karachi in early 1948.
(*Courtesy*: Henri Cartier-Bresson/Magnum Photos.)

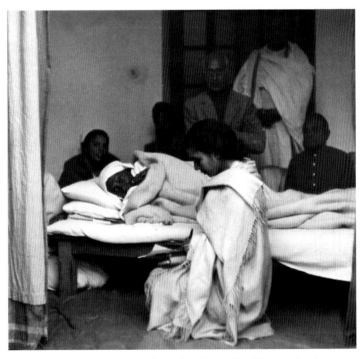

Gandhiji after breaking his fast a few days before his assassination on
30 January 1948 at Birla House, New Delhi.
(*Courtesy*: Henri Cartier-Bresson/Magnum Photos.)

its very first act was to let loose a tribal invasion through the north-west. Srinagar today, Delhi tomorrow.[42]*

Uri (where we found Akbar Khan stranded), Naoshera to Uri's south on the southern side of the Pir Panjal range and Tithwal to Uri's north were approximately at the eastern extremities of the belt of territory which General Douglas Gracey had argued was necessary for Pakistan's security. Pakistani raiders advancing in early November 1947 had occupied a large portion of this area. After the tribal *lashkar* had fled from the Kashmir Valley and Uri had been recaptured on 14 November 1947, India considered the question of recovering all of this territory, including the Jhelum Valley road from Uri to Domel, situated on the Pakistan border. Before we proceed further, let us focus on two factors that played a significant role in the struggle for the above territory.

The first was Mountbatten's metamorphosis. From being 'almost neutral' with even a slight pro-Indian edge, by the end of October, following the directions received from London, he began to tilt towards Pakistan. On learning of the tribal invasion of J&K, his first thought was to somehow avoid an interdominion war, which would undo all the good work he had done for Britain in the subcontinent in the past six months. He explained this dilemma to the King as follows:

> It would still be legally correct to send troops at [its] request to a friendly neighbouring country even if it did not accede but the risk of Pakistan also sending troops would be considerable. The accession would fully regularize the position, and reduce the risk of an armed clash with Pakistan forces to a minimum because then they will be entering a foreign country.[43]

India was committed to holding plebiscites in the princely states which became disputed. Mountbatten was confident that he could

---

* 'The Kashmir dispute started life as a contest over rights to a territory, not to establish the wishes of people', remarks the historian Alistair Lamb in his work *Incomplete Partition: The Genesis of the Kashmir Dispute 1947–1948* (Roxford Books, Hertingfordbury, 1997).

subsequently arrange matters, with Indian agreement, to Pakistan's satisfaction, through either a plebiscite or a partition of the state of J&K. In his report to the King, he continued that 'forming an Interim Government under Sheikh Abdullah [had]...increased India's chances of retaining Kashmir in the ultimate plebiscite...though I still think that a country with so large a Muslim population will finally vote for Pakistan'.[44]

Mountbatten had accepted the maharaja's accession in his capacity as governor-general. With the cabinet's approval, he simultaneously wrote a personal letter to the maharaja in which he declared:

> As soon as law and order have been restored in Kashmir and her soil cleared of the invaders, the question of the State's accession should be settled by reference to the people.[45]

This letter was not the legal acceptance of the Instrument of Accession. Such an acceptance had been given on the instrument itself in accordance with the Government of India Act, 1935, as amended and in force on 15 August 1947; the letter was a supplementary written due to the extraordinary situation in which the accession was sought. Its contents would later form the background of the basic conflict between India and Pakistan.*

✶

---

* Almost all non-Pakistani writers have come to the conclusion that the accession of J&K was legally complete when the governor-general had signed the Instrument of Accession on 27 October 1947. The US Government recognized the accession. For a discussion on this issue see Lars Blikenberg, *India and Pakistan: The History of Unsolved Conflicts*, Vol. I (Odense University Press, Odense, Denmark, 1998, pp. 79–82). A few writers believe the accession did not come into force because of the letter written by Mountbatten; its coming into force is conditional on an approval by the population of Kashmir.

In this controversy, the intention of the man who accepted the Instrument of Accession is important. Mountbatten, in an aide mémoire, to Lord Ismay after he had left India has explained: 'This decision to hold a plebiscite in no way invalidated the legality of the accession of Kashmir to India. The position then was that Kashmir was legally part of the Dominion of India and the voluntary, unilateral, decision to hold [a] plebiscite to confirm this was only intended to be held after the tribesmen had been withdrawn and peaceful conditions had been restored throughout Kashmir.'[46]

A factor that had weighed with Mountbatten was the necessity to save the British residents living in and around Srinagar from the fate that had befallen the nuns of the Convent of Jesus and Mary in Baramullah at the Pathans' hands. General Claude Auchinleck, the supreme commander, wanted to send British troops to escort the British residents out of J&K. Mountbatten, however, prohibited this. 'Blood will be on your hands', Auchinleck had protested.

Mountbatten's metamorphosis started on 31 October 1947. On that day a policy directive on J&K issued by the Commonwealth Relations Office (partly quoted at the start of this chapter) was brought to Mountbatten's notice by the British high commissioner. Besides stating that Kashmir had to go to Pakistan, though 'on agreed terms', this directive went on:

> On the one hand Pakistan had connived at the tribal invasion into Kashmir, "supplied artillery and transport" for the same and on the other *India had made "provocative mistakes" in accepting Kashmir's accession since that was not really required for sending military help (to prevent tribal depredations)... "had not consulted Pakistan and* [had] *used Sikh troops"* [italics added].[47]

Prime Minister Attlee was obviously not sure that the accession could be so easily made to 'vanish' by the Mountbatten magic in Delhi, as the governor-general believed. Other means would, therefore, have to be employed to offset the advantage gained by India through this legal process. The first of these would be to establish Pakistan's locus standi in J&K, using the presence of the Pakistani tribals and volunteers inside Kashmir for the purpose. The second would be to bring in the weight of international, particularly US, opinion, to pressurize India to make concessions. This explains Attlee's icy blast directed at Nehru when the latter explained to him the reasons for his government accepting Kashmir's accession to India:

> I do not think it would be helpful if I were to comment on the action your Government has taken.[48]

Side by side Noel-Baker wired to Lord Ismay: 'Prime Minister is...unwilling to send a message to Jinnah (drawing his attention to the help the tribals had obtained from Pakistan) which, in fact, charges him (Jinnah) with responsibility.'[49]

On the same day, Attlee wired to Liaqat Ali Khan: 'If in the talks with the Indians [scheduled for the next day] there was agreement that accession "is not to prejudice in any way the ultimate decision of the future of Kashmir" [Attlee trusted] he [Liaqat] and Jinnah would make such appeal in the way you will know best to ensure those not immediately under your control may fully weigh your counsel to them.'[50] This was an extraordinarily convoluted way of referring to the tribesmen in order to absolve Pakistan of blame for the invasion. But the message was clear: If there was no agreement and if India used the Instrument of Accession to justify its position in Kashmir, you stay put (do not pull back the tribals).

Attlee had disapproved Mountbatten's action on accession. Like the good soldier that he was, Mountbatten immediately fell in step with HMG. On the very next day (1 November) on meeting Jinnah at Lahore (for nearly four hours), he launched, together with Ismay, a far-reaching initiative taking into account Attlee's objectives:

> It is the sincere desire of the Government of India that a plebiscite should be held in Kashmir at the earliest possible date and in the fairest possible way.... They suggest that UNO might be asked to provide supervisors for this plebiscite, and they are prepared to agree that a joint India–Pakistan force should hold the ring while the plebiscite is being held.[51]

★

Mountbatten had no authority from the Government of India to suggest a reference to the UN or for the induction of Pakistan's forces into J&K. His hope was that if Jinnah gave a nod to the proposal, he would try to get India to agree to it. Jinnah refused for reasons mentioned earlier; he was not confident of winning the plebiscite. It was during this conversation that Jinnah suggested 'both sides should withdraw simultaneously'. When Mountbatten asked him: 'How the tribesmen [who, Pakistan maintained, were acting independently] were to be called off?' Jinnah replied (in the oft-quoted remark): 'All he had to do was to give them an order to come out.'[52]

At the meeting, Mountbatten upbraided Jinnah for making out that the accession 'rested on fraud and violence'. He said that the accession was perfectly legal and that the tribesmen, for whom Pakistan was responsible, had indulged in violence. On 28 October 1947 General Auchinleck, the supreme commander, had threatened to pull out all British troops from the Pakistan Army, which Pakistan could ill afford to allow to happen. This threat had resulted in Jinnah cancelling his order to General Douglas Gracey, the acting commander-in-chief of the Pakistan Army, to send in regular troops into the Kashmir Valley to clear the Indian troops arriving there by air and to secure the Banihal Pass. London had welcomed Auchinleck's intervention, which probably averted an interdominion war. Mountbatten's warning was part of the same British effort to restrain Pakistan from further adventures. The British, throughout the crisis, supported Pakistan but restrained it from taking actions that might result in an Indian invasion of West Punjab and a full-scale war.

Another factor that distinctly influenced the situation was Nehru's offer to Mountbatten to chair the Defence Committee of the Indian Cabinet. It was this committee and not the Indian Cabinet as a whole that made the decisions on Kashmir war policy. This position gave the governor-general enormous power to influence the course of the fighting. After Mountbatten had lived up to his bargain to place the princely states in the Indian Union in July and August 1947, Nehru (as well as Patel and Gandhiji) had come to trust his word. The Indian leaders were also moved by Lady Edwina Mountbatten's indefatigable efforts to provide solace to the suffering by touring refugee camps and hospitals day in and day out. Nehru and the Mountbattens had come close to each other. The Indian was less able to separate affairs of state from personal feelings than the Englishman.

★

General Kulwant Singh, GOC, Kashmir Operations, had prepared a plan in November 1947 to clear the invaders from the entire belt (referred to above) along the Pakistan border. General Roy Bucher, the acting British commander-in-chief of the Indian Army, with support from Mountbatten (chairing the Defence Committee), opposed Kulwant Singh's plan as being too risky. And though Nehru and the other ministers pressed for an attack, Kulwant Singh was instructed 'not to take unnecessary risks'. On 9 November, Mountbatten left for London to attend the wedding of Princess Elizabeth with Prince Phillip.* Mountbatten's absence gave Kulwant Singh an opportunity to interpret his chief Bucher's order in his own way and, within fifteen days, his troops had relieved the towns of Kotli, Jhangar and Naoshera from tribal occupation and were able to reinforce the besieged town of Poonch. He could not, however, take back Mirpur, Domel and Muzaffarabad, situated near the Pakistan border.

On returning from London on 14 November, Mountbatten wrote to Nehru as follows: 'I have on several occasions repeated my views on the question of sending Indian troops into western areas.... During my absence in London this object changed. It thus evidently became the purpose of the Government of India to impose their military will on the Poonch and Mirpur areas.'[53]

Admittedly, some portions of the uncharacteristically stiff letter to Nehru were meant for Attlee's eyes. In London, he had been made wise to the alarming allegations being made against him for siding with India against Pakistan. The cheerleader of this campaign was none other than his former godfather, Winston Churchill: 'Muslims were Britain's friends and that it was terrible that an Englishman and a cousin of the King should now support Britain's enemies against them.'[54] Mountbatten later said: 'He accused me of having planned and organized the first victory of Hindustan against Pakistan by sending British-trained soldiers and British equipment to crush and suppress the Muslims in Kashmir.'[55]

---

* Patel encouraged Mountbatten to go to England: 'At the present juncture such a visit would be both tactically and politically wise.'

The Indian success in stemming the Pakistani advance by flying in troops into the state had resulted in the welling up of frustration in all those Englishmen who saw India and the Hindus as their enemy. Most of the British officers who had decided, at the time of withdrawal, to serve on in the subcontinent had opted for service in Pakistan. Over 500 British personnel held positions in the Pakistan Army, and many in the Civil Service and the Political Department. The governors of Pakistan provinces such as Sir Francis Mudie in West Punjab and Sir George Cunningham in the NWFP were Britishers. Only some of them would fight for Pakistan in Kashmir, but most supported Pakistan's efforts there. When the Indians complained to London about British officers taking part in the Kashmir war, some of whom were killed, A.V. Alexander, the minister of defence, agreed with Noel-Baker that: 'It would be wise not to probe too deeply into the matter.'[56]

C. Dasgupta has written:

The course and outcome of the first India–Pakistan war cannot be understood if we overlook the fact that the two contestants had yet to establish full national control over their respective armed forces.... The international factor is particularly important in wars in the third world.... Decisive results must be speedily achieved before major powers can intervene. The role of Mountbatten and the British Service Chiefs made it virtually impossible for India to meet this requirement in 1947–48.... The British Government was kept informed at every stage and was thus enabled to take diplomatic steps to close India's military options.[57]

The truth of these observations was proved time and time again during the struggle for the possession of the western belt of Kashmir's territory during 1947–48. In November 1947 Nehru proposed a 'cordon sanitaire', or a demilitarized zone, to be established along the frontier with West Punjab with orders that any observed movement within it should be attacked from the air after due notice. According to H.V. Hodson:

They [Indians] were so insistent that Lord Mountbatten had to temporize by getting the proposal referred to Joint Planning Staff. He made sure meanwhile that the report would be adverse and so it was. The Ministers then gave up the idea without argument.[58]

On 3 December 1947 Bucher made an effort to get the Defence Committee to accept the evacuation of Poonch, which, according to British thinking, had to be left with Pakistan. However, Nehru was able to shoot down this proposal despite the support Bucher received from Mountbatten. On the other hand, the commander-in-chief succeeded in getting shelved the push from Uri to Domel to clear the Jhelum Valley till the next spring. He also succeeded in getting dropped the plan to destroy the bridges across the Kishan Ganga river, which would have cut off Muzaffarabad from Pakistan.

The struggle for control of this territory continued throughout 1948. During March that year, General K.M. Cariappa, the new GOC-in-C in the area, was able to reoccupy Jhangar and beat back a powerful Pakistani attack on Naoshera. In April the Indian troops entered Rajouri town and thus the Jammu–Naoshera lines of communication were restored. Cariappa had taken care not to inform the Army Headquarters about his operational plans. According to his biographer, Cariappa had to fight 'two enemies, Army Headquarters headed by Roy Bucher, and the Pakistan Army headed by [Frank] Messervy'.[59]

Bucher admitted to Gracey, the Pakistan C-in-C, that he had no control over Cariappa but hit upon an intriguing scheme to now stop the advance of his own army. Graffety Smith, British high commissioner in Karachi, reported to London the arrangements reached privately between the commanders-in-chiefs of the two dominions. General Bucher indicated to General Gracey that 'he had no wish to pursue an offensive into what is effectively Azad Kashmir-controlled territory, i.e., to Mirpur and Poonch sector.... The object of these arrangements is to reach a situation in which each side will remain in undisputed military occupation of what are roughly their present positions.... *An essential part of the process...is that three battalions of the Pakistan army should be employed in Kashmir opposite the Indian forces at*

Jhangar in or around Poonch and at Uri [italics added].... The Pakistan Prime Minister is aware of the exchanges I have reported above, but I understand he feels unable at present to endorse this officially.'[60] Further, Bucher told Gracey that he would try to get Indian troops withdrawn from Poonch.

Sardar Mohammad Ibrahim Khan, the leader of the so-called 'Azad Kashmir' Government, spilled the beans on this secret pact. He was so delighted that the Indian side had referred to, and thus recognized, 'Azad Kashmir' that he issued a press statement on 31 March 1948 to proclaim the same. It said: 'His Government had been approached by India for a ceasefire.' The Indian Government repudiated Bucher's initiative, but there is no record of his being pulled up.

Mountbatten too wanted to neutralize Indian military initiatives. He told General Gracey, the Pakistani Army's commander-in-chief, who visited Delhi on 2 May 1948:

I pointed out [to Gracey] that, if we could get the two Governments to...feel themselves thoroughly militarily impotent, then this appeared to be the best chance of reducing the risk of war after my departure.*[61]

Nehru and the Indian Cabinet had no such intention. Terence Shone, the UK high commissioner in India, warned London on 14 May 1948 that the Indians intended to press ahead from Uri to Domel.[62] The regular Pakistan Army had by now entered Kashmir. On 8 May 1948, the US military attaché in Delhi had cabled Washington:

Pakistan has three regular...Army battalions in Kashmir now one vicinity Uri, one vicinity Poonch and one vicinity Mirpur.... Pakistan on practical war footing along entire India–Pakistan border Bahawalpur State to Domel.... Lack [of] supplies and reserves would mean short but bloody engagement; with India certain and quick victor...[63]

---

* Mountbatten was to leave India on the conclusion of his governor-generalship at the end of June 1948.

As a result of the Pakistani reinforcements, the Indian two-pronged attack to capture Domel and Muzaffarabad fizzled out. Tithwal, north of Uri, was captured but the advance on the Jhelum road did not proceed beyond 10 kilometres west of Uri. Soon thereafter, the members of the United Nations Commission for India and Pakistan (UNCIP) arrived and India suspended operations for the duration of their stay in the subcontinent.

How the ceasefire was agreed to is for the next chapter, which deals with the story as it unfolded at the UN. The intensified fighting and the diplomacy that preceded it are also touched upon.

Notes and References

1. File L/P&S/13/1845 B (Oriental and Indian Collection, British Library, London). Cited in C. Dasgupta, *War and Diplomacy in Kashmir: 1947–48* (Sage, New Delhi, 2002, pp. 54–55).
2. Ibid.
3. V. P. Menon, *The Story of the Integration of the Indian States* (Orient Longman, New Delhi, 1961, p. 415).
4. Alistair Lamb, *Incomplete Partition: The Genesis of the Kashmir Dispute 1947–1948* (Roxford Books, Hertingfordbury, 1997, p. 191).
5. *Bulletin of Military Historical Society of Great Britain*, Vol. 46, No. 182, 1995 (OIC, British Library, London).
6. Alistair Lamb, *Incomplete Partition*, p. 239, and *Birth of Tragedy* (Wisdom Books, Ilford, Essex, 1994, p. 120).
7. MSS EUR D670 (OIC, British Library, London).
8. Alistair Lamb, *Incomplete Partition*, p. 193.
9. File MSS EUR F200/246 (OIC, British Library, London). Cited in Dasgupta, op. cit., p. 100.
10. Quoted in Josef Korbel, *Danger in Kashmir* (Oxford University Press, New York and Karachi, 2002, p. 138).
11. US FR 1948, Vol. V, p. 434.
12. Ibid., pp. 448–49.
13. Ibid., p. 456.
14. Nehru to Attlee, 25 October 1947 in *Selected Works of Jawaharlal Nehru*, Vol. IV (Nehru Memorial Museum and Library, New Delhi, pp. 274–75).

15. Stanley Wolpert, *Nehru: A Tryst with Destiny* (Oxford University Press, New York, 1996, p. 435).
16. US FR 1948, Vol. V, p. 356.
17. Korbel, op. cit., p. 124.
18. Ibid., p. 131.
19. Lars Blinkenberg, *India and Pakistan: The History of Unsolved Conflicts*, Vol. I (Odense University Press, Odense, Denmark, 1998, p. 116).
20. Ibid.
21. US FR 1948, Vol. VII, pp. 729–30. US consul (John Hall Paxton) in Tihwa to the secretary of state.
22. Quoted in Korbel, op. cit., pp. 138–39.
23. V.P. Menon, op. cit., p. 394.
24. H.V. Hodson, *The Great Divide: Britain-India-Pakistan* (Oxford University Press edition, Delhi, 2000, p. 442).
25. Mountbatten's report of talk with Jinnah on 1 November 1947. *Sardar Patel's Correspondence*, Vol. X (Nehru Memorial Museum and Library, New Delhi).
26. Karan Singh, *Heir Apparent* (Oxford University Press, Delhi, 1982, pp. 47–48).
27. Philip Ziegler, *Mountbatten* (Collins, London, 1985, p. 445).
28. V.P. Menon, op. cit., p. 395.
29. Report on 'The Last Viceroyalty', Part E, Para 69 (OIC, British Library, London).
30. Governor-general's Interview No. 17, 10 October 1947, Broadland Archives (BA), University of Southampton, D 74.
31. File L/P&S/13/1226, W.P. Webb's reports (OIC, British Library, London).
32. H.V. Hodson, op. cit., p. 446.
33. File L/P&S/13/1226, W.P. Webb's reports (OIC, British Library, London).
34. File L/P&S/13/1845B, General Victor Scott's reports (OIC, British Library, London).
35. Lars Blinkenberg, op. cit., p. 76.
36. *Sardar Patel's Correspondence*, Vol. X (Nehru Memorial Museum and Library, New Delhi, pp. 49–50).
37. Ibid., p. 42.
38. Major General Akbar Khan, *Raiders in Kashmir* (Army Publishers, Karachi, 1992 edition, p. 33).

39. Alan Campbell-Johnson, *Mission with Mountbatten* (New Age Publishers, Delhi, 1994, p. 230).
40. Major General Akbar Khan, op. cit., p. 68.
41. Ibid., p. 191.
42. V.P. Menon, op. cit., p. 413.
43. Governor-general's personal report to the King, 7 November 1947, Para 28 (other personal reports from 15 August 1947 to June 1948 not released).
44. Ibid., Para 30.
45. Government of India's White Paper, March 1948, on Jammu and Kashmir, pp. 47–48. Cited in Lars Blinkenberg, op. cit., p. 78.
46. MBI/G25, BA, University of Southampton.
47. File L/P&S/136/1845–46 (OIC, British Library, London). Cited in Dasgupta, op. cit., p. 59.
48. Ibid. Cited in Dasgupta, op. cit., p. 56.
49. Ibid. Cited in Dasgupta, op. cit., p. 59.
50. File L/P&S/136/1845–46, Attlee to Liaqat Ali Khan, 29 October 1947 (OIC, British Library, London). Cited in Dasgupta, op. cit., p. 60.
51. *Sardar Patel's Correspondence*, Vol. X (Nehru Memorial Museum and Library, New Delhi, p. 81).
52. Mountbatten's personal report, 7 September 1947, Para 63.
53. File L/WS/1/1139, telegram from high commissioner to CRO, 28 November 1947 incorporating the text of the message (OIC, British Library, London). Cited in Dasgupta, op. cit., p. 68.
54. Ziegler, op. cit., p. 461.
55. Ibid.
56. Alistair Lamb, *Incomplete Partition*, p. 242.
57. Dasgupta, op. cit., p. 109.
58. H.V. Hodson, op. cit., p. 403.
59. Brigadier C.B. Khanduri, *Field Marshal Cariappa: His Life and Times* (Lancer, New Delhi, 1995, pp.165–66).
60. File L/WS/1/1141, Graffety Smith to CRO, Telegram No. 294, 26 March 1948/1 April 1948 (OIC, British Library, London). Cited in Dasgupta, op. cit., pp. 138–39.
61. Larry Collins and Dominique Lapierre, *Freedom at Midnight* (Vikas Publishing House, New Delhi, 1976, pp. 292–94).
62. File L/WS/1/1142, Terence Shone to CRO, 14 May 1948 (OIC, British Library, London). Cited in Dasgupta, op. cit., p. 144.
63. US FR 1948, Vol. V, pp. 340–41.

13

The Kashmir Imbroglio II: At the UN

UNTIL THE EARLY PART OF THE TWENTIETH CENTURY, INDIANS BELONGING to the Hindu faith, on returning home from journeys abroad, were required to take a dip in the holy Ganga as part of a purification ritual.* If contact with the outside world was shunned to such a great extent, how could they be expected to know much about other people: their customs and cultures, their politics and passions, their strengths and weaknesses? In the nineteenth century, an English observer described the character of the Hindus as a mixture of 'arrogance, political blindness...and misplaced generosity.... So far as politics goes they were novices and unfit to preserve their liberties'.[1] In this respect, those Indians who were converted to Islam gradually acquired a different frame of mind. Islam was a universal faith with a global perspective (every country is our country because it is our God's country). Even an uneducated Muslim in an Indian village would have heard about Jerusalem, Istanbul, Baghdad, Bokhara, and even Cordoba, besides of course Mecca and Medina. However

---

* In 1931, on coming back to India from the First Round Table Conference held in London, my father avoided the ritual dip by agreeing to have some drops of Ganga water sprinkled on him, thereby denoting that the custom was being gradually eroded.

Islam-centric, and however limited their vision, the Muslims of India were much more the citizens of the world than their Hindu compatriots.

Most Indian leaders in the forefront of the independence movement continued to be victims of the age-old legacy. They did not devote much thought during the freedom struggle to external relations or how the defence of the country would be organized after independence had been achieved. They pursued preconceived ideas. They tended to ignore the reality of power politics in world affairs. They were indeed novices as far as external politics was concerned. There were exceptions. Jawaharlal Nehru was one of the few who was intensely interested in global affairs and kept in touch with world leaders. However, he did not prove knowledgeable on how the United Nations' Security Council functioned: that its members acted in the context of power pulls and in their own national interests, rather on the basis of merit or the high ideals enshrined in the UN Charter.

Alan Campbell-Johnson, the governor-general's press attaché and confidant, told me in London in the early 1990s that Mountbatten did pressurize Nehru to take Kashmir to the UN; he was worried about international repercussions if war broke out between India and Pakistan. In his book, Campbell-Johnson has written:

> Since returning to Delhi [from London] Mountbatten had seen Gandhi and V.P. [Menon] who were both favourably inclined to the invocation of [the] UNO. And today [11 November 1947] he had a further talk with Nehru whose attitude to the idea is now less inactive than it was at Lahore [at the meeting between Nehru and Liaqat Ali Khan three days earlier].[2]

Earlier, in September 1947, Gandhiji had approached Mountbatten with the suggestion that Attlee be requested to mediate between India and Pakistan to avert a clash between the two countries as a result of the conflagration in the Punjab. Gandhiji wanted Attlee to ascertain 'in the best manner he knows who is overwhelmingly in the wrong and then withdraw every British Officer in the service of the wrong party'.[3] Attlee had parried the request: 'When political tragedies occur', he informed Gandhiji, 'how seldom it is that, at all events at the time, the blame can be cast, without a shadow of doubt substantially on one party alone'.[4] Gandhiji was very disappointed.* Mountbatten, after a while, wrote to him as follows: 'An alternative means is to ask UNO to undertake this enquiry and you would have no difficulty in getting Pakistan to agree to this.'[5] Nothing came of this proposal, but this was how a reference to the UN came to be broached.

Vallabhbhai Patel and Mountbatten had worked together on the division of India and the integration of the princely states into the Indian dominion, but after independence, Mountbatten found him less tractable than Nehru. Mountbatten was aware of the growing rift between Nehru and Patel. When Nehru had submitted to him the list of independent India's first cabinet in August 1947, according to H.V. Hodson, Patel's name was missing from it. It was Mountbatten who, on V.P. Menon's prompting, made Nehru include Patel in the cabinet. V.P. Menon argued that an open clash in the Congress Party Working Committee between the two might result in Nehru's defeat.[6]** Nehru's main misgiving about Patel was that he would oppose a socialistic economic policy.† Morevover, Nehru wanted to be all in all.

Records of conversations between Mountbatten and Gandhiji will bear recapitulation as they reveal the fissures appearing in the Indian leadership that naturally had an impact on India's handling

---

* Mountbatten's own comment on Gandhiji's proposal (in a letter to Lord Ismay) was as follows: 'He seems to ignore the fact that if we expelled Pakistan from the Commonwealth, Russia would obviously step in or if we expelled India, America might.'

** S. Gopal in *Nehru*, Vol. I (Oxford University Press, Delhi, 2003, p. 361) calls this 'an absurd story'. But Hodson was meticulous in his research and had access to Mountbatten while writing his book *The Great Divide* in the 1960s. Hodson said that the Mahatma possibly wanted Patel to lead the recast Congress Party that he was then planning.

† Patel believed that 'the Government would not be able to produce a sufficient number of trained and educated administrators to run the nationalized industry. The Government without the credit to raise loans would not be able to finance all these great schemes'. (Larry Collins and Dominique Lapierre, *Mountbatten and Independent India*, Vikas Publishing House, New Delhi, 1985, p. 113).

of J&K. On 16 September 1947 Mountbatten and Gandhiji discussed the communal situation. Mountbatten records:

> I told Mr Gandhi that it was not a bit of good preaching to the people unless he had converted the leaders and I urged him to devote his full energy towards keeping the leaders, and particularly the Deputy Prime Minister [Patel], as straight as possible.... Mr Gandhi said he entirely agreed with every word I had spoken that he already knew it but that he was interested to see that I had summed up the position so correctly. He [Gandhiji] promised to do his very best and that never to mention my name in this matter or that he had had these conversations.[7]

After the Pakistani invasion of J&K in October 1947, Mountbatten had arranged for Nehru to fly to Lahore in order to meet Jinnah. Nehru avoided going. 'Why was it', Mountbatten asked Gandhiji on 29 October 1947, 'that Sardar Patel and the rest of the Indian Cabinet had been against the Governor-General and Pandit Nehru going to Lahore?' (Ismay was present on this occasion and recorded the conversation.)

> Mr Gandhi replied: It was wrong for him [Nehru] to plead illness as an excuse for not going.... When again pressed by Lord Mountbatten to answer his question as to why the Indian Cabinet was against Nehru's visit to Lahore, Mr Gandhi (rather coyly) said that Sardar Patel, and indeed the whole of the Cabinet, except the Prime Minister, could never forget that they had been the underdogs for so long. Nor could they rid their minds of the suspicion that all the British in India, including Field Marshal Auchinleck and (this still more coyly) Lord Ismay, were anti-Hindu and pro-Muslim.
> This did not however apply in any way to Lord Mountbatten who enjoyed the complete confidence of all of them, including Sardar Patel. When further questioned as to how this alleged pro-Pakistan attitude affected the question of the Governor-General going to Lahore, Mr Gandhi said that this visit would increase

the prestige of Mr Jinnah and was therefore encouraged by Lord Mountbatten's British advisers.[8]*

There was another problem at that time over which British policy and Patel clashed. This problem concerned the division of the assets of undivided India between the two dominions. The crux of the issue was one of transferring the second instalment of Rs 550 million (equal to about half a billion US dollars today) to Pakistan. (Until then only the first instalment of Rs 200 million had been transferred.) Nehru had told C. Rajagopalachari** on 26 October 1947: 'It would be foolish to make this payment until this Kashmir business had been settled.'[9] However, Mountbatten knew that it was Patel who was influencing the other ministers to hold back on the transfer. 'Why should we give them the money to buy the arms to shoot our soldiers?'[10] was the refrain in Delhi, according to Campbell-Johnson. Pakistan was hard up for cash. It had obtained a loan of Rs 20 crore from the Nizam of Hyderabad only the previous month.†

To the Indians, delaying the payment appeared to be a non-belligerent way of restraining Pakistan in Kashmir. The other view was that an agreement reached before independence had to be honoured, despite the subsequent fighting in Kashmir.

Mountbatten has recorded how he convinced Gandhiji of the validity of the Pakistani claim:

I told him that I considered it to be unstatesmanlike and unwise (not to pay) and that it was the only conscientious act which I

---

* Mountbatten posed the same question to Patel: 'I then asked how my own going to Lahore would be harmful? He replied that I must remember that I had been invited by the Government of India to be their constitutional governor-general. Thus, I represented the honour of the state and, being an Englishman, should be all the more careful not to act in an unconstitutional manner against the advice of the whole cabinet who were one and all bitterly opposed to my going.' (This, not Gandhiji's, was the correct response.)

** C. Rajagopalachari, a prominent Congress leader from South India, succeeded Mountbatten as the governor-general of India.

† These constraints did not prevent Jinnah from ordering a 'cavern green' Cadillac super limousine for $6000 and a Vicker's Armstrong aircraft whose price it was noted 'was not unreasonable' (exact price withheld) compared to a converted B23 beach craft he wanted (costing more than £150,000). These are 1947 prices; for equivalent prices today, multiply the figures by fifty.[11]

was aware of that the Government of India had taken which I regarded as dishonourable. The Mahatma expressed regret that he had not appreciated earlier the significance of this act as he should have done something about it.... I made one request that...he should make it clear that it was he who had started this conversation and asked my advice and not I who tried to get him to bring pressure to bear upon the Government. He readily gave this undertaking and asked for more details.... The Mahatma was of the opinion that the only honourable course for India was to pay out the [Rs] 55 crore at once and he now proposed to talk to the Prime Minister and Deputy Prime Minister and the Ministers concerned. "Once my fast has started they may not refuse me."[12]

✯

Sardar Baldev Singh, the defence minister, told Mountbatten on 23 January 1948: 'The sole reason [for Gandhiji's fast] was to force the Government of India to hand over [Rs] 55 crore to Pakistan.'[13] Indeed, it was to save Gandhiji's life that the Indian cabinet members made this payment against their own better judgement. The payment was also responsible for Gandhiji's assassination a few days later.

Mountbatten's growing caution about Patel had not affected the relationship between the two. 'I had a long talk with Patel yesterday', wrote Mountbatten to Ismay on 4 October 1947. (The topic was Pakistan.) Mountbatten added: 'He [Patel] had also attacked Nehru for the first time saying "I regret our leader has followed his lofty ideas into the skies and has no contact left with earth or reality".'[14]

This outburst probably reflected Patel's frustration with Nehru at the time, for refusing to accept the Maharaja of Kashmir's accession to India unless and until a government under Sheikh Abdullah was installed. But neither Patel nor Nehru took Mountbatten into confidence with regard to their actual contacts with the maharaja.

✯

The matter of India making a reference to the United Nations on J&K came under serious consideration in mid-December 1947, after Mountbatten's mediatory efforts between Nehru and Liaqat Ali Khan collapsed and the war hotted up. At the meeting of the Indian Defence Committee on 20 December 1947, Nehru spoke of striking at the invaders' camps and lines of communication inside Pakistan. Mountbatten immediately intervened to suggest a reference to the UN, as mentioned in Chapter 12. 'India had a cast-iron case', he asserted. On 22 December 1947 Nehru handed over a letter to Liaqat Ali Khan formally asking the Government of Pakistan 'to deny all help to the raiders'.[15] This letter created serious concern in London. If an interdominion war broke out, the British Government would be obliged to withdraw all its officers serving in the Indian and Pakistan Armies. Also, Mountbatten's own retention in India would come into question. With the departure of the 500 British officers manning the top posts in Pakistan, its armed forces would be crippled. The restraining hand of the three British commanders-in-chief of the Indian armed forces on India would be removed.

On Christmas day, Mountbatten wrote a long letter to Nehru. He urged that it was 'a fatal illusion' to believe that war between India and Pakistan could be confined to the subcontinent or be finished off quickly in favour of India without further complications. He shrewdly added that 'embroilment in war with Pakistan would undermine the whole of Nehru's independent foreign policy and progressive social aspirations'.[16] Nehru replied as follows: 'Under international law we can in self-defence take any military measures to resist it [the invasion], including the sending of our armies across Pakistan to attack their bases near the Kashmir border.'[17] Despite this firm posture, the Indian prime minister agreed, in the operative part of his reply, to refer the matter to the United Nations, adding that side by side preparations should be made to enter Pakistan if it refused to pull out. Meanwhile, Attlee also wrote to Nehru:

I am gravely disturbed by your assumption that India would be within her rights in international law if she were to send forces to Pakistan in self-defence...I think you are very optimistic in concluding that your proposed military action would bring about a speedy solution.[18]

When the Indian Cabinet members agreed to complain about Pakistan's aggression to the United Nations, they did so under the impression that it was a prelude to India marching towards the invaders' bases if they did not withdraw within a short time. However, the fact remains that though the complaint to the UN was lodged on 1 January 1948, no military preparations were made by the Indian C-in-C for carrying out any operation. A few days earlier, i.e., on 29 December 1947, Nehru had written to Patel:

Among the consequences [of war] to consider are the possible effect on the British Officers in the Army and also the reaction of the Governor-General (i.e., that he may decide to leave India).[19]

This suggests that the above factor had started to weigh on the prime minister's mind. Did the possibility of Mountbatten's departure weaken his resolve regarding the military option?

On the same day, i.e., 29 December 1947, Sir Paul Patrick of the Commonwealth Relations Office in London sent for the US chargé d'affaires to the UK and brought to his notice Nehru's letter to Liaqat Ali Khan (written on 22 December 1947). The US official reported to Washington that Patrick had described the situation as follows:

An ultimatum...the seriousness of which can hardly be exaggerated. India was likely to attack Pakistan simultaneously with filing the complaint with the Security Council.... Government of India [GOI]...is driven to its rash course by Nehru's "Brahmin logic", which argues that now Kashmir has adhered to GOI it is part of India.[20]

The next day (30 December) the US chargé d'affaires was again summoned to the Commonwealth Relations Office. Sir Archibald Carter, the permanent undersecretary of the CRO, with Patrick present, received him. Carter said:

Prime Minister [Attlee] is disturbed by GOI assumption [that] GOI will be within its rights in international law...to move forces into Pakistan in self-defence. Prime Minister doubts whether it is in fact juridically correct and is afraid that it would be fatal from every other point of view. Carter and Patrick then came to the operative part of the démarche [they enquired] whether the US Government would be willing to instruct the US Embassy in Delhi to approach Nehru immediately, and without reference to the Nehru–Attlee correspondence, advise him "not to take any rash action such as invading Pakistan territory which would also prejudice irretrievably world opinion against India's case".[21]

The US chargé d'affaires asked whether there was a recourse other than a reference to the Security Council. The Englishmen replied, '...afraid not'.

British diplomacy recorded its first success – though a partial one – when, the next day (31 December), the US Embassy in India was instructed by the State Department to deliver a formal note to India. The US Embassy in Karachi was intimated to address a similar note to Pakistan. The identical notes stated that the US hoped that India and Pakistan would restrain 'irresponsible elements' – this was aimed at Pakistan – and that precipitous action by either government would seriously jeopardize international goodwill and prestige – this was directed at India.[22] The US, while disposed to work with Britain 'in glorious harness' (Dennis Kux's phrase), wanted to maintain its neutrality between the two countries at that stage.

The beginning of the new year (1948) saw Lord Ismay being transferred from Delhi and installed as the principal adviser to the Commonwealth secretary, Noel-Baker, no doubt to guide the latter through the Kashmir thicket at the United Nations. Attlee had great confidence in Ismay, as had had his predecessor, Winston Churchill. We are aware of the position that Ismay took on Kashmir from his days in Delhi. This was that the international community should recognize the presence of the Pakistani raiders in Kashmir, thus establishing Pakistan's locus standi in the state; the Abdullah administration should be replaced; and an UN-supervised plebiscite should be organized. Alternatively, the Indian troops should withdraw to the Hindu-majority areas of Jammu and the Pakistani troops should be given control of the western and northern areas, with a 'neutral' force in the Kashmir Valley (Ladakh on Tibet's border was ignored). These were, by and large, the very propositions put forward by Noel-Baker at the UN in New York. Ernest Bevin, the influential secretary of state for foreign affairs, meanwhile, warned Attlee that 'we should be very careful to guard against the danger of aligning the whole of Islam against us'.[23]

The other officer in the thick of things was General Sir Geoffrey Scoones, the principal staff officer of Noel-Baker, who, along with Lord Ismay, accompanied his chief to New York. It may be recalled that we met him briefly in Chapter 12, expressing doubts about the viability of a polyglot India as against a cohesive Islamic Pakistan. He was an influential officer who attended the cabinet meetings when India was discussed. Records show that, on 16 October 1947, a top-secret appreciation was prepared in the Commonwealth Relations Office that was signed by Scoones. This was done a week *before* the Pakistani invasion of J&K and soon after Carter had paid a visit to Karachi. Carter marked a copy of the appreciation to Ismay in Delhi:

> If war developed (and even Gandhi has hinted at this possibility)...it is likely to unite India and to bring about the downfall of Pakistan. Before Pakistan was finally liquidated it seems probable that frontier tribes of Afghanistan would enter the struggle and it is not impossible that Soviet Russia might play a part. The effect of the disappearance of Pakistan on the Middle East would be very considerable.... In neither case would the object of HMG be achieved.
> One of the root causes of this dangerous and unfortunate situation seems to be the weakness of Pakistan. It invites attack...if Pakistan were strong or showed signs of strong backing her potential enemies would probably hesitate before thinking in terms of offensive action. The first problem, therefore, seems to be to

stabilize the newly set up Pakistan, with the object of removing, or at any rate reducing, one of the main causes of danger in the situation.... Up to the present HMG's policy has been one of strict impartiality towards each of the new Dominions. Can this achieve the object?... Any change from a purely impartial policy to a more defined one may result in India leaving the Commonwealth. This may happen in any case. The decision is a political matter.[24]

Attlee's instructions to Noel-Baker, as the latter prepared to leave for New York on 10 January, were to

(1) pressurize India through public debate in the Security Council to discourage it from attacking Pakistan;
(2) play on Indian respect for legal processes to make India accept the Security Council's recommendations; and
(3) avoid giving Pakistan the impression that Britain was siding with India against it.[25]

The consideration of the entire issue in the Security Council can be broadly divided into four phases. First, the charge of the Ismay–Scoones heavy brigade led by the former professor, Noel-Baker, with Senator Warren Austin, the US delegate to the UN, happily galloping along 'in glorious harness', though at times outstripping his colleagues as an American would be wont to do. Second, the efforts in February 1948 by the US secretary of state, George Marshall, in Washington and Attlee in London to rein in the heavy brigade. The third phase saw the formation of the United Nations Commission for India and Pakistan (UNCIP) without Britain participating in it. Finally, the ceasefire on the basis of the somewhat ambiguous UNCIP proposals at the end of the year.

Noel-Baker, accompanied by the two generals, reached New York hard on the heels of the Indian complaint lodged at the UN. Their first call was on Senator Austin on 8 January 1948. They told Austin that a UN decision should be firmly and promptly made and that military policing would be required for a plebiscite, for which the Pakistani troops would be the most suitable because peace in

Kashmir had to guarantee the security of the Muslims there. 'The whole affair, according to my visitors, started with the massacre of Muslims instigated by the Prince [Hari Singh]', wired Austin to the US secretary of state on 8 January 1948.[26]

On 10 January 1948 the delegation shifted to Washington where Noel-Baker and Ismay met undersecretary of state, Robert Lovett. They suggested to him a joint Anglo–US approach at the UN based on the following points:

(1) Movement of Pakistan forces to the Northern Areas;
(2) the withdrawal of Indian troops to the southern (Hindu) part;
(3) a joint occupation of the [Kashmir] Valley by the Indian and Pakistani forces; and
(4) the establishment of an UN Commission in Srinagar, the military commander of which might exercise Interim Governmental administration in Kashmir [i.e., Abdullah to be out].

Noel-Baker told Lovett that 'Kashmir would probably go to Pakistan under a fair plebiscite'. Lovett was cautious. He thought it should be enough at that stage to call on the parties to desist from military action, to affirm the intention expressed by both to hold a plebiscite at an early date and to establish a commission to that end.[27]

The support for Pakistan that developed in the Security Council in January 1948 was mainly the result of British lobbying based on the argument that since J&K had a 77 per cent Muslim population, it should 'naturally' go to Pakistan. The views of the ex-colonial powers were given due weight by the Western members of the Security Council.* The performance of the Indian delegate at the Security

---

* Besides the USA, the USSR, China (Nationalist), the UK and France, which were permanent members with veto power, the non-permanent members in 1948 were Argentina, Belgium, Canada, Columbia, Syria and Ukraine.

Council also swung opinion in favour of the accused. Gopalaswamy Ayangar thought that 'high statesmanship' required him not to condemn Pakistan directly for aggression. He took pains to differentiate between 'the raiders' and the armed forces of Pakistan, focusing on the former. In a further effort to appear 'objective', Ayangar made it appear as if the accession was absolutely conditional on the result of the plebiscite. This statement was taken as an indication that India would be willing to accommodate Pakistan. He failed to insist on a time-bound vacation of Pakistani aggression to be followed by a plebiscite and to make it clear that if the Security Council was unable to ensure such vacation, India would be forced to do so itself. Nor did he point out that the division of India had left millions of Muslims behind in India and was essentially a political settlement. In contrast, the Pakistani delegate, Sir Zafrullah Khan, accused India of obtaining the accession 'by fraud and violence' and went hammer and tongs to attack India on a variety of issues totally unconnected with India's complaint. Whereas the Indian delegate's statement was seen as apologetic, as if India had something to hide, Pakistan's strident approach was taken as the cry of the wronged.

Sheikh Abdullah, who was a member of the Indian delegation, while talking to the Americans on 28 January 1948, raised the possibility of a third alternative, that of independence for Kashmir: 'It would be much better if Kashmir were independent and could seek American and British aid for development.' Austin did not encourage the idea.[28]*

The rethinking in Washington and London, on their pro-Pakistan stance at the UN, started after India sought an adjournment in the

---

* Abdullah raised the same proposition with the US ambassador, Henry F. Grady, in Delhi on 21 February 1948, except that this time he whittled down his demands to 'internal independence with defence and foreign affairs controlled by India and Pakistan'. (US FR 1948, Vol. V, p. 292). Josef Korbel (a member of the UNCIP) has confirmed that when the commission visited Srinagar in July 1948, Abdullah suggested the 'division of the country'. According to Korbel, the Kashmiri leader asserted that 'if this is not achieved the fighting will continue...and our people's suffering will go on'. The UNCIP was perplexed whether he was speaking on his own or reflecting the latest Indian view. [Korbel, *Danger in Kashmir* (Oxford University Press, New York and Karachi, 2002, p. 147).]

discussion on 9 February 1948 and the Indian delegation returned home. This move gave rise to the possibility of India withdrawing from seeking UN mediation. The debates and the manoeuvrings in the Security Council had caused outrage in India. Grady's report to Washington on 28 February 1948 confirms this as follows:

Ayangar publicly accused both Governments [of the UK and the US] and the SC of bias...Nehru likewise has bitterly accused [the] SC without singling out HMG and USG. On the other hand, [Karachi's] *Dawn* newspaper frequently indicates belief in successful outcome for Pakistan of Kashmir dispute at UN.... General feeling here is Abdullah has the confidence of people of Kashmir as no other Kashmiri could possibly have.[29]

Strong reaction in India even before this report was received in Washington had made the secretary of state, George Marshall, sit up and focus more carefully on the issue. On 29 February 1948, Marshall wired to Austin, outlining his views as follows:

We believe it highly doubtful that GOI...will acquiesce in or assist in implementation of British plan in present form contemplating as it does virtual UN trusteeship in Kashmir for indefinite period.... It provides no alternative to an acceptance by India of Pakistan troops in Kashmir, and by setting up UN Interim Government, which would completely supersede the present Kashmir regime; the British excluded any possibility of a compromise solution in which both parties would cooperate.... We question advisability of UN at the present stage attempting to assume broad responsibilities for interim civil and military administration in Kashmir as envisaged in the British draft as well as that of establishing "popular" government after plebiscite and transferring power thereto...it appears questionable that British scheme would receive necessary minimum of seven votes in SC; nor should the possibility of Soviet veto be overlooked.

We further believe that section on "Procedure for stopping the fighting" should be given more prominent place than is accorded it in British plan; *also that accent given therein to communal aspects should be eliminated* [italics added].... It would also be essential to include under this heading, provision for GOP...to withhold material assistance to tribal elements and Kashmir insurgents as part of general procedure for termination of hostilities.[30]

This stand differed from the one adopted so far by Austin, who had unquestioningly accepted Noel-Baker's prognosis that pressure on India was necessary to make it accept a compromise and that the question was a communal one. Austin had gone so far as to tell Ayangar that there had to be a settlement between India and Pakistan 'before [the] United States or its nationals could, with a sense of security, establish political and economic relations of a permanent character with India'.[31]

Marshall's intervention resulted in the immediate dispatch of a British delegation to consult American officials in Washington. This delegation was headed by B.R. Curson of the Commonwealth Relations Office. The American team was led by Dean Rusk (the future secretary of state). Ismay and Scoones did not appear. When the British argued that Kashmir was a 'territory in dispute', Rusk corrected them by pointing out that *Kashmir was a State about which a dispute had arisen between India and Pakistan* [italics added]'. Rusk also said that 'they [the US] found it difficult to deny the legal validity of Kashmir's accession to India'. He argued that 'they were disturbed by the possibility [of] far-reaching implications of a Security Council Resolution recommending the use of foreign troops from one party to a dispute in the territory of another party to the dispute'. The British answered that they were assuming 'that India would in the last analysis agree to the induction of Pakistani troops in Kashmir but only if "morally compelled" to do so by virtue of a UN recommendation'. But ultimately conceded that 'we had to proceed on the assumption for the time being at any rate [that] India had legal jurisdiction over Kashmir'. In response, Rusk said that 'the farthest we [the US] could go would be to envisage the use of Pakistani troops as a result of an agreement between the Government of Kashmir and the Governments of India and Pakistan'.[32] The

British also appeared to have given up their objection to the continuation of Sheikh Abdullah.

On 4 March 1948, Marshall (through a telegram) cautioned Austin: 'An Anglo–American split [on] this question must be avoided "but the SC cannot impose settlement under Chapter 6 [of the] UN Charter but can only make recommendations to parties. Such recommendations must necessarily be made in the light of India's present legal jurisdiction over Kashmir".'[33] On the proposal for the partition of Kashmir, he said: 'We shall certainly take no initiative in this regard but carefully consider proposals calling for partition by agreement between GOI and GOP.'[34]

Marshall wanted Austin and Noel-Baker to remain 'yoked' together but with the American setting the pace rather than the British, as had happened hitherto. Austin, however, failed to establish this ascendancy.

In London too there was a review of the UK policy. On 8 February Attlee received a message from Nehru complaining that Noel-Baker, in a conversation with Sheikh Abdullah, had dismissed as untrue that Pakistan had assisted the raiders:

> You will forgive me if I say frankly…that the attitude revealed by this conversation cannot but prejudice continuance of friendly relations between India and the UK.[35]

Attlee's impression that the British delegation to the UN had to be reined in was reinforced by a message from Patrick Gordon Walker, junior minister in the Commonwealth Relations Office, who had passed through Delhi. Walker warned: 'The Indians will be mortally wounded if we put forward the idea of admitting Pakistani troops into Kashmir publicly….' He added: 'Grady [the American ambassador in New Delhi] was telling Indians that Warren Austin had been under pressure from the British delegation at the United Nations.'[36]

Mountbatten also sent a message to Attlee: 'Everybody here [New Delhi] is now convinced that power politics and not impartiality

are [sic] governing the attitude of the Security Council' and hinted
that this may result in India leaving the Commonwealth and falling
'into the arms of Russia'.[37]

Attlee's reply to this message was rather sharp: 'Russia's aim was
to prevent a settlement of the Kashmir issue and then bring about
anarchy and chaos throughout the subcontinent.'[38]* Attlee could
not, however, so easily brush aside Marshall's views. In early March
1948, the Commonwealth Affairs Committee of the cabinet was
summoned to discuss the British delegation's stand on Kashmir at
the UN. Its minutes read as follows:

> The US proposals...would be wholly unacceptable to the
> Government of India and that the relations between the HMG
> and the Government of India would be seriously prejudiced if
> the former were to support them.... These were the sort of terms
> which might be imposed on a defeated country.[39]

Now where was the question of any US proposals? All the
proposals put forward were inspired by the UK delegation. Austin
was taking the lead because of British pleas that the ex-colonial
power should not come to the forefront. Marshall's telegram of
20 February 1948 (quoted earlier) makes it abundantly clear that
the plan that had been pursued was British and not American.

Attlee was actually trying to kill two birds with one stone. On
the one hand, backtrack slightly by issuing revised instructions for
supporting the withdrawal of the Pakistani raiders and leaving the
Sheikh Abdullah Government in place, though insisting that India
should abandon Poonch. And, on the other, to lay the blame for the
course adopted so far on the US. As a cockney once put it:

> Tis on'y ar-rmies fights in th'open.
> Nations fights behind threes an' rocks.[40]

---

* Mountbatten did not take this response lying down: 'I later replied [to Attlee]
that I could not believe that Russia would consider her interests well served
by this as by the emergence of a strong, stabilized India activated by a deep
feeling of gratitude and admiration towards Russia.'

Nehru was promptly informed of the cabinet decision, probably by Sir Stafford Cripps or Krishna Menon, who could be counted upon to embellish the supposed 'mischief' played by the US. In a conversation between the US ambassador to Pakistan and Jinnah on 10 April 1948 in Karachi, the latter attributed the British 'somersault' to 'wire pulling instigated by Cripps whose operations...had many "wheels within wheels"'.[41]

Mountbatten has recorded: 'I told him [Nehru] that I claim practically the whole credit for this change.... He smiled and said "I suspected as much".'[42] But nothing changed very much in the UN, as we shall shortly see.

*

On 27 January 1948, the Belgian ambassador to India, Prince de Ligne, told Nehru that 'the US approach to [the] Kashmir issue would be influenced less by intrinsic merits than by effect of solution on broad considerations of American world strategy in [the] present state of tension between [the] USA and [the] USSR.... If Pakistan should be willing to cooperate similarly with the USA it is to be expected that the USA would try to befriend Pakistan in solution of her dispute with India over Kashmir'.[43] The Belgian ambassador at the UN, Fernand van Langenhove, who was the president of the Security Council in January 1948, had been the closest collaborator with the British delegation. There is no record of American intentions to tie Pakistan to the West in early 1948. Therefore, it would appear that Prince de Ligne was roped in to help Attlee fight from 'behind threes an' rocks'. The ambassador's words impressed Nehru. On 28 January 1948 he lashed out at Senator Austin. When Nehru met Patrick Gordon Walker, he vented his anger on the USA, without blaming the UK. He recounted to the British minister what 'a foreign ambassador' had told him, adding 'that India was receiving a very rapid education in the field of international relations'.[44]

Kingsley Martin, the editor of the leftist New Statesman, visited Delhi in February 1948. There, he propounded the same thesis as Prince de Ligne: 'American ideas on global strategy did indeed bulk much in the affair. Pakistan was believed to be staunchly anti-communist. India was at the best ambivalent; naturally the United States felt that the former's cause over Kashmir should be given a favourable hearing.' He went on to dismiss the attitude of the British delegation at the UN, stating that Noel-Baker was 'in matters of high policy, weak as water'.[45]

Kingsley Martin also exchanged views with Mountbatten. In this context, Philip Ziegler writes:

> He [Mountbatten] was concerned that Britain should continue to play the leading role in development of the Indian economy and in particular the US should be kept at bay. He told Sir Terence Shone [the British high commissioner to India]: "Mr Grady has been sent here for one purpose only as US Ambassador, and that was to sell the American industrialization to the Indians at the earliest possible moment." Grady on the other hand complained to the State Department that Mountbatten was warning Indians against the perils of dollar imperialism.... What dictated [the attitude of] Mountbatten was not anti-Americanism but desire for the growth of Commonwealth ties.[46]

The truth emerges from Hugh Dalton's (the chancellor of the exchequer in Attlee's Government) diary, wherein he jotted down that Ernest Bevin attached importance to Pakistan's role in his strategy of organizing the 'middle of the planet' and promoting cordial relations with the Arab states.[47] Later in the year, Bevin did ask Liaqat Ali Khan to get in touch with the Arabs.

In March 1948, at the UN, it was the turn of the Chinese (Nationalist) delegate to assume the presidentship of the Security Council. On 10 March 1948 he submitted a draft, which sought to

(1) secure the withdrawal of the raiders;
(2) lay down the conditions for a plebiscite; and
(3) ensure that the plebiscite administrator appointed by the UN secretary-general would act "as an Officer of the J&K (Abdullah) Government" and the "interim government in Kashmir would be expanded to take in other political groups".

The US endorsed the first two points of the Chinese draft, but sought a tighter control by the UN Commission. The British delegation opposed the draft altogether. It continued to lobby for the induction of Pakistani troops into J&K and for the removal of Sheikh Abdullah.

On 6 April Krishna Menon conveyed to Attlee and Cripps Nehru's strong feelings against Noel-Baker continuing to pursue his own line, despite assurances given to India by London that revised instructions were being sent to him. Noel-Baker explained to Attlee by alleging 'that Ayangar had left him with the impression that India might well accept his suggestions if a little more pressure was applied'.[48] Attlee answered as follows: 'I find it very hard to reconcile the view which you express as to the attitude of the Indian delegation...with the representations I have received through the High Commissioner from India here.... [Christopher] Addison [a cabinet member] and Cripps share my view that all the concessions are being asked from India...'[49]

The Security Council resolution that was finally adopted after many revisions on 21 April 1948[50] constituted a five-member commission (UNCIP) that was to proceed immediately to the subcontinent in order to mediate between India and Pakistan. As guidelines, the Security Council recommended that

(1) Pakistan should "use its best endeavours" to secure the withdrawal of the raiders – tribesmen and other Pakistani nationals from J&K;
(2) after fighting had ceased, India should withdraw its forces reducing them to the minimum level required for support of the civil power in the maintenance of law and order; and
(3) for the purposes of pacification, the UN Commission could employ Pakistan troops *but with the consent of India* [italics added].

Pakistan immediately proposed an amendment to the last point to enable the administrator to deploy Indian or Pakistani troops at his discretion, i.e., without having to seek the consent of India. This proposal was defeated by seven votes to nil with four abstentions.* The 21 April resolution was not accepted by either India or Pakistan but both countries agreed to receive the commission and confer with its members.**

The charge of the Ismay–Scoones heavy brigade had been halted, even after they had broken through the Indian lines. However, little by little India was being made to compromise its stand.

★

The Soviet Union had taken no interest in the proceedings of the Security Council on Kashmir. Stalin had shown no interest in India after independence. He considered India still to be under British tutelage. Nehru then sent his sister, Vijayalakshmi Pandit, as ambassador to the USSR. She was not granted an audience with Stalin even once throughout her stay in Moscow.

Attlee's greater flexibility towards India at this point of time may be attributed to the exploration going on, through Krishna Menon in London and Mountbatten in New Delhi, to find a formula that would enable India to remain a member of the British Commonwealth, despite the fact that it was committed under its Constituent Assembly resolution of 9 August 1946 to become a Republic. Mountbatten wrote to Patrick Gordon Walker on 27 February 1948: 'I believe that you have it in your power to save India for the Commonwealth and to keep both India and Pakistan within the Anglo–US line-up if you can only persuade the Prime Minister and Noel-Baker to follow the line as agreed upon [i.e., not rubbing India the wrong way at the UN on Kashmir].'[51]

---

* The abstaining members were Argentina, Syria, the Soviet Union and Ukraine.
** Its members were from Argentina (nominated by Pakistan), Czechoslovakia (nominated by India), Columbia and Belgium (selected by the Security Council) and the USA (nominated by the Security Council president). India selected a Czechoslovakian but does not appear to have verified the credentials of its nominee. Dr Josef Korbel was an émigré to the US from his country. His book, *Danger in Kashmir*, shows that he was vehemently anti-Soviet and not particularly friendly to India. He was replaced in 1949 by a Czech from Czechoslovakia. According to Korbel his replacement was the cause of the UNCIP being wound up.

On 11 March 1948 Attlee, in a long private and personal letter to Nehru, put forward the case for India remaining in the British Commonwealth. Its central point was as follows:

> We have now reached another stage in the development of the Commonwealth...for the British the content is always more important than names.... The functions of our King are very different from those of King Ibn Saud, but their titles are the same. The same incidentally applies to the term "Republic". The actual position in Australia and New Zealand gives far more real freedom and democracy than the position in some of the South American Republics...I know how much you have at heart the unity of India. It will, I think, be of very material assistance in promoting this unity if India and Pakistan are both within the Commonwealth, and it will also help relations with Ceylon [now Sri Lanka] and Malaya, for in my view it is right and natural that India should increasingly take a leading part among the nations of Asia.[52]

Attlee then seeks Nehru's 'views on these high matters'. Nehru replied to Attlee on 18 April 1948 as follows:

> It is his [Nehru's] as also his colleagues' desire that the association of India with the UK and the British Commonwealth of Nations should be close and intimate. He was more interested in the content – real friendship and cooperation – than merely a formal link. Indeed it is remarkable what Lord Mountbatten, and may I add Lady Mountbatten also, have done to remove many of the old causes of distrust and bitterness between India and England.... We are anxious not to come to any hurried decision and we hoped that the lapse of time would make it easier to decide. That decision was bound to be influenced by the events which preceded it. [Here was the rub]: Since the Indian Constitution will be drafted in the Hindi language...the words used in Hindi will not have the same historical background and associations which English words might have...I shall not say much more at this

stage except to repeat the hope that India and England will be closely associated to their mutual advantage.[53]

*

The UNCIP delegation visited Pakistan and India in July 1948. At Karachi came the first 'bombshell', discloses Korbel, who was presiding over the commission at that stage. 'Sir Zafrullah Khan [Pakistan's delegate at the UN] informed the Commission that three Pakistani brigades were fighting on Kashmir territory since May.'[54] It had been known for some time that Pakistani forces were operating in Kashmir but mediators could proceed only on the basis of admissions by parties.

If, in Karachi, the UNCIP members encountered distrust and tantrums, in Delhi they found disarray and imprecision. Some of the conflicting Indian views that Korbel came across in Delhi have been noted in Chapter 12. He further writes: 'The Prime Minister told them that: "We do not insist upon the right of our Army to advance and occupy the territory which would be vacated by Pakistan. On the other hand there must not be a vacuum there and we shall be satisfied with the recognition of the authority of the State over all its territories and with the occupation of advanced positions important to us strategically and economically."' Korbel continues: 'He [Nehru] revealed skepticism about a plebiscite and [as noted earlier] expressed the thought that we [India] would not be opposed to the idea of dividing the country between India and Pakistan'.[55]

The UNCIP recommendations were finalized in the form of a resolution on 13 August 1948.[56] Taken together with the explanations given by the commission to the two sides, these may be briefly enumerated as follows:

(1) Ceasefire within four days after their acceptance;
(2) Withdrawal of Pakistani troops from Kashmir "as the presence of troops of Pakistan in the territory of the State of J&K constitutes a material change in the situation since it was represented by the Government of Pakistan before

the Security Council" [thus the Pakistani withdrawal was sought not because Pakistanis had committed aggression but because they had lied about their presence in Kashmir];

(3) "The territory evacuated by the Pakistanis to be administered by the local authorities under the supervision of the UN Commission" [who would be the "local authorities"? Was the Azad Kashmir Government to be left in place?];

(4) "Withdrawal of the bulk of Indian forces in Kashmir to begin after the Commission had notified India that the Pakistani nationals had withdrawn *and the Pakistani forces were being withdrawn*" [italics added] [this clause indirectly recognized Indian sovereignty over Kashmir but to some extent equated Indian and Pakistani withdrawals, creating possibilities of misunderstandings on the issue, as happened];

(5) Pending the acceptance of the conditions for a final settlement, India would remain within the lines as existing at the moment of the ceasefire [thus the control over Gilgit and the Poonch– Muzaffarabad sector would not be handed over to India. A clarification was sought by India on this last proviso and the UNCIP replied that it had noted the point but a decision would be left to the commission to resolve. India did not pursue the matter further];

(6) Finally, both the Governments would affirm their agreement that the future of Kashmir would be determined in accordance with the will of the Kashmiri people.

The foregoing proposals, however unsatisfactory to India, were a setback for Pakistan. After the success Pakistan had recorded at the UN, at the time of the Ismay–Scoones offensive in early 1948, it had hoped that the world body would recognize the presence of its troops in Kashmir and displace Abdullah. Now the UNCIP was proposing that Pakistan withdraw its Army from Kashmir. Liaqat Ali Khan thereupon decided to approach Britain for help and played his major card. He offered a defence alliance with Britain. This factor he knew would move Attlee more than any argument on the merits of the Kashmir question. Walter Cawthorn, the Australia-born deputy commander-in-chief of the Pakistan Army, was dispatched on a secret mission to London in September. Noel-Baker met the Pakistan envoy on 18 September 1948. During the meeting, Cawthorn explained to him that:

> He had come to explore the possibility for joint defence arrangements with [the] UK as soon as possible. Pakistan was greatly alarmed by the danger posed by communism. It was resolutely determined to play [its] part in collective defence against Russian aggression. Pakistan would move formally in the matter after Britain was agreeable for such a proposal.[57]

Thereafter, Cawthorn was received by Attlee, who after consulting the chiefs of staff, authorized the Commonwealth Relations Office to inform him orally that a formal proposal from Pakistan on this request would be welcome. London did not immediately respond to the Pakistani request for a military pact. However, Britain started to ship arms to Pakistan and agreed to press for an unconditional ceasefire by the Security Council in order to stop the Indian advance. Britain also agreed to work to bypass the UNCIP proposal for the withdrawal of Pakistani troops. It further decided to press India directly for a ceasefire. Britain evidently did not wish to enter into a military pact with Pakistan without the US also joining in. But

> The beat was on,
> The flags were out,
> Th'animal moving
> Towards the machan.

★

On 4 October 1948, Sir Paul Patrick of the Commonwealth Relations Office sent for the US chargé d'affaires in the UK and tried to impress upon him that 'it might be better for Kashmir Commission Report never to be made public even though it is as even-handed as Department [of State] suggests'.[58] Simultaneously, Sir Alexander Cadogan, the UK's permanent delegate to the UN, took up the issue in Paris where the UN General Assembly was meeting that year.

According to the US secretary of state's telegram to Washington: 'From his [Cadogan's] remarks we gather Britain have in mind almost immediate action in SC.... With UNCIP meanwhile taking back seat.'[59]

Britain simultaneously explored the Mountbatten channel. On 8 October 1948, Sir Archibald Carter, the permanent undersecretary in the Commonwealth Relations Office, wrote to the former governor-general. By that time, Mountbatten had left India but Whitehall was aware of Nehru's continuing contacts with him and Lady Mountbatten. Carter suggested that Nehru be brought round 'to go back to his earlier idea of a partition of Kashmir, with the plebiscite confined to the Valley'.[60] Carter knew that during his visit to England to attend the Commonwealth Prime Ministers' Conference, Nehru would spend some time with the Mountbattens at their country seat in Hampshire where he could be approached at leisure. In fact, Nehru spent four days relaxing in picturesque Broadlands. Though Mountbatten was busy in London most of the time, he did raise the matter with Nehru and wrote to Noel-Baker on 25 October:

I feel I can reassure you about India making war on Pakistan... India is now so strong (in Kashmir) that any question of their contemplating invasion of Pakistan territory [to offset Pakistan's advantage in Kashmir] seems to be extremely remote; thus I do not see open warfare developing out of the present situation though I agree with you that it is highly desirable to bring even the present and unofficial war to an end as soon as possible.

Mountbatten had also raised with Nehru the Commonwealth issue, so dear to his heart:

I had already made it clear to Nehru that I was certain that he would have to make some concession to Commonwealth sentiment and Stafford [Cripps] came down with the idea of asking India to accept the King as the fountain of honour for the Commonwealth. Nehru gladly accepted this and in general expressed himself as most anxious to meet our sentimental difficulties, provided that in so doing he did not get a substantial vote against remaining in the Commonwealth from the Constituent Assembly.... Stafford and Krishna [Menon] drafted a memo on these lines to which Nehru agreed.[61]

Unknown to Nehru, Ernest Bevin and Noel-Baker, at the same time, were holding separate talks with Liaqat Ali Khan, the Pakistan prime minister, in London, on the likely communist threat. In these talks they informed the delighted Liaqat Ali Khan that 'it was time to return the Kashmir question to the Security Council'[62] (i.e., bypass the UNCIP). (The unsuccessful British push for an unconditional ceasefire at the United Nations and for the pigeonholing of the UNCIP proposals has already been mentioned earlier.)

After the Commonwealth Prime Ministers' Conference Liaqat Ali travelled to Paris (where the UN Security Council was meeting) and raised the bogey of the communist threat in his talks with the Americans. (I am unaware whether or not he was encouraged to do so by Bevin.) On his very first call on George Marshall, the US secretary of state, on 29 October, he straightaway hinted at a defence alliance against the communist powers. The following telegram to Washington gives the gist of Marshall's conversation with the Pakistani prime minister:

> After exchange of pleasantries, Liaqat commenced conversation by saying that he wished, besides having opportunity to meet Secretary, to discuss strategic position in Middle East and the world. He reviewed great difficulties Pakistan has encountered in becoming established. Citing vast refugee problem, economic difficulties and relations with India, particularly in Kashmir, he declared it unthinkable that Pakistan could fall prey to communism since (a) the latter was contrary to tenets of Muslim religion, in respect of democratic ideals, property ownership and individual position; (b) States outside communist orbit should fully know that communist ideology was oppressive in extreme. Pakistan was anxious to maintain stand against communist infiltration. Liaqat then said frankly that since the United States was strongest most powerful among free nations, it...should strengthen Middle Eastern Areas economically and militarily. Turning to

India–Pakistan relations, Liaqat Ali termed Indian attitude towards Pakistan as hostile, adding, "Pakistan had been struggling to obtain peaceful settlement" in Kashmir.[63]

The secretary of state spoke to Liaqat Ali Khan at some length to explain American policy to build up Europe, which he called a 'nerve centre'. He declared that the US was also planning to help the Near East. Regarding communism and USSR policy he said that 'he was glad to know of Pakistan's attitude'. Marshall also observed: 'One very important way by which the states outside Police States' orbit [carefully avoiding the word communist] could strengthen themselves would be to settle all their major difficulties quickly and peacefully.' In this connection he expressed the hope that the Kashmir question 'would be settled in conformity with UN principles'. Finally, he remarked that the US had not been able to ship arms to India or Pakistan while Kashmir was the point of friction.[64]

According to Zafrullah Khan the meeting had gone off rather well.

*

In November 1948, the Indian Army had crossed the Himalayan range at Zojila and also raised the one-year-old siege of Poonch. The latter development had caused serious concern in Karachi – and London – for it could lead to Pakistan losing the entire Poonch–Muzaffarabad strip. On 18 November 1948, Attlee, while replying to Liaqat Ali Khan's SOS for help, affirmed: 'I am taking action to do anything I can to secure the halting of any offensive that may be taking place.'[65] Having failed to budge the Americans, Attlee now put his faith in British diplomats and soldiers, who had stayed behind in India and Pakistan, to stop the Indian offensive.

General Archibald Nye had taken over as the UK high commissioner in Delhi from Terence Shone. He had been the deputy chief of staff to Churchill during the war. Also, he was an accomplished soldier-diplomat. On 22 November 1948, General Nye called on Nehru. In his report to the Commonwealth Relations Office on his conversation with the Indian PM, he has stated:

'He [Nehru] gave me opportunity to give him my views on Kashmir situation which I did as follows:

The nature of the country was such that it was not possible for either side to drive the other out of Kashmir; indeed, in these conditions unless the morale of one side broke, no really substantial advance could be made by either side. Moreover...attacks would be costly in human life. (Neither Commander-in-Chief need have any fears so long as he was required to act on the defensive.) Pakistan forces were on the whole far better placed than Indian forces because their communications were short...and not vulnerable.

But even if my military appreciation was wrong, still there was no military solution to the Kashmir problem, for, even if Indian forces were able to clear Kashmir entirely of Pakistan forces (the proposition which I reiterated seemed to be out of the question) there is nothing to prevent the tribesmen from coming back whenever they wished, and it was unthinkable that India would maintain for an indefinite period immense forces in Kashmir against such a contingency. It followed therefore there is no military solution to the Kashmir problem; only a political one....

He [Nehru] was very thoughtful, a trifle gloomy, but did not dispute anything I said; indeed by questions and comments gave the impression that he agreed.

If Nye had stopped here, his statement could have been taken as disinterested advice. However, his report continued:

There is one other relevant point which I did not mention to him...but which I am arranging to be fed into him from other and more professional sources. It is this. There are signs that the morale of the troops of the Indian Army is beginning to wear a little thin. The first flush of enthusiasm has subsided. Troops have been fighting for a long time, including one winter and the prospect of another winter does not appeal to them very much.... The great majority of the troops of the Indian Army have never operated in such trying conditions...(they) have little or no enthusiasm on the Kashmir issue. Due to the very rapid promotions in the Indian Army and to the inexperience of their Regimental Officers and in particular the Commanding Officers...leadership is lacking. I hope by making these various representations to Nehru, that it will be possible to bring home to him that there is no military solution to this problem.[66]

On the original of this inward telegram to London somebody in Whitehall wrote the word 'Nonsense' opposite where the prowess of the Indian Army was questioned. This comment could have been made only by an Englishman, military or civilian.

*

After Mountbatten left India in June 1948, from July to September that year, Nehru wrote as many as eleven fairly lengthy letters on the situation in India, including Kashmir, to him.*

On 15 August 1948, Mountbatten warned Nehru as follows:

There was no alternative to the UN approach; if war came the world would blame India because Pakistan was seen as too weak to seek belligerency; war would mean the Indian leaders abandoning all they have stood for; if the UN declares India an aggressor, even India's best friends would have to conform to the world body's decision; war would result in a communal carnage inside India; and, finally, India did not have the means to prevail on its own. "What have you got? A few old Dakotas..."**

Mountbatten then wrote: 'You might feel that this [the ceasefire] would give an unfair advantage to Pakistan. But will it? If there were any competent and honest observers...they can prevent any form of consolidation by Pakistan, or at least report any infringement, which

---

* On 3, 8, 21 and 28 July; on 1, 4, 9, 23 and 29 August; and on 10 and 18 September.
** The argument about communal carnage was disproved during the 1965 and 1971 Indo–Pak wars.

would finally put Pakistan out of court before UNO and the world'.[67] Did Mountbatten really believe that Britain would support putting Pakistan in the dock if that country tried to consolidate its hold on Kashmir?

General K.M. Cariappa had planned to reconquer Mirpur and Muzaffarabad situated on the Pakistan frontier in November. Bucher in Delhi, with the concurrence of the Defence Committee had, however, denied Cariappa fresh troops for carrying out the assault. The argument used was that such an attack would expose East Punjab (India) to a Pakistani counterattack.

On 20 November 1948, Graffety Smith, the British high commissioner to Pakistan, wired the Commonwealth Relations Office in London as follows: 'Bucher will meet Gracey in Karachi on...26 November for Joint Defence talks and might be able to propose a formula [for ceasefire] acceptable to both sides...'[68]

Graffety Smith followed this up by informing London that Bucher had told Gracey: 'There would be no (repeat no) attack on Mirpur or any stage (repeat stage) attack on Kotli or Bhimbar.... After much difficulty he [had] succeeded in getting one RIAF [Royal Indian Air Force] Squadron withdrawn from Jammu.'[69]

On 26 November General Nye informed the CRO that Bucher had warned Nehru, in writing, that the Army was running seriously short of transport and lacked spares as well as certain types of ammunition. Nehru thereupon conceded that 'Muzaffarabad and Mirpur are out of our reach at present...Kotli is of somewhat different category.'[70] Thus, despite Cariappa's plan to capture all the above three towns, the advance was made only towards Kotli.

To reinforce its diplomatic moves for a ceasefire, Pakistan, on 14 December 1948, launched an offensive, termed 'Operation Venus',* in the Naoshera area. This offensive succeeded in badly

---

* 'Operation Venus' was carried out under the command of Major General Loftus Tottenham and several British officers were responsible for planning and executing the attack.

mauling the strategically important bridge at Beri Patan. The Pakistanis had withdrawn troops in West Punjab for this offensive, thereby taking the great risk of exposing themselves in the Sialkot–Lahore area – a risk that the stronger Indian Army had refused to take in East Punjab. According to the Indian generals, India could have taken back most of Pakistan-occupied territory in the southwest despite the latter's improved defence preparations, if more troops had been available. However, the warning sounded by Nye and earlier by Mountbatten (and possibly by others when he visited the UK) kept ringing in Nehru's ears.

By this time, the Pakistanis were agreeable to a ceasefire, something they had rejected when speaking to the UNCIP in July. They were also now willing to drop their demand for the removal of Sheikh Abdullah. Therefore, the chances of their accepting the UNCIP proposals for the withdrawal of their forces from Kashmir and for an early plebiscite had improved, or so the Indians thought. Even if two-thirds of the inhabitants there and in western Jammu voted for India, the plebiscite could be won.

This change in the Pakistani position had come largely because the Americans had remained adamant that the Pakistanis had to pull out. On 23 November 1948, John Foster Dulles, the acting chairman of the US delegation to the UN (who was in Paris), sent the following message to the secretary of state in Washington:

> Strong UK pressure past two weeks for early SC meeting on Kashmir. They [the UK] are not keen on August 13 provision [the UNCIP resolution] regarding withdrawal Pakistan troops.... Present UK approach to Kashmir problem appears extremely pro-GOP [Pakistan].[71]

The secretary of state wired back the next day:

> Re: withdrawal Pakistan troops we continue feel this aspect so essential acceptable overall settlement that failure its inclusion as integral part plan would probably certainly prejudice GOI [India] acquiescence in plan.[72]

On 7 December 1948, Dulles reported to Marshall that the British were still holding out. They had proposed a draft of a resolution, on which Dulles commented as follows:

In effect UK resolution in present form is to tie both parties formally to ceasefire against present benefit GOP; to leave GOI without any definite commitment re withdrawal GOP troops.[73]

It was on 27 December 1948 that Pakistan eventually gave in. On that day the American chargé d'affaires in Pakistan wired to the secretary of state:

He [Zafrullah Khan] asked me what I thought about the matter [the UNCIP resolution]. I told him that in my opinion Pakistan was over a barrel and they had better accept the proposal.... Sir Zafrullah then said that he himself had arrived at that conclusion.[74]

But Pakistan did not yield before it had succeeded in resisting the provisos for an absolutely unconditional withdrawal.

The ceasefire came into effect on 1 January 1949.

It was only after the Cold War started in real earnest and 'pact mania' gripped American foreign policy that mutually agreed terms could be found for a defence pact between Pakistan and the Western powers. In the first such alliance, known as 'the Baghdad Pact' (which was signed in February 1955), Pakistan, Iran, Iraq and Turkey joined Britain and created the 'brick wall' to thwart Soviet ambitions. This concept was first thought of by Sir Olaf Caroe. A few years later, in 1959, this defence pact was translated into CENTO (Central Treaty Organization), the US taking over command from Britain as the captain of the Western team against the Soviets in the old Great Game that had by then assumed global dimensions and had come to be called the Cold War.

Notes and References

1. Colonel James Todd, *Annals and Antiquities of Rajputana* (Munshiram Manoharlal, New Delhi, 2001).
2. Alan Campbell-Johnson, *Mission with Mountbatten* (New Age Publishers, Delhi, 1994, diary entry of 11 November 1947).
3. MBI/E/193/2, Broadlands Archives (BA), University of Southampton.
4. Ibid. Message to Gandhiji from Attlee.
5. Ibid. Mountbatten to Gandhiji, 29 September 1947.
6. H.V. Hodson, *The Great Divide: Britain-India-Pakistan* (Oxford University Press edition, Delhi, 2000, p. 381).
7. MBI/D4, Interview No. 43, 16 September 1947, BA, University of Southampton.
8. MBI/E/193/3, 29 October 1947, BA, University of Southampton.
9. Stanley Wolpert, *Nehru: A Tryst with Destiny* (Oxford University Press, New York, 1996, p. 426, Nehru to Rajagopalachari, 26 October 1947).
10. Campbell-Johnnson, op. cit., diary entry 18 December 1947.
11. Jinnah–Isfahani correspondence September 1947, pp. 525–26. Cited in Stanley Wolpert, *Jinnah of Pakistan*, ninth edition (Oxford University Press, London, 2002, p. 348).
12. Record of governor-general's Interview No. 80, 12 January 1948, BA, University of Southampton.
13. Mountbatten's interview with Sardar Baldev Singh, 23 January 1948. Cited in Larry Collins and Dominique Lapierre, *Mountbatten and Independent India* (Vikas Publishing House, New Delhi, 1985, p. 126).
14. MBI/E/193, BA, University of Southampton.
15. Jawaharlal Nehru, *Selected Works*, Vol. IV (Nehru Memorial Museum and Library, New Delhi, pp. 391–92).
16. File L/WS/1/1139, IOR, London, cited in telegram from Terence Shone to CRO, 28 December 1947.
17. Jawaharlal Nehru, op. cit., pp. 399–403, 24 December 1947.
18. File L/WS/1/1140, IOR, London. Cited in C. Dasgupta, *War and Diplomacy in Kashmir: 1947–1948* (Sage, New Delhi, 2002, p. 105).
19. Jawaharlal Nehru, op. cit., pp. 411–12.
20. US FR 1947, Vol. III, p. 185, 29 December 1947.
21. Ibid., p. 190, 30 December 1947.
22. Ibid., p. 192.

23. File FO 80/470, CRO, London. Minute, 6 January 1948, to prime minister.

24. MBI/D/241, BA, University of Southampton.

25. File L/WS/1/1148, Attlee to Noel-Baker, 10 January 1948 (OIC, British Library, London).

26. US FR 1948, Vol. V, p. 274, 8 January 1948.

27. Ibid., pp. 291–92, 28 January 1948.

28. Ibid., pp. 308–09, 28 February 1948.

29. Ibid.

30. Ibid., p. 300, 29 February 1948.

31. Austin's cable to Ayangar, 22 January 1948, referred to in Ayangar's cable No. 25-S to Nehru, 22 February 1948 in Jawaharlal Nehru, op.cit., Vol. V.

32. US FR 1948, Vol. V, p. 306, 27 February 1948.

33. Ibid., p. 311, 4 March 1948.

34. Ibid.

35. Jawaharlal Nehru, op. cit., Vol. V, p. 211. Cited in Dasgupta, op. cit., p. 122.

36. File L/WS/1/1148, Walker to Carter, 1 February 1948, IOR, London. Cited in Dasgupta, op. cit., p. 122.

37. File L/WS/1/114, Mountbatten to Attlee, 8 February 1948, IOR, London. Cited in Dasgupta, op. cit., p. 123.

38. Philip Ziegler, *Mountbatten* (Collins, London, 1985, p. 450). Governor-general's personal Report No. 9, 19 March 1948, D 88, BA, University of Southampton.

39. File CAB/134/55, Public Relations Office (PRO), London, minutes of CAC meeting of 5 March 1948.

40. Wavell's collection of notes and ideas 1939–46 (privately printed). The verse is attribute to one Dooley.

41. US FR 1948, Vol. V, pp. 327–28.

42. Ziegler, op. cit., p. 451. Governor-general's Interview No. 129, 20 March 1948, D 77, BA, University of Southampton.

43. Nehru's cable to Ayangar. Jawaharlal Nehru, op.cit., Vol. V, p. 188.

44. File L/P&9/13/1865/O/R, 28 January 1948 (OIC, British Library, London).

45. According to governor-general's Interview No. 108, 17 February 1948, D 76, BA, University of Southampton.

46. Ziegler, op. cit., p. 467.

47. Hugh Dalton's diary entry dated 15 October 1948. Quoted in S. Gopal, *Nehru* (Oxford University Press, Delhi, 2003, p. 35).
48. Noel Baker to Attlee, 2 April 1948, FO 800/470, PRO, London, p. 129. Cited in Dasgupta, op. cit., p. 129.
49. Ibid., 4 April 1948, Attlee to Noel-Baker. Cited in Dasgupta, op. cit., p. 129.
50. Josef Korbel, *Danger in Kashmir* (Oxford University Press, New York and Karachi, 2002, p. 307).
51. Mountbatten's letter to Walker, 27 February 1948, No. 72, BA, University of Southampton.
52. Attlee's letter to Nehru, 11 March 1948, BA, University of Southampton.
53. Nehru's personal letter to Attlee, 18 April 1948, BA, University of Southampton.
54. Korbel, op. cit., p. 121.
55. Ibid., p. 129.
56. Ibid., p. 312.
57. File Prem 8/997, PRO, London.
58. US FR 1948, Vol. V, p. 419.
59. Ibid.
60. MBI/F40, Carter to Mountbatten, 8 October 1948, BA, University of Southampton.
61. Ibid., Mountbatten to Noel Baker, 25 October 1948, BA, University of Southampton.
62. File Prem 8/997, PRO, London. Note by Cumming Bruce, 26 September 1948 and extract from minute of COS (48)/36 meeting, 4 September 1948.
63. US FR 1948, Vol. V, pp. 435–36.
64. Ibid.
65. File L/WS/1/1144, Attlee to Liaqat Ali Khan (OIC, British Library, London). Cited in Dasgupta, op. cit., p. 180.
66. Ibid., General Nye to CRO, 22 November 1948 (OIC, British Library, London).
67. MBI/F40, Mountbatten to Nehru, 15 August 1948, BA, University of Southampton.
68. File L/WS/1/1144, 20 November, 1948 (OIC, British Library, London).
69. Ibid.
70. Jawaharlal Nehru, op.cit., Vol. V, p. 87.

71. US FR 1948, Vol. V, pp. 459–60.
72. Ibid., p. 461.
73. Ibid., p. 471.
74. Ibid., pp. 481–82.

14

Postscript

BRITAIN'S 'PAKISTAN STRATEGY' SUCCEEDED BRILLIANTLY. PAKISTAN, together with Iran, Iraq, Turkey and Britain, joined the Baghdad Pact and later, CENTO, which the US also joined, to form the defence barrier against Soviet ambitions in the Middle East. In 1954 Pakistan entered into a bilateral pact with Britain's ally, the USA, and, in 1958, provided an air base in Peshawar to the CIA for U-2 spy planes to keep a watch on military preparations in the Soviet Union. Then, in the 1970s, Pakistan helped the US establish relations with China, to pressurize the Soviet Union from the east. And, in the 1980s, Islamabad provided the forward base from which the US could eject the Soviet forces from Afghanistan, precipitating the collapse of the USSR and altering the world balance of power.

On the other hand, the 'Pakistan strategy' did not prevent the Soviet Union from reaching out to India. This it did by supporting India against Pakistan, which had the backing of the Western powers, on Kashmir, in the 1950s. In August 1971 an Indo–Soviet treaty, with a defence-related clause in it, was signed. This treaty restrained China from interfering in the forthcoming Indo–Pakistan war on Bangladesh. Treaties may be like flowers and young girls that last while they last, as Charles de Gaulle said, but the process of India purchasing Soviet arms on rupee payment and barter that started in the early 1960s has become an important and long-standing feature of Indo–Soviet relationship. Would the collaboration between these two countries have developed but for partition?

Partition also helped China extend its influence right up to the mouth of the Persian Gulf – via Pakistan. In 2004, hundreds of Chinese were building a port in Gwadur in Baluchistan, at the mouth of the Gulf. What facilities China will get from Pakistan remain undisclosed. To begin with, China befriended Pakistan so that the latter would not permit separatist Islamic influences to reach the Muslims of Sinkiang through the British-built road from the subcontinent via northern Kashmir to Kashgar – 'the main artery into Central Asia', as Ernest Bevin once described it to George Marshall. From the 1980s, China has helped Pakistan neutralize the larger Indian conventional force, by supplying it directly, and through North Korea, nuclear weaponry and missiles. One may indeed ask: Would the 1962 Sino–India clash have occurred had India remained united? Would the Indian subcontinent have been nuclearized in the twentieth century but for partition?

The unobtrusive, but steady, pressure exerted by the US on Britain in favour of India's independence and unity from 1942 to 1947 has been (strangely) neglected by historians so far. Roosevelt made several attempts to persuade Churchill to grant self-government to India after the fall of Singapore, but in vain. As soon as an Interim Government under Jawaharlal Nehru was formed in 1946, the US recognized it and sent an ambassador to Delhi, to the consternation of the British. The Americans thereafter advised Britain to keep India united. They feared that India's Balkanization would help the communists. It was only after March 1947, when the Congress Party itself accepted the division of the Punjab and Bengal, that the US found itself helpless to do any more. 'The Congress leaders had in fact abandoned the tenets which they supported for so many years in the campaign for united India', wired the American Embassy in Delhi to Washington.

The US pressure on Britain led to one predictable result. To fend it off, Churchill, in 1942, played the 'Muslim' or the 'Pakistani' card: that it was *not* British reluctance to grant self-government to India, but the serious differences amongst Muslims and Hindus on India's future that were creating the problem. Such a move brought Jinnah's 1940 scheme for partition and his two-nation theory to centre stage. The theory of 'the provincial option', which created the constitutional channel by which partition could be put into effect, was concocted in London in 1942.

That by 1943 India had become an important adversarial factor in Anglo–US relations is not well known. This factor could have been liquidated by Indian disenchantment with America, or vice versa, or both. The record shows that Mountbatten, Krishna Menon and Attlee worked on Nehru to raise his suspicions about the US motives in Asia. Side by side, British speakers and diplomats propounded the idea in the US that the Indian Muslim had better imbibed the Western legacy and was a more reliable partner than the basically feeble and unreliable Hindu. The Indian leaders' ambitious foreign policy after independence, combined with their inexperience, took no time to collide with the Americans' impatient and demanding nature, mixed with their ignorance about India.

The Americans, to begin with, showed more understanding of India's position on Jammu and Kashmir than did Britain. Throughout 1948, the US insisted that J&K's accession to India could not be brushed aside unless it lost the plebiscite that India itself had offered and, meanwhile, Pakistani forces that had entered the state had to be withdrawn. It was this US stand that prevented J&K's accession to India being negated, at British behest, by the UN Security Council. But while Britain was able to maintain good relations with India, the neutral Americans were cast as the villains of the piece. This was largely due to Nehru's basic distrust of capitalist America, his faith in socialist Britain and the personal ties that the Mountbattens had developed with him.

To bring to light an important, but ignored, historical truth is by itself worthwhile. This is all the more appropriate because India has never recognized the goodwill that the US showed for India's independence and unity during the end game of Empire. Admittedly, today, given Russia's retreat from Central Asia and the growing mutual concern about terrorism and political Islam, a new chapter is opening up in Indo–US relations.

The story is also a cautionary tale for Indians. The leaders of the Congress Party were inspired by high ideals. They built up a broad-based all-India organization without which the struggle for independence would not have been possible. They revived the sagging morale and confidence of a fallen people, contributing to 'India's great recovery', to use K. M. Pannikar's phrase. They devised instruments such as satyagraha (peaceful mass protest or resistance), answering violence by non-violence. Such measures put moral pressure on the democratic British people to push their government to recognize India's legitimate demands. These were great achievements.

But the Indian leaders remained plagued by the Indians' age-old weaknesses of arrogance, inconsistency, often poor political judgement and disinterest in foreign affairs and questions of defence. Overconfidence made them ignore the dangers of rejecting, from the Congress Party's fold (in the 1920s), the secular and very able, though egocentric, Jinnah. They failed to include, after the party's massive victory in provincial elections, in their governments, in 1937, those Muslim League leaders who wanted to taste the plums of office. The British archives reveal that in their negotiations with the viceroys in the 1940s, there was no consistency – without which there could be no success in diplomacy or war – or indeed a clear, realistic policy. In fact, they could not even make up their minds on whether or not to accord priority above all else to India's unity or to consider non-violence a higher duty.

Resigning from governments in British provinces in 1939 and launching the Quit India movement in 1942 proved counterproductive. For Nehru to agree to include Muslim League ministers in the Interim Government in September 1946, before the League had entered the Constituent Assembly and agreed to stop 'direct action' or terrorism, was another blunder. To prematurely declare in December 1946 that India would become a republic, while engaged in delicate negotiations with the Attlee Government on a future

406 II THE SHADOW OF THE GREAT GAME

settlement, was a mistake. By the end of 1946, they had been manoeuvred into such a corner that if Sardar Patel had not stepped forward 'to have a limb amputated', as he put it, and satisfy Britain, there was a danger of India's fragmentation, as Britain searched for military bases in the bigger princely states by supporting their attempts to declare independence.

Protected by British power for so long and then focused on a non-violent struggle, the Indian leaders were ill prepared, as independence dawned, to confront the power play in our predatory world. Their historic disinterest in other countries' aims and motives made things none the easier. They had failed to see through the real British motivation for their support to the Pakistan scheme and take remedial measures. Nor did they understand that, at the end of the Raj, America wanted a free and united India to emerge and to find ways to work this powerful lever. Glaring mistakes were made in handling the Kashmir imbroglio, as recounted in Chapter 13.

The Mahatma, who galvanized and united the heterogeneous Indian people in the 1920s with his mystical appeal that amazed the world, was of little help to his countrymen as they faced aggression, not from the British police, but from jihadi forces. Jinnah, though playing a weaker hand, had a better grasp of what the British were after and offered a realistic quid pro quo, threatening the use of violence to hammer home his demands.

The documents also bring out the anti-Congress Party and anti-Hindu sentiments of the British officers serving in the country even as they prepared to quit India. Most such officers, who stayed on after independence, went over to serve Pakistan and did their damnedest against India.

★

Was it possible to have avoided partition by 1946–47? It may be worth dwelling on this question for a moment.

Besides the strategic factor, there were other reasons for Britain to favour partition. One was the doubt in the British mind that India might not have a very good chance of surviving as an independent state. A top-secret appreciation, prepared in the Commonwealth

Relations Office soon after British withdrawal (partly quoted in Chapter 9), elaborates this doubt. Factors such as India's heterogeneous population, the North–South divide, the communal problem, the unruliness of the Sikhs and the policy of the Indian communists to spread dissension are cited in this context. One can't say how far Attlee, or how many of his colleagues, accepted this analysis. But notions of India's instability were deeply embedded in the thinking of British officials, senior Conservative politicians and many journalists, including editors of newspapers. In the circumstances, it is not surprising that the British would hesitate to put *all* their eggs in the Indian basket.

There was another reason for the British tilt towards the creation of Pakistan. I have referred to the hatred for Indian leaders in general and for the Hindus in particular that most British civilians and military men in India had started to feel by 1947. The nationalists' non-cooperation in the war effort had created deep distrust for them in Britain; so also in several countries of the British Commonwealth, particularly in South Africa, Australia and New Zealand. Therefore, the emotion among the English in favour of Pakistan was very great. (It has not subsided entirely even to this day.)

The Indians too faced difficulties in cooperating with Britain. The British support for the Muslim League as well as for the Pakistan scheme had created a general and widespread suspicion of their intentions among the public. Besides, there were specific points of disagreement. Jawaharlal Nehru was willing to cooperate with Britain on several issues, including that of supporting the Commonwealth concept, which, he believed, would help to balance American influence in the world. But he was absolutely opposed to getting entangled in any schemes to contain or confront the Soviet Union and China. Also, he was bent upon fighting European colonialism as well as apartheid, even if his stance embarrassed Britain and its friends. A possibility that greatly excited him was the opportunities independence would offer India to mediate for peace between the West and the East and, in so doing, strike out a new path in world affairs. By appealing to the deep-felt urges of mankind for freedom, equality and peace, he believed that India could develop a diplomatic reach, which would be as effective in influencing world events as power politics and military strength. These concepts, of course, would be difficult to marry with British ideas,* and were unlikely to persuade Britain to abandon the Pakistan scheme.

★

The findings in this book go against the conventional wisdom in India and abroad. The Indians, by and large, believe that the Imperial power supported the partition plan to weaken India, so that it remained dependent on Britain even after independence. This is less than half the truth. The British left no stone unturned to push their allies, the princes – whose territories constituted one-third of the Raj – into the arms of India, except for Jammu and Kashmir. This step helped unify disparate and fragmented parts into a cohesive country. If the British were out to weaken India, why should they have done this, or left the Andaman and Nicobar as well as the Lacadive Islands in Indian hands, which increased India's naval reach in the Indian Ocean? Or, indeed, why should they have whittled down Jinnah's territorial demands to the minimum required for Britain to safeguard its defence requirements?

The English and people abroad generally believed that India was divided because Hindus and Muslims could not live peacefully together in one country and, a separate state – Pakistan – needed to be carved out of India for the Muslims. But the fact is that such a division of the two communities was never made. Nearly thirty million Muslims, or a third of the total Muslim population of India, were *excluded* from Pakistan. These Muslims residing in Indian provinces, in which they were minorities, were the only ones who could be said to be vulnerable to Hindu pressure or domination. The creation of Pakistan was justified in order to protect them, but they were left behind in India.** The areas placed in Pakistan (the NWFP, West Punjab, Baluchistan and Sind) had Muslim majorities with no

---

* 'Overidealistic, inexperienced in foreign affairs, and far too vain' was the British High Commission's (in India) top-secret assessment of Nehru.[1]
** The Muslim population of India has more than quadrupled in fifty years and today about 145 million Muslims live here with people of other faiths.

fear of Hindu domination and were being ruled by governments dominated by Muslims. Indeed, the NWFP and the Punjab had governments opposed to Jinnah's Muslim League. But they were placed in Pakistan.

These four provinces/units, however, had one common feature: the British chiefs of staff considered their territories of absolute importance for organizing a defence against a possible Soviet advance towards the Indian Ocean.

Partition was a politico-strategic act. It was not to 'save' Muslims from Hindus; nor was it to weaken India. 'Everyone for home; everyone for himself.'

The British adopted the policy of divide and rule in India after the bloody revolt or the Great Mutiny of 1857. This was a policy to control Indians, not to divide India. The latter question arose when the British started to plan their retreat from India, the facts about which are the subject of this story. If the impulse was Churchill's, it was Attlee who implemented the scheme. Working behind a thick smoke screen, he wove circles around Indian leaders and persuaded them to accept partition.

★

The belief that the Cabinet Mission plan sought to avoid, or would have succeeded in avoiding, partition is mistaken. This plan would have intensified communal tension and most probably Balkanized India, as explained in Chapter 8. However, it served HMG's purpose as follows. It delivered a shock to Jinnah that the Attlee Government might move away from partition and prepared the ground for him to accept the smaller Pakistan. The entry of the Congress leaders into the Interim Government kept them from revolting; it softened them up to ultimately accept the Wavell–Attlee plan. The exercise served British public relations; it created the impression in the United States that Britain was working for Indian unity.

The plan for the smaller Pakistan was not worked out by Mountbatten in 1947, as generally believed, but by Lord Wavell in 1945, who submitted its detailed blueprint to London in February 1946. Mountbatten implemented the plan by persuading the two main Indian parties to accept the same. Advancing the date of British departure from June 1948 to August 1947 is often blamed for the chaos and killings in Punjab. The date was advanced after the Congress Party, in May 1947, agreed to accept the transfer of power on a dominion status basis, provided Britain pulled out of India *forthwith*. The Indian acceptance of dominion status, even temporarily, was important for Britain. ('The greatest opportunity ever offered to the Empire.') It would facilitate the passage of the Indian Independence Bill in the British Parliament, by appeasing the Conservative opposition. It would prove to the world that India had willingly accepted partition; otherwise why should it agree to remain a British dominion? It would gain time to persuade Nehru and his friends to abandon their commitment to leave the British Commonwealth.

Penderel Moon, civil servant and historian who was on the spot, has written: 'The determination of the Sikhs to preserve their cohesion was the root cause of the violent exchange of populations which took place; and it would have operated with like effect even if the division of the Punjab had been put off another year.' Admittedly, the Muslim attacks on Sikh farmers in the villages around Rawalpindi in March 1947 confirmed this community's worst fears that the Muslim League was out to cleanse West Pakistan of non-Muslims, which actually happened. However, Linlithgow and Wavell cannot escape the responsibility for the Punjab massacres. They ignored the warnings of their governors, Henry Craik and Bertrand Glancy, that strengthening Jinnah's Muslim League in the Punjab at the expense of the Muslims of the Unionist Party, who were opposed to partition – Shaukat Hayat used to call it 'Jinnahstan' – would result in a blood bath in the province. Wavell did forward Glancy's warning to London, but the policy to build up Jinnah as the sole spokesman of the Muslims continued.

The view that Britain, by staying on longer, might have avoided the Punjab troubles ignores the fact that the British neither had the troops nor the administrative capacity to control events in India by the summer of 1947. The vigour and speed with which Lord Mountbatten acted at least had the merit of confining the conflagration to the Punjab.

★

The British focus was no doubt on Pakistan as a future defence partner in the Great Game, but India too had its value. If it remained in the British family of nations, i.e., in the Commonwealth, this retention would add to British prestige and influence in the post-war world. How Mountbatten juggled the above two British goals, none-too-easy a feat, has been covered in the earlier chapters. While viceroy of India, he prized away the North West Frontier Province from the Congress Party's control and, while India's governor-general after independence, he restrained it from occupying the whole, or more areas, of Kashmir. This made it possible for Pakistan to be formed as a defence bastion. Simultaneously, he was able to build bridges between the British and India that led to the latter remaining a member of the British Commonwealth.

The view that Mountbatten helped India to gain Kashmir, by persuading Sir Cyril Radcliffe to allot parts of the Muslim-majority areas of Gurdaspur district (in the Punjab) to India, is not well founded. A fair-weather road through this district was indeed the only route that connected the state with India. But it was Wavell's blueprint for Pakistan, sent to London on 6 February 1946, which has to be studied in this context. The allotment had nothing to do with Kashmir or Mountbatten. Wavell had recommended:

> In the Punjab the only Muslim-majority District that would not go into Pakistan under this demarcation is Gurdaspur (51 per cent Muslim). Gurdaspur must go with Amritsar for geographical reasons and Amritsar being [the] sacred city of Sikhs must stay out of Pakistan.

In 1947 the territory of Kapurthala state, then an autonomous entity, blocked access to Amritsar from East Punjab. That was why Radcliffe awarded certain areas of Gurdaspur to India to connect the Sikh holy city with the Sikh-dominated East Punjab (and India).

Mountbatten continues to receive flak in Britain, Pakistan and India. Some of the British frustration at India's independence ('Of course he lost it'), not unnaturally, got rubbed off on the man who actually handed over power. The ex-viceroy, in his old age, talked a bit too much – about his success in India – which played into his detractors' hands, with India being vilified in the process. His achievements for his country were very great, and as they say in England: Good Wine Needs No Brush!

Regarding the princes, unless some organic relationship could be established between the Central Government and the princely states, as was actually done through the process of accessions – into which the princes were no doubt stampeded by Mountbatten – a much worse fate awaited them. Ninety per cent of the princely states were too small to resist agitators entering from the Indian or Pakistani provinces and overrunning them, threatening their rulers' lives and property. If some bigger states tried to break away by declaring independence, they would not have succeeded, because Britain was not in a position to come to their aid, and the United States was against the further Balkanization of India. The accessions saved the princely order, if not the princely states. They laid the foundation for a peaceful revolution. (It is another matter that the British paid scant regard to solemn treaties signed with the princes, whereas they laid so much stress on their obligations to mere declarations made in the British Parliament to safeguard minority rights. After all, Pakistan would be a partner in the Great Game after they quit India; the princes had outlived their utility.)

*

Many, including some prominent historians,* are of the view that Mahatma Gandhi remained opposed to partition till the very end. His absenting himself from Delhi on Independence Day is cited as proof. However, his conversation with Mountbatten on 2 June 1947, a day before the partition plan was announced, his statement at his prayer meeting that afternoon, and his advice to the All-India Congress

---

* Stanley Wolpert, after reading this manuscript, wrote to me that he believes that Gandhiji had *not agreed* to partition.

Committee on 14 June, all suggest that he had accepted the division of India as a necessary evil. He absented himself from the Independence Day celebrations probably for a different reason. He would not have fitted in. His stature in India was far higher than that of either Nehru or Mountbatten. But these two alone would represent their respective countries at the official ceremony for the Transfer of Power. Can one imagine the Mahatma sitting propped up in an open landau with Lord and Lady Mountbatten and Nehru, the foursome driving through the Delhi crowds throwing back flowers hurled at them? It would be ridiculous!

Britain's pro-Pakistan policy on Kashmir was based on its desire to keep that part of its old Indian Empire, which jutted into Central Asia and lay along Afghanistan, Soviet Russia and China, in the hands of the successor dominion that had promised cooperation in matters of defence. In the open forum of the UN, Britain could not conceal its pro-Pakistani stand. The Americans, in their internal telegrams, have left a record of Britain's pro-Pakistani tilt on Kashmir.

It is not my purpose in this book to pontificate on the rights and wrongs of actions of countries whose interests were involved in Kashmir. It is primarily to suggest that the Kashmir imbroglio in 1947–48 proved once more that all that happened during the end game of Empire cannot be understood unless one keeps in view the overwhelming concern of the withdrawing power, as it pulled out, to secure its strategic agenda.

Nevertheless, I would like to touch upon two aspects of the Kashmir imbroglio.

First, to begin with, Kashmir was considered a territorial issue, not a communal one. The communal argument was injected by Britain and Pakistan in the UN debates to bolster the latter's claim. Be it noted that when Sir Zafrullah Khan told the Americans that 'Kashmir was essential to the strategic defence of Pakistan',[2] he was referring to Kashmir's territory, not its people. Pakistan's acquisition of Kashmir would compensate it for the 'smaller' territory it received than it had hoped for by partition, enhance its profile as a crucially strategic state in Asia touching the roof of the world – and help it to build relations with powerful states. Pakistan's attempt to capture Buddhist Ladakh on Tibet's border could not by any stretch of imagination be described as 'a move to protect Muslims'.

In July 1947, Jinnah personally approached the Maharaja of Jodhpur and the Maharaj Kumar of Jaisalmer (as we have seen in Chapter 11) and offered favourable terms to the rulers of these wholly Hindu-populated states to accede to Pakistan. He also approached the rulers of the Hindu-populated states of Baroda, Indore and others through the Nawab of Bhopal. Jinnah did so because he knew very well that the affiliation of the princely states to one or the other dominion was left entirely to their rulers by the same British act that created Pakistan. It was not a Hindu–Muslim question. That is also why Pakistan accepted the accession of the Nawab of Junagadh, a Hindu-majority state.

Secondly, it would be wrong to believe that because Kashmir was 77 per cent Muslim, its people would, in 1947, have automatically wished to join Pakistan. The NWFP, next door, was 95 per cent Muslim but we have seen how its people resisted the Muslim League and British pressure and remained with the Congress Party, till 1947, when, this party's leaders, in a quid pro quo with the British, abandoned them. In 1947, the overwhelming majority of Muslims of the Valley of Kashmir, where well over half of the people of the state lived, supported Sheikh Abdullah and his National Conference Party. Whatever his other ambitions, Abdullah was absolutely opposed to Pakistan. Similarly, Jammu and its Dogra belt would have voted against Pakistan. The only Muslims of the state who would have supported Pakistan in large numbers at that time were those living along Pakistan's border in the Poonch–Mirpur area.

Since Pakistan was created, the communal virus has spread to large parts of the subcontinent. I can't say how the Kashmiris would vote today. But, in 1947–48, the majority, in all probability, would have supported the maharaja's accession to India. And 1947–48 is the pertinent date, when considering the issue. In all fairness, the position that existed then cannot be brushed aside.

★

The successful use of religion by the British in India to gain political and strategic objectives was replicated by the Americans in Afghanistan in the 1980s by building up the Islamic jihadis, all for the same purpose of keeping the Soviet communists at bay. The Muslim League's 'direct action' before partition in India was the forerunner of the jihad in Afghanistan. However, Al-Qaida's attacks on the World Trade Center towers in New York and the Pentagon in Washington on 11 September 2001 woke up the West to the dangers of encouraging political Islam.

It was the Pakistan Government that, through the Jamaat-i-Islami, Pakistan, and their intelligence service, the ISI, created the Taliban movement in Afghanistan. The preachings of the Jamaat's founder, Abdul Al Mawdudi, a migrant from India, envisaged a clash of civilizations and governments founded *strictly* on the tenets of the Shariat; he counselled jihad against non-believers. These views found an echo in many Muslim lands; they influenced Osama bin Laden. Even after the US-backed jihad in Afghanistan had succeeded, Pakistan continued to help the Taliban train terrorists to fight non-believers in the name of Allah. Without Pakistan's backing, it is doubtful whether Islamic terror could have spread so far and wide in the world, despite Osama bin Laden, Saudi and Gulf petro dollars and Arab suicide bombers. The Americans are now taking steps to rein in the export of terror from Pakistan. But the genie has escaped the bottle. Some of the roots of the present Islamic terrorism menacing the world surely lie buried in the partition of India.

The British brought the 'New Learning' to India as well as the notion of the separation of religion from politics that had become the norm in Christian Europe after the Renaissance. These features opened up the possibility for secularism – anathema to orthodox Muslims – to take root among the Muslims of India and for them to work a democratic constitution together with people of other faiths; indeed, for India becoming a laboratory for enlightened Islam. At the same time, Western social mores helped foster among the individualistic Hindus a greater sense of responsibility for society and feeling of brotherhood between man and man. Shashi Tharoor, the writer, speaking of Hindus has asked: How can the followers of a faith without any fundamentals become fundamentalists? But lack of parameters and a sense of social responsibility can also lead to intolerance as well as to parochialism. The good done by the spread of British liberal ideas in India in the nineteenth century was undone in the twentieth by British politicians and viceroys, who introduced divisive policies such as separate electorates for Muslims (besides, of course, self-serving economic policies that overtaxed the farmers). British rule, to the end, maintained its duality: the civilizing mission and extreme selfishness mixed with cunning – though during its last days, 'the Raj was about neither plunder nor civilization but rather survival', as Fareed Zakaria, the columnist and writer, has put it.

There is, of course, the view that partition averted a worse disaster for India in the years to come. The past half a century has seen a phenomenal rise in Islamic fundamentalism and in the forces of political Islam. Such a development has drawn and deepened fault lines within many states with mixed populations of Muslims and others. Would it be possible in such circumstances, for the nearly 500 million Muslims (by the year 2010) of an *undivided* India to settle down peacefully under a democratic, secular constitution? Partition, by compartmentalizing Muslim political power in the two corners of the subcontinent, has weakened the jihadis and given time for the pressure from economical globalization and the technological revolution sweeping the world to overhaul or temper the intensity of the globalization of jihad and political Islam and ensure peaceful co-existence in the subcontinent.

All these are questions for the reader to ponder over. I can only express the hope that the knowledge of the hitherto not so well-known facts about the politics surrounding the partition of the subcontinent might help to ease the mutual misunderstanding in the relations between India and the West that crept in around half a century back with the forging of the alliance between Pakistan and the West. The awareness that it was global politics, Britain's insecurity and the errors of judgement of the Indian leaders that resulted in the partition of India might help India and Pakistan in search for reconciliation.

Notes and References

1. The quotation is from the top-secret report of the British High Commission in India for the third quarter of 1950, written by Frank Roberts, the acting high commissioner. It fell into Indian hands and crossed my desk as private secretary to Sir Girja Shanker Bajpai, the secretary-general of the Ministry of External Affairs. The words of the analysis appeared so appropriate that they stuck in memory. Roberts was a highly thought-of diplomat who later became the UK's ambassador in Moscow.

2. US FR 1948, Vol. V, p. 137.

Index

Abdullah, 19
Abdullah, Omar, 68
Abdullah, Sheikh, 320, 344-50, 370, 376-81, 384, 388, 396, 414
Abell, George, 233, 251
Abyssinia, 169
Acheson, Dean, 200, 215-16, 228, 256, 258, 259, 263, 265
Addison, Christopher, 384
Advance in date (of British departure), 410
Afghani, Maulana, 69
Afghanistan, 10, 11, 15, 16, 17, 19, 26, 30, 31, 68, 70, 124, 129, 163, 168, 188, 219, 244-46, 303, 304, 311, 331, 334, 335, 337, 341, 343, 374, 402, 413, 415
Afghan war, second, 244
Agra, 35, 66
Ahmedabad, 35
Ain-ud-Din, Sayed, 73
Air Force
  Indian, 339
  Pakistani, 338
Akali Dal, 284
Akalis, 284-85

Akbar the Great, 75, 342
Alexander, A.V., 203, 208, 211, 359
Ali, Agha Shaukat, 347
Ali, Aruna Asaf, 230
Ali, Asaf, 230, 257
Ali, Captain Mohammad, 174
Aligarh, 75
Aligarh Muslim University, 206
Ali, Ghanzafar, 72
Ali, Rahmat, 69-70
Allahabad, 100, 125, 153, 173
Allenbrooke, Field Marshal Viscount, 23
Allied cause, 158
Allied war effort, 153
All-India All-Party Conference, 83-84
All-India Congress Committee, 194, 307, 412-13
All-India Federation, 35, 48, 53, 70, 86
All-India Federation Act, 316
All-India Momin Conference, 69
All-India Muslim Conference, 85
Al-Qaida, 11, 68, 176, 224, 415
Amanullah, King, 19
Ambedkar, B.R., 142

American Civil War, 18
American Consul, 224
American forces in India, 151-52
American hegemony, 287
Amery, Leopold, 53-54, 56, 60,
    65, 98, 99, 100-02, 111, 123,
    149, 153, 176, 188, 199
Amritsar, 81, 195, 285, 411
Andaman and Nicobar Islands,
    200, 240, 312, 408
Anglo-American collaboration,
    156, 161
Anglo-American misunderstanding,
    156
Anglo-American relations, 154-56,
    165
Anglo-Congress Party rupture, 45
Anglo-Oriental College, 75
Anglo-Pak alliance, 197
Anglo-Soviet relations, 181
Anglo-US lend lease, 155
Ansari, Dr Mukhtar Ahmed, 83-84
Anwar, Major Khurshid, 334
Apartheid, 238, 242, 407
Arabs, 204
Argentina, 385
Army, 35, 167, 171, 172, 173,
    174, 185, 198, 201, 217,
    234, 237, 246, 292, 323
    Indian, 335, 340, 341, 371,
    372, 392-96
    Pakistani, 335, 357, 359, 360,
    361, 371, 388
Asia for Asiatics Movement, 184
Asia Relations Conference, 275-76
Assam, 179, 195, 211, 212, 214,
    216, 225, 233, 250, 252,
    253, 258, 273, 289
Assets (of undivided India),
    Nehru's opinion on, 369
Ataturk, Mustafa Kemal, 19, 69
Atlantic Charter, 150, 153, 159,
    161, 185, 188-89
    signing of, 152

Atom bomb, dropped on
    Hiroshima and Nagasaki, 188
Attenborough, Sir Richard, 142
Attlee, Clement, 26, 28, 45, 82,
    97, 100, 102, 149, 183, 188,
    189, 192, 199, 200, 202,
    203, 205, 208, 210, 212,
    214, 215, 216, 220, 221,
    228, 230, 233, 234, 235,
    239, 243, 250, 251, 255,
    261, 262, 263, 272-74, 280,
    285, 287, 293, 295, 304,
    308, 309, 312-14, 330, 355,
    356, 358, 366, 371, 373-75,
    380-82, 384-86, 388, 389,
    392, 403, 405, 407, 409
Auchinleck, Field Marshal
    Claude, 24, 25, 75, 173,
    218-19, 220, 240, 326, 327,
    355, 357, 368
Aurangzeb, 284
Australia, 163, 256, 287, 386, 407
Austin, Senator Warren, 375-76,
    378, 380, 381, 382
Axis Powers, 148, 152
Ayangar, Sir Gopalaswamy, 338,
    377-78, 384
Azad, Maulana Abul Kalam, 34,
    60, 84, 127, 173, 247
Azerbaijan, 181

Bacon, Lieutenant-Colonel Roger,
    332-34
Baghdad, 365
Baghdad Pact, 29, 204, 397, 402
Bahawalpur, 315, 361
Bailey, Colonel F.M., 343
Bajpai, Sir Girja Shanker, 105,
    108, 115, 146, 256, 257
Baksh, Colonel Elahi, 94
Baku, 19
Baldwin, James, 87
Balkanization, 200, 255, 300,
    301, 311, 403

Baltistan, 336, 337
Baluchistan, 16, 22, 31, 66, 71,
   195, 206, 211, 218, 234,
   244, 246, 289, 294, 303, 408
Banaras, 35
Bandung Conference, 276, 308
Bangladesh, 255
Banihal Pass, 342, 357
Bannu, 282
Baramullah, 351, 355
Baroda, 317-20
Battenberg, Prince Louis of, 270, 271
Battle for Asia, 154
Battle of Badr, 224
Battle of Plassey, 75
Beaverbrook, Lord (Maxwell
   Aitken), 105, 168
Beck, Theodore, 75
Belgium, 408
Bengal, 66, 161, 162, 176, 178,
   179, 190, 191, 195, 201,
   203, 204, 206, 215, 218,
   222, 233, 253, 264, 273,
   278, 280, 283, 292-95, 300
   East, 211, 237, 289
Bengal Muslim League, 60
Benn, Wedgewood, 56
Berlin, 124
Berlin-Baghdad railway, 18
Berry, J.L., 145
Bevin, Ernest, 15, 28, 30, 243,
   255, 258, 287, 308, 336,
   337, 374, 383, 391, 403
Bhabha, C.H., 279
Bhabha, Homi, 77
Bhave, Vinobha, 58
Bhavnagar, diwan of, 317
Bhimbar/Bhimber, 340, 395
Bhopal, 317, 318
Bhopal, Nawab of, 279, 306,
   317-20
   accession to India, 320
Bihar, 179, 206, 211, 233, 237,
   259

Bikaner, 322-23
bin Laden, Osama, 11, 68, 415
Birkenhead, Earl of (Frederick
   Edwin Smith), 82
Birla, Ghanshyam Das, 56
Blake, David, 10
Blikenberg, Lars, 339, 348, 354
Bokhara, 365
Bolan Pass, 16, 246
Bolitho, Hector, 179
Bombay, 35, 38, 48, 66, 74, 77,
   89, 125, 172-73, 179, 206,
   211, 233
Bombay Chronicle, 232
Bose, Subhash Chandra, 40, 55,
   123-25, 171, 192
Boundary Commission, 294, 327
Brabourne, Lord (John Ulick
   Knatchbull), 92
Bright, John, 75
Britain/England/Great Britain/UK,
   9, 15-31, 34-62, 74-75,
   97-119, 127-42, 145-65, 183,
   188-91, 192, 199, 214, 219,
   220, 232, 233, 238, 240,
   243, 253, 256, 265, 274-75,
   286, 288, 293-95, 303,
   308-10, 314, 325, 335, 340,
   343, 346, 353, 358, 375,
   380, 382, 383, 386, 389,
   390, 396-98, 402, 404-13,
   416
British Cabinet, 254, 208, 294,
   301
British Foreign Office, 241, 243
British Government, 28, 155,
   201, 222, 229, 242, 263,
   325, 332, 359, 371
British Labour Party
   Annual Conference 1947, 15, 243
British Military Academy, 174
British Military Intelligence, 171
British provinces (in India), 35,
   66

British War College, 174
British withdrawal plan, 299
Broadlands, 13, 390
Brown, Judith, 143
Brown, Major William Alexander,
    332, 333, 334, 337
Bucher, General Roy, 358, 360,
    361, 395
Buck, Pearl, 156
Buddhism, 67
Buddhists, 336
*Bulletin of Military Historical
    Society of Great Britain*, 233,
    334
Bundi, 323
Burma, 99, 173, 205, 240, 242,
    245
Burrows, Sir Frederick, 222, 224
Butler, Harcourt, 323

Cabinet Delegation, 220, 256
Cabinet Mission, 102, 204, 205,
    207, 208, 212, 213, 215,
    217, 219, 222, 225, 231,
    233, 409
Cadogan, Sir Alexander, 337,
    389-90
Cairo, 152
Calcutta, 71, 84-85, 191, 212,
    222-25, 231, 234, 278, 283,
    306
Calcutta killings, 222-25, 231
Cambridge, 163
Campbell-Johnson, Alan, 199,
    288-89, 317, 366, 369
Canada, 163, 256
Canberra Conference, 326
Cariappa, K.M., 324, 360, 395
Caroe, Sir Olaf, 30, 31, 176,
    248, 246, 249, 280, 281,
    299, 300, 302-04, 331, 397
Carter, Sir Archibald, 372, 373,
    374, 390
Casey, Lord Richard, 187

Cawthorn, General Walter Joseph,
    326, 388-89
Ceasefire (1949), 397
CENTO, 21, 29, 397, 402
Central Asia, 17, 18, 141, 142,
    163, 209, 336, 343, 413
Central Government, 253, 254,
    258, 261, 313, 314, 317, 412
Central Legislature, Lower House
    of, 316
Central Provinces, 179, 206, 241
Ceylon (Sri Lanka), 242, 386
Chagla, M.C., 77, 82, 84
Chamberlain, Neville, 39, 53
Chamber of Princes, 279, 315,
    316, 317, 321, 345
Chaplin, Charles, 270
Chauri Chaura, 81-82
Chiang Kai-shek, 103, 147-48,
    149-50, 151, 152, 269
Chiang Kai-shek, Madame, 150
China, 100, 105, 126, 129,
    146-48, 155, 156, 163, 189,
    209, 238, 243, 257, 332,
    334, 346, 402, 403, 407, 413
Chinese communists, 276
Chinese delegation to UN, 238
Chinese démarche, 148
Chitral, 30, 335, 337
Chittagong, 145, 195, 322
Christianity, 67, 74, 196
Christian missionaries, 324
Churchill, Pamela, 104
Churchill, Randolph, 105
Churchill, Winston, 10, 16, 22,
    25, 31, 36, 38, 53-56, 70,
    87, 97-119, 122, 130, 132,
    146, 149, 150, 155, 157,
    158-59, 162, 164, 168-70,
    172, 177, 178, 181, 183-85,
    188, 191, 199, 200, 216,
    221, 269, 271, 272-74, 295,
    296, 306, 372-74
CIA, 29, 402

Ciano, Count Galaezzo, 124
Clash of civilizations, 415
Clemencau, M., 207
Clive, Robert, 75
Cochin, 290, 323
Cold War, 11, 164, 165, 181, 397
Collins, Larry, 367
Columbia, 385
Colville, Sir John, 304
Commonwealth Affairs Committee, 381
Commonwealth, British, 24-27, 218-20, 229, 231, 235, 239, 240, 241, 243, 254, 265, 273, 274-75, 278, 279, 286, 287, 288, 289, 291, 294, 295, 312, 325, 367, 375, 381, 383, 385, 386, 390, 391, 407, 411
Commonwealth Relations Office, 254, 347, 355, 372, 374, 379, 380, 389, 390, 395, 406-07
Communism, 196, 389, 392
Communists, 255, 310, 407, 415
Congress Party, 25, 29, 34, 35, 37-39, 40-45, 47-50, 55-59, 60, 61, 68, 69, 73, 78, 82, 83, 84, 86, 90, 98-99, 102, 107, 109-11, 117, 119, 122, 123, 125, 131, 132-34, 138, 141, 142, 146, 149-51, 154, 157, 158, 160-63, 170, 173, 177-79, 187, 188, 189-94, 199, 202, 205, 210, 211-18, 221, 222, 228, 230-36, 241, 242, 245, 246-48, 250, 251, 253-55, 259, 260-64, 273, 277, 279-83, 287, 289, 291, 294, 296, 299, 300, 302, 304, 305, 312, 314, 317, 319-21, 325, 326, 350, 367, 403, 405, 406, 410, 411, 414

Congress Working Committee, 149, 153, 184, 194, 195, 233, 264, 275
Connally, Thomas, 104
Conservative Party, 57, 170, 188
Constituent Assembly, 191, 211, 214-16, 218, 222, 229, 231, 233, 234, 236, 247, 249, 250-53, 256, 259, 260, 262, 263, 265, 278-80, 282, 289, 292, 294, 385, 391, 405
Constitution, Central, 263
Indian, 386
Cooch Behar, 218
Cordoba, 365
Craik, Henry, 53, 410
Crete, 271
Cripps Mission, 100, 145, 154, 184, 200
Cripps, Sir Stafford, 44, 46, 56, 100, 101, 102, 108, 110-14, 123, 125, 129, 130, 132, 154, 162, 167, 189, 190, 191, 192, 200-03, 207, 208, 220, 221, 228, 231, 232, 250, 255, 272-73, 308, 325, 327, 358, 382, 384, 390-91
Crown, 169, 175, 234, 284
Cunningham, Sir George, 110, 334, 350, 350
Cunningham, Sir John, 27
Currie, Lauchlin, 151
Curson, B.R., 379
Curzon, Lord, 169
Cyrenica (North Africa), 169
Czechoslovakia, 385

Dacca, 195
Dalmia, R.K., 322
Dalton, Hugh, 383
Darjeeling, 195, 283
Darling, Malcom, 46
Das, C.R., 82

Dasgupta, C., 359
Dass, Dewan Jermani, 321
Dass, Durga, 186
Das, Vishvanath, 127
Dawn, 161, 378
Defence Committee, 357, 360, 395
de Gaulle, Charles, 402
Delhi, 10, 15, 30, 57, 66, 68, 71, 83, 102, 108, 109, 113, 114, 124, 130, 145-46, 151, 155, 157-60, 170, 171, 173, 186, 192, 207, 219, 224, 229, 231, 234, 238, 239, 256, 258, 269, 272, 281, 284, 299, 305, 306, 309, 311, 330, 332, 338, 339, 347, 348, 353, 355, 360, 361, 366, 369, 374, 380, 385, 395, 403, 413
Delhi Secretariat, 238
de Ligne, Prince, 382
Deliverance Day, 38
Deo, Acharya Narendra, 127
Deoband, 68
Dera Ismail Khan, 282
Dholpur, 320
Dir, 315
Direct Action Day, 222, 224
Directorate of Intelligence, 167
Divide and rule, 75, 169
Domel, 353, 358, 360, 361, 362
Dominion status, 254, 296, 307, 410
Dostoyevsky, Fyodor, 18
Dube, Major General Udey Chand, 174
Dulles, John Foster, 21, 31, 216, 238-39, 337, 396, 397
Durand line, 244, 304, 331
Dutch, 242
Dyer, Reginald, 81

East India Company, 169

Economic and War Supplies Mission to India, 104
Eden, Sir Anthony, 184
Edward VII, 270
Edward VIII (Prince of Wales), 272, 343
Egypt, 204
Eisenhower, Dwight, 216, 269-70
Elections
of 1937, 88-90
to Central and Provincial Legislatures, 192
to assembly (1946), 251
Elizabeth (Queen), 296
wedding of (with Prince Phillip), 358
Elmherst, Air Marshal Thomas, 339
Emergency Powers Act (the Rowlatt Act), 81
Empire (British), 253, 274, 278, 283, 293, 313, 332, 343, 410, 413
end game of, 299-327
Europe, 18
Eastern, 164
European Association, 130

Faizal, King, 19-20
Fakir of Ipi, 300, 302, 341
Far East, 184, 185, 240
Fazal-ul-Haq, 57, 60, 89, 91, 124
Federal Legislature (in India), 36
Fisher, Louis, 59, 114, 154, 155
Fitze, Sir Kenneth, 324
Fortune, 157
France, 34, 57, 67
French, Patrick, 67

Gallman, Waldemar, 257-58
Gandhi, Feroze, 77
Gandhi, Mahatma, 34-35, 38, 39, 41-44, 46, 48, 49, 54-55, 58, 59, 73, 78-79, 81, 82, 86,

88, 100, 114, 115, 122-42,
146-48, 149-50, 153, 157,
159, 160, 163, 164, 170,
173, 179-80, 184, 186, 193,
203, 207, 224, 231, 237,
241, 245, 276-77, 299, 301,
306, 307, 309, 368-70, 374,
406, 412, 413
Gandhi, Rajiv, 77
Ganga, 365
George VI, 286
Germany, 18, 20, 22, 35, 54, 55,
124, 127
Ghazni, Mahmud, 72, 352
Ghose, Sudhir, 236
Gilbert, Sir Martin, 88
Gilgit, 16, 30, 332, 333-41, 343,
388
Gilgit Agency, 303, 331
Gilgit-Astore, Republic of, 334
Gilgit Scouts, 332, 333
Giliat, Elizabeth, 88
Glancy, Sir Bertrand James, 187, 410
Gold Coast, 157
Golden Temple, 284
Gopal, S., 367
Gorchakov, Prince Aleksandr
Mikaylovich, 18
Government of India (GOI), 157,
228, 230, 256, 305, 316,
337, 338, 352, 358, 361,
369, 370, 371, 373, 378-81,
396, 397
Act (1935), 354, 356
Government of Pakistan, 333,
371, 378, 379, 380, 387,
396, 397, 413
Gracey, Sir Douglas, 335, 340,
346, 353, 357, 360, 361, 395
Grady, Henry, 230, 288, 310,
378, 380, 383
Great depression of 1930, 20
Great Game, 9-12, 15-31, 188, 242,
244-45, 278, 343, 397, 411

Green, Nathan, 104
Grew, Joseph, 184
Gunther, John, 48
Gurdaspur, 195, 411
Gurkha/s, 216
Gwadur, 403
Gwalior, 322

Hailey, Lord Malcolm, 86
Halaku, 72
Halifax, Lord, 114, 138, 145-46,
153, 155, 159, 185
Hallet, Sir Maurice, 151
Hamidullah, Nawab Muhammad
(see also Bhopal), 71
Han Sui Yen, 13
Hare, Raymond A., 310
Harijan, 132, 141
Harriman, Averil, 103, 104, 106
Hayat, Shaukat, 410
Heathenism, 224
Hebrew University, 276
Himalayas, 219
Hindu-Muslim differences, 11,
160
Hindus, 48, 50, 67, 80, 90, 93,
98-99, 170, 178, 183, 190,
191, 194, 223, 225, 237,
265, 282, 285, 305, 307,
340, 347, 348, 359, 365,
404, 407, 408, 409, 415
Hitler, Adolf, 34, 39, 41, 54, 55,
60, 124, 125, 150, 163, 324
His Majesty's Government
(HMG), 48, 51, 56, 57, 70,
82, 86, 100, 103, 129, 134,
151, 154, 157, 169, 188,
190, 191, 199, 203, 207,
230, 234, 235, 242, 250,
251, 261, 262, 291, 312,
314, 347, 356, 374, 375,
378, 381, 409
Hizb-ul-Mujahideen, 68
Hodson, H.V., 108, 109, 111,

187, 236, 290, 299, 344, 347, 359, 367
Holkar (Maharaja of Indore), 163
Hollis, Sir Leslie, 26, 241
Hollywood, 163
Hong Kong, 240
Hopkins, Harry, 150, 271
Hormuz, Straits of, 103
Horton, Ralph Albert, 320
House of Commons, 261, 295
  Churchill's speech in, 296
  debate in, 205
Hull, Cordell, 104, 107, 113, 114, 145-46, 149, 151, 153, 154, 159, 161-62
Hunt, John, 174
Hunza, 331
Hussain, Ghulam, 89
Hussain, Imam, 206
Hussein, Saddam, 20
Hyderabad (Deccan), 71, 117, 213, 218, 263, 313-15, 317, 322, 330
  Nizam of, 315, 317, 322, 330, 344
  separatist move by, 263
Hyderabad (Sind), 318

Imam, Sir Ali, 84
Imperial Legislative Council, 78, 81
Independence, announcement of, 306
Independence Day
  celebrations, 327
  of India, 327
  of Pakistan, 327
India, 10-11, 25-31, 35, 40-41, 66, 72, 74-75, 97-119, 145-65, 168, 181, 199, 200, 201, 203, 205, 209, 214, 215, 219, 229, 230, 233, 235, 239, 240, 242, 245, 252-56, 259, 261, 262, 264, 265, 278, 282, 283, 287, 289, 290-93, 294, 296, 307,

309, 312, 326, 330, 334-36, 338, 340, 341, 343, 347, 352, 353, 355, 358, 359, 361, 362, 366, 367, 371-75, 377, 379, 381-86, 388, 391, 392, 394, 396, 402, 404, 405-07, 409, 411, 412, 415, 416
India Committee, 199
India League, 15
Indian Cabinet, 335, 357, 361, 372
Indian Civil Service (ICS), 16, 193
Indian Communist Party, 125, 310
Indian Independence Bill, 410
Indian National Army (INA), 171-72, 193
  trial of officers of, 192-93, 200-01
Indian National Congress (see under Congress Party)
Indian Ocean, 17, 21, 22, 25, 29, 31, 170, 181, 205, 219, 220, 239, 309, 313
Indian Police (IP), 193
Indian Political Service, 205, 350
Indian princes, 200
Indian troops, overseas, 240
Indian Union, 349, 357
India Office, 200, 207, 241, 258
India Office Records, 13
India-Pakistan war (on Kashmir), 359
India-Pakistan war (on Bangladesh), 402
Individual Peaceful Disobedience, 58-60
Indo-British relations, 312
Indo-China, French action in, 242
Indo-Soviet treaty, 402
Indo-US relations, 265, 405
Indonesia, 193
Indore, 317, 318, 322

Indus, 336
Indus Valley, 335
Instrument of Accession, 314,
    317, 319-20, 354, 356
Intelligence Bureau, 193, 225
Inter-Asian Conference, 309
Inter-Services Intelligence (ISI),
    68, 415
Interim Government, 210, 214,
    215, 218, 225, 228, 230,
    231, 233, 236, 239, 240,
    241, 249, 250, 254, 256,
    260, 265, 276, 354, 403,
    405, 409
Inverchapel, Lord (Sir Archibald
    Kerr), 230
Iqbal, Mohammad, 90, 352
Iran/Persia, 10, 15, 19-21, 24, 29,
    103, 163, 164, 181, 242, 326
Iraq, 19-21, 29, 103, 126, 204
Ireland (Eire), 256
Irish Republican Army, 48
Iron Curtain, 164
Irwin, Lord (Edward Frederick
    Lindley Wood), 85, 86, 290
Isfahani, M.A., 89, 260
Islam, 11, 196, 204, 224, 254,
    346, 374
    political, 11, 304, 405, 415, 416
Islamabad, 402
Islamic brotherhood, 204
Islamic fundamentalism, 416
Islamic jihadis, 415
Islamic terrorism, 11
Ismay, Lord Hastings, 178, 192,
    221, 239, 274, 280, 286,
    289, 292, 293, 303, 312,
    345, 354, 356, 367, 368,
    370, 373, 374, 376
Ismay-Mountbatten plan, 280, 283
Ismay-Scoones heavy brigade, 375,
    379, 385, 388
Istanbul, 365
Iyer, Sir C.P. Ramaswamy, 321-22

Jaikar, R., 84
Jainism, 67
Jaipur, 321, 323
Jaisalmer, 318
Jallianwala Bagh, massacre at, 81
Jalpaiguri, 195
Jamaat-i-Hind, 68
Jamaat-i-Islami, 68, 415
Jamaat-ul-Ulema, 68
Jama Masjid, 66
Jammu, 337, 342, 347, 348, 360,
    374, 395, 396, 414
Jammu and Kashmir (see under
    Kashmir)
Jamrud, 248
Japan, 21, 23, 62, 97, 98, 99,
    103, 112, 125-29, 132, 137,
    145, 159, 169, 240
Japanese troops, 150
Jat tribe, 204
Jerusalem, 365
Jessore, 195
Jhangar, 358, 360, 361
Jhelum bridge, 341
Jhelum river, 342
Jhelum Valley, 353, 360
Jihad, 224, 305
Jinnah, Mohammad Ali (Quaid-e-
    Azam), 9, 25, 27, 34, 35, 37,
    38, 41-62, 65-94, 106, 111,
    123, 133, 151, 160-61, 168,
    170, 173, 177, 178-80, 183,
    186, 187, 190, 193, 194,
    202, 204-06, 210, 211,
    215-17, 221, 222, 225, 228,
    231-33, 235-37, 245, 247,
    249, 250, 253, 257-60, 262,
    264, 265, 273, 277, 278,
    280, 281, 283, 284, 286,
    289, 296, 299, 302, 304-06,
    310, 313, 315, 320, 326,
    331, 346-49, 351, 356, 357,
    368, 369, 382, 404-06,
    408-10, 414

Jinnah, Ruttie, 80
Jirga (assembly), 247, 249
Jodhpur, 323
Jodhpur, Maharaja of, 318, 319
Johnson, Colonel Louis, 104,
    109, 113, 114, 139, 146,
    150, 151, 158, 162
Joint Defence Committee, 340
Joint Intelligence Committee, 173
Joint Planning Staff, 360
Jordan, 19
Junagadh, 313, 317, 322
    Nawab of, 414

Kabul, 17, 19, 124, 244
Kakinada, 109
Kak, Ram Chandar, 348, 350
Kalat, 315
Kandy, 272
Kapurthala, 321, 411
Karachi, 29, 31, 93, 94, 172,
    173, 209, 260, 311, 318,
    320, 327, 330, 333, 335-37,
    373, 374, 378, 382, 395
Karakoram, 16, 336, 337, 343
Karakoram Pass, 343
Kargil, 335, 337
Kashgar, 336, 337, 343, 403
Kashmir, 16, 68, 213, 218, 219,
    303, 312, 313, 317, 322,
    326, 327, 330, 331-39,
    340-46, 347-50, 352, 354,
    355, 357, 358, 359-61, 370,
    372, 373, 376, 378-85, 387,
    388, 390-92, 395, 396, 402,
    404, 405, 408, 411, 413, 414
Kashmir Commission Report, 389
Kashmiriyat, 342
Kathiawad, 313
Kenya, 157
Keynes, John Maynard, 189
Khaliq-uz-Zaman, 42, 72, 91, 263
Khan, Agha, 67, 70, 76, 85, 86
Khan, Akbar, 350, 351, 353

Khan, Chenghez, 72
Khan, Khan Abdul Ghaffar, 38,
    89, 173, 245, 247, 248, 281,
    300-02, 304, 305, 341, 350
Khan, Liaqat Ali, 88, 91, 94, 237,
    238, 251, 259, 305, 350, 351,
    372, 383, 388, 391, 392
Khan, Major Aslam, 334
Khan, Mohammad Ayub, 174
Khanna, Meher Chand, 110
Khan, Sardar Mohammad
    Ibrahim, 361
Khan, Sikandar Hayat, 44, 52,
    57, 60, 89, 90, 178
Khan, Syed Ahmad, 75-76, 85
Khan (Mohd.) Zafrullah, 318,
    377, 392, 397, 413
Kher, B.G., 91
Kherpur, 315
Khilafat Movement, 69, 79, 81
Khiva, 16
Khoja sect, 87
Khokand, 16
Khyber, 302, 332
Khyber Pass, 16, 247, 284
Kidwai, M.B., 72
King/King Emperor, 167, 171,
    316, 334, 353, 390
Kipling, Rudyard, 18
Kishan Ganga river, 360
Kitchlu, Saif-ud-din, 84
Kolhapur, 319
Korbel, Josef, 338, 339, 377, 385
Korea, North, 403
Kotli, 358, 395
Kriplani, J.B., 126
Kuomintang, 276, 331
Kutch, 319
Kux, Dennis, 260, 373

Labour Party, 43, 57, 86, 100,
    168-69
    Government, 188, 222, 243,
    309, 312

Lacadive Islands, 408
Ladakh, 335, 337, 342, 374
la Follet, Dewey, 104
Lahore, 48, 51, 195, 284, 285,
    315, 340, 344, 347, 356,
    368, 369
Laithwaite, Sir John Gilbert, 46,
    192
Lal, Pyare, 307
Lamaistic Buddhists, 342
Lamb, Alistair, 332-34, 353
Landikotal, 247
Landsdowne, Lord (George
    Granville), 244
Langenhove, Fernand van, 382
Lapierre, Dominique, 367
Lawrence, Sir John, 17
Lawrence, T.E., 19
Leach, R.S., 30
Leftist forces, 199
Legislative Assembly, 277
Leh, 335, 342, 343, 347
Life, 157
Linlithgow, Lord (Victor
    Alexander John Hope), 25,
    30, 34, 35, 37-39, 41-44,
    46-48, 50-56, 58, 60, 65, 70,
    88, 99, 110, 111, 123, 134,
    139, 151, 159, 162, 167,
    168, 170, 176-78, 188, 192,
    199, 235, 262, 308, 410
Lippmann, Walter, 216
Listowel, Lord (William Hare),
    200
Lockhart, General Robert, 302
London, 15, 42, 46, 47, 57, 58,
    61, 86, 88-89, 97, 101, 102,
    104, 106, 113, 130, 149,
    152, 154, 157, 159, 173,
    176, 178, 183, 184, 187,
    189, 190, 200, 204, 207,
    221, 224, 225, 234, 240,
    251, 254, 257-58, 259, 261,
    283, 284, 286, 290, 293,

294, 300, 306, 312, 346,
    347, 358-61, 366, 371, 372,
    375, 377, 380, 389, 391,
    394, 404, 410
London Gazette, 334
London News Chronicle, 179
London School of Economics,
    163
London Times, 154
Lothian, Sir Arther, 314
Lovett, Robert, 376
Luce, Henry, 157
Lucknow, 35,73, 306
    Pact, 78
Lutyens, Edwin, 93, 207

MacArthur, Douglas, 269
Madras, 66, 109, 135, 173, 179,
    206, 211, 233, 311, 321
Madrasas, 68
Mahajan, Mehr Chand, 348
Mahbub, Sheikh, 249
Mahsud tribe, 247
Makinlay, J.P.C., 223
Malakand, 247-49, 332
Malakand Field Force, 16
Malay, 240, 242
Malaya, 386
Maliks, 244
Mandela, Nelson, 140
Manekshaw, Field Marshal Sam,
    77
Manipur, 216, 223
Mao Ze Dong, 331
Mardan, 248
Marshall, General George, 113,
    239, 257, 261, 263, 265,
    269, 311, 336, 375, 378,
    379, 380, 381, 391, 392, 403
Martin, Kingsley, 382, 383
Mathieson, Captain, A.S., 332-34
Mawdudi, Abdul Al, 11, 67, 68,
    415
Maxwell, Sir Reginald, 160

Mayne, Rupert, 240
McDonald, Sir Ramsay, 86-87
McGhee, George, 308
McGrigor, Admiral Rhoderick, 23
Mecca, 365
Medina, 365
Menon, Krishna, 15-16, 28, 30,
   189, 239, 240, 275, 286-88,
   338, 382, 384, 385, 391, 403
Menon, Vapal Panguni (V.P.), 37,
   38, 61, 101, 253, 254, 275,
   279, 288-92, 294, 300, 306,
   313, 327, 332, 338, 344,
   345, 352, 366, 367
Menzes, General Stan, 175
Merrell, George R., 133-34, 145,
   161-62, 239, 256, 258, 259,
   260, 264
Mesopotamia, 20
Messervy, Frank, 360
Middle East, 152, 164, 169, 170,
   173, 181, 196, 204, 213,
   240, 243, 287, 303, 304,
   310, 374, 391, 402
Mieville, Sir Eric, 286, 294
Mintaka Pass, 16, 336, 343
Minto, Lord Gilbert Elliot, 77
Miranshah, 247
Mirpur, 338, 340, 358, 360, 361,
   395
Mirza, Humayun, 305, 306, 350
Mirza, Iskander, 305, 334, 350
Mishra, D.P., 237
Mohammad, Prophet, 206
Mohand country, 305
Mohan, Brij Kishen, 350
Molotov, Vyacheslav, 240
Monteath, Sir David, 241
Montgomery, Field Marshal
   Bernard Law, 27, 326-27
Moon, Penderel, 253, 410
Moore, R., 158
Moscow, 19, 181, 385
Mossadeq, Mohammad, 21, 204

Mountbatten, Edwina, 270, 272,
   273, 276, 357, 386, 413
Mountbatten, Lord Louis, 10, 15,
   30, 37, 94, 168, 174, 191,
   199, 235, 254, 255, 262,
   264, 269, 270-83, 286, 287,
   289-96, 299-301, 304,
   306-08, 311-26, 327, 331,
   335, 338, 343-48, 353-55,
   357-61, 366-69, 370-72,
   380-83, 385, 386, 390, 394,
   396, 404, 409, 410-13
Mountbatten, Pamela, 324
Mountbatten, Patricia, 271
Mudie, Sir Francis, 72, 325, 359
Mughal Empire, 17
Mujaheedin, 188
Multan, 195
Murray, Wallace, 115, 160
Murshidabad, 195
Muslim/s, 46, 47, 50, 51, 52, 57,
   65, 66, 67, 72, 73, 76-77,
   80, 83, 85, 86, 88, 90-93,
   98, 99, 105-06, 133, 150,
   157, 170, 176, 178, 183,
   186, 190, 192, 194-96,
   202-07, 212, 218, 221, 222,
   224, 225, 230, 232, 235,
   237, 265, 274, 277, 285,
   287, 303, 305, 307, 336,
   340, 347, 348, 358, 365,
   366, 377, 403, 404, 408-10,
   414-16
   Bengali, 213, 250
   Punjabi, 285, 345, 346
Muslim fundamentalist groups,
   67, 70
Muslim League Party, 10, 25,
   34-62, 57, 60, 66, 70-73, 77,
   78, 81-83, 89, 92, 113, 123,
   133, 154, 161, 168, 170,
   178-80, 187, 194, 202, 205,
   206, 212-14, 216, 217,
   222-25, 228, 231-34, 236-38,

245, 246, 248, 251-53,
258-63, 277-78, 281-84,
299-301, 304, 307, 325, 346,
347, 350, 405, 407, 409,
410, 415
Muslim National Guards, 60,
221-22
Muslim states, autonomous, 42, 46
Muslim sultanates, 16
Mussolini, Benito, 124
Mutinies in
Engineers, 201
Royal Air Force, 201
Royal Indian Navy, 201
Royal Signal Corps, 201
Mutiny (1857), 17, 68, 75, 135,
176, 315, 323, 409
Muzaffarabad, 338, 340, 358,
360, 362, 395
Muzaffarabad-Kohala, 341
Mysore, 117, 315, 322, 323

Nadia, 195
Nadwain Tul Ulema, 68
Nagpur, 80-81
Naipaul, V.S., 141
Naoroji, Dadabhai, 77
Nasserism, 204
Nation, 154
National Conference, 344, 347,
349, 414
Nationalists, 9, 45, 125, 235,
242, 253, 254, 265, 407
Naushera/Naoshera, 340, 341,
353, 358, 360, 395
Naval Mutiny (1946), 172-73
Nawanagar, Maharaja of, 317
Nehru, Jawaharlal, 15, 25, 39,
40, 42, 46, 48, 54, 55, 58,
59, 60, 73, 82, 83, 84, 90,
91, 100, 110, 113-15, 126,
129, 130, 131, 133, 146,
147, 150, 162, 165, 173,
186, 189, 200-03, 214, 215,

221, 228, 230-42, 244,
247-53, 256-59, 263-65,
273-81, 286, 288, 291-92,
300-02, 305-06, 308, 310,
311, 320, 321, 323, 330,
331, 334-37, 339, 344-46,
349, 357-61, 366-69, 370-73,
378, 380, 382, 385, 386,
390-92, 395, 396, 403-05,
407, 408, 410, 412, 413
Nehru, Motilal, 82, 83
Nehru Report, 83-84
Nesselrode, Count K.V., 18
New Statesman, 382
New York, 10, 176, 374, 375,
415
New York Times, 154
New Zealand, 256, 386, 407
Niven, David, 174
Nizam-ud-din, 124
Noakhali, 237
Noamani, Maulana Shoam, 68
Noel-Baker, Philip, 255, 373,
374, 376, 380, 383-85,
388-91
Non-violence, 54-55, 58, 123
Noon, Sir Firoz Khan, 72
Northern Areas, 331, 339, 340,
342, 346, 376
North-South divide (in India), 407
North West Frontier Province
(NWFP), 30, 38, 49, 66, 69,
71, 90, 178, 179, 186, 195,
202, 205, 211, 212, 214,
216, 225, 237, 244, 245-47,
249, 258, 262, 273, 275,
280-83, 289, 293-95,
299-303, 305, 311, 315,
330-32, 408, 409, 411, 414
Nye, General Archibald, 392-95,
396

Oilfields, 9
Ootacommand, 322

Orissa, 206, 211, 233
Ottoman Empire, 19, 69, 79
Oudh, 306
Oxford, 163

Packmans, K.C., 247
'Pact mania', 397
Pahlavi, Shah Reza, 20
Pakistan, 10, 11, 12, 16, 25, 26,
    29, 30, 38, 52, 57, 61,
    65-94, 103, 123, 141, 158,
    168, 179, 180, 186-91, 194,
    195-96, 199-215, 218-20,
    221, 228, 233, 234, 246-50,
    254, 255, 260, 262, 263,
    265, 273, 275, 278, 280,
    282-84, 290, 293, 294, 296,
    299, 303, 304, 307, 308-13,
    315, 318-20, 325-26, 330-49,
    352-55, 357-61, 366-67, 370,
    371, 373-80, 382-86, 388,
    389, 391, 392, 394-97, 402,
    403, 405-09, 411-16
  East, 213, 278, 334
  West, 278, 334, 410
Pakistan-Iran axis, 204
Palestine, 152, 193
  Arabs and Jews in, 152, 204
Palit, D.K., 175
Palmer, Ely E., 30, 303, 331
Pamirs, 245, 342
Pandits, Kashmiri, 342
Pandit, Vijayalakshmi, 238, 385
Panna, 320
Pannikar, K.M., 405
Pant, Govind Ballabh, 307
Paramountcy, 234, 261, 294, 314,
    332, 348
Paris, 164, 337, 389, 391, 396
Parliament, British, 167, 168,
    170, 287, 296, 319, 410, 412
Partition, 10, 15, 50, 53, 122-42,
    262-63, 306, 403, 409, 416
  schemes for, 202-03

Patel, Sardar Vallabhbhai, 58,
    173, 214, 215, 228, 231-33,
    237, 241, 247, 250-51, 253,
    254, 264, 275-77, 289, 290,
    300, 302, 306, 307, 308,
    313, 314, 319, 321, 344,
    346, 349, 358, 367-70, 372,
    406
Pathans, 212, 245-47, 280, 300,
    302, 304, 305, 324, 352
Patiala, 321
  Maharaja of, 279
Patliputra/Patna, 35, 306
Patrick, Sir Paul, 34-35, 372,
    373, 389
Patwardhan, Achyut, 127
Paxton, John Hall, 340
Pearl Harbor, Japanese attack on,
    62, 97
Pearson, Drew, 185
Persia, see under Iran
Persian Gulf, 9, 11, 16, 31, 181,
    196, 239, 240, 246, 403
Peshawar, 29, 30, 31, 35, 124,
    244, 249, 302, 332, 333,
    340, 402
Pethick-Lawrence, Frederick
    William, 190, 203, 208, 221,
    240, 254, 258, 262
Petit, Sir Dinshaw, 80
Petro dollars, 415
Petrov, I., 309
Philippines, 159
Phillips, William, 139, 158-62,
    160, 185
Pilditch, Denys, 126, 129
Pillai, Shanker, 327
Pir Panjal, 341-42, 353
Plebiscite, 346, 347, 354
Poona, 142, 173, 315
Poonch, 338, 341, 347, 348, 358,
    360, 361, 381, 392
Poonch-Mirpur area, 414
Poonch-Muzaffarabad, 388, 392

Portuguese, 242
Post-Hostilities Planning Staff of War Cabinet, 22, 24, 181, 246
Powers, Gary, 29
Prasad, Dr Rajendra, 42, 126-27
Princely states, 36, 202, 218, 241, 251, 290, 300, 308, 313, 412, 414
Princes, 253, 254, 261, 408
Provincial option, 119, 250, 404
Puckle, Sir Frederick, 155-58
Punjab, 66, 71, 78, 179, 186, 190, 191, 195, 201, 211-13, 216, 218, 233, 250, 253, 264, 273, 278, 280, 285, 287, 292, 327, 342, 347, 348, 410, 411
East, 395, 411
Pakistani, 331, 340, 341
West(ern), 275, 284, 289, 340, 357, 359, 396, 408

Qasim, Mohammad Mir, 72
Quaroni, Alberto, 124
Quetta, 246, 303
Quit India resolution, 125-26, 134-35, 147, 153, 155, 158, 159, 214, 284, 405
draft for, 125-26
Quran, 224

Racism, 173-75, 324-26
Radcliffe, Justice Lord Cyril, 327, 411
Raikes, Charles, 324
Raj, 246, 283, 290, 291, 315, 406, 408, 416
Rajagopalachari, C., 115, 127, 134, 160, 369
Rajasthan, 318
Rajouri, 360
Rajputs, 319
Rampur, 306, 317

Rangoon, 192
Rawalpindi, 195, 285, 410
Rawlinson, Sir Henry, 17, 176
Razmak, 247
Reading, Lord (Rufus Issacs), 272
Red Army, 331
Red Star, 309
Referendum, 179, 301
Rehman, Abd-ur, 244
Reuters, 162, 238, 256, 311
Roberts, General Frederick, 17, 247
Rome, 124
Roosevelt, Franklin Delano, 10-11, 97-119, 129, 147-52, 157, 159, 161, 162-64, 169, 181, 184, 285, 403
Round Table Conference, 70, 86, 87, 290, 365
First, 365
Second, 87, 290
Third, 87
Royal Indian Air Force (RIAF), 395
Rusk, Dean, 379
Russia (see also Soviet Union), 18-19, 21, 23, 103, 131, 219, 240, 244, 246, 325, 343, 348, 367, 381, 404

Sahib, Dr Khan, 246, 247, 281, 282, 301, 302, 305
Sahib, Raja (of Mahmoodabad), 84
Samarkhand, 16
San Francisco conference, 184
Sapru, Sir Tej Bahadur, 84
Sardaryah, 248
Saturday Evening Post, 154
Saudi Arabia, 19, 68, 204
Scheduled Castes, 185
Schemes A and B (for India), 208, 209
Scoones, General Geoffrey, 347, 374, 379

Scott, General Victor, 347, 348
Scott, Ian, 233
Segal, B.M., 248, 305
Sen, L.P., 141
Sevagram, 114
Shahi Jirga, 294
Shahs (Persia), 17
Sharma, K.L., 13
Shia Political Conference, 69
Shone, Sir Terence, 242, 311, 361, 383
Short, Major John Mclaughlin 'Billy', 285
Sialkot-Lahore area, 396
Sikhism, 67, 90
Sikhs, 90 178, 185, 191, 195, 205, 212, 224, 251, 252, 255, 282, 284-86, 305, 342, 347, 407, 410
Simla, 10, 39, 288, 291, 303
Conference (1945), 88, 185-87
Simon Commission, 82-83
Simon, Sir John, 82
Sind, 66, 71, 195, 206, 211, 233, 250, 264, 289, 408
Singapore, 171, 184, 269
Singh, Amrinder, 321
Singh, Baldev, 212, 251, 283-84, 306, 370
Singh, Bhawani, 321
Singh, Bhupinder (Maharaja of Patiala), 321
Singh, General Kulwant, 358
Singh, Ghansara, 332, 333
Singh, Gulab, 342
Singh, Hanwant, 319
Singh, Hari (Maharaja of Kashmir), 320, 333, 343-46, 348-50, 376
Singh, Karan, 321, 345, 350
Singh, Khushwant, 175
Singh, Maharaja Bahadur, 323
Singh, Maharaja Ranjit, 284, 285, 342

Singh, Master Tara, 284-85
Singh, Rajindar, 351
Singh, Sukhjeet, 321
Sinkiang, 10, 16, 31, 219, 315, 331, 336, 340, 343, 403
Sino-Indian clash (1962), 403
Siraj-ud-Daula, Nawab, 75
Sitalvad, Chamanlal, 59
Skardu, 335-37
Slade, Madeleine (Mira-ben), 125
Slim, Sir William, 324
Smith, Graffety, 360, 395
Smith, N.P.A., 225, 228, 232
Smith, Sir Arthur, 325
Smuts, Jan Christian, 169-70, 287
Snow, Edgar, 114, 154-55
Soong, T.V., 148
South Africa, 238, 242, 287, 407
South-east Asia, 169, 189, 200, 213, 312
South-east Asia Command (SEAC), 240, 272
Soviet Central Asia, 209
Soviet press, 309
Soviet Union (USSR), 11, 15, 20, 21, 22, 23, 25, 29, 30, 163, 181, 191, 204, 240, 257, 259, 303, 309, 310, 331, 337, 374, 378, 382, 385, 392, 402, 407, 409, 413
Spain, 39
Spectator, 211
Spry, Graham, 114-15
Srinagar, 332, 342, 346-48, 351-52, 355, 376
Stalin, Joseph, 9, 169, 181, 309, 385
Standstill Agreement, 348-49
States Ministry, 320
Stettinius, Edward R., 184
Suez Canal, 103
Sufis, 342
Suhrawardy, Huseyn, 222-25, 283
Swaraj Party, 82

Swat, 315, 331, 335
Sylhet, 195
Syria, 193, 204, 385

Taj Mahal, 66
Taliban, 11, 68, 415
Tandon, Purshotamdas, 307
Tank, 282
Tashkand/Tashkent, 16, 343
Taskin-ud-din, Captain, 352
Tata, Jamshedji, 77
Tedder, Air Marshal Arthur
    William, 23, 27
Terrorism, 405, 415
Tharoor, Shashi, 416
Tibet, 342, 374
Tihwa (Sinkiang), 340
Time, 157, 260
Time-Life, 260
Tirah, 305
Tithwal, 353, 362
Tiwana, Khizar Hayat Khan, 178,
    188, 285
Tobruk, 135
Tories, 177, 200
Tottenham, Major General Loftus,
    395
Transfer of power, 333, 410
Travancore, 117, 213, 311, 317,
    321, 322
Travancore-Cochin, 317
Tribesmen, 350-53
Trinidad, 157
Tripura, 213, 237
Truman, Harry S., 229, 256, 308
Tsar Paul, 31
Turkey, 19, 21, 29
Turnbull, Francis, 207
Two-nation theory, 49, 73, 93

Udaipur, 318, 323
Ukraine, 385
Unionist-Akali Alliance, 285
Unionist Party, 90, 410

Unionists, 178, 187, 205
United Nations (UN), 152, 184,
    238, 239, 312, 336, 356,
    362, 367, 371-76, 378, 379,
    381-85, 392, 394-96, 413
    Charter, 366, 380
    Commission for India and
        Pakistan (UNCIP), 336-38,
        340, 362, 375, 377, 384,
        385, 387-91, 396, 397
    General Assembly, 238, 239,
        242, 336, 389
    secretary-general, 283
    Security Council, 335, 337,
        339, 366, 372, 373, 375-84,
        387, 389-91, 396, 404
    Trusteeship Council, 242
United Provinces, 91, 151, 179,
    206, 211, 233
United States of America (US/
    USA), 10, 18, 21, 29, 52, 62,
    97-119, 126, 128, 145-65,
    169, 183, 199, 215, 216,
    229-31, 239, 256, 257, 261,
    265, 303-04, 311, 325, 337,
    338, 340, 354, 355, 373,
    378, 379, 381-83, 392, 397,
    402-05, 409, 412
    State Department, 160, 162,
        185, 186, 228, 230, 256,
        258-60, 264, 287, 310, 336,
        340, 373, 383
Uri, 341, 351, 353, 360-62
Uri-Poonch-Naoshera, 341
U-2 spy planes, 402
Uzbekistan, 16

Vandenberg, Arthur H., 104
Viceroy's Executive Council, 56,
    66, 167, 186, 211, 228, 231,
    236, 237, 250, 252
Viceroy's House, 207-08
Vietnam, 232
Villiers, Sir Edward, 130-32

Visakhapatnam, 109
Vyas, Jaya Narain, 319

Wahhal, Mohammad ibn Abd al,
    68
Walker, Patrick Gordon, 380,
    382, 385
War Cabinet, 98, 100, 109, 115,
    183, 199
War Consultative Committee, 56
Wardha, 41, 130-31
Washington, 30, 104, 113-16,
    124, 146, 152, 154, 159,
    160, 176, 228, 230, 257,
    261, 337, 361, 372, 375-79,
    390, 391, 396, 403
Wavell, Lord Archibald, 24, 25,
    30, 37, 53, 88, 113, 168,
    169, 183, 185, 167-96, 199,
    203-07, 208, 210-11, 215-21,
    225, 231-37, 240, 246,
    248-49, 251, 254, 262-64,
    289, 308, 314, 331
    and blueprint for Pakistan, 168,
    195, 208, 411
Wavell-Attlee plan, 409
Wazirstan, 247, 305
Webb, W.P., 347
Weigold, Auriol, 155
Wells, Sumner, 114, 148, 160
Whitehall, 235, 242, 255, 339,
    390, 394
White House, 185
'White man's burden', 324

Willingdon, Lady, 81
Willingdon, Lord (Freeman
    Freeman-Thomas), 80, 274,
    345
Winant, John G., 103, 184-85
Wolpert, Stanley, 70, 85
World Trade Center, terrorist
    attack on, 11, 176
World War
    First, 19, 38, 40, 79, 177, 223,
    271
    Second, 10, 31, 35, 37, 40-41,
    91, 177, 323
Wyatt, Major Wilson, 256
Wyatt, Woodrow, 194, 202, 211-12
Wylie, Sir Francis, 313-14

Yalta Conference, 181
Yarkhand, 343
Young, Desmond, 46
Yunus, Mohammad, 89, 301, 350

Zahedi, Ardershir, 20
Zakaria, Fareed, 416
Zetland, Lord (Laurence John
    Dumley Dundas), 39, 41, 42,
    43, 46, 49, 50, 51-53, 56,
    70, 72, 92, 123, 262
Zhou En Lai, 308
Zhukov, Yuri, 309-10
Ziegler, Philip, 271, 272, 327,
    345, 383
Zionist policy, 152-53
Zojila Pass, 335, 392
Zoroastrianism, 67, 77